363. Forchuk, Cheryl.
597   Homelessness, housing,
409   and mental health
71
FOR

HOMELESSNESS, HOUSING, AND MENTAL HEALTH

FINDING TRUTHS—CREATING CHANGE

HOMELESSNESS, HOUSING, AND MENTAL HEALTH
FINDING TRUTHS—CREATING CHANGE

Cheryl Forchuk, Rick Csiernik, and Elsabeth Jensen

Canadian Scholars' Press
Toronto

Homelessness, Housing, and Mental Health
Edited by Cheryl Forchuk, Rick Csiernik, Elsabeth Jensen

First published in 2011 by
Canadian Scholars' Press Inc.
180 Bloor Street West, Suite 801
Toronto, Ontario
M5S 2V6

www.cspi.org

Copyright © 2011, Cheryl Forchuk, Rick Csiernik, Elsabeth Jensen, the contributing authors, and Canadian Scholars' Press Inc. All rights reserved. No part of this publication may be photocopied, reproduced, stored in a retrieval system, or transmitted, in any form or by any means, electronic, mechanical, or otherwise, without the written permission of Canadian Scholars' Press Inc., except for brief passages quoted for review purposes. In the case of photocopying, a licence may be obtained from Access Copyright: One Yonge Street, Suite 1900, Toronto, Ontario, M5E 1E5, (416) 868-1620, fax (416) 868-1621, toll-free 1-800-893-5777, www.accesscopyright.ca.

Every reasonable effort has been made to identify copyright holders. CSPI would be pleased to have any errors or omissions brought to its attention.

Canadian Scholars' Press Inc. gratefully acknowledges financial support for our publishing activities from the Government of Canada through the Canada Book Fund (CBF) and the Government of Ontario through the Ontario Book Publishing Tax Credit Program.

Library and Archives Canada Cataloguing in Publication

Homelessness, housing, and mental health : finding truths, creating change / Rick Csiernik, Cheryl Forchuk, Elsabeth Jensen.

Includes index.
ISBN 978-1-55130-390-1

1. Mentally ill homeless persons—Canada. 2. Mentally ill—Services for—Canada. 3. Mentally ill—Economic conditions. 4. Homelessness—Canada. I. Csiernik, Rick II. Forchuk, Cheryl III. Jensen, Elsabeth

RA790.7.C3H66 2010   363.5'9740971   C2010-906930-7

Cover design by Colleen Wormald
Cover image © Mudassar Ahmed Dar/shutterstock.com
Text design by Em Dash Design

09 10 11 12 13   5 4 3 2 1

Printed and bound in Canada by Marquis Book Printing, Inc

Canada

DEDICATION

We would like to dedicate this book to the hundreds of mental health consumer-survivors, family members, peer supports, and community professionals who so willingly gave of their time and shared their stories and experiences as participants and collaborators in this endeavour.

This book is also dedicated to all those with or without a mental health issue who do not have a safe place to sleep tonight.

Community-University Research Alliance
on
Mental Health and Housing

CONTENTS

Preface xi

Acknowledgements xiii

SECTION I. OVERVIEW

1. Creating a Process of Inquiry and Change
   Cheryl Forchuk, Rick Csiernik, and Elsabeth Jensen 3

2. Methodologies Employed
   Cheryl Forchuk, Rick Csiernik, Elsabeth Jensen, and Heather Atyeo 13

SECTION II. UNDERSTANDING THE ISSUE

Introduction 31

3. Housing, Income Support, and Mental Health: Points of Disconnection
   *Cheryl Forchuk, Ruth Schofield, LiBbey Joplin, Rick Csiernik,
   Carolyne Gorlick, and Katherine Turner* 35

4. Surviving the Tornado: Mental Health Consumer-Survivor Experiences of Getting, Losing, and Keeping Housing
   *Cheryl Forchuk, Catherine Ward-Griffin, Rick Csiernik,
   and Katherine Turner* 49

5. Families Caring for Members with Mental Illness: A Vicious Cycle
   *Catherine Ward-Griffin, Ruth Schofield, Sandra Vos,
   and Robin Coatsworth-Puspoky* 59

6. De-"Myth"-ifying Mental Health
   Rick Csiernik, Cheryl Forchuk, Mark Speechley, and Catherine Ward-Griffin ... 77

7. "It's Important to Be Proud of the Place You Live in": Housing Problems and Preferences of Mental Health Consumer-Survivors
   Cheryl Forchuk, Geoffrey Nelson, and G. Brent Hall 91

8. Current and Preferred Housing of Mental Health Consumer-Survivors
   Geoffrey Nelson, G. Brent Hall, and Cheryl Forchuk 107

SECTION III. HOMELESSNESS AND ITS PREVENTION

Introduction 123

9. Perceptions of Health and Health Service Utilization among Homeless and Housed Mental Health Consumer-Survivors
   Ruth Schofield, Cheryl Forchuk, Elsabeth Jensen, and Stephanie Brown 127

10. Homelessness and Health in Adolescents
    Amy Haldenby, Helene Berman, and Cheryl Forchuk 143

11. From Psychiatric Ward to the Streets and Shelters
    *Cheryl Forchuk, Gord Russell, Shani Kingston-MacClure,
    Katherine Turner, and Susan Dill* 167

12. An Intervention to Prevent Homelessness among Individuals Discharged from Psychiatric Wards to Shelters and "No Fixed Address"
    *Cheryl Forchuk, Shani Kingston-MacClure, Michele Van Beers,
    Cheryl Smith, Rick Csiernik, Jeffrey S. Hoch, and Elsabeth Jensen* 179

13. Using Electronic Patient Records in Mental Health Care to Capture Housing and Homelessness Information of Mental Health Consumer-Survivors
    Richard G. Booth 191

SECTION IV. ADDITIONAL CHALLENGES

Introduction 201

14. The Changing Face of Diversity in the Context of Homelessness
*Helene Berman, Carolyne Gorlick, Rick Csiernik, Susan L. Ray,
Cheryl Forchuk, Elsabeth Jensen, and Fatmeh Al Zoubi* 205

15. Gaining Ground, Losing Ground: The Paradoxes of Rural Homelessness
*Cheryl Forchuk, Phyllis Montgomery, Helene Berman, Catherine
Ward-Griffin, Rick Csiernik, Carolyne Gorlick, Elsabeth Jensen, and
Patrick Riesterer* 229

16. Exploring Differences between Community-Based Women and Men
with a History of Mental Illness
*Cheryl Forchuk, Elsabeth Jensen, Rick Csiernik, Catherine Ward-Griffin,
Susan L. Ray, Phyllis Montgomery, and Linda Wan* 243

17. Uprooted and Displaced: A Critical Narrative Study of Homeless,
Aboriginal, and Newcomer Girls in Canada
*Helene Berman, Gloria Alvernaz Mulcahy, Cheryl Forchuk,
Kathy Edmunds, Amy Haldenby, and Raquel Lopez* 257

18. Is Substance Abuse Even an Issue? Perceptions of Male and Female
Community-Based Mental Health System Consumer-Survivors
Rick Csiernik 287

SECTION V. MOVING FORWARD

Introduction 301

19. Margaret's Haven: The Story and the Process
*Elsabeth Jensen, Cheryl Forchuk, Rick Csiernik, Katherine Turner,
and Pamela McKane* 303

20. Why Should Communities Be Involved in Research?
Cheryl Forchuk 315

Appendix A: Glossary of Housing Terms
Cheryl Forchuk, Pamela McKane, Jim Molineux, Ruth Schofield, and Rick Csiernik 321

Appendix B: CURA Fact Sheets 335

List of Contributing Authors 339

Copyright Acknowledgments 349

Index 353

PREFACE

> I am amazed by what an incredible group of people have been able to create together through this CURA. I understand what an exhausting, traumatic, unending process of commitment and recommitment is involved (particularly for the community partners) as they engage in the work that they do every day.
>
> —Katherine Turner, inaugural community director of the Community-University Research Alliance on Mental Health and Housing

Most research is conducted as a specific *project*. The research in this book is part of a *program* of research focusing on housing and mental health. Although the majority of the chapters have been published elsewhere, they appeared as single projects rather than as small parts of a much larger endeavour. This book weaves the various projects into the much greater tapestry of one program of research. In Chapter 1, we describe how the Community-University Research Alliance (CURA) on Mental Health and Housing started. The purpose of this book is to present the finished "tapestry" as a complete work. It is the culmination of nearly a decade of study of the topic of mental health and housing by an inter-professional team of researchers, community groups, students, and mental health consumer-survivors. The ongoing impact of the CURA in the community has been such that a few of the studies included actually occurred after the formal conclusion of the project. By collecting and tying the various threads of this process together, we hope the full beauty of the larger picture will inform and inspire others pursuing this topic.

A critical question in developing this book has been that of labelling. Those affected by mental health issues have worn many labels over time, some very clinical, others very pejorative. Some labels, while attempting to be inclusive, were not necessarily so and many have become oppressive and stigmatizing in some manner, even if this was not the original intent. Thus, we have chosen, after consultation with mental health consumer-survivors, to use that term throughout this book. While this label is not one that all members of this group necessarily accept or even like, it is intended to present and represent the population in an empowering manner. In general the idea of "consumer" is of one who participates and works collaboratively with others, be they helping professionals or policy and program developers. As well, it typically also connotes a self-advocacy function. The idea of survivor refers to surviving the illness as well as surviving the systems put in place to help, though just as often to control.

The book is divided into five sections, plus appendices. Section I provides the environmental and research contexts that led to the development of the book, with a separate chapter summarizing the methodologies used to collect both the quantitative and the qualitative information used in the main project. Section II consists of six chapters that provide an understanding of the issue of homelessness and housing as it pertains to mental health consumer-survivors. Section III focuses on preventative issues, including the perceptions of members of the population and a discussion of an actual intervention that arose directly from the CURA. It has been successfully implemented and has already led to a reduction in the number of individuals who became homeless in the London community. Section IV looks at five specific themes pertaining to mental health consumer-survivors: (1) diversity, (2) rural homeless, (3) male-female differences, (4) the idea of uprootedness and displacement, and (5) the specific perceptions of the population with regard to their use of psychoactive substances. Section V provides a closer examination of the specific project that was at the heart of the CURA—Margaret's Haven—discussing the process that began the initiative and concludes with an examination of why communities should be engaged in the process of research and in developing new knowledge and innovative solutions to difficult social problems.

We hope that you learn from the book, from our experiences, and from the voices of the mental health consumer-survivors who shared their knowledge and their experiences with us. We also hope that, like the CURA itself, reading this book will not only be an academic exercise but lead you to participate in active change in your community. Enjoy our tapestry!

Cheryl Forchuk, Rick Csiernik, and Elsabeth Jensen, January 2011

ACKNOWLEDGEMENTS

The editors would like to thank all the members of the Community-University Research Alliance on Mental Health and Housing who volunteered thousands of hours of their time over the course of this project: Heather Atyeo, Reta Bere, Helene Berman, Bruce Brown, Stephanie Brown, Julia Capaldi, Kathleen Chalmers, Bill Cline, Martha Connoy, Betty DaCosta, Susan Dill, Betty Edwards, Lance Evoy, Carolyne Gorlick, Brenda Fuhrman, Brent Hall, Kerri Hallas, Allison Hargreaves, Jeff Hoch, Paul Huras, LiBbey Joplin, Norma-Jean Kelly, Shani Kingston-MacClure, Lisa Kraw, Janet Kreda, Eric Levitan, Kathy Lewis, Susan Macphail, Jane Martin, Kathryn Maver, Pamela McKane, Jim Molineux, Phyllis Montgomery, Jeanette Naisbett, Geoff Nelson, Leaurie Noordermeer, David Norton, Walter Osoka, Sue Ouseley, Wally Parsons, Maureen Pennington, Stewart Perry, Nancy Powers, Dick Rastin, Gordon Russell, Ruth Schofield, Linda Sibley-Bowers, Rob Skirving, Cheryl Smith, Mark Speechley, Katherine Turner, Michele Van Beers, John Van Damme, Sandra Vos, Judy Wakem, Catherine Ward-Griffin, Barbara Warnok, Mary Wiktorowicz, and Catherine Wilson.

The editors also wish to thank Dr. Susan Silva-Wayne of Canadian Scholars' Press Inc. for her support for this project and the reviewers of the book for their insights and assistance.

This original CURA on Mental Health and Housing was funded by grant 833-2000-1018 from the Social Sciences and Humanities Research Council of Canada.

Additional funding was provided by:
The University of Western Ontario and the City of London, for Chapter 12: An Intervention to Prevent Homelessness among Individuals Discharged from Psychiatric Wards to Shelters and "No Fixed Address"

The Social Sciences and Humanities Research Council of Canada, for Chapter 14: The Changing Face of Diversity in the Context of Homelessness

The Housing and Homeless Branch, Canada, for Chapter 15: Gaining Ground, Losing Ground: The Paradoxes of Rural Homelessness

The Canadian Institutes of Health Research, New Perspectives on Gender and Health, for Chapter 17: Uprooted and Displaced: A Critical Narrative Study of Homeless, Aboriginal, and Newcomer Girls in Canada

Section I

OVERVIEW

Chapter 1

CREATING A PROCESS OF INQUIRY AND CHANGE

Cheryl Forchuk, Rick Csiernik, and Elsabeth Jensen

1. PREAMBLE

As so often occurs, real change in this story begins with one person. That person was "Margaret," a pseudonym. Margaret was a well-known regular in the London community. She stood out, she was different, she was flamboyant, and she was a risk taker. However, what most people noticed was that Margaret was mentally ill and homeless. Margaret did have a formal clinical diagnosis and she clearly owned the title "survivor" for she had survived one of Canada's largest, most complex, and most bureaucratic systems. While what follows is very much the product of a rigorous, professional, well-funded, and well-resourced project that constitutes thousands of hours of research and just as much volunteer time and commitment, without Margaret, an old, homeless, mentally ill woman whom many knew of but few knew, there would have been no Community-University Research Alliance and thus there would have been no process of inquiry and change.

2. BACKGROUND

The Issue Area

Housing has been identified as one of the key determinants of health (Health Canada, 1996) and also as one of the essential social determinants of health (Raphael, 2008). In fact, of the social determinant 10 tips for better health, three relate to housing (don't live in damp, low-quality housing; don't live next to a busy major road or near a polluting factory; learn how to fill in complex housing benefit forms before you become homeless) two relate to poverty (don't be poor; don't have poor parents), and two relate to employment (don't work in a stressful, low-paid manual job; don't become unemployed), all of which relate to the theme of mental health, housing, and homelessness (Raphael, 2008).

There are many paths to homelessness and a wide range of variables that can affect an individual's likelihood of becoming homeless. Of these, mental health, mental illness, and addiction play prominent roles (Canadian Institute for Health Information, 2007). Mental health is not only absence of any formal diagnosis of a mental illness. It is also "a state of well-being in which the individual realizes his or her own abilities, can cope with the normal stresses of life, can work productively and fruitfully, and is able to make a contribution to his or her community" (World Health Organization, 2001: 1). Issues of adequate housing and homelessness can be fully addressed only with a comprehensive mental health policy (Pan-Canadian Planning Committee for the National Think Tank on Mental Health Promotion, 2009).

The Funding Opportunity

In 1999 the Canadian Social Sciences Humanities Research Council (2008) introduced a new funding opportunity to encourage and support the collaboration of university-based researchers with community-based partners, resulting in the Community-University Research Alliance (CURA). Through a process of ongoing collaboration and mutual learning, the goal of a CURA is to foster innovative research, training, and the creation of new knowledge in areas of importance for the social, cultural, or economic development of communities across Canada. CURAs were also given funding to develop strategies for intervention, action research, program delivery, and policy development.

CURAs are based on equal partnerships between the community and the academy, and provide coordination and support for planning and carrying out community-based and university-supported research activities that are of mutual importance to all partners. Each CURA was to have distinct research, education, and knowledge creation and dissemination strategies that met the needs of both academic and community partners (Social Sciences and Humanities Research Council, 2008).

However, when we started this work we did not know about the CURA program. We did know that many people in our community who had mental illnesses also had many serious problems in relation to housing. We knew that many such individuals were homeless. We did not know why this was happening, what could prevent homelessness, or what kind of housing would be best to meet various needs.

3. BEGINNING THE PROCESS OF INQUIRY AND CHANGE

Margaret's circumstances had been the catalyst that brought together a contingent of community agencies and activists. A significant difference that would not have occurred previously was that academics were also invited to assist in developing a unique demonstration housing project for single vulnerable women with mental health issues and challenges in the greater London, Ontario, area who had either been homeless or were at imminent danger of homelessness. The project was to be called "Margaret's Haven."

The advisory group was staffed by Katherine Turner and Janet Kreda of LIFE*SPIN, an organization that assisted individuals experiencing poverty, and that also had, as part of its mission, community development and advocacy. LIFE*SPIN had ties to several post-secondary institutions by providing field placements for social services students. A key community member of the Margaret's Haven advisory committee was Norma-Jean Kelly, a representative of Can-Voice. Can-Voice was and remains a mental health consumer-survivor group based in London. At this time Can-Voice was just completing its first involvement as a collaborating partner in a university-driven research project examining effective transitional discharge processes that included the role of peer supports. It was not surprising, then, that when the advisory group discussed evaluation plans for this new project, it was suggested that the university researcher already involved with Can-Voice be approached to assist. Dr. Cheryl Forchuk, a professor of nursing at the University of Western Ontario and a scientist at the Lawson Health Research Institute, and a member of her research staff, Elsabeth Jensen, who was completing her doctorate in nursing at Wayne State at this time, were invited to a meeting to discuss the possibility of conducting an evaluation as one component of the housing funding proposal. Forchuk and Jensen were keenly interested in the idea as housing problems were identified as a critical element in their transitional discharge study, and agreed to meet with the advisory group to make a few suggestions and act as resources on an as-needed basis. Ironically, at this same time, Forchuk had a homeless person staying in her basement on a fairly regular basis—a teenage classmate of her eldest son had been evicted with his mother. The mother was hospitalized with schizophrenia shortly before the eviction. The struggle to find services and housing underscored the research and community issues that all involved in the project were grappling with.

Coincidentally, at this time Forchuk was contacted by a Victorian Order nurse, Betty DeCosta, who was running an outreach program at the Salvation Army men's homeless shelter. She asked if Dr. Forchuk would be interested in meeting with her and other Salvation Army staff as they were finding an increasing number of men with mental health challenges who were experiencing homelessness, and were thinking about pursuing funding to develop a specific long-term housing project to assist this population. They asked Forchuk if she would be interested in assisting the Salvation Army to conduct an evaluation to determine the need for such an endeavour. Since both were fairly small projects, Forchuk suggested that the two should be looked at as parallel processes. Unbeknownst to the parties involved, Dr. Rick Csiernik, a social work professor at King's University College in London who had a background in addiction, community housing, and advocacy, had just been assigned to supervise social work practicum interns at LIFE*SPIN and the Salvation Army shelter.

While Forchuk began meeting with the community agencies, she was also conducting regular meetings with staff from the Ontario Ministry of Health and Long-Term Care (MHLTC) to update them on the transitional discharge project. Members of the ministry staff were encouraging her to examine housing more broadly, rather than just from a homelessness perspective. They described the dilemma they faced as the literature from the United States indicated that individuals preferred independent living above all other choices, but in the absence of Canadian literature, the housing providers in Ontario had and continued to have a focus primarily on group homes. Ministry staff asked if perhaps the research focus could be expanded to include independent living and group homes along with an examination of the homeless. As the issues grew, so did the emerging advisory group.

To address the opportunity and the synergy occurring in the community on this issue, and in order to adequately address the complex nature of mental health and housing, it was determined that more program-focused funding was required. It was the Margaret's Haven advisory group that found the call for proposals related to Community-University Research Alliances (CURA) from the Social Sciences and

Humanities Research Council of Canada (SSHRC). By the time the final draft of the funding proposal was prepared, the group had met and worked together for over a year. The last person added to the proposal—literally days before it was forwarded for consideration—was Rick Csiernik from the King's University College School of Social Work. The funding request was successful and the Community-University Research Allowance on Mental Health and Housing was provided with three years of stable funding to examine mental health and housing from numerous perspectives, which was subsequently followed by an additional two years of funding.

4. IMPLEMENTING THE CURA

The CURA on Housing and Mental Health had two community directors and an academic director, and functioned with an advisory group of key stakeholders. These stakeholders included consumers of mental health services, housing providers, mental health agencies, hospitals, policy and decision makers, and researchers from nursing, social work, epidemiology, psychology, economics, urban planning, and geography.

Figure 1.1: **CURA Committee Structure**

The CURA was organized with a very flexible and organic committee structure (Figure 1.1). The advisory committee was central and included membership from homeless shelters (the Salvation Army and Mission Services), hospitals (including the Homes for Special Care program), community mental health agencies (Canadian Mental Health Association local program, Western Ontario Therapeutic Community Housing [WOTCH]), consumer-survivors, researchers, students, and policy decision makers (from both the City of London and the Ontario Ministry of Health and Long-Term Care).

Several subcommittees encircled the Advisory Group. All subcommittees included membership from the various stakeholder groups. These included the following.

Annual Conference Planning Committee
The annual conference was key to setting the annual CURA agenda. This activity was to provide feedback and obtain direction from a broad range of community stakeholder groups. There were typically 100 participants each year. Of this one-fifth to one-third were consumer-survivors. The stakeholder groups represented

on the advisory groups were able to have more members present at these conferences than at the smaller advisory and subcommittee groups, thereby broadening their representation. There were presentations from community groups, as well as from researchers and students. Group discussions and consensus exercises were conducted to establish priorities for the following year.

Research Committee

The research committee oversaw the collection and analysis of quantitative and qualitative data. For each of the five years of the study, structured interview data from 300 mental health consumers who were living in the greater London and surrounding community were collected. The sample was stratified by sex (150 women and 150 men) and housing type (independent living, group home, homeless). Attempts were made to maintain the same participants where possible from year to year despite the transient nature of some groups being examined. If participants could not be located the following year, they were replaced with someone of the same sex and housing type. The qualitative data were primarily collected through focus groups. Key stakeholders representing consumers, family members, mental health service providers, housing service providers, landlords, and employers were identified each year for inclusion in focus groups. There were 63 groups with 550 participants interviewed over the five years of the CURA.

Policy Committee

The policy committee collected and analyzed policies related to mental health and housing. A policy library was developed that included over 200 documents on housing, income support, and mental health.[1]

Media and Political Action Committee

This committee planned creative and diverse dissemination strategies, including press releases, media events, one-page summaries (see Appendix B), plays, and all-candidates meetings at municipal, provincial, and federal elections.

Staffing Committee

The staffing committee dealt with the concrete issues related to hiring and staff planning.

Margaret's Haven Evaluation Committee

This committee dealt with the issue that had kick-started the entire process, the evaluation of Margaret's Haven (see Chapter 19).

Specific Project Committees

Specific projects emerged over the course of the program that required specific subgroups. Examples included the evaluation of a Salvation Army project, the issues of discharge to "no fixed address" (chapters 11 and 12), concerns related to employment, and questions related to diversity issues with homelessness (Chapter 14).

Students

Although not a specific committee, the inclusion of students was an important component of the CURA. Multiple students—including several master's students, a doctoral candidate, and a post-doctoral student—used the data for secondary data analysis. Research assistantships were provided to a wide breadth of students at the graduate and undergraduate level; clinical and research placements were offered; and an interprofessional graduate course on housing and mental health was provided based on the CURA. In total, just under 300 students were directly involved in CURA learning opportunities.

The movement of members between the advisory committee and the subcommittees was dynamic and flexible. Anyone on any subcommittee could join the advisory committee, and anyone on the advisory committee could join any subcommittee. This was very important for maintaining momentum over the years. People regularly moved around between committees, bringing a fresh perspective to each group, and preventing individuals from becoming bored with topics. Day-to-day operation was overseen by an executive committee consisting of the research coordinator, the academic director (Cheryl Forchuk), and two community directors (initially Janet Kreda and Katherine Turner, followed by Pamela McKane from Margaret's Haven, and then Sue Ouseley and Betty Edwards from Can-Voice).

5. CREATING A PROCESS OF INQUIRY AND CHANGE

Partnerships were key to the success of this CURA. The year prior to applying for funding was a critical period for relationships to be formed and tested. This was particularly important due to the number and diversity of partners. A considerable effort went into ensuring that the community was sufficiently empowered to participate. Having two community directors and only one academic director for most of the CURA is one concrete example of structurally keeping the community empowered and an equal partner in the process. Meals were frequently provided at meetings and travel costs were reimbursed. For many consumer-survivors and/or homeless individuals, it made the difference between coming or not coming. In consideration of the time constraints of community agency partners, the CURA process attempted to structure an entire day for various committee meetings to avoid having to regularly disrupt work schedules. Although this was difficult for staff and the directors, it was easier for community members to take time off for less frequent but full days rather than more frequent but short meetings.

What was learned from all the committee meetings, through the creation and evolution of the partnerships, via the collection and analysis of data, and as a result of all the various products produced is presented in the following chapters. Although much new knowledge has resulted from the CURA on Mental Health and Housing, and new innovative programs have arisen, each is still only a glimpse of the process of change that emerged from a process of inquiry created by this large coalition. Every paper, each activity, and all the endeavours have more people in the background, more underlying issues, and more activities than can be conveyed through a traditional print format. However, this book not only allows us to provide a comprehensive presentation of the work produced because of Margaret, it also allows us to demonstrate the interrelationships of the various projects. We hope, through this book, to show how a process of inquiry can bring greater clarity to the complex issues regarding the questions pertaining to mental health and housing. We hope that this clarity can lead to meaningful change that will improve the lives of people struggling with mental illness and the lack of secure housing.

NOTE

1. The list is available at: publish.uwo.ca/~cforchuk/cura/Reference%20Manager1.htm. A more structured list specific to housing that has numerous links to original sources can be found at: publish.uwo.ca/~cforchuk/chl/index.html.

REFERENCES

Canadian Institute for Health Information. (2007). *Improving the health of Canadians: Mental health and homelessness.* Ottawa: Canadian Institute for Health Information.

Health Canada. (1996). *Towards a common understanding: Clarifying the core concepts of population health.* Ottawa: Health Canada.

Pan-Canadian Planning Committee for the National Think Tank on Mental Health Promotion. (2009). *National mental health promotion and mental illness prevention policy for Canadians.* Ottawa: Pan-Canadian Planning Committee for the National Think Tank on Mental Health Promotion.

Raphael, D. (2008). *Social determinants of health: Canadian perspectives*, 2nd ed. Toronto: Canadian Scholars' Press Inc.

Social Sciences and Humanities Research Council. (2008). *Community-University Research Alliance.* Retrieved March 14, 2009, from http://www.sshrc-crsh.gc.ca/site/apply-demande/program_descriptions- descriptions_de_programmes/cura-aruc-eng.aspx.

World Health Organization. (2001). *Mental health: Strengthening mental health promotion.* Geneva: World Health Organization.

Chapter 2

METHODOLOGIES EMPLOYED

Cheryl Forchuk, Rick Csiernik,
Elsabeth Jensen and Heather Atyeo

1. THE CONTEXT

Partnerships in Capacity Building: Housing, Community Economic Development, and Psychiatric Survivors was a Community-University Research Alliance (CURA) initiative, funded by the Social Sciences and Humanities Research Council of Canada. The population of interest was individuals who were diagnosed with a mental illness at some point in their lives and who were currently living in the community. The inaugural research group consisted of academics from five different universities, representing seven different disciplines (nursing, social work, psychology, geography and urban planning, epidemiology, law, and economics), working in collaboration with a range of community partners, including providers of housing for people with mental health issues, community agencies serving individuals with a mental illness, and consumer-survivors of the mental health system. The goal of this alliance was to promote understanding of the housing situation for mental health consumer-survivors on an individual, community, and societal level. Using a participatory action research approach, both qualitative and quantitative methods were employed with the purpose of improving the capacity for appropriate housing for this marginalized, stigmatized, and oppressed population.

The research was conducted in the city of London, located in Middlesex County, Ontario, and the surrounding four counties. London, which has a census metropolitan population of just under half a million, had been the location of a large provincial psychiatric hospital that served the city and the surrounding regions, and had another psychiatric hospital in St. Thomas, only 36 kilometres away, which served the population. In 2001, both psychiatric facilities had their governance moved to a community hospital as part of province-wide mental health reform. This transfer was one aspect of a larger plan that called for a large reduction in the total number of psychiatric beds and the redeployment of mental health resources to the communities served by the former provincial hospitals. The reduction in hospital beds and the movement of people and resources into the community provided a need and opportunity to examine housing issues related to mental health consumer-survivors.

The original study used a mixed-methods approach collecting both quantitative and qualitative data between 2001 and 2006. Personal interviews and focus groups were held in a range of community locations, including shelters, group homes, community agencies, and drop-in centres. This chapter describes the methodological issues pertaining to the majority of the remaining chapters in the book. Rather than repeatedly discussing the methodology that was utilized to examine different perspectives of the issues faced by mental health consumer-survivors in finding housing, this chapter will provide an overview of the key methodological approaches employed. Subsequent chapters will provide additional relevant methodological information and also discuss in greater detail when different approaches and methods were used.

2. GOAL AND OVERALL APPROACH

As stated, the goal of the overall program was to understand the complex issues related to housing and mental health at individual, community, and societal levels. Rather than do this through a series of related studies, we chose instead to have large quantitative and qualitative data sets that included a breadth of information. The program was designed for multiple "secondary analysis" of the quantitative, qualitative, and policy data. The research committee, with broad community input, planned the nature of the information gathered through individual quantitative interviews and focus groups, but all this information was never intended to be used as a single "primary" analysis.

This approach of planned multiple analysis worked well as a participatory, collaborative approach. Any team/committee member could "claim" an interest in a particular sub-analysis. The list of "claimed" topics was circulated at all meetings so that others could join. As long as the volunteers made a significant contribution, they would be authors on the designated topic. Generally, people interested in a particular topic met over several months to complete their work. Several students were also able to use the data for master's or doctoral theses.

3. QUANTITATIVE METHODOLOGY

Who to Include

There is a general awareness of the distinction between a community-based sample and a clinical sample. Yet, a simple and routine component of designing a controlled clinical study is not necessarily a method that will provide a representative or accurate picture of a real-world community. A standard sampling frame that is intended to produce a "representative" sample can, during its implementation, produce a skewed sample by excluding segments of the population that are not amenable to the classical methods of sampling.

At the beginning of this study, the research team developed a hypothesis about what type of consumer-survivor of mental health services would function best in what type of housing. Housing decisions were based on a combination of available housing and professional judgment. There was little empirical evidence available to guide either placements of individuals or development of housing to meet the needs of the population. Policy-makers relied almost exclusively on practice wisdom in the funding of housing for people with mental health problems, with varying degrees of success.

Community partners identified sex as another important variable to be studied due to growing requests for female-only housing. Some of the sites included both women and men, while others housed only one sex. It was decided early in the planning phase to have equal numbers of men and women in the sample in order to assess similarities and differences. Sample calculations, based upon Cohen (1988), using conventional values of 80 percent power, 5 percent alpha, to detect a moderate effect size of .25, determined that 150 people would be required for each stratum.

As well, a cross-section of people residing in the available housing options was desired. Data were collected regarding how many people were housed in the settings that represented each type of housing used by the population of study. Shelters for the homeless, group homes, apartments with support staff available, and independent apartments and houses without supports represent the types of housing settings included in the study. Of these groups, only those living in supported living situations constituted a known population. Homeless people and people living independently who have been diagnosed with mental illness at some time in their lives are largely invisible and hence impossible to enumerate. All of these factors were considered in developing the sampling strategies for the research. However, all participants, regardless of their housing situation, were required to have a history of a mental health issue for a minimum of one year. A mental health issue was defined as having experienced symptoms of an Axis I diagnosis, as outlined in the *Diagnostic and Statistical Manual IV–TR* such as depression, anxiety, bipolar disorder, or schizophrenia.

Issues in Quantitative Sampling

Sampling is one of the necessary steps in the conduct of research. Entire books have been dedicated to it (Barnett, 1991; Henry, 1990; Levy & Lemeshow, 1999; Lwanga, 1991; Rao, 2000; Thompson, 2002), and every student of research is familiar with the topic. Researchers take care to define their population, and then to draw samples that will be most representative of the population. Such care is required in order to secure reliable data. Sometimes, though, the real world does not co-operate despite careful preparation and planning. As health care research moves from clinical to community settings, the approaches to the process of sampling demand increasing creativity and flexibility in order to balance the ideal with the possible.

Ideally, researchers study samples in order to learn about the population as a whole at less cost than would be involved in studying the entire population. For this technique to be effective, the sample population must be large enough to ensure that it is representative of the population being studied (Caplan, Slade & Gansky, 1999). This convention also relies on having access to a known population. Due to the stigma, discrimination, and oppression associated with mental illness, segments of this population remain largely invisible in the community. Faugier and Sargeant (1997) pointed out that innovative sampling methods need to be used to study hard-to-reach or hidden groups. The study of a captive, known population, such as the people living in group homes and other supported living situations, is amenable to traditional sampling methods. However, the other two populations—homeless people or people living independently—required more innovative and less routine approaches. Thus, as the research evolved, it became apparent that to successfully study people in the continuum of housing types, a mix of sampling methods would be required.

Women and men residing in group homes and supported living environments constituted a known population. The community research partners representing these housing services were able to provide a complete list of their residents from which a random sample was drawn. One challenge arose because some very specialized homes had a very small number of residents. It was decided to include the entire population from some homes with special programs in order for the final sample to adequately capture the full range of supported housing. This would assure that adequate data would be available for the analysis. Thus, for this group, sampling was a mix of simple random sampling (Polit & Beck, 2004) and inclusion of an entire population from some select sites. The use of a traditional approach offered confidence that the results would be generalizable to the population.

The remaining two housing categories presented substantive sampling challenges. It is impossible to generate a sampling frame for either people who are homeless or for people who are living independently in the community. Shelters experience an extremely unpredictable population each evening. Of the people who used each of the four shelters in the study on a given day, no one could predict how many would have had a psychiatric diagnosis at some point in their lives or even who these people might be. Of those who did meet the criteria, it was unknown how many would agree to participate in the study. It became clear that the shelter group and the independent group each required a distinct sampling method. The approaches used to sample the homeless population and the people living independently in the community would need to differ. Each of these will be discussed in turn.

The second major category in the sampling plan was the homeless group. The research team decided to randomly choose the dates for data collection at each shelter site and to interview all those who met the criteria for inclusion in the study. This would be repeated until the quota for homeless people with a history of mental illness was met. The sampling method chosen was an example of simple random sampling, using dates as the element that was randomized (Polit & Beck, 2004). The team acknowledged that recruitment from shelters might not truly represent homeless people with a history of mental illness as those not accessing the shelter would be excluded. The resources required to seek out homeless people who were not shelter users in order to draw a true probability sample are substantial (Henry,

1990) and were generally beyond those available to this team. One additional strategy was employed in an attempt to at least partially address this issue. Sampling was conducted on random days at agencies that provided services for homeless individuals in the hope that some individuals living under bridges, in parked cars and outdoors, as well as those who were couch surfing would be included.

The third major category consisted of the people who lived independently. It would not be possible to create a list from the population in order to draw a random sample as there was no master list of the population available. People with a history of mental illness living independently are usually indistinguishable from members of the general population. Thus, participants living independently were located using a variation of convenience sampling known as the network sampling method (Polit & Beck, 2004). Posters were circulated to places attended by consumer-survivors, and letters were distributed to professionals working in the mental health field in order to find members of this subgroup. People who were interviewed were asked if they knew of others who would qualify and if they indicated that they did, they were asked to facilitate contact with their networks. The drawback of this method is that people who are not out and about or who do not have relationship skills would be underrepresented, as would the people who did not want to disclose their history of mental illness (Faugier & Sargeant, 1997).

As the study progressed, yet another sampling challenge emerged. There were generally more men than women available to be interviewed, particularly in the shelters and the supported housing sites. In fact, the single most ongoing challenge with respect to data collection arose due to difficulties in locating adequate numbers of women available to participate at the various sites, other than group homes and supported apartments. While the specific reasons for this were largely unknown at the time, the research team did, in consultation with community partners, infer some possible explanations for this occurrence. Of note is that homeless women who have a history of abuse, and who have children in their care are considered a priority for subsidized apartment units through the municipality and are thus fast-tracked into independent living. Women may also have a wider social support network and may have access to friends and family willing to assist and/or provide accommodation, thus avoiding shelter stays or the need for supported living environments, such as group homes. To deal with the challenge in locating sufficient numbers of women eligible to participate in the study, it was agreed that in the sites housing fewer women, all consenting women who met the study's inclusion criteria were included in the study while only the targeted number of male participants were included at each site.

The Interviewing Process

The interview team was large and consisted of researchers, research staff, and students employed as research assistants on the CURA. At the beginning of the project, all interviewers underwent extensive training of a minimum of two days, including criterion referenced testing to assure that inter-rater reliability was maintained at 90 percent. In addition, new students and staff added to the interview team after the project was underway would observe an actual interview and be observed doing a second interview before independently interviewing participants. Interviewers carried cellphones in case they needed support or clarification, but for this study no one required using the phone during the interviews. Participants were paid $20 Canadian as compensation for their time in the interview, which typically lasted one to two hours. Interviews were done in a mutually agreeable location, most often in the participants' current housing location.

The Sample

Over the five years of data collection, the quantitative data were drawn from a total stratified sample of 1,503 participants (though some chapters used data collected from only one or select years of the study). Of these, 887 individuals completed quantitative questionnaires during the five-year study period. All of these people were located in London, Ontario, and its surrounding 100 kilometre area. In three of the study's five years, the targeted community sample size was 300 individuals, while in 2004 and 2005, there were 267 and 336 participants, respectively. Inclusion criteria required that participants have a history of mental illness for a minimum of one year, be 16 years of age or older, be able to provide informed consent, and be proficient in English. Individuals were excluded from the study if they had a diagnosis of an organic brain disorder to the extent that it would interfere with their ability to participate in an interview. Some participants were included in more than one year of the study; however, if repeated participants were not found, they were replaced with new participants of the same sex and housing arrangement. All participants who took part in the study were offered the chance to participate in the following year. The samples were stratified by sex (female or male) and housing type (supported apartment units, group homes, independent apartments, an AIDS hospice, emergency shelters, and long-term homeless shelters).

Participants were recruited through various clinical, housing, and other community partners of the research team using a predetermined sampling target. Community partners and agency representatives were apprised of research questions to be asked and were given copies of the study letter of information to share with potential participants at their various locations. At housing interview sites with on-site supports, agency staff were consulted regarding chosen dates and the total number of individuals to be interviewed, according to the predetermined sample target. Generally, interviews were conducted early in the week so that staff supports would be available if participants found they wanted to explore issues raised later with staff. This is important since some of the questions involved potentially difficult issues such as childhood trauma and abuse. Letters of information were posted within the agency/home identifying those dates. Individuals who met study criteria and who showed interest advised the housing staff, who then referred them to the interview team. As well, potential participants could also communicate their interest with research staff by phone or in person directly. Where the number of available participants exceeded the target for the site, a random sample was drawn. Study participants represented people housed in homes for special care, large houses with private or shared bedrooms for four to 20 people per house, meals provided, and 24-hour staffing, operated for profit; temporary shelters, primarily large dormitory-style rooms with up to 20 people, set up as emergency housing for the homeless; supportive housing units, group homes, or individual apartments within one apartment block with support staff available provided by two non-profit agencies; and independent living settings, either apartments or houses.

Data Collection Instruments

Instruments were chosen in consultation with the community and consumer-survivor members of the research team. In-depth quantitative interviews gathered information on demographics, severity of mental illness, current utilization of health and social services, housing preferences, life satisfaction, income history, and childhood trauma. Each of the instruments used is described in greater detail below.

DEMOGRAPHIC FORM

The original CURA research team developed specific items to address information regarding mental health consumer-survivors in the community. Questions covered age, sex, marital status, the highest level of education, and primary psychiatric diagnosis of participants. Participants reported their sex as male or female; their marital status as single/never married, separated/divorced, widowed, or married/common law; and their highest level of education as less than grade school, grade school, high school, or university/community college. Primary psychiatric diagnoses were self-reported by participants and were categorized as schizophrenia, mood disorder, anxiety disorder, other, or unknown. As issues were identified through the focus groups, some additional items were added to the demographic form in later years. This included information on parent roles, employment history, experience of stigma/discrimination, issues of diversity, and information on rural/urban concerns.

THE COLORADO CLIENT ASSESSMENT RECORD (CCAR)

Participants' severity of psychiatric symptomatology and level of functioning were measured using the Colorado Client Assessment Record (CCAR), a standardized clinical assessment of problems, strengths, and functioning. The CCAR groups individuals' personal and social functioning into 12 major areas, with each of these areas having a single measure that assesses general dysfunction (Ellis, Wackwitz & Foster, 1991; 1996). The CCAR contains 29 specific items, each of which is measured on a Likert scale ranging from 1 to 9. A rating of 1 denotes the individual had no problem and they function consistently average or better than what is standard for their age, sex, and culture. In contrast, a rating of 9 represents an extreme problem, suggesting the individual's behaviour or situation is out of control, intolerable, and possibly life-threatening.

Problem severity was rated for the following domains: emotional withdrawal, depression, anxiety, hyperaffect, attention problems, suicide/danger to self, thought processes, cognitive problems, self-care/basic needs, resistiveness, aggressiveness, legal, violence/danger to others, family issues, family problems, interpersonal problems, role performance, substance abuse, medical illness, security/management issues, and overall degree of problem severity. Level of functioning consisted of five subscales: (1) societal/role, (2) interpersonal, (3) daily living/personal care, (4) physical, and (5) cognitive/intellectual, and one overall scale.

Altschul, Wackwitz, Coen, and Ellis (2001) examined the inter-rater reliability for the CCAR by employing adult-focused study-raters. The reliability coefficients for clinical judgment data were expected to range from 0.5 to 0.8. Four areas of the CCAR were examined: (1) problem severity, (2) strengths and resources, (3) levels of functioning, and (4) overall CCAR instrument. Overall CCAR instrument, problem severity, and level of functioning were the three out of the four correlations that fell within the expected range: 0.588, 0.644, and 0.538, respectively. Thus, specific questions targeted toward determining problem severity and level of functioning fell within the 95 percent confidence interval, indicating a reliable instrument for adult consumers. Nevertheless, the strengths and resources domain may be less reliable for evaluating adult consumers.

Research staff was trained in the administration of the CCAR and did not participate in interviews unless they had 90 percent concordance with ratings previously established by an expert clinical panel on two consecutive videotaped interviews. Retraining and rating a further videotape were mandatory at each six-month interval, in order to ensure the maintenance of this degree of inter-rater concordance across all four years of data collection.

THE UTILIZATION OF HOSPITAL AND COMMUNITY SERVICES FORM

Information regarding participants' utilization of health services was collected using the Utilization of Hospital and Community Services Form (modified from Browne et al., 1990). The presence or absence of an admission to hospital in the past month was recorded. For those who had reported an admission, the number and length of stay (in days) of admission in the past month to psychiatric hospital, general hospital, and psychiatric ward of a general hospital were specified. Reasons for admission to general hospital were also recorded. As well, the number of psychiatric hospitalizations in the two years prior to interview was collected using the CCAR.

The Utilization of Hospital and Community Services instrument consisted of 30 questions regarding social support, type and cost of housing, use of services such as individual therapy or social skills training, and contacts or visits with service providers and/or medical health care providers. The questions referred to the use of services within the past month. Other inquiries related to medication use and income support programs. Browne et al. (1990) validated part of the form by comparing 141 cardiac patients' self-reports on laboratory tests to the actual tests and frequencies on clinical records. Observed agreement among testers ranged from 0.7 to 0.9 and, when adjusted for chance agreement, the kappa statistics were from 0.48 to 0.89. To assist with accuracy on this instrument, the investigators kept the period of recall to one month for this study.

LEHMAN QUALITY OF LIFE SCALE

The Brief Version of the Lehman Quality of Life Interview (Lehman, Postrado & Rachuba, 1993) was used to collect information regarding participants' perception of their physical and emotional health, as well as their perception of their health in general. Participants rated their feelings regarding their health according to a 7-point scale, ranging from "terrible" (1) to "delighted" (7).

CHILDHOOD TRAUMA QUESTIONNAIRE

The Childhood Trauma Questionnaire was utilized to obtain retrospective information about childhood trauma resulting from sexual abuse, as well as physical and emotional abuse and neglect (Bernstein et al., 1994).

HOUSING PREFERENCE

To assess preferences for housing, living companions, and supports, the short version of the Consumer Housing Preference Survey Instrument was used (Tanzman Wilson & Yoe, 1992). This frequently employed survey instrument (Tanzman, 1993) includes questions regarding current housing, preferred housing, preferred living companions, and supports needed. The format for most of the items is that of fixed-choice alternatives, which yield categorical data. For example, the question used to assess a preferred living situation is "Ideally, what kind of place would you like to live in?" Consumers respond to this question by choosing one of 11 fixed-choice options (e.g., in a group home run by a community mental health centre, in an apartment, in my family's home, in a shelter) or by indicating some other choice. In addition to these fixed-choice questions, there are also a few open-ended questions (e.g., "What is it about that place that would be most important to you?" "What kinds of supports or services do you think you might need in order to be able to live where you want?").

4. QUALITATIVE METHODOLOGY

The inclusion of a qualitative component was particularly appropriate for this investigation as it is intended for the in-depth exploration of a phenomenon about which we have little knowledge (Morse & Field, 1995). The qualitative approach utilized in the research was ethnography, which involved detailed descriptions of housing circumstances for people with mental health issues. Ethnography uses both interaction and observation to describe and analyze life ways or particular patterns of groups or cultures in their environment (Leininger, 1985: 35). A focus group method was used to collect all qualitative data. Focus groups are carefully planned discussions designed to obtain perceptions in a non-threatening environment (Krueger, 1994). They are also commonly used to create an opportunity for participants to provide mutual support for one another throughout the research process (Brown, 1999; Greenbaum, 1993; Morgan, 1988)

Consumer-Survivor Focus Groups

The consumer-survivor focus groups involved people with a diagnosed mental health issue who were either current or former consumers of mental health services. The initial focus group interviews were conducted in collaboration with district health councils in the southwestern region of Ontario between July 17, 2001 and

August 22, 2001. Fourteen specific mental health consumer-survivor focus groups (n = 133) were conducted at this time. Each of the focus groups was led by one of the district health council staff and assisted with the identification of concerns and problems experienced by mental health consumer-survivors with respect to housing and social services. Focus groups ranged in size from one to 24, with a mean of 10.6 running between 60 and 90 minutes.

An additional nine focus groups were conducted by members of the CURA research team in both urban and rural areas in southwestern Ontario between July 5, 2002 and September 3, 2002, with five to 13 participants per group. The total sample included 51 women and 39 men. Five groups included both men and women. Two groups were for women only, and two were for men only.

Another set of consumer-survivor focus groups were held between February 10, 2005 and November 8, 2005 with five to 14 participants per group. There were a total of 13 groups including men and women with a total sample of 109. Five groups were for men only and seven groups were for women only. Two groups included both men and women.

The final set of focus groups with consumer-survivors took place between January 10, 2006 and June 14, 2006. A total of eight groups were held with a total sample size of 67, including 18 males and 49 females. There were three groups with only female participants, two groups with only males, and four groups consisting of males and females.

Participants lived in shelters, group homes, supported apartments, and independent housing. No direct demographic information was obtained from participants; however, field notes indicated that participants ranged in age from late teens to late sixties, though the majority appeared to be in their forties and fifties. The groups were predominantly Caucasian, with some representation from members of minority groups, including Asian, African, and First Nations.

Participants were recruited for the focus groups through posters and word of mouth. Posters were placed in a variety of locations in order to recruit individuals living in a range of housing types, including shelters, group homes, transitional housing programs, and public housing units. Posters were also sent to community mental health agencies, a consumer-survivor self-help organization, and the public library. Posters indicated that the research team was interested in recruiting people with a history of mental illness to discuss issues related to housing and mental health, and gave the time and location of the next group. Letters of information, describing the project in more detail, accompanied the posters and were also distributed and reviewed before beginning each group.

Groups were held in a variety of community locations, including shelters, group homes, community agencies, and drop-in centres. Staff members at the group locations were also helpful in using word of mouth to encourage people to attend. Food, usually pizza, was available at each of the group discussions to encourage and acknowledge attendance. Research team members led all the groups. A common set of open-ended research questions and prompts were used as guides for all groups. The initial interview guide consisted of three sections, each with three questions:

1. *housing:*
   Briefly describe your current housing situation.
   Do you have any problems or concerns with your current housing?
   Describe the type of housing in which you would like to live.
2. *services:*
   What has your experience been?
   Which have been helpful?
   Have you had any problems or concerns with the services you have used?
3. *social supports:*
   Who are key people in your life?
   What types of supports do you use and do you need?
   If you could change your relationships with your supports, how would you make them better?

In the second year additional questions focused on barriers and solutions, and in the later groups we included issues related to diversity and stigma.

Group discussions were audiotaped and transcribed verbatim. Two note takers were present during each group to record field notes. Field notes were completed during and immediately after each group. They included a description of the setting and participants, as well as general impressions. The notes were added to the transcripts and included in the analysis. Each was coded independently by a minimum of two investigators.

Family Focus Groups

Eleven specific family focus groups were held between 2001 and 2004 as a distinct component of the CURA. Each participant had at least one family member who was living with a mental illness (n = 75). In the summer of 2001, the Ontario Ministry of Health and Long-Term Care funded several district health councils across southwestern Ontario to conduct a community housing study through a consultation process. Mental health consumer-survivors and their families were recruited from consumer-survivor groups and family support networks to participate in focus groups. Unfortunately, only half (n = 4) of these family group interviews were audiotaped and transcribed verbatim. Due to the limited comprehensive descriptions of this secondary data set, only preliminary data analysis (i.e., identification of initial themes) was possible. Therefore, three additional focus groups with families caring for individuals with mental illness were conducted in 2003 and 2004 to ensure data adequacy. Adequacy is attained when such sufficient data have been collected that saturation occurs and no new patterns emerge (Morse & Field, 1995). For these additional focus groups, participants were recruited through posters and telephone calls to group homes, transitional housing programs, local community mental health agencies, and family support networks. Potential participants were invited to participate in a focus group to discuss issues related to mental health and housing from a family perspective. If interest was expressed, a focus group was mutually arranged, including the date, time, and location.

Verbal consent to participate in this component of the study was gained immediately prior to the focus group interview, and confidentiality was promised to the participants (e.g., use of pseudonyms). In-depth focus group interviews averaging 60 minutes in length (range 45–90 minutes) were conducted by three researchers using a semi-structured interview guide. This guide elicited the participants' thoughts and feelings about their experiences as family members living with mental illness. Using an open-ended process, participants were asked the following questions:

1. Generally speaking, what has been your experience as a family living with mental illness?
2. Describe the living arrangement of your family member with mental illness.
3. Is this living arrangement your preferred choice and how was this decision made?
4. Have you and/or your family member encountered any problems?
5. Describe the adequacy and utility of the supports (formal and informal) that your family member and/or you use on a regular basis.
6. What do you envision as the "ideal" situation in relation to family members with mental illness and how can we get there?

Sampling continued until theme saturation (Morse, 1991) to elicit an in-depth understanding of the experiences of families caring for members with mental illness. Ultimately, a total sample of 75 participants who varied in age, sex, marital status, family relation, living arrangement with member with mental illness, and geographical location was obtained. The CURA advisory committee decided at the outset of the project that written demographic information would not be directly collected from the people with mental illness or their families due to the stigma associated with mental illness. However, participant observations at each of the focus groups were recorded. The vast majority of the family participants were White, Anglo-Saxon, Canadian middle-aged individuals caring for adult family members (mostly males) with mental illness, such as schizophrenia and bipolar disorder. Most were parents (usually mothers), but other family relationships included siblings, an uncle, and a cousin. Study participants lived in both rural and urban settings. Housing arrangements for family members with mental illness reflected a range of possibilities, including living away from home in an apartment, in a board-and-care facility, in a hospital, or with a family member, who was generally a mother. Finally, many spoke about the financial difficulties they encountered in caring for family members with mental illness, especially those who lived in rural areas, which tended to have fewer mental health resources.

Other Non-consumer Groups
"Peer support worker" focus groups were also held. These groups comprised consumer-survivors who were successfully living in the community and who provided help to other consumers as they attempted to reintegrate into the community themselves. "Service providers" were the last group of informants interviewed. Participants included nurses, doctors, landlords, employers, and police officers. Aside from these service providers, most of the participants came from low socio-economic strata.

Focus groups generally consisted of eight to 14 participants; the trained interviewers ensured that everyone present had an opportunity to participate. All interviews were audio-recorded and transcribed verbatim as soon as possible. Transcripts were reviewed by the interviewer for accuracy. All identifiers were removed during transcription.

Feedback Process
A written summary of the results was provided to all participants who indicated interest in receiving the information. All participants were also invited to attend an annual conference, which provided research results and sought further input

from community stakeholders on priorities for the CURA for the following year. Participation in the conferences was at no cost to participants, and transportation and child-care costs were reimbursed. Approximately 40 consumer-survivors participated each year in the conference. This process was implemented to help ensure that results were quickly fed back to the consumer-survivor community and used to increase the level of information that the community has about housing preferences relative to the current housing available to them.

5. ETHICS REVIEW

Ethics approval was received from the Research Ethics Board at the University of Western Ontario in 2001. Participants provided informed consent prior to participating in the study and were informed that their participation would not impact the level of services or care they were currently receiving. Participant confidentiality was maintained.

6. CONCLUSION

The community is a messy place to do research, so researchers need to be flexible and respond to the needs and realities of the communities within which they work. This also demands flexibility in response to non-academic research partners, particularly when relationships can be intangible and fluid. The combination of three different sampling methods to address the question is one example of flexibility. This response was necessitated when the real world did not align perfectly with the proposed theoretical plan. The sampling frame thus evolved through a filtering process involving academic researchers, community-based service providers, and the consumers of service. Likewise, the need for additional consumer-survivor and family focus groups to reach saturation, highlights the need for a flexible methodological approach when conducting community-based research.

In community-based research, methodology itself needs to be a process, especially when engaging a dynamic community such as was encountered in the mental health consumer-survivor population. In this instance, standard rigid procedures could have become quite problematic, but instead, with the assistance of community partners, the academics on the team were able to develop a more responsive multifaceted approach. While this outcome may not have been a pure process, it was relevant to the environment and led to a more accurate snapshot of the community of interest. It is also offered here as a solution that may be followed by others studying difficult-to-reach or hidden groups in the community.

The methodology for much of this book was ultimately a CURA—a Community-University Research Alliance. It is the product of the collaboration of researchers, service providers, and consumer-survivors working together to address and to begin to resolve housing issues facing people with mental illness. As this collaboration discovered, standard research and standard process will not necessarily work in a community setting, particularly when working with populations invisible to society … and thus you create.

REFERENCES

Altschul, D.B., Wackwitz, J., Coen, A.S. & Ellis, D. (2001). *Colorado Client Assessment Record Interrater Reliability Study.* Denver: Colorado Mental Health Services.

Barnett, V. (1991). *Sample survey principles and methodology.* New York: Oxford University Press.

Bernstein, D.P., Fink, L., Handelsman, L., Foote, J., Lovejoy, M., Wenzel, K., et al. (1994). Initial reliability and validity of a new retrospective measure of child abuse and neglect. *American Journal of Psychiatry, 151,* 1132–36.

Brown, J.B. (1999). The use of focus groups in clinical research. In B.F. Crabtree & W.L. Miller (Eds.), *Doing qualitative research,* 2nd ed. (pp. 109–24). Thousand Oaks: Sage.

Browne, G.B., Arpin, K., Corey, P., Fitch, M., & Gafni, A. (1990). Individual correlates of health service utilization and the cost of poor adjustment to chronic illness. *Medical Care, 18,* 43–58.

Caplan, D.J., Slade, G.D. & Gansky, S.A. (1999). Complex sampling: Implications for data analysis. *Journal of Public Health Dentistry, 59,* 52–59.

Cohen, J. (1988). *Statistical power analysis for the behavioral sciences.* Mahwah, New Jersey: Lawrence Erlbaum Associates.

Ellis, R.J., Wackwitz, J.H. & Foster, M. (1991). Uses of an empirically derived client typology based on level of functioning: Twelve years of the CCAR. *Journal of Mental Health Administration, 18,* 88–100.

Ellis, R., Wackwitz, J. & Foster, M. (1996). *Treatment outcomes using level of functioning and independent measures of change: An alternate approach for measurement of change.* Denver: Decision Support Services, Colorado Department of Mental Health.

Faugier, J. & Sargeant, M. (1997). Sampling hard to reach populations. *Journal of Advanced Nursing, 26,* 790–97.

Greenbaum, T. (1993). *The handbook of focus group research.* Toronto: Maxwell Macmillan Canada.

Henry, G.T. (1990). *Practical sampling.* London: Sage Publications.

Krueger, R.A. (1994). *Focus groups: A practical guide for applied research.* Thousand Oaks: Sage.

Lehman, A., Postrado, L. & Rachuba, L. (1993). Convergent validation of quality of life assessments for persons with severe mental illnesses. *Quality of Life Research* issue 2(5), pp. 327–33.

Lehman, A., Postrado, L., Roth, D., McNary, S. & Goldman, H. (1994). An evaluation of continuity of care, case management, and client outcomes in the Robert Wood Johnson program on chronic mental illness. *Milbank Quarterly,* 72, 105–22.

Leininger, M.M. (1985). Ethnography and ethnographic nursing: Models and modes of qualitative data analysis. In M.M. Leininger (Ed.), *Qualitative research methods in nursing.* 73–117. Orlando: Grune and Stratton.

Levy, P.S. & Lemeshow, S. (1999). *Sampling of populations: Methods and applications,* 3rd ed. New York: John Wiley & Sons.

Lwanga, S.K. (1991). *Sample size determination in health studies: A practical manual.* Geneva: World Health Organization.

Morgan, D. (1988). *Focus groups as qualitative research.* Beverly Hills: Sage.

Morse, J.M. & Field, P.A. (1995). *Qualitative research methods for health professionals,* 2nd ed. London: Sage.

Morse, T. (1991). *Qualitative nursing research: A contemporary dialogue.* Newbury Park: Sage.

Polit, D.F. & Beck, C.T. (2004). *Nursing research: Principles and methods,* 7th ed. Philadelphia: Lippincott Williams & Wilkins.

Rao, P.S.R.S. (2000). *Sampling methodologies: With applications.* Boca Raton: Chapman & Hall/CRC.

Tanzman B. (1993). An overview of surveys of mental health consumers' preferences for housing and support services. *Hospital and Community Psychiatry,* 44, 450–55.

Tanzman, B., Wilson, S. & Yoe, J. (1992). Mental health consumer preferences for housing and supports: The Vermont consumer housing preference study. In J. Jacobson, S. Burchard & P. Carling (Eds.), *Community living for people with developmental and psychiatric disabilities.* 155–166. Baltimore: Johns Hopkins University Press.

Thompson, S.K. (2002). *Sampling,* 2nd ed. New York: John Wiley & Sons.

Section II

INTRODUCTION: UNDERSTANDING THE ISSUE

Mad, insane, lunatic, deranged, abnormal, unhinged, aberrant, unbalanced, diseased, unsound, batty, cracked, cuckoo, or just simply crazy. These are hardly empowering or affirming words, yet this language and imagery are still often associated with a distinct oppressed minority who have very poor or no permanent housing. Of course there are no simple reasons why people become homeless. It is a complex phenomenon that requires a holistic and interdisciplinary approach to even begin to comprehend, let alone properly address, in order to create positive change, which is what Section II attempts to do.

The opening chapter by Forchuk, Schofield, Joplin, Csiernik, and Gorlick, entitled "Housing, Income Support, and Mental Health: Points of Disconnection," examines the lack of integration and cohesion of policies in the mental health, housing, and income support fields. One of the complexities associated with analyzing the intersection of these policies is that federal-, provincial-, and municipal-level policies are all involved. Canada is one of the few developed countries without a national mental health policy and because of the federal policy reforms of the 1970s, the provincial governments now oversee the process of deinstitutionalization from the hospital to the community level. During this same period, the availability of affordable housing has dramatically decreased as responsibility for social housing has been transferred from the federal government to the provincial and/or municipal levels of government. Canada is also now the only developed nation without a national housing policy. Instead, what is considered "affordable" housing is partially dependent on each individual's personal economic resources. As well, over the past decade rates of income supports have been reduced despite increasing costs of living. Mental health consumer-survivors have long been identified as being at risk for homelessness, with the disconnection between housing, income, and mental health policies and the lack of a national policy in any of these areas further contributing to this risk.

Chapter 4, "Surviving the Tornado: Mental Health Consumer-Survivor Experiences of Getting, Losing, and Keeping Housing," by Forchuk, Ward-Griffin, Csiernik, and Turner, is a qualitative exploration of consumer-survivors' experiences related to housing. Participants provided descriptions of their devastating experiences of losing much of what was important to them, including their housing status, and going through a long arduous process to rebuild their lives after they were struck with mental illness. Group discussions revealed that mental health consumer-survivors encountered three levels of upheaval, loss, and destruction, similar to the effects of a tornado: losing ground, struggling to survive, and gaining stability. Within each of these levels, five major themes were identified: (1) living in fear; (2) losing control of basic human rights; (3) attempting to hold onto and create relationships; (4) identifying supports and seeking services; and (5) obtaining personal space and place. It was found that a caring community response, including adequate housing, income support, and community care, can help overcome the devastation brought on by the tornado of mental illness.

Ward-Griffin, Schofield, Vos, and Coatsworth-Puspoky follow with another qualitative study in Chapter 5's "Families Caring for Members with Mental Illness: A Vicious Cycle." The four nurses explore the perspectives of individuals caring for a family member with a mental illness, with a particular focus on housing, quality of supports, and formal care services. The authors found that many family caregivers who remained involved with their loved ones experiencing mental illness became part of a "circle of care," supporting the independence of their family members, while at the same time trying to protect them from the external world and its often too harsh realities. However, the focus group interviews also led to suggestions that this circle of care resulted in a "vicious cycle" of unrelenting caregiving. Three major themes were identified: (1) witnessing inadequacies; (2) working behind the scenes; and (3) creating a better world.

Chapter 6, "De-'Myth'-ifying Mental Health," by Csiernik, Forchuk, Speechley, and Ward-Griffin, brought together academics from the fields of social work, epidemiology, and nursing to examine some of the many myths that relate to mental illness and those with mental health issues. The chapter examines and disputes beliefs about four popular myths: that people with mental health problems are a homogeneous population; are violent and dangerous and thus spend extended periods of time incarcerated; are unemployed because they are uneducated; and are unsupported by their families, which then leads to housing problems. Challenging these and other equally erroneous myths are essential for all helping professionals in their response to the oppression faced by mental-health consumer-survivors.

In Chapter 7, "'It's Important to Be Proud of the Place You Live in': Housing Problems and Preferences of Mental Health Consumer-Survivors," Forchuk, Nelson, and Hall bring together authors from nursing, community psychology, and geography. The authors explore the importance of understanding housing and mental health issues from the perspective of mental health consumer-survivors. This chapter presents findings from a series of focus group meetings held with survivors of mental illness to address issues concerning housing preferences and housing needs. Most consumer-survivors' first choice for housing was an independent living arrangement where supports would be available as needed. The authors describe dilemmas that consumer-survivors face of having to choose between the housing they wanted and the supports they needed, as supports were often contingent on living in a less desirable housing situation. Thus, helping professionals working in this area need to be aware of the forced choices that mental health consumers-survivors are often faced with during discharge planning. As well, professionals should work to ensure that the voices of clients are heard by decision makers at various levels of government in order for housing policy to become more receptive to their realities.

In the concluding chapter of Section II: Understanding the Issues, Nelson, Hall, and Forchuk return to discuss "Current and Preferred Housing of Mental Health Consumer-Survivors." The three authors discovered that while 79 percent of the sample of 150 men and 150 women preferred living independently, 76 percent were living in some other type of setting such as a temporary shelter, supportive housing, or sheltered care. Those living in temporary shelters reported the lowest levels of housing satisfaction, and those who were living in the type of housing they preferred had the highest levels of housing satisfaction. This information collected was subsequently used by stakeholder groups to help build the community's capacity to provide the types of housing that are preferred by mental health consumer-survivors.

The chapters as a whole in this section illustrate the disconnection between policies that have brought us to the current situation and the impact of these disconnections on people's lives. We hope that juxtaposing these analyses will help create more desire for action to improve the housing situation that some consumer-survivors can't survive.

Chapter 3

HOUSING, INCOME SUPPORT, AND MENTAL HEALTH: POINTS OF DISCONNECTION

Cheryl Forchuk, Ruth Schofield,
LiBbey Joplin, Rick Csiernik,
Carolyne Gorlick, and Katherine Turner

1. INTRODUCTION

There is a well-known relationship between the presence of a mental illness and increased rates of poverty and homelessness. However, the exact dynamics of this relationship has remained unclear. While early literature suggested that increased rates of homelessness and unstable housing were due to a mental illness (Drake, Wallach & Hoffman, 1989; Lamb & Lamb, 1990), subsequent research has suggested that these increased rates are more likely the result of an overall lack of affordable housing (Draine, Salzer, Culhane & Hadley, 2002; Drake & Wallach, 1999; Koegel, Burnam & Baumohol, 1996). In Canada, the lack of national housing, mental health, and income policies have further added to the basic problems related to the issues of housing and mental health. At the provincial level in Ontario, Canada's most populous province, an examination of the policies pertaining to the issues of housing development, income support, and mental health brings to light a large area of disconnection among these policy realms. The purpose of this chapter is to answer, by analyzing the available research literature, these questions: What are these areas of policy disconnect? What is their impact on those who rely on these policies?

2. HOUSING DEVELOPMENT

Under section 92 of the *Constitution Act*, 1867, responsibility for the development of social housing rests with the provincial governments in Canada. However, the federal government has the ability to unilaterally initiate social housing programs under the Peace, Order, and Good Government Clause of the *Act*, as long as these programs are determined by the courts to be in the national interest. Until the 1990s the Canadian federal government was involved with a number of different partners, including the various provincial governments, in the development of social housing stock. However, at that time, the federal government transferred administrative responsibility for the majority of this housing stock to the provincial governments, and has since proceeded to further cut the funding of programs supporting the development of new housing. Presently, the federal government continues to have only an administrative role in the federal co-operative social housing sector.

After the 1995 election of Mike Harris's ideologically and politically conservative government, the province of Ontario transferred ownership of administrative responsibility for the existing social housing stock to newly created municipal service managers. A one-time allocation of funds and a substantial body of operational regulations accompanied this transfer. At the same time, the Harris provincial government cancelled the previously existing housing development agreements and signalled that any subsequent affordable housing developments would be the responsibility of the private sector.

The definition of affordable housing, according to the Canada Mortgage and Housing Corporation (CMHC) (2007), varies with the number of bedrooms, number of levels, and the location of a given home within Ontario. For instance, according to the CMHC, for a one-bedroom, one-level apartment to be considered affordable in the city of London, Ontario, in 2005, the rent must have been below the maximum of $700 a month, while an apartment having the same number of levels and bedrooms in the city of North Perth must have been below a maximum of $575 a month, and in the city of Toronto it must have been below the maximum of $990 a month. Between 1995 and 2002, almost no new affordable housing developments arose in the province of Ontario due in part to private housing developers' reluctance to invest in the development of new affordable housing, a venture they considered to be somewhat less than attractive.

Throughout this period, community-level pressure for the creation of new affordable housing developments escalated, fuelled by increasing levels of homelessness in cities across the country (Begin, Casavant, Chernier & Depuis, 1999). This has led to renewed federal interest in the development of affordable housing stock. As a result, in 2001 the federal government initiated a federal–provincial partnership regarding the development of affordable housing and proceeded to negotiate agreements on a province-by-province basis. The agreements were intended to leverage matching provincial dollars of $25,000 per unit to provide the upfront capital funds necessary for housing development.

In Ontario the provincial government signed an agreement with the federal government in 2002, in which the Ontario government would provide a provincial sales tax rebate of $2,000 per unit, while the participating municipalities and the participating housing developers would provide an additional $2,000 per unit. In 2004, a number of housing developments were proposed, but still not implemented despite the election of an Ontario Liberal government in October 2003 that had expressed a commitment to the development of new subsidized and supportive housing units within the province, nor did it become an issue discussed by the governing Liberals as part of the 2007 provincial election.

As a result of the downloading through the various governmental levels and reliance on the private sector, affordable housing generally and public housing in particular are more scarce. Municipalities have long waiting lists for available units. For example, in London there are typically 3,000 family units on the waiting list for approximately 5,000 public housing units. Although generally approximately 1,000 units turn over each year, they are often the less desirable units. An undesirable unit may turn over several times within a year and in reality, some individuals and families in need will never be housed in this system.

3. INCOME SUPPORTS

Individuals with mental illnesses in Ontario are most likely to obtain public income support through either the Ontario Works or the Ontario Disability Support Program. Other sources of income support for such individuals first require a period of employment, requirements that people with serious mental illnesses may have difficulty achieving. For example, to obtain income support through the Canada Pension Plan (Disability) (CPP [D]), a person must be employed for at least four of the previous six years, a criterion that individuals with serious mental illnesses often have difficulty meeting. As well, the CPP (D) requires a potential recipient to have an "ongoing" illness, which is a barrier for those with mental health issues given that many mental illnesses are episodic and not ongoing in nature. Similarly, those individuals with mental illnesses in Ontario would be eligible for private insurance coverage only if they became ill while employed or if the Workplace Safety and Insurance Board (WSIB) determined that the employee suffered an injury while at work. However, it would be very unlikely for a person suffering a mental illness to be eligible for such coverage given that the development of mental illnesses has rarely been linked to workplace injuries.

Ontario Works (OW)

In May 1998, the *Ontario Works Act* replaced the existing General Welfare Assistance program, though no increase in actual financial support accompanied this change in program direction. As of December 2008, the amount of income support meant to meet the basic needs of a single person with no dependants was $216 per month, the shelter costs (inclusive of utilities) was a maximum of $356 for a total monthly income of $572. That value increased to the sum of $429 for basic needs and $607 for shelter for a total family income of $1,036 per month if the person had a partner and dependent child over the age of 13.

The Harris provincial government was very clear in that Ontario Works was to serve as a labour market adjustment program with the provision of employment assistance as its primary goal. This program, therefore, was intended to provide only temporary financial assistance to people in need; it was not conceptualized as a social assistance program. The government believed that previous welfare rates had been so generous that they failed to encourage self-reliance and instead gave rise to widespread dependency on welfare, thus discouraging people from seeking employment in Canada's most prosperous province. In accordance with the government's interpretation of social assistance programs, a mandatory welfare-to-work program was instituted in the province along with a diligent crackdown on any perceived systematic or individual fraud. The fundamental philosophy underlying the Ontario Works program was that the shortest route to paid employment must be the overriding principle of all of the program's activities (Gorlick & Brethour, 1998a). The program's eligibility rules were designed to encourage individuals in financial need to seek employment as a first resort and to seek social assistance only when all other resources and possibilities had been exhausted. It was believed that these rules would help to ensure that social assistance funds were given to those considered to be the most in need of them: the deserving poor.

A range of employment assistance activities was introduced, including programs to provide those participants who were not job-ready with employable skills, programs to assist participants who were job ready in the process of finding paid employment, and programs designed to support participants in finding the shortest route possible to paid employment through community participation and various employment measures. Everyone involved with Ontario Works is required to participate in one or more employment assistance programs to be considered eligible for financial assistance unless these requirements are deferred under special circumstances (Gorlick & Brethour, 1998a). This stipulation, like many other Ontario Works stipulations, was intended to make people more self-reliant. The *Ontario Works Act* provides a legislative framework that mandates local delivery agents to offer specific types of assistance, including referrals to basic education opportunities where appropriate, making available skills training initiatives to assist participants in becoming job-ready, and to help put each participant on the shortest route possible to the goal of paid employment. This training is intended to be job-specific, with the goal of providing an entry into or a return to employment in the shortest amount of time possible.

The *Act* does provide for basic financial assistance to be paid to those who meet the eligibility requirements (Gorlick & Brethour, 1998b). Basic financial assistance under this Act includes:

- income assistance provided for basic needs and shelter
- benefits as prescribed in the regulations, e.g., prescription drugs
- emergency assistance to help with basic needs and shelter on an emergency basis

The *Ontario Works Act* also provides employment assistance to recipients based on their individual skills, experience, and circumstances (Gorlick & Brethour, 1998b). Employment assistance offered under the Act includes *community participation* in activities that allow people to contribute to their community and to improve their level of employability. *Other employment measures* include:

- job search support services, including employment resource centres
- literacy screening tests
- literacy assessment, literacy training, or both
- other basic education and job-specific skills training sessions, including sessions pertaining to life skills
- employment placements

- education or training programs
- self-employment activities
- supports pertaining to self-employment
- substance abuse recovery programs
- LEAP—Learning, Earning, and Parenting—a program designed to help teen parents receiving social assistance to finish high school, to learn more about what it takes to be good parents, and, most importantly, how to get a job as quickly as possible.

In May 2001, the government announced a five-point action plan designed to make Ontario Works an even more responsive program, including:

- following through on the government's commitment to the practice of double placements in order to provide more people with the opportunity to gain the job-related experience they need to find and keep a job
- providing additional supports for people on welfare who face significant employment barriers
- mandatory literacy testing and training to help people who cannot read and write well enough to find and keep a job to break through the literacy barrier and overcome these obstacles
- advanced caseworker training in order to provide recipients with the skills that they need to better assist those facing employment barriers take the steps required to move from welfare to work
- mandatory addiction treatment to help people overcome addictions that are obstacles to employment

The goals of Ontario Works, as outlined in the *Ontario Works Act*, is the establishment of a program that recognizes individual responsibility and promotes self-reliance through employment, that provides temporary financial assistance to those most in need while they satisfy obligations to become and stay employed, and that holds the government sufficiently accountable to the taxpayers of Ontario (Gorlick, 2002).

Ontario Disability Support Program (ODSP)

The Ontario Disability Support Program is an adjunct to Ontario Works as indicated by the transitional provisions listed under Schedule D of the *Social Assistance Reform Act* of 1997. The intent of this program is to provide income and employment supports to people with disabilities and their dependants who meet the strict criteria stipulated by the *Act*. According to the ODSP *Act*, a person is considered disabled if:

(a) the person has a substantial physical or mental impairment that is continuous or recurrent and expected to last one year or more;
(b) the direct and cumulative effect of the impairment on the person's ability to attend to his or her personal care, function in the community, and function in a workplace results in a substantial restriction in one or more of these activities of daily living; and,
(c) the impairment and its likely duration and the resulting restrictions it places on the person's activities of daily living have been verified by a person having the prescribed qualifications (Ontario Ministry of Community and Social Services, 1997).

While the ODSP *Act* does not precisely define what is meant by the term "substantial," given the context in which the term is used, it can be inferred to mean a disability that results in a number of obstacles in one's life that can be overcome only with government assistance.

The ODSP application process entails completion of a health status report, activities of daily living report, a medical consent form, and a self-report. However, single-status people are not eligible for the program if they have over $5,000 in liquid assets, cash, Registered Retirement Savings, or insurance policies, while those with a partner may have up to $7,500 in assets and still qualify for the program (Ontario Ministry of Community and Social Services, 2003a). In addition, in direct opposition to human rights legislation, people are deemed ineligible for ODSP if they are found to be dependent on or addicted to alcohol or any other psychoactive drug unless otherwise authorized (Ontario Ministry of Community and Social Services, 1997).

Becoming qualified for ODSP has become extraordinarily difficult since its evolution from the former GAINS-D (Guaranteed Annual Income Supplement for the Disabled) program. In 1998, there were 189,442 active cases on file, three-quarters of which pertained to single-status individuals. By 2003, the caseload had grown by 11,718 to a total of 201,160, a rate of just slightly over 1 percent per year (Ontario Ministry of Community and Social Services, 2003b).

While the income support provided by ODSP is substantially greater than that provided by Ontario Works, it still provides recipients with an income significantly below any of the established poverty line levels. In 2002, the National Council of Welfare Reports (2003) conducted an analysis comparing income support benefits in constant dollars and found that a single individual receiving ODSP that year could have obtained a maximum amount of $11,466, nearly double that of an individual on Ontario Works at the time. However, the equivalent income in 1997 when the legislation was first introduced was $12,682, while the equivalent income in 1992 would have been $13,449. Thus, a single person without any substantial assets and who, under government policy, is considered to be permanently unemployable has seen the amount of income support he or she is eligible to receive decreased by 10.6 percent since the new legislation was passed and has seen the amount of real dollars support decreased by 17.7 percent in a single decade. In this same time period, income support for a single employable person receiving Ontario Works benefits fell in the province by nearly half from $9,741 per year to $6,623, a pattern that has been repeated across Canada.

4. MENTAL HEALTH CARE: DEINSTITUTIONALIZATION

Bachrach (1978) defined deinstitutionalization as a process having two main elements: the avoidance of traditional institutions/hospitals, and the concurrent expansion of community-based facilities (p. 573). The "deinstitutionalization" of individuals diagnosed with a mental illness has been evolving for decades. Goldman and Morrissey (1985) described cycles of institutional reforms such as the early 19th-century introduction of moral treatment through the use of asylums; the mental health hygiene movement and psychopathic hospitals; and the mid-20th-century community-focused mental health movement. They argue that the fourth cycle in this evolutionary process is the establishment of a broad network of mental health and social welfare services. However, according to Goldman and Morrissey, the "failure to address the basic social problems themselves has resulted in a repeating cycle of policies which only partly accomplish the goals of their activist proponents" (1985: 727).

Sussman (1998) described the evolution of psychiatric facilities across Canada as a process that has occurred with little communication or collaboration among the provinces. Sussman also differentiated between the process of "deinstitutionalisation" and the process of "dehospitalization," and discovered that many so-called "community" programs were, in actuality, simply smaller institutions. The movement associated with making the community the focus of care instead of psychiatric hospitals began with the introduction of effective antipsychotic drugs after the 1950s (Smith & Hart, 1975). In Ontario, the total number of patients in provincial psychiatric hospitals peaked in 1959–61, with the largest decrease occurring between 1965 and 1968. In 1960, there were 19,501 hospitalized patients in Ontario, while in 1982, there were only 4,514 (Heseltine, 1983).

In recent decades there have been a number of provincial discussion papers and policy documents written that advocate for mental health policy reform. The Ontario branch of the Canadian Mental Health Association (2004) has noted that 20 such documents and papers have been produced in as many years. The process of deinstitutionalization and the corresponding movement of the focus of care to the community have been the predominant focus of these documents and papers. Since the Ontario Ministry of Health's *Putting People First* report of 1993, this proposed recommendation has included an explicit shift in funding such that 60 percent of the funding for mental health services would be distributed to community-based programs, while the remaining 40 percent would be distributed to hospital-based programs. This recommendation, therefore, was in essence the mirror image of the funding situations existing at that time.

In 1999, the Health Services Restructuring Committee recommended that the provinces transfer the provincial psychiatric hospitals (PPHs) to local community service centres and/or community hospitals. The document called for a reduction in hospital beds and stated that "the proposed hospital bed targets are achievable once the appropriate community services and supports are in place to reduce reliance on institutional care, especially PPHs, and dramatically reduce the need for hospital-based treatment services" (Ontario Ministry of Health, 1999). The report further stated that "in 1995–96 there were 2,900 mental health beds in PPHs. The number of beds that will be available post-restructuring [2003] is estimated at 1,767 beds, resulting in a decrease of 1,133 beds (39 percent)" (Ontario Ministry of Health, 1999: 6). All of these decreases in the number of hospitalized patients occurred as the province's overall population steadily grew with each passing year.

Despite this dramatic decrease in the funding of psychiatric hospitals and the reduction of the number of available beds, a concurrent shift of resources to community-based mental health programs did not occur. In addition, given that psychiatric hospitals provided patients with housing as well as mental health services, the need for new homes has increased as the process of dehospitalization and bed reductions have also increased. In fact, there has been no corresponding increase in the funding of community mental health programs in Ontario since 1993, despite the larger numbers of people seeking these community-based services. With the change in government to the Liberal Party led by Premier Dalton McGuinty, there was a promise of increased community mental health funding, and after years of no increases, some increases have been made since 2004 in key areas such as crisis response, early intervention for psychosis, and case management.

The Rhetoric of Mental Health Reform Policy paper (Wasylenki, Goering & MacNaughton, 1992) and the *Putting People First* policy document (Ontario Ministry of Health, 1993) that appeared the following year both recognized the need to better take into account recognized health determinants and to provide a more comprehensive vision of health rather than narrowly focusing on the alleviation of illness in the delivery of mental health services. In 1998, the Ministry of Health policy document entitled *2000 and Beyond: Strengthening Ontario's Mental Health System* further recognized that one of the principles guiding the reform of mental health policies should be the adoption of a holistic approach that addresses broader determinants of health such as housing and income support. Unfortunately, in the subsequent policy document *Making It Happen—Implementation Plan for Mental Health Reform* (Ontario Ministry of Health, 1999) this holistic principle was rejected as a guiding principle underlying mental health policy reform while at the same time, the document stated that increasing the quality of life of the mentally ill must be a goal of all subsequent reforms. The question that then arises is how can the government expect the quality of life of the mentally ill to improve if such well-established determinants of health, such as housing and poverty (Raphael, 2008), are not taken into account in the relevant policies?

5. IMPLICATIONS

There appears to be a large area of disconnection between the evolving policies regarding housing, income support, and mental health care. The move to shift the focus of care of mental health consumer-survivors to community-based centres away from the hospital and institutional setting occurred while the availability of affordable housing was decreasing. The increased restrictions placed on income support further reduced the availability of housing that could be considered affordable to this population. The disconnection between these policy areas has created a situation that has increased an already vulnerable population's risk of being reduced to a state of homelessness. Since these policy changes have occurred simultaneously throughout multiple policy sectors, the resulting areas of disconnection are often poorly understood even by service providers within each policy sector. Solutions to the problems resulting from the existing areas of disconnection can arise only by re-establishing and strengthening the connections among these diverse policy arenas.

What is often neglected in the discussion of mental health policy and practice is the actual voice of the consumers or recipients of these services. Consumers of these services have described the disconnection at the mental health service provider level and client level as "resembling a false ploy doubling as an art form in practice." In some circumstances, no matter how unhealthy a situation becomes, the service provider's credo remains essentially "Don't worry, dear, we have everything under control," even when circumstances are clearly beyond their control. Hence, there is also policy disconnection at the interpersonal level when fending off a complainant's concerns. Given the disconnection between evolving policies in the areas of mental health, income support, and housing, it becomes evident why the term "mental health consumer-survivors" has become so accurate in describing this group.

Health care and social service professionals, as well as policy-makers, need to understand and acknowledge the areas of disconnection among the various policies related to mental health, income maintenance, and housing. Clearly, there is a role for advocacy to increase community awareness and to promote system level change. However, proper acknowledgement of the disconnection includes working on a personal level with clients and avoiding the use of therapeutic euphemisms or pathologizing very real poverty-related fears. On the whole, the disconnection among housing policy, income support policies, and mental health policies adversely impacts many whose lives were meant to be improved by these policies. This disconnection causes many of these individuals to feel as though they've been disregarded by society, are harmed even further, and minimizes the experiences of those with mental health issues. These disconnections hold people back and erode their sense of dignity, worth, stability, and security. It effectively revictimizes the already aggrieved, disenfranchised, and at-risk. It is our hope that by reforming the aforementioned practices, programs, and policies, we can reverse this trend and better serve those individuals whom these programs are intended to benefit.

REFERENCES

Bachrach, L.L. (1978). A conceptual approach to deinstitutionalization. *Hospital & Community Psychiatry, 29*(9), 573–78.

Begin, P., Casavant, L., Chenier, N. & Depuis, J. (1999). *Homelessness* (Ottawa Library of Parliament PRB 99-1E). Ottawa: Parliamentary Research Branch.

Candian Mental Health Association, Ontario (2010). Chronology of reports, Retrieved October 25, 2010, from recommendations and plans for mental health reform. www.ontario.cmha.ca/policy_and_research.asp?cID=23000.

Canadian Mortgage and Housing Corporation. (2007). *Affordability criteria.* CMHA. Retrieved October 25, 2008, from www.cmhc-schl.gc.ca/en/inpr/afhoce/fias/upload/criteria.pdf.

Draine, J., Salzer, M.S., Culhane, D.P. & Hadley, T.R. (2002). Role of social disadvantage in crime, joblessness, and homelessness among persons with serious mental illness. *Psychiatric Services, 53*, 565–73.

Drake, R.E. & Wallach, M.A. (1999). Homelessness and mental illness: A story of failure. *Psychiatric Services, 50*(5), 589.

Drake, R.E., Wallach, M.A. & Hoffman, J.S. (1989). Housing instability and homelessness among aftercare patients of an urban state hospital. *Hospital and Community Psychiatry, 40*(1), 46–51.

Goldman, H. & Morrissey, J. (1985). The alchemy of mental health policy: Homelessness and the fourth cycle of reform. *American Journal of Public Health, 75*(7), 727–31.

Gorlick, C. (2002). *Policy expectations and program realities: Welfare to work programs in Canada (final report)*. Ottawa: Human Resources Development Canada.

Gorlick, C. & Brethour, G. (1998a). *Welfare to work programs in Canada: A national inventory*. Ottawa: Canadian Council on Social Development.

Gorlick, C. & Brethour, A. (1998b). *Welfare to work programs in Canada: A discussion paper*. Ottawa: Canadian Council on Social Development.

Health Services Restructuring Commission. (1999). *Building a community mental health system in Ontario: Report of the health services restructuring commission*. Toronto: Ministry of Health and Long-Term Care.

Heseltine, G.F. (1983). *Towards a blueprint for change: A mental health policy and program perspective discussion paper*. Toronto: Ontario Ministry of Health.

Koegel, P., Burnam, M.A. & Baumohl, J. (1996). The causes of homelessness. In J. Baumohl (Ed.), *Homelessness in America* (pp. 24–33). Phoenix: Oryx Press.

Lamb, H. & Lamb, D. (1990). Factors contributing to homelessness among the chronically and severely mentally ill. *Hospital and Community Psychiatry, 41*(3), 301–5.

National Council of Welfare Reports. (2003). *Welfare incomes 2002* (Cat. no. H68-27/2002E). Ottawa: Minister of Public Works and Government Services.

Ontario Ministry of Community and Social Services. (1997). *Ontario disability support program act*. Toronto: Queen's Printer for Ontario.

Ontario Ministry of Community and Social Services. (2003a). *ODSP handbook*. Toronto: Queen's Printer for Ontario.

Ontario Ministry of Community and Social Services. (2003b). *ODSP quarterly statistical report*. Toronto: Queen's Printer for Ontario.

Ontario Ministry of Health. (1993). *Putting people first: The reform of mental health services in Ontario*. Toronto: Ministry of Health.

Ontario Ministry of Health. (1998). *2000 and beyond: Strengthening Ontario's mental health system*. Toronto: Ministry of Health.

Ontario Ministry of Health. (1999). *Making it happen—Implementation plan for mental health reform* (Cat. no. 2231504). Toronto: Queen's Printer for Ontario.

Raphael, D. (2008). *Social determinants of health: Canadian perspectives*, 2nd ed. Toronto: Canadian Scholars' Press Inc.

Smith, W. & Hart, D. (1975). Community mental health: A noble failure? *Hospital and Community Psychiatry, 26*(9), 581–83.

Sussman, S. (1998). The first asylums in Canada: A response to neglectful community care and current trends. *Canadian Journal of Psychiatry, 43*(3), 260–64.

Wasylenki, D., Goering, P. & MacNaughton, E. (1992). Planning mental health services: 1. Background and key issues. *Canadian Journal of Psychiatry, 37*, 199–205.

Chapter 4

SURVIVING THE TORNADO: MENTAL HEALTH CONSUMER-SURVIVOR EXPERIENCES OF GETTING, LOSING, AND KEEPING HOUSING

Cheryl Forchuk, Catherine Ward-Griffin, Rick Csiernik, and Katherine Turner

1. INTRODUCTION

The recent trend in deinstitutionalization from hospital to community for mental health consumer-survivors has frequently led to housing problems. Mental health consumer-survivors are consistently overrepresented in homeless populations (Koegel, Burnam & Baumohl, 1996; Drake & Wallach, 1999; Robertson, 1992), so housing stability has become an important concern for this group. The Centre for Addiction and Mental Health (2001) examined the issue of housing stability for consumer-survivors and subsequently emphasized the importance of preference in determining an individual's ability to maintain stable housing. The authors noted that the process of making a house a home is based on interactions among three key factors: person, support, and housing. For a housing situation to be stable, an individual should receive appropriate support within a physical and social housing environment suited to the individual's goals, characteristics, preferences, strengths, and needs. The authors noted that housing stability is often defined as duration of stay. They suggested that an appropriate measure of stability should include consideration of the quality or desirability of housing mobility rather than simply the quantity of moves. Research from New Zealand has expanded on the concept of designing housing for consumer-survivors to facilitate housing stability (Peace & Kell, 2001). This work focused on the issue of sustainability in the context of mental health and housing as an attribute of the wider environment rather than of a particular house. A "sustainability framework" was developed that details the array of supports and resources necessary to maintain independent living. Access to four categories of resources is necessary for true sustainability. First, a supportive regulatory environment is needed, which implies well-enforced statutory government frameworks to safeguard human rights; combating discrimination; and regulating the labour market, building codes, and housing standards. Second, material resources must be available, including adequate and suitable housing to choose from, income to pay for it, and access to basic necessities. Third, service resources are necessary, including clinical services, housing facilitation services, and personal support services tailored to individuals' needs. Fourth, social resources are needed, including community supports, groups, families, and cultural and social networks.

The issue of housing preference has been explored in the literature to address the housing needs of people with mental illnesses. This research has consistently found that independent living is preferred (Carling, 1993; Forchuk, Nelson & Hall, 2006, Nelson, Hall & Forchuk, 2003; Tsemberis & Eisenberg, 2000). Unfortunately, mental health consumer-survivors often face many obstacles to obtaining and keeping independent housing.

A review of existing research on supported and supportive housing undertaken by the Cochrane Review (Chilvers, Macdonald & Hays, 2004) found a lack of conclusive evidence regarding the effectiveness of supportive housing as opposed to supported housing options. The authors concluded that further research is required in this area. A cautionary note was injected by O'Malley and Croucher (2003), who indicated that assuming that individuals will progress from higher to lower levels of supported accommodation over time may marginalize the needs of people with particularly challenging behaviour who require long-term, permanent accommodation with higher levels of support.

In summary, although housing issues are known to be of concern for mental health consumer-survivors, the literature has many gaps. Studies have focused on issues such as homelessness, housing stability, and housing preference. Subjective experiences related to housing remain largely unexplored. The purpose of this investigation was to explore experiences of mental health consumer-survivors in relation to housing, and identify potential solutions to difficulties encountered by this population. The study used descriptive qualitative methods and focus groups. Ethics approval was granted through the University of Western Ontario, and data were compiled in July and August 2002.

2. A METAPHOR, THEMES, AND PHASES

The study used an ethnographic method of analysis (Leininger, 1987). While a full ethnography would require a longer period of observation, a broad approach was still desired to help us understand the patterns related to housing and mental health in the social and cultural contexts of the participants across multiple settings. The ethnographic analysis first identified and listed descriptors and then developed them into patterns. Patterns were then synthesized to obtain broad themes. Themes were then tested by reviewing them against raw data. Data were initially analyzed independently by each research team member. Team members then met on three different occasions to compare and further develop the identified themes. A matrix was used to assist in the development of identified patterns— for example, living with fear or losing control—into larger themes. Team members who made slight revisions to the interpretation of themes and patterns then reviewed the matrix and transcripts.

On the basis of the analysis of the focus group data, the team members proposed a metaphor of a tornado to describe the upheaval and loss encountered by the study participants (Figure 4.1). Few phenomena can form as quickly as a tornado and create such devastation in such a short time and in such a random way. Although the probability of actually being touched by a tornado is quite small, and surviving a tornado is likely, it is nonetheless a substantive force that cannot be ignored. Tornadoes not only enter lives unexpectedly, they rip them apart and scatter the accumulated possessions of a lifetime haphazardly, often across great distances and usually without warning.

Participants saw their experiences related to housing as part of broader experiences related to supports. In other words,

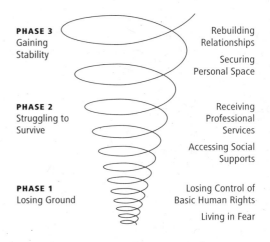

Figure 4.1: Three Overlapping Phases within the Tornado of Mental Illness

obtaining and maintaining housing were related to obtaining and maintaining a broad base of supports, ranging from assistance with psychiatric symptoms to income supports.

Three overlapping phases within the tornado of mental illness were proposed: (1) losing ground, (2) struggling to survive, and (3) gaining stability. Depending on certain environmental forces, mental health consumer-survivors moved between and among the three phases. Five major themes were also identified within the phases. Living in fear and losing control of basic human rights were dominant themes in the losing-ground phase, and gaining access to social supports and receiving professional services were the most common themes within the struggling-to-survive phase. Finally, the themes of securing personal space and rebuilding relationships were identified in the gaining-stability phase.

In November 2003 the findings from the initial data analysis were presented to a group of 75 key stakeholders, including consumer-survivors, researchers, and members of community agencies. They were asked for oral or written feedback about the analysis and the metaphor used. Feedback was received from six consumers (four oral and two written), and all their feedback supported the analysis and metaphor. Supportive written feedback was also received from two community mental health service providers. Written feedback tended to be brief—for example, "Tornado a great metaphor."

Phase 1: Losing Ground

Losing ground was the first and most destructive phase of the tornado identified in the study findings. Metaphorically speaking, the tornado is at its greatest strength in this phase, uprooting people and causing the most damage, perhaps even death. Indeed, some individuals with mental illness may not survive these "killer" tornadoes, especially if they have experienced consistent loss and destruction as a result of poor housing conditions.

The words of two participants illustrate this destructiveness. "Some of the homes have been condemned…. Four of them I had to leave because they burned right down. I lost everything." "So I had to leave everything, and that isn't the first time. I had lost a lot of belongings, seven times to fire and five times to just up and leaving, and carrying whatever I could. So I am getting pretty tired of it."

Loss of current living arrangements also frequently occurred when individuals needed to be hospitalized because of their mental illness. As one woman explained, "They made me give up my apartment…. I left everything behind—my couch, my TV, everything, my fish tank, everything. I left it all behind because they said I wasn't well enough to go back. I wasn't able to look after myself."

Living in fear was the dominant theme in this phase. Participants were fearful of many things; they were afraid of being hurt and of losing their lives or their possessions. One young man remarked, "There has been a lot of violence in my building.... One guy here tells me he is going to kill me, daily." A woman commented that she did not want to live in a house—even one with affordable rent—where there may be people who would harm her or her family: "Even if I were to get housing and they said, 'Oh, you could pay $97 a month for a one bedroom,' I wouldn't take it, considering what is out there. I mean, the guy next door may be a pyromaniac, and the other one might be a pedophile for all I know."

Women who lived in shelters and other living arrangements that housed both men and women shared additional concerns: "Him and me were in [a facility] together. He attempted to rape me on the ground.... Went back there this year, after finally a year and a half, only to find out that this guy's been let off."

Others agreed that women and men living together constituted a risk to women's safety. One man stated, "If there is a female ... three rooms over, hey, you're going to have, like, ten dogs [males] over, right? So to put it more plainly, it would just be a festival. It wouldn't work.... It would be trouble."

Losing control of basic human rights was the second predominant theme in this phase. It was apparent that people with mental illnesses felt deprived of adequate income, which led to inadequate food and housing. One woman explained, "The comfort allowance [personal needs allowance] is the same today as it was 10, 12 years ago in 1990. It is like the government has something against people with mental illness. We are being punished and held down financially. If you have a mental illness, they say, 'Here's this,' and shove you into a corner.... I have nothing."

The cramped conditions under which many people with mental illness are expected to live are at times deplorable. Residents frequently must share limited toilet facilities. A man living in a shelter described his experience: "You are living with, and sleeping with, 25 other guys, and you gotta deal with their noise when they come in and out of the room. And as far as the rest goes, I mean we're all men and we all do what men do, so if you gotta do it, you do it."

Other participants reported that they were treated "like children" who had no choice but to comply with the rules. One man explained, "You have to beg for a drink when you want one. I find I get thirsty a lot. You're not supposed to be around the kitchen. You get yelled at."

Phase 2: Struggling to Survive

Struggling to survive was the second phase of the tornado identified in the study findings. As people started to pick up the pieces from the destruction caused by the tornado, they still struggled with meeting their basic needs. As one woman explained, "I was in an apartment of my own, and I was trying to cope with it, but I didn't have any support. They just dumped me here."

For others, energy was expended toward gaining access to social supports. Such supports were seen as critical to maintaining more independence in housing. One man explained how he needed to use a variety of supports to survive, and yet at times these social programs were inadequate to meet his basic needs: "I am sorry, but a can of beans and a little bit like that once a month is not going to go anywhere, ... and the food bank is here, but it is only going to feed you for two days, and when you have no money, what do you do for the other 28 days?"

Other participants attended church programs to acquire adequate food and shelter. "In the wintertime, they have suppers at the church over there. I go for a free meal. Meals are usually on at some of these churches all around the city."

In addition to providing meals, some of the churches and housing providers offered professional counselling services. Many participants also relied heavily on the services of health professionals to survive this phase of the tornado. However, many spoke of the difficulties they experienced in gaining access to and receiving professional services in a timely fashion. If their symptoms are not treated, they fear losing their housing.

Phase 3: Gaining Stability

Gaining stability is the final phase of the tornado. Participants in this phase reported that they were beginning to rebuild their lives. As most of their basic physical and medical needs were met, they were free to concentrate on securing personal space and rebuilding relationships. Some of the participants spoke about the importance of having their own place and of setting down roots again: "I am in my fifth home.... But this one I know that I can stay for two years and I can finally go to a permanent home after that. So I know I'll finally be able to have a home that I can call home for quite a while."

Others commented on the differences between their current living arrangements and their previous types of housing. Most notably, participants mentioned that they appreciated living in a "nice" neighbourhood, being "allowed" to have pets, and having their own bathroom and kitchen appliances. One woman aptly described this aspect of gaining stability: "In this house I used to live in, there were 20 people in the same house. So, now there is eight, and there's a huge difference.... There is more space to yourself."

The final theme—building relationships—was most evident in this last phase of the tornado. In the early phases, relationships were usually tenuous or destructive.

Participants who were gaining stability spoke about the importance of relationships and how strong relationships with friends or family were key to their health and well-being. One participant described how sharing meals with someone led to a strong friendship: "I was on the main floor and I had a lady friend on the other floor, and we switched back and forth for meals. One night I would cook, the next night she would cook and she'd supply the vegetables, or if she was coming to my place I'd supply the meat.... We are still good buddies even though I have been out of there all these years. And she is out of there too, and we still communicate."

3. QUESTIONS AND IMPLICATIONS

A question to consider is: What is the tornado? Is the tornado the experience of mental illness or the experience of society's response to mental illness? The participants' descriptions would suggest the latter. The loss and destruction experienced were not linked to the experience of symptoms, such as depression or hallucinations. Rather, the loss and destruction were related to the loss of home, possessions, relationships, and human dignity. The consequences of such loss after experiencing a mental illness would seem to have more to do with society's response to the illness, rather than the illness per se. When an actual tornado strikes, disaster relief is usually immediate. Government aid is available, and community organizations from near and far move quickly to provide tangible supports. What happens when mental health consumer-survivors experience their more personal tornadoes? It may be that the initial tornado is visible only to family and close friends, who, because of their proximity, feel the strong winds of disaster. Perhaps these forces are invisible to those more distant. Or perhaps the disaster is visible from a distance, but simply does not provoke a need to respond in others.

Certainly government aid is not quick to arrive, particularly in Ontario. At the time of data collection, there had been no increase in community mental health funding or disability income support for over a decade despite inflation and continued policies of deinstitutionalization. Since then small increases have been made. Individuals who receive assistance from the Ontario Disability Support Program actually risk having the housing portion of the assistance cut during a hospitalization on the assumption that because they are hospitalized, rental support is not required. Few landlords cease to charge rent during a hospitalization. Therefore, as some of our participants described, people with mental illnesses can lose not only their apartment but also their furniture and their memories when their family photos and albums are thrown into the garbage. Other participants in our study lost their belongings when the treatment team believed that they could not live independently because of their illness. They were discharged to a group living situation that could not accommodate many of their possessions, including furniture and pets.

The issues described by participants suggest some strategies. As participants initially lost ground, the issues of living in fear and losing control over their basic human rights surfaced. Such feelings were primarily related to being forced into unsafe or otherwise inappropriate housing. Participants struggled to survive by gaining access to social supports and obtaining professional services. Timely availability of such supports and services might assist consumer-survivors to move more quickly to the phase of gaining stability. Stability was maintained by securing personal space and rebuilding relationships. These consumers described accommodation, which includes personal space and control, as critical in rebuilding their lives. Relationships can be facilitated through consistent professional relationships. In addition, support for peer-support and consumer-survivor organizations can give back a sense of belonging. Many participants described the role of churches in facilitating their recovery through tangible supports that went beyond traditional spiritual support.

The metaphor of a tornado was used to capture the experiences related to housing and illness that consumer-survivors described. Many described a devastating experience of losing much of what was important to them and going through a long arduous process to rebuild their lives after the devastation. Health care providers and policy decision makers need to be aware of the losses that are not simply a result of the symptoms of mental illness but more the result of response to the illness. A caring community response, including adequate housing, adequate income support, and available community care, may help people rebuild their lives.

REFERENCES

Carling, P.J. (1993). Housing and supports for persons with mental illness: Emerging approaches to research and practice. *Hospital and Community Psychiatry, 44*, 439–49.

Centre for Addiction and Mental Health. (2001). *Evaluating housing stability for people with serious mental illness at risk for homelessness: Final report.* Toronto: Centre for Addiction and Mental Health, Community Support and Research Unit.

Chilvers, R., Macdonald, G.M. & Hayes, A.A. (2004). Supported housing for people with severe mental disorders. *Cochrane Database of Systematic Reviews*, Issue 4 DOI: 10.1002/14651858.CD000453.pub2.

Drake, R.E. & Wallach, M.A. (1999). Homelessness and mental illness: A story of failure. *Psychiatric Services*, 50, 589.

Forchuk, C., Nelson, G. & Hall, G.B. (2006). "It's Important to Be Proud of the Place You Live in": Housing problems and preferences of psychiatric survivors. *Perspectives in Psychiatric Care*, 42(1), 42–52.

Koegel, P., Burnam, M.A. & Baumohl, J. (1996). The causes of homelessness. In J. Baumohl (Ed.), *Homelessness in America* (pp. 24–33). Phoenix: Oryx Press.

Leininger, M.M. (1987). Importance and uses of ethnomethods: Ethnography and ethnonursing research. *Recent Advances in Nursing*, 17, 12–36.

Nelson, G., Hall, B. & Forchuk, C. (2003). Current and preferred housing of psychiatric consumer/survivors. *Canadian Journal of Community Mental Health*, 22(1), 5–19.

O'Malley, L. & Croucher, K. (2003). *Supported housing services for people with mental health problems: Evidence of good practice?* Toronto: York University, Centre for Housing Policy.

Peace, R. & Kell, S. (2001). Mental health and housing research: Housing needs and sustainable independent living. *Social Policy Journal of New Zealand*, 17, 101–23.

Robertson, M. (1992). The prevalence of mental disorder among homeless people. In R. Jahiel (Ed.), *Homelessness: A prevention-oriented approach*. Baltimore: Johns Hopkins University Press.

Tsemberis, S. & Eisenberg, R.F. (2000). Pathways to housing: Supported housing for street-dwelling homeless individuals with psychiatric disabilities. *Psychiatric Services*, 51(4), 487–93.

Chapter 5

FAMILIES CARING FOR MEMBERS WITH MENTAL ILLNESS: A VICIOUS CYCLE

Catherine Ward-Griffin, Ruth Schofield, Sandra Vos, and Robin Coatsworth-Puspoky

1. INTRODUCTION

One of the most important issues on the health promotion agenda in many countries is mental health (McMurray, 2003). However, a forgotten population in health promotion work is families caring for members with mental illness. Deinstitutionalization, health care restructuring, and movement toward community living have shifted the care of individuals with serious mental illness from hospital to community and, more specifically, to families (Lefley, 1991). In the United States, between 50 percent and 90 percent of people with mental illness have regular contact with family (Anthony, Cohen & Farkas, 1990). Clearly, families are a major source of support for people with serious mental illness (Kaufman, 1998; Tryssenaar & Tremblay, 2002), with 35–60 percent of family members with serious mental illness living with or receiving care from families (Lefley, 1987; National

Institute of Mental Health, 1994). In Canada, between 40 percent and 50 percent of people with schizophrenia live with their families.

Social support and housing are key determinants of health for people living with serious mental illness. Strengthening and supporting families who care for a member with mental illness, either living at home or in the community, are crucial in promoting family health. A cornerstone principle of primary health care, understanding family perspectives of caring for a member with mental illness is of particular importance in the promotion of family health (Community Health Nurses Association of Canada, 2003).

2. MENTAL ILLNESS AND FAMILY HEALTH

Investigations about mental illness and family health conducted in the 1970s and even earlier focused more on the family's impact on the member's illness than on the experiences or perspectives of the family (Biegel, Sales & Schulz, 1991). In particular, these studies reported that the family had a negative influence on the stability and recovery of the family member with mental illness and, in certain cases, was a "causal agent" of the illness (Biegel et al., 1991; Lefley, 1991; Spaniol & Zipple, 1988). This tendency to "lay blame" either on the family or on the individual with mental illness can be found in a variety of studies. Vaughn and Lefley (1976) found that the family member with mental illness whose family rated "high" in expressed emotion, meaning the emotional environment of families, was more likely to experience a relapse. In a British study of parents of 22 adult children with schizophrenia, more than half of the parents blamed themselves for their son's or daughter's illness (Ferriter & Huband, 2003). Conversely, in a survey of 51 caregivers, Casten and colleagues (1999) found that a significant reason why 35 percent of the members with mental illness did not improve resulted from family caregivers "blaming" them or holding them responsible for controlling their illness symptoms, thereby perpetuating the illness and hindering recovery.

The impact of mental illness on family health has also been investigated in relation to "family burden" over the past two decades. Objective family burden was considered a disruption of family life caused by the family member with mental illness, and subjective family burden was the emotional impact of the ill member upon his or her family (Biegel et al., 1991; Rose, 1996). An early study on family burden found that 50 percent of the families not only felt responsible for supervising the family member with mental illness, but also felt some form of embarrassment (Thompson & Doll, 1982). As well, 33 percent of these families experienced financial and/or role strain, and 66 percent reported feeling overloaded. In this study, families caring for members with mental illness experienced financial strain and caregiver burden as their family member became more ill. More recently, Doornbos (2002) found that a major factor that influenced family health in mental illness was the extremely high economic burden of mental illness, including both direct costs related to health care expense and indirect costs such as loss of productivity. In a randomized control trial to determine the costs of hospitalization and discharge, one half of the families reported financial strain associated with travel, personal items, and phone bills (Solomon, Beck & Gordon, 1988). Similarly, Milliken (2001) found that personal costs and loss of paid work were extensive sources of stress in mothers caring for an adult child with schizophrenia in addition to an increased prevalence of illness in caregivers, such as psychiatric problems, sleep disorders, and physical illnesses. In a study of 108 Thai families with a member with schizophrenia, Rungreangkulkij, Chafetz, Chesla, and Gilliss (2000) found that stresses of family life, such as employment and marriage, had a stronger impact on the psychological status of the family members than did the mental illness itself.

Although the above research helps us to understand the association between mental illness and family health, these investigations tend to use an individualistic, medical definition of health, with a tendency to blame either the individual or the family for the negative outcomes of mental illness. Although quantitative studies on caregiver burden move beyond the medicalization of mental illness, a deficit view of family health is portrayed and lacks a family perspective of the caregiving process within mental illness.

3. FAMILY PERSPECTIVES OF THE CAREGIVING PROCESS WITHIN MENTAL ILLNESS

During the past few years, research guided by qualitative methodologies has advanced our understanding of the family caregiving process with respect to mental illness. Research shows that parents of adult children with mental illness are most often the primary caregivers (Johnson, 2000), with mothers feeling the strain more than fathers (Milliken, 2001). In an ethnographic study of 40 francophone Québécois family caregivers of frail elders or relatives with mental illness, Guberman, Maheu, and Maille (1992) found that many interrelated factors affect women's decisions to become primary caregivers, such as the "inadequacy of institutional and community resources" (p. 610) and their "feelings of duty and obligation" (p. 611). Perhaps mothers' strong sense of familial duty compounds their stress.

However, it is rare for the legal system, the mental health practitioner, or sometimes the person with mental illness to recognize the parent's role in the decision-making process in mental health care.

Milliken (2001) found in a grounded theory study of 29 parent caregivers of adult children with schizophrenia that stress in the caregiving experience emerged from multiple sources and included a sense of helplessness and powerlessness as their family member's health declined, frustration due to multiple caregiving demands and competing roles, fear of the nature of the illness, and fear for the child's safety. In addition, parents in this study described two transitions that redefined their parental identity. Normally, parents go through identities such as a parent of a teen or young adult to an emancipated parent. With a child who has mental illness, parents experienced two new identities of "disenfranchised parent" to "parent suffrage" prior to becoming emancipated. In contrast, the transitions experienced by parents of a child with a mental illness were "becoming marginalized" when they experienced grieving, no sense of recognition, and feelings of stigma. The next identity, "embracing the collective," led them to learn more about mental health and community services, to "parental suffrage," when they became advocates, to "evaluating their life," which moved them toward some degree of emancipation.

Using semi-structured interviews, Riebschleger (1991) found that 20 adult sibling caregivers also grieved the loss of a "healthy" brother or sister. In addition, sibling caregivers felt that they received mixed messages from the mental health system; they were often called on by the professionals in time of crisis and yet were not included in a treatment plan. Similarly, Saunders and Byrne (2002) found that caregivers of people living with schizophrenia encountered legal system difficulties that reduced access and receptivity to family input.

Tryssenaar and Tremblay (2002) explored the life experience of people aging with serious mental illness, living in rural northern Ontario, from the perspective of the family member. Using interviews and focus groups, several themes were identified: the challenges of rural life, such as the lack of continuity of services and attrition of health care professionals; the exclusion of family members in health care planning, though they were often viewed as essential supports; family members' desire to enhance the collaborative partnership with providers; and physical and mental health changes increased with age, yet the symptom acuity and hospitalization related to the mental illness decreased. The families described the caring experience as having a "lifelong influence" on their lives (Tryssenaar & Tremblay, 2002: 261). They also experienced what they considered a "sequelae of the disability, not only as caregiver responsibility, but as mourning the lost future and the ruined past, while trying to live in the present" (p. 261). Many of these family members expressed concern for the future of their member with mental illness upon their death. Based on the findings of the studies above, it appears that caring for a member with a mental illness does not usually require family caregivers to tend to physical ailments but rather to address a variety of personal, interpersonal, and systemic challenges, such as the invisibility of their caregiving roles, the stigma of mental illness, and poor relations in the mental health, legal, and social assistance systems. However, still more research is required in order to identify strategies and solutions that will help families in their efforts to care for a member with mental illness.

4. SOURCES OF SUPPORT AND FAMILY HEALTH

A few studies have examined the sources of stress and support for families caring for a member with mental illness. Several studies have reported that frequently the health care system is a source of stress rather than a source of support for families living with mental illness (Rose, 1996; Spaniol & Zipple, 1988; Tryssenaar & Tremblay, 2002). Spaniol and Zipple (1988) found, in a survey of 187 families and 192 health professionals, that nearly one half of the families reported dissatisfaction with the mental health services related to lack of information about the benefits and side effects of medication and resources available in the community. Similarly, Ferriter and Huband (2003) reported that parents found health care providers the least helpful in alleviating caregiver burden and providing support, and viewed other family members and self-help groups as the most helpful. However, in Spaniol and Zipple's study, mental health professionals stated that 82 percent of the families were satisfied with mental health services. This discrepancy suggests that families and health professionals may hold different perspectives on what are useful supports.

In a cross-sectional, predictive study with 126 National Alliance for the Mentally Ill (NAMI) family members, it was found that family coping, family stressors, and professional communications were most predictive of outcome variables of family health (Doornbos, 2002). In the qualitative component of this study, 76 caregivers indicated that they needed better information about the illness, medication, and interventions (Doornbos, 2001). Family caregivers also believed that professionals needed greater understanding of the impact of mental illness on families, and described the amount of time devoted to caregiving as "24-7-52" (Doornbos, 2001: 339). It is not surprising that family caregivers reported that most of the information acquired was through family support groups and self-research as opposed to professional health sources.

Similarly, Kaufman (1998) reported that the coping ability of 20 parents was positively influenced by a high level of social support. Parents indicated that most of their support came through relief and some practical help from relatives and friends. In an interpretative study of 15 family caregivers, Rose (1998) found three key themes emerge from their ongoing interactions with an ill family member: (1) staying connected, (2) finding the essence of the person obscured by the mental illness, and (3) reflecting on their own identities as family members and caregivers. The last theme motivated them to help the relative with mental illness move forward by making sense of the future, by sustaining hope, and by holding a sense of self apart from their caregiving role.

Finally, the lack of affordable housing and supportive housing options (Forchuk, Schofield, Joplin, Csiernik & Gorlick. 2007) available in the community may intensify the stress experienced by families caring for their members with mental illness. However, research on the effectiveness of community housing supports available to individuals with mental illness residing in various living arrangements is limited. Only two studies were found that examined the family's perspective on housing options for their member with mental illness. One cross-sectional survey of 118 family members examined housing perceptions and preferences of housing needs and problems (Friedrich, Hollingsworth, Hradek, Friedrich & Culp, 1999). This study found that families preferred higher levels of support than those of clients. In addition, as the level of support decreased, families perceived more problems with housing. The second cross-sectional study compared the views of consumers, family members, and providers on living arrangements (Holley, Hodges & Jeffers, 1998) and found that clients desired more independence than expressed by either family or providers. Although professional-supported housing schemes may have potential, there is lack of conclusive evidence that these housing options would provide the supports needed by individuals with mental illness and their families (Chilvers, MacDonald & Hayes, 2003).

In summary, the literature reviewed revealed a shift in family research in mental health from one that was primarily medically problem-oriented to one that focuses more on the subjective experiences of families living with mental illness. However, more interpretive research on the family health promotion perspective of families living with mental illness is still needed. Although the unpredictable course of a chronic mental illness, associated with relapse and frequent need for hospitalization, ambiguity of mental illness, and the nature of disability (Rose, Mallison & Walton-Moss, 2003), contributes to a lack of understanding of the need for mental health services for people with mental illness and their families (Biegel et al., 1991; Milliken, 2001), more research about appropriate community supports for individuals with mental illness and their families and how these affect family health is sorely needed. To address these gaps in the literature, the purposes of this qualitative, descriptive study were to explore the experiences of families living with mental illness, with particular attention to family perspectives on housing, quality of supports, and formal care services and to identify potential solutions to difficulties encountered by families.

5. METHOD

This chapter reports qualitative findings from the 11 family focus group interviews with family members who had one member living with a mental illness (n = 75) conducted over a three-year period. In-depth focus group interviews averaging 60 minutes in length were conducted by three researchers using a semi-structured interview guide (see Chapter 2's "Issues in Quantitative Sampling").

Study participants lived in both rural and urban settings. Housing arrangements for family members with mental illness reflected a range of possibilities, including living away from home in an apartment, in a board-and-care facility, in a hospital, or with a family member, who was generally a mother. Finally, many spoke about the financial difficulties they encountered in caring for family members with mental illness, especially those who lived in rural areas, which tended to have fewer mental health resources.

The investigators used the immersion and crystallization analysis strategy as described by Lincoln and Guba (1985). Immersion consisted of reading the transcription of each interview while also listening to the audiotape, noting and categorizing sensitizing concepts (i.e., fear, hopelessness, protection) until themes and patterns emerged. The analysis was undertaken by the individual researchers for each interview and repeated until interpretations of the experiences of all three groups were inductively developed and crystallized into a holistic interpretation of the participants' shared experience.

6. FINDINGS

The central theme that emerged from this study was that families are part of a "circle of care," supporting the independence of their family members with mental illness while attempting to protect them from the inadequacies of the health care and social services sectors. Due to inadequate system supports for individuals with mental illness and their families, this circle of care frequently led to a "vicious cycle" of caregiving, depicted in three major themes: (1) witnessing inadequacies, (2) working behind the scenes, and (3) creating a better world (Figure 5.1). All family members expressed a range of emotions within each of these themes, such as anger, frustration, fear, and a sense of hope. The following section describes each of these themes accompanied with illustrative quotes.

Figure 5.1: Families Caring for Members with Mental Illness

Witnessing Inadequacies

All families were very aware of numerous housing inadequacies faced by their family members with mental illness. The following quotes illustrate how families witnessed terrible living conditions:

> "It's supposed to be furnished, but it has a decrepit single bed, one easy chair that sinks to the floor when you sit in it, two kitchen chairs, one of which is broken, no cupboards or shelves or anything like that. There's no kitchen as such, just this little bar fridge and microwave, so you have to do your dishes in the bathroom sink."

Families identified unscrupulous landlords and neglectful operators as part of the problem:

"And the people that run these places, I guess you call them 'slum landlords'—they know that these people get a welfare cheque for these awful little holes."

Unsafe housing was also recognized by all the families, which included those conditions that threatened one's physical health. As noted by one concerned mother:

"One of my concerns with those apartments is the stores above them are really old, and there's been a lot of fires.... He was actually evacuated during the last fire because the smoke was so toxic."

Other parents noted that poor living conditions compromised the mental health of their family member.

"If you are schizophrenic and you're hearing voices and you're paranoid, and there are many other people sleeping in the same room with you, and there's a lot of theft—it's just terrifying for my son. Because of this, most of them would prefer to actually sleep on the streets than go to a shelter."

Inappropriate placements were also identified by families. The placement was perceived as inappropriate if it did not meet their family members' needs due to factors such as health condition and/or age. In the words of one father:

"My daughter lives in a nursing home. She is 49 years old. She has many medical problems in addition to her psychiatric problems, which require a high level of care; therefore, she has been placed in a nursing home—to live with the dying. She doesn't belong there, but I'm told by the doctor, 'That's the way life goes.' We can't move her out of here—there is no other place for her."

Finally, limited staffing was identified as another inadequacy within the system. Frequently, there was not enough qualified staff, as mentioned by one parent:

"My son lives in a domiciliary hospital. The staff is unfamiliar with his medication and they are always short-staffed. One person is expected to be nurse, cook, and bottle washer."

As a result of these housing inadequacies, families were fearful for the well-being of their family members with mental illness. One parent expressed anger at the system and its inadequacies:

"Two years ago our daughter went into a coma—too much clozapine. My husband was very angry. He said, 'I've never seen so much abuse.'"

Working behind the Scenes

In response to the housing and other system inadequacies, the second major theme that emerged from the data was "working behind the scenes," as one parent aptly remarked, "As a family member, you can do quite a bit behind the scenes because you're a part of the circle of care."

Furthermore, because of the deplorable conditions described above, family members assumed many roles, such as movers, housecleaners, and landlords.

"The cooking stove was condemned so he had nothing to cook on. There are cockroaches everywhere. No housecleaning or anything like that was done unless the person themselves did it, and most people who are mentally ill can't do that—I have seen toilets that are absolutely black. So I would mop and vacuum and scrub and clean his cupboards and put his hangers and drapes and things to try to make it look decent, but they were still awful places."

"Our daughter has paranoid schizophrenia. We bought a semi-detached home. We rent it to her. She needs to know this is a place where she won't get kicked out."

"Right now my son couldn't survive anywhere else but home.... I do everything.... I am his everything."

In addition, many families paid out-of-pocket expenses for items such as travel to appointments, rent, food, and medical personnel.

"I had to pay $22.50 for travelling to get blood tested, and I had to pay all the travelling expenses because she was there for six months. I tried to get reimbursed from Ontario Works ODSP for all the expenses, but I am still trying two years later."

"The money my son gets covers his rent, but he has almost nothing left over, so we provide him with food. He won't go to the food bank. I don't know if he's ashamed, but he won't go, so we feed him. And his sisters, once in a while, send him a bit of money. If that were not happening, he would be homeless."

Families were frustrated when resources were unavailable. One mother spoke about her son's experiences with homelessness and the factors that prevent people with mental illness from escaping homelessness: "They can't get welfare unless they have an address, and without money they can't get an address.... They are one cheque away from homelessness all the time."

Parents were especially frustrated because, during the years of caring for their son or daughter, they usually understood their family member's needs, but were unable to obtain adequate assistance, nor were they consulted about their member's treatment plan, as the following quotes illustrate:

"We were not involved in any of her [daughter's] treatment. She was certified and kept at [name of hospital] and our involvement was somewhat limited—well, there was no involvement. Nobody talked with us. Whenever we called to ask how she is, we didn't really get any answers. It just seems like an endless cycle trying to get anything for her."

Creating a Better World

In their quest to break the vicious cycle of caregiving, a third theme emerged from the study findings, creating a better world. Despite the negative experiences reported by all the families in this study, most were hopeful that changes within the system would improve the care for people with mental illness and their families. Suggested changes included the need for more affordable housing that was safe, located close to the family, and appropriate to meet the needs of the person with mental illness.

"What I would like may not be what my son would like, but I would like him to have his own apartment, not necessarily in an apartment building but, you know, his own space. And it would be nice if they were staffed in some way ... where there would be a nurse or a social worker that would call in periodically, depending on the needs of the ill person—more than to just check the smoke alarm."

"It would be beneficial to have staff support in housing agencies who have knowledge of mental health issues. It is also important to consider the potential of the person looking for housing and match them with appropriate housing."

"People can rise above those surroundings, but they need people around and need good staff with psychiatric training.... It is also unfair to remove the person from their community.... That can be very frightening to some of these people."

In addition, participants emphasized that supports must be put into place if families are to continue in their role as primary caregivers.

"There is no respite where we live—we cannot have a holiday or a weekend away because there are no supports for that. We are near retirement so we don't know how much longer we can continue to provide this care, and what will happen to our son when we are gone?"

"Families are a great resource, but they need help, too. They need help to understand these illnesses. Families need resources to help them cope. If there were more funds available, you could have better staff and a subsidy for the family who is trying to support their family member."

Many families stated that a more coordinated, individualized system needed to be created to address the ongoing problems encountered by families living with mental illness.

"We need to focus on what they [people with mental illness] can do, more than what they can't do.... We'll have it made when the mentally ill receive the same respect and dignity as the physically ill."

Furthermore, families commented that health care providers must change their approach to families, particularly to include them in the care of their member with mental illness. During the discharge process, one mother explained:

"I think the main thing is to get in there before they [people with mental illness] are discharged ... to tell them [hospital care providers] to sit down with us and we'll decide as a team how this is to be resolved; if you want us to be a part of it, then involve us."

Another parent with a son suffering from suicidal episodes for 15 years commented that a change in attitude toward people with a mental illness and their families among health professionals, particularly those in the general hospital, needed to occur.

"Many health professionals have a different attitude when treating the mentally ill, compared with other diseases.... When our son was released from the hospital, he had no place to go. There was no discharge plan—just visit the doctor each month to get more pills. Everything we have read indicated that medication along with counselling is necessary."

Some families acted as advocates for their member with mental illness, hoping to address the barriers that prevent family-centred care. One father explained:

"We found the [health care] system daunting and, in most cases, unresponsive to the needs of both the patient and the family. It wasn't until we came up against the Mental Health Act [MHA] that we realized it does as much to hinder treatment as help.... On a provincial scale, the MHA needs to be reformed to give loving family a voice in the treatment and care of their loved ones."

Finally, one parent who is heavily involved in the local and provincial community mental health associations strongly suggested that families must become actively involved in changing the system.

"It is up to the families to advocate.... We certainly are not very organized and the politicians aren't going [to] do anything without a good shove because we have limited resources—they have to be allocated and they're certainly not coming our way.... First of all, family members should be picking the topic to advocate for. Secondly, families should all be working together because we've got family members associated with 33 schizophrenia societies and now we've got 35 CMHAs in Ontario and all these people are not connected in any way. They're all doing their own thing, duplicating their efforts. We're not going to get anywhere with politicians until we do it ourselves!"

In summary, families are part of the circle of care, offering emotional and instrumental support to their members with mental illness while attempting to protect them from the inadequacies of the system. However, findings also suggest that inadequate and inappropriate resources propel family caregivers into a vicious cycle of caregiving that compromises both their own and their family members' health.

7. DISCUSSION

The findings presented here were based, in part, upon secondary analysis and hence should be viewed as suggestive and tentative. Further research, particularly longitudinal studies, would result in a more complete understanding of families caring for members with mental illness. This study was also restricted to the perspectives of White, middle-class, Canadian families who provided ongoing care, especially parents of adult children. No doubt the perspectives of family members who do not actively provide care to members with mental illness would differ somewhat, if not dramatically. In addition, sampling a wider range of family members to include siblings and other members from ethnically diverse families would be helpful in broadening our knowledge about family networks and caregiving in mental illness. According to Keating, Otfinowski, Wenger, Fast, and Derksen (2003), future research on family caregiving, in which caregiving is examined as a series of interconnected relationships, needs to be conducted.

Despite these limitations, the insights gained from this qualitative study are particularly significant for health care practitioners and policy-makers. The family caregivers in this study were motivated to create a better life for themselves and their family members with mental illness. In particular, they articulated areas requiring change at both the family and system level. These changes included increased affordable and safe housing for their family member, available and accessible respite programs that provide relief from the stressors associated with caregiving, government financial assistance to assist with the economic burden associated with caregiving, and changes in mental health legislation that recognizes them as partners in the circle of care for their family member with mental illness. There is evidence in this study and others (Doornbos, 2001; Milliken, 2001; Riebschleger, 1991; Saunders & Byrne, 2002) that the implementation of these changes could have a positive impact on the health of families caring for members with mental illness.

First, family caregivers clearly expressed the need for health care providers to examine their own beliefs and attitudes about family caregiving and mental illness. Although an underlying principle of community care is social justice in addressing essential determinants of health (Raphael, 2008), it is evident that the families in our study faced incredible inequities and discrimination. Clearly, families working behind the scenes deserve a better world that challenges those working in the mental health system to listen, reflect, and develop new ways in their care practices. In this call for action by families, those working in the mental health system need to build trusting and respectful collaborations with families of members with mental illness and to take action through advocacy for policy and service changes at the various levels and sectors of local, municipal, and federal government.

Second, there is an opportunity for mental health practitioners to strengthen and support families in their desire to inform policy through the mental health care reform process. In the Ontario Ministry of Health and Long-Term Care (2003) mental health reform report, families are recognized as valuable in the planning, evaluation, and service delivery of mental health services. Mental health practitioners involved with the various planning and service structures can advocate and support the participation of families and be a voice with them for a better world. Lobbying for affordable housing through provincial and national family support organizations such as the Schizophrenia Society of Canada, national and provincial professional organizations, and federal/provincial/municipal elections are further advocacy opportunities for helping professionals and families to work together.

Finally, study findings underscore the need for change in mental health legislation. Even though families caring for members with mental illness wished to be a partner in the care of their family members, the Ontario *Mental Health Act* recognizes only families with children younger than 16 years as it relates to age of consent. However, the *Substitute Decisions Act* does give families—but only if they are deemed a substitute decision maker—the power to participate in care decisions when their ill family member is deemed incapable of making decisions through a capacity assessment. As a result of the last provincial mental health care reform document, the *Mental Health Act* did go through a review process in 2000 called Brian's Law (Mental Health Legislation Review), which amended the *Mental Health Act* and the *Health Care Consent Act*. However, the amendments to the Act primarily affected practitioners and legal services but not families. These legislations have given those identified above the power to care for individuals in the community rather than in the hospital through community treatment orders. Therefore, under these amended legislations, there is a possibility for families, if they are substitute decision makers, to be involved with the community treatment plan.

In conclusion, study findings highlight the need for a number of changes if primary health care is to become a reality for families caring for members with mental illness. In the future, mental health practitioners need to collaborate, advocate, and support families in their quest to care for members with mental illness. Only then will the vicious cycle of caregiving among these families be broken.

REFERENCES

Anthony, W.A., Cohen, M. & Farkas, M. (1990). *Psychiatric rehabilitation.* Boston: Boston University Centre for Psychiatric Rehabilitation.

Biegel, D., Sales, E. & Schulz, R. (1991). *Family caregiving in chronic illness.* Newbury Park: Sage.

Casten, R., Rovner, B., Shmuely-Dulitzki, Y., Pasternak, R., Pelchat, R. & Ranen, N. (1999). Predictors of recovery from major depression among geriatric psychiatry inpatients: The importance of caregivers' beliefs. *International Psychogeriatrics, 11*(2), 149–57.

Chilvers, R., MacDonald, G. & Hayes, A. (2003). Supported housing for people with severe mental disorders (Cochrane Review). Retrieved August 24, 2004, from http://www.mrw.interscience.wiley.com.libaccess.lib.mcmaster.ca/cochrane/clsysrev/articles/CD000453/frame.html

Community Health Nurses Association of Canada. (2003). *Canadian community health nursing standards of practice.* Ottawa: Author.

Doornbos, M. (2001). The 24-7-52 job: Family caregiving for young adults with serious mental and persistent mental illness. *Journal of Family Nursing, 7*(4), 328–44.

Doornbos, M. (2002). Predicting family health in families of young adults with severe mental illness. *Journal of Family Nursing, 8*(3), 241–63.

Ferriter, M. & Huband, N. (2003). Experiences of parents with a son or daughter suffering from schizophrenia. *Journal of Psychiatric Mental Health Nurses, 10,* 552–60.

Forchuk, C., Schofield, R., Joplin, L., Csiernik, R. & Gorlick, C. (2007). Housing, income support and mental health: the point of disconnection. Health Research Policy and Systems, 5(14) DOI: 10.1186/1478-4505-5-14.

Friedrich, R., Hollingsworth, B., Hradek, E., Friedrich, B. & Culp, K. (1999). Family and client perspectives on alternative residential settings for persons with severe mental illness. *Psychiatric Services, 50*(4), 509–14.

Guberman, N., Maheu, P. & Maille, C. (1992). Women as family caregivers: Why do they care? *The Gerontologist, 32*(5), 607–17.

Holley, H., Hodges, P. & Jeffers, B. (1998). Moving psychiatric patients from hospital to community: Views of patients, providers, and families. *Psychiatric Services, 49*(4), 513–17.

Johnson, E.D. (2000). Differences among families coping with serious mental illness: A qualitative analysis. *American Journal of Orthopsychiatry, 70,* 126–34.

Kaufman, A. (1998). Older parents who care for adult children with serious mental illness. *Journal of Gerontological Social Work, 29*(4), 35–55.

Keating, N.C., Otfinowski, P., Wenger, C., Fast, J.E. & Derksen, L. (2003). Understanding the caring capacity of informal networks of frail seniors: A case for care networks. *Aging & Society*, 23, 115–27.

Kruger, R. (1994). *Focus groups: A practical guide for applied research*. Thousand Oaks: Sage.

Lefley, H.P. (1987). Aging parents as caregivers of mentally ill adult children: An emerging social problem. *Hospital and Community Psychiatry*, 38, 1063–69.

Lefley, H.P. (1991). *Family caregiving in mental illness*. Newbury Park: Sage.

Lincoln, Y.S. & Guba, E.G. (1985). *Naturalistic inquiry*. Beverly Hills: Sage.

McMurray, A. (2003). *Community health and wellness: A socioecological approach*, 2nd ed. Sydney: C.V. Mosby.

Milliken, J. (2001). Disenfranchised mothers: Caring for an adult child with schizophrenia. *Health Care for Women International*, 22, 149–66.

Ministry of Health. (1998). *Mental health: 2000 and beyond: Strengthening Ontario's mental health system*. Toronto: Queen's Printer of Ontario.

Morse, T. (1991). *Qualitative nursing research: A contemporary dialogue*. Newbury Park: Sage.

National Institute of Mental Health. (1994). *Statistics on prevalence of mental disorders*. Washington, DC: Government Printing Office.

Ontario Ministry of Health and Long-Term Care. (2003). *Mental Health Accountability Framework Act*. Retrieved October 25, 2010, from http://www.health.gov.on.ca/english/public/pub/ministry_reports/mh_accountability/mh_accountability_e.html

Raphael, D. (2008). *Social determinants of health: Canadian perspective*, 2nd ed. Toronto: Canadian Scholars' Press Inc.

Riebschleger, J. (1991). Families of chronically mentally ill people: Siblings speak to social workers. *Health and Social Work*, 16(2), 94–103.

Rose, L. (1996). Families of psychiatric patients: A critical review and future research directions. *Archives of Psychiatric Nursing*, 10(2), 67–76.

Rose, L. (1998). Gaining control: Family members relate to persons with severe mental illness. *Research in Nursing & Health*, 21, 363–73.

Rose, L., Mallison, B. & Walton-Moss, B. (2003). Families of patients with mental illness revised their ideas of what it means to live a "normal" life. *Evidence-Based Nursing*, 6(2), 61.

Rungreangkulkij, S., Chafetz, L., Chesla, C. & Gilliss, C. (2000). Psychological morbidity of Thai families of a person with schizophrenia. *International Journal of Nursing Studies*, 39, 35–50.

Saunders, J. & Byrne, M. (2002). A thematic analysis of families living with schizophrenia. *Archives of Psychiatric Nursing, 14*(5), 217–23.

Solomon, P., Beck, S. & Gordon, B. (1988). Family members' perspectives on psychiatric hospitalization and discharge. *Community Mental Health Journal, 24*(2), 108–17.

Spaniol, L. & Zipple, A. (1988). Family and professional perceptions of family needs and coping strengths. *Rehabilitation Psychology, 33*(1), 37–45.

Thompson, E. & Doll, W. (1982). The burden of families coping with the mentally ill: An invisible crisis. *Family Relations, 31,* 370–88.

Tryssenaar, J. & Tremblay, M. (2002). Aging with a serious mental disability in rural northern Ontario: Family members' experience. *Psychiatric Rehabilitation Journal, 25*(3), 255–64.

Vaughn, C. & Lefley, J. (1976). The influence of family and social factors on the course of psychiatric illness: A comparison of schizophrenia and depressed neurotic patients. *British Journal of Psychiatry, 129,* 125–37.

Chapter 6

DE-"MYTH"-IFYING MENTAL HEALTH

Rick Csiernik, Cheryl Forchuk, Mark Speechley, and Catherine Ward-Griffin

1. INTRODUCTION

When we consider things that are mythical we often think of things that are fanciful, fictitious, non-existent, or relating to ancient gods (Knox, 1964). Archaic myths arose from the oral traditions of hunter-gatherers, nomadic tribes, and rudimentary agricultural societies that, while crude or basic, provided a foundation for what would become considered sacred and true. Archaic myths evolved over time to become intermediary myths that served, among other things, as a source of propaganda as they became more refined, helping in part to substantiate the positions of the power elite, including reinforcing gender stereotypes (Day, 1984). Contemporary ideological myths have become more complex yet still serve a variety of societal functions. They awaken and maintain a sense of awe about the universe as did archaic myths, while at the same time helping to explain the mysteries of seemingly unknowable things. Contemporary myths also validate, support, and imprint societal norms, particularly about complex realities that produce ideological contradictions (Campbell, 1994; Scheid-Cook, 1988). Myths also helped mediate the transition of humanity to the Age of Reason (Morgan, 2000), though with certain social issues, such as mental health, that transition is still incomplete. The first to openly link and critique the mythology of mental illness was Thomas Szasz (1961). However, despite four decades of debate, there still remain many entrenched myths regarding mental health that lead to oppression for mental health consumer-survivors.

Oppression, stigma, and discrimination are all significant issues that impede the community integration and support of both men and women with mental health issues. This population has been identified as among the most devalued of all people with disabilities (Lyons & Ziviani, 1995). Mental health consumer-survivors of both sexes face negative attitudes and discriminating behaviours from employers, politicians, the communities they call home, and from health care providers (Drake et al., 1999; Geller, 2001; Mann & Himelein, 2004; Schulze & Angermeyer, 2003; SEARCH Conference, 2003; Underhill, 2002; Wahl, 1999). Two common sets of characteristics associated with former psychiatric patients are that they are violent and unpredictable (Arboledda-Florez, 2003; Hyler, Gabbard & Schneider, 1991; Link et al., 2001; Penn et al., 1999; Torrey, 1994), and that they lack intelligence and are thus unemployable (Arboleddda-Florez, 2003; Community Living Ontario, 2003; Freidl, Lang & Scherer, 2003; Mechanic & Aiken, 1987). Drake and his colleagues (1999) also illustrated how health care professionals' unsupported beliefs have led professional helpers to underestimate mental health consumer-survivors' capacity to cope with work in the competitive marketplace. In turn, diminished access to employment opportunities contributes to poverty and inadequate housing.

The negative perceptions of mental health consumer-survivors also affect their ability to obtain and maintain adequate housing. The ongoing use of labels such as "borderline personality" or "paranoid schizophrenic" by not only the media and the general public but also by helping professionals negatively affects interpersonal interactions (Geller, 2001). Despite studies indicating that the majority of neighbours report no problem or adverse effects on their property value (Arens, 1993) once a group home is created and residents move in, the "Not in My Backyard" (NIMBY) syndrome remains a significant barrier to providing affordable, appropriate housing for people with mental health problems in residential communities (Piat, 2000). This situation is exacerbated by the lack of available, affordable housing in Canada. While several studies (Holland, 1996; Zapf, Roesch & Hart, 1996; Zima et al., 1996; City of London Task Force Report, 2000) show that from one-quarter to one-half of the homeless population suffer from psychiatric disability, current discussions in Ontario about resource allocation have isolated the provision of supports to individuals with psychiatric needs from the housing and community context within which these supports will be provided. If the community is already suffering from a shortage of available housing, it will be more difficult for oppressed groups to access this limited resource. This occurs even though stable housing has been identified as a crucial factor for their successful integration of individuals diagnosed with psychiatric illness into the community (Baker & Douglas, 1990; Drake & Wallach, 1988; Elliott, Taylor & Kearns, 1990; Nelson, Hall & Walsh-Bowers, 1998; Newman, 1994; Segal & Moyles, 1979).

The academic literature indicates that there is a general ignorance of this population and a general level of discomfort in getting to know mental health consumer-survivors as people rather than as stereotypes such as "the neighbourhood bag lady" (Merves, 1992). Huxley (1993) conducted a national survey in the United Kingdom on the public attitude toward mental illness. Nearly half of the respondents (47 percent) believed that few or no people recovered from mental illness. A large majority (82 percent) also believed that most people were embarrassed by mental illness, though when asked about personal comfort, less than one-third stated that they themselves were personally embarrassed in dealing with or discussing mental health issues. Despite our increased academic understanding and knowledge of mental illness, many societal myths still abound and are prominent in the minds of government officials, the media, and the general public, creating ongoing oppressive conditions for this entire group (George, 2000; Laudet et al., 2002; SEARCH Conference, 2002, 2003). The multiple levels on which stigma exists—individual, family, community, and society—dehumanizes, delegitimizes, and negatively portrays mental health consumer-survivors (Hinshaw & Cicchetti, 2000). This is exacerbated by collective oppressed group behaviour where those with mental health issues do not acknowledge their actual mental illness but rather identify with those who discriminate against them, thus further perpetuating stigma. These behaviours are based on myths that, if examined empirically, can readily be discerned as being socially constructed products of ignorance and fear. Deinstitutionalization policies and approaches have not provided an adequate response or a sufficient solution, so that unmet needs regarding housing, medical care, employment, and opportunities for community participation for those with mental health issues are increasing (Mechanic & Aiken, 1987).

Individual interviews using a survey instrument, focus groups, and results from a 2002 SEARCH conference were used in this deductive process, which examined data collected through the CURA process. The research question examined was: To what extent does the CURA data confirm or contradict myths of mental illness?

2. RESULTS

In examining the data, one of the first differences was that between men and women. While there was only a one-year difference in mean age of first contact with the mental health system (21 for men and 22 for women), women in the sample had been hospitalized in a psychiatric facility an average of 9.5 times while men had been hospitalized an average of only 6.2 times. The average duration of the most recent hospital stay was 63 days for women and 53 days for men. There were also distinct differences in primary diagnosis (Table 6.1) and in marital status, the latter reflecting current and previous social supports (Table 6.2).

Table 6.1: Primary Diagnosis

	Male	Female
Schizophrenia	72 (48.0%)	50 (33.3%)
Mood disorder	49 (32.7%)	59 (39.3%)
Developmental disability	7 (4.7%)	13 (8.7%)
Not reported	22 (14.7%)	28 (18.7%)
Total	150	150

Table 6.2: Marital Status by Gender

	Male	Female
Never married	117 (78.0%)	78 (52.0%)
Married	5 (3.3%)	9 (6.0%)
Separated/divorced	26 (17.3%)	51 (34.0%)
Not reported	2 (1.3%)	12 (8.0%)
Total	150	150

Only two (1.3 percent) women in the study reported that their substance abuse was a moderate problem, none reported it as any more severe, and 58 (38.7 percent) stated it was no problem at all. On the other hand, 14 (9.3 percent) men stated that their drug use was a moderate to severe problem, twice as many men than women stated it was a slight problem, and 12 percent fewer men than women stated that substance abuse was not an issue in their lives. Significantly more women than men had been victims of sexual abuse (54.7 percent vs. 28.0 percent) and physical abuse (59.3 percent vs. 41.3 percent) and had attempted suicide (60.7 percent vs. 45.3 percent).

Of the study's 300 participants, over one-half were unable to work, though one-quarter of men and 15 percent of women were actively seeking employment at the time of the study (Table 6.3). However, it was not a lack of education that accounted for this very low participation in the workforce. While there were more study participants who had not been able to complete high school compared to the general London, Ontario, population (40.0 percent vs. 21.7 percent), 67 (22.7 percent) had completed high school. This percentage is equivalent to the general London population. As well, 37 (12.5 percent) participants had some post-secondary education, while 35 (11.9 percent) had obtained either a college diploma or university degree. Thus, while nearly half the sample had a least a high school diploma, only 13 percent were employed and of those, only two people had a full-time position.

Table 6.3: Employment Status

	Male	Female	Total
Unable to work	76 (50.7%)	96 (64.0%)	172 (57.3%)
Seeking employment	38 (25.3%)	23 (15.3%)	61 (20.3%)
In school	5 (3.3%)	7 (4.7%)	12 (4.0%)
Employed	23 (15.4%)	16 (10.7%)	39 (13.0%)
Not reported	8 (2.7%)	8 (2.7%)	16 (5.4%)
Total	150	150	300

Two hundred-sixty of 300 participants reported that they currently had no legal issues—criminal, civil, or family. Only 4.0 percent (n = 12) reported legal issues of moderate or greater severity on the nine-point CCAR scale, with 11 individuals (3.7 percent) stating that committing a violent act against another person or against themselves was more than a moderate concern. Only three study participants (two women and one man, 1 percent of the sample), had been incarcerated during the past month—one for three days, one for four days, and one for five days. At the time of the study, one (.3 percent) participant was living in the community on condition of bail, two (.7 percent) were on parole, and 13 (4.4 percent) were on probation. In contrast, focus group findings indicated that many mental health consumer-survivors lived in fear:

> "I lost my apartment, but now that I've lived with people, I wouldn't want to go back to getting up in the morning and having nobody all day.... I wouldn't want to be home by myself all day, alone 24 hours a day, around the clock, seven days a week. Not again."

> "... and you're wondering 'Okay, what am I gonna do now? Who's going to help me?' All these questions go through your mind. You get scared, you get panicky. You get used to being pushed around, shunted around like a piece of dirt, so after a while, you just say 'Okay, let the system do it.'"

Table 6.4a outlines the living arrangements of the study's participants at the time of interview. Only 4.0 percent were living with their partner, while an additional 3.0 percent were living with other relatives. Just under one-quarter were living alone, with the majority living with unrelated people. Women were slightly more likely than men to be living with a relative than with an unrelated person (Table 6.4a). Place of residence was somewhat evenly divided between homes for special care, private homes or apartments, and shelters or hostels. Men, however, were much more likely to be living in a shelter or group home than were women, who were more frequently housed in a home for special care or private accommodation (Table 6.4b).

Table 6.4a: Living Arrangement

	Women (n = 149)	Men (n = 150)	Total (n = 299)
With partner	9 (6.0%)	3 (2.0%)	12 (4.0%)
With other relative	7 (4.7%)	2 (1.4%)	9 (3.0%)
Alone	37 (24.8%)	35 (23.8%)	72 (24.1%)
With unrelated person	96 (64.4%)	107 (72.8%)	203 (67.9%)

Table 6.4b: Place of Residence

	Women (n = 150)	Men (n = 149)	Total (n = 299)
Group home	10 (6.7%)	24 (16.1%)	34 (11.4%)
Homes for special care	54 (36.0%)	38 (25.5%)	92 (30.8%)
Private home/apartment	58 (36.7%)	30 (20.1%)	88 (29.4%)
Shelter/hostel	28 (18.7%)	54 (36.2%)	82 (27.4%)
Other	0	3 (2.0%)	3 (1.0%)

Women in particular shared concerns about safety during the focus groups. Comments included:

> "She was in there [hospital] because she was sexually abused. She was placed in a home with two guys. When she complains, they tell her that she is lucky to be out of hospital."

Other focus group participants commented:

CHAPTER 6

"You should see the dump I live in."

"There are affordable apartments, but you wouldn't believe the neighbours you have to live with."

"Where I'm at, you can't call that home."

A proportion of the study's participants did have stable housing situations, with over one-third having lived in the same accommodation for the past two years and 45.2 percent having experienced no undesirable moves in the past five years. However, there was a significant minority who had experienced the opposite. Over one-third of the respondents had moved four or more times in the past 24 months, with 21 having moved 10 or more times in two years. Likewise, nearly half had been forced to move at least once in the past 24 months against their wishes, with 18.0 percent averaging at least one undesirable or forced move per year for the past five years (Table 6.5).

Table 6.5: Housing History

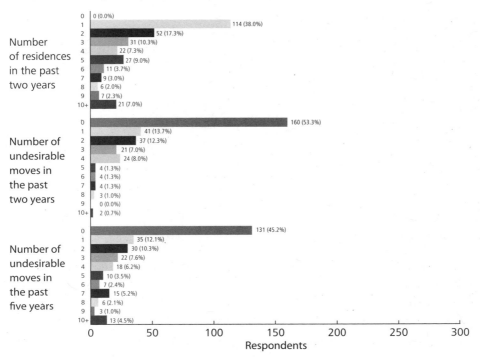

When asked where they would like to live, the vast majority of the study's participants (n = 212, 70.7 percent) indicated that they would like to have their own apartment or home, while only seven (2.3 percent) stated that they would like to move back to their family home. Only one person indicated that he would prefer to live in a shelter environment, and three stated that their first choice would be a community care home. Another 18 chose a group home as their ideal living option. A significant minority of respondents stated that if they had a choice, they would prefer to live on their own (46.5 percent), while just under one-quarter (23.4 percent) stated that they preferred living with other mental health consumer-survivors; 20.7 percent wished to live with a friend; 9.7 percent would opt to live with a family relative, and 7.3 percent with their partner. Moreover, the focus group findings showed that many families provide instrumental and emotional support to mental health consumer-survivors. As well, families were well aware of the inadequate and sometimes deplorable housing conditions. One father explains:

> "My son lives in a house—a cesspool. I was incensed when I visited last Christmas and his bathroom wasn't working, and hadn't been for weeks. He explained that he would go to the bathroom in a bag and then put the bag in the garbage!"

Contrary to the myth that families abandon members with mental illness, the study's findings illustrated that families attempt to "work behind the scenes." In the words of one parent: "As a family member, you can do quite a bit behind the scenes because you are part of the circle of care." Due to the unsafe, deplorable living conditions, families often assumed multiple roles, such as movers and landlords:

> "I have moved him [son] 22 times.... We're always ready for him to lose his housing."

3. DISCUSSION

Every myth contains some mixture of truth and falsehood. When misinterpretations are based on some factual foundation and then perpetuated, they can become a dangerous fiction (Crystal, 1988). This becomes even more problematic and oppressive when those who are mythologized themselves begin to construct their own personal realities in response to society's false impressions of them (Feinstein, 1997). Thus, stereotypes that are used to categorize complex ideas and organize the excessive amount of information that we must routinely process can emerge. Stereotypes may be based on facts or real occurrences, although if those occurrences are rare at a population level, the resulting stereotype is a fallacy, a false generalization about a group based on a selected set of observations. Furthermore, once ingrained and accepted, stereotypes are not routinely subjected to critical examination by the people who use and perpetuate them. When stereotypes grow to mythical proportions, they can be damaging and problematic as has occurred with beliefs about mental health and mental health system consumer-survivors.

Originally, archaic myths were stories regarding some type of supernatural person or occurrence that, if not heeded, created ruin, thus serving as a warning to the listener or reader. These oral and written histories were often created to explain unusual events or perceived anomalies in nature that were not fully understood, and thus typically feared. Mental illness is such an occurrence. While historically, those with mental health problems have at times been revered as mystics or shamans, more commonly they have been feared and ostracized (Antoniou, 2004; Lukoff, 1985; NorthEast Ohio Consumer Quality Review Team, 1999; Silverman, 1967). In contemporary Canadian society, there remain many oppressive factors that impede community integration of mental health consumer-survivors, many of which have become ideological myths serving a greater purpose.

The first myth is that ex-psychiatric patients are a homogeneous group. Mental health consumer-survivors, while having one distinct commonality, are, not surprisingly, quite a diverse group, particularly when examining issues of gender. Prominent differences that were found included primary diagnosis, frequency and average length of psychiatric hospitalization, perceptions of severity of problems, psychoactive substance use and abuse, interpersonal relationships, family histories, and histories of sexual and physical abuse. The findings support those practitioners who believe that distinct approaches by gender are warranted when working with this group of individuals.

The most well-documented societal myth pertaining to mental health consumer-survivors is that they are to be feared because of their unpredictable and violent behaviour. This belief was also challenged by this community-based study's findings. There was virtually no criminality, civil, family, or criminal or violence reported with this community-based population. In fact, many consumer survivors were living in fear not only for their immediate safety, but for what was to become of them within the ongoing neo-conservative agenda of shrinking health and social service funding.

Another myth is that mental health consumer-survivors do not work because of a lack of education. While the study participants did have less education than the general London, Ontario, population, the rate of high school completion was equivalent, with nearly one-quarter of the research participants having attended a post-secondary institution or having either a college diploma or university degree. Despite this, only two of 300 people interviewed during the course of the research had full-time employment of any type, though nearly one-quarter were either actively searching or in an educational program.

While some mental health consumer-survivors certainly are ignored, separated, or even disowned by their families, others become the central focus of their families' lives (see also Chapter 5). Family members continue to care for them well into adulthood, and even in situations of independent living, they continue to worry and support their family member with mental illness (Ward-Griffin et al., 2005). However, families should not be expected to maintain consumer-survivors in perpetuity. It is imperative that appropriate government programs and policies be created to adequately support both mental health consumer-survivors and their families.

This Community-University Research Alliance was initiated to assist in building the capacity of the community to create, support, and evaluate housing for mental health consumer-survivors. In order to do that, this population needs to be seen as members of the community and not deviants, objects of research, or mythical stereotypes. The CURA has attempted to address this not only through a formal research project that includes dispelling myths commonly associated with this group, but also making members of this oppressed group part of the research process. Input from participants was not only sought, their individual voices were deemed to be vital in addressing the myths of society.

Despite the findings of this research, participants in the study and others like them regularly experience oppression due to the perpetuation of the myths discussed. The increasing importance of, and growing reliance on, community-based support and services for mental health consumer-survivors exposes the need for comprehensive knowledge of the obstacles and disadvantages that oppression creates for this vulnerable population. Understanding these fears and the myths concerning mental health consumer-survivors is essential in order to educate the public, change policies, provide adequate resources, and assist with community integration. Reducing oppression by educating the public to the realities, in light of these myths, can enhance quality of life across multiple domains. Facts derived from research are essential in combating fear-based myths, and conveying this knowledge in academic, political, educational, and public forums by both consumer-survivors and their advocates is essential if we are to de-"myth"-ify mental health and allow for true societal participation of this oppressed group.

REFERENCES

Antoniou, J. (2004). Does crime literature contribute to the stigmatisation of those with mental health problems? *Psychiatric Bulletin, 28*(3), 95–97.

Arboleda-Florez, J. (2003). Considerations on the stigma of mental illness. *Canadian Journal of Psychiatry, 48*(10), 645–50.

Arens, D. (1993). What do the neighbors think now? Community residences on Long Island, New York. *Community Mental Health Journal, 29*(3), 235–45.

Baker, F. & Douglas, C. (1990). Housing environments and community adjustments of severely mentally ill persons. *Community Mental Health Journal, 26*(6), 497–505.

Beckwith, D. & Lopez, C. (1997). *Community organizing: People power from the grassroots.* Center for Community Change. http://comm-org.utoledo.edu/papers97/beckwith.htm.

Campbell, J. (1994). Joseph Campbell on myth and mythology. In R. Sartore (Ed.), *Myth and mythology.* New York: University Press of America.

City of London Task Force Report. (2000). *Affordable housing.* London: City of London.

Community Living Ontario. (2003). Inclusion difficult in resource-scarce north. www.acl.on.ca/Daily_News/2003/March/mar27.htm.

Crystal, D. (1988). Asian Americans and the myth of the model minority. *Social Casework, 70*(7), 405–13.

Day, M. (1984). *The many meanings of myth.* New York: University Press of America.

Drake, R.E., McHugo, G.J., Bedout, R.R., Becker, D.R., Marris, M., Bond, G.R. & Quimby, E. (1999). A randomized clinical trial of supported employment for inner-city patients with severe mental disorders. *Archives of General Psychiatry, 56,* 62.

Drake, R. & Wallach, M. (1988). Mental patients' attitude toward hospitalization: A neglected aspect of hospital tenure. *American Journal of Psychiatry, 145*(1), 29–34.

Elliott, S., Taylor, M. & Kearns, R. (1990). Housing satisfaction, preference, and need among the chronically mentally disabled in Hamilton, Ontario. *Social Science and Medicine, 30*(1), 95–102.

Feinstein, D. (1997). Personal mythology and psychotherapy: Myth-making in psychological and spiritual development. *American Journal of Orthopsychiatry, 67*(4), 508–21.

Freidl, M., Lang, T. & Scherer, M. (2003). How psychiatric patients perceive the public's stereotype of mental illness. *Social Psychiatry and Psychiatric Epidemiology, 38,* 269–75.

Geller, J.L. (2001). Taking issue: Ain't no such thing as a schizophrenic. *Psychiatric Services, 52*(6), 715.

George, T. (2000). Defining care in the culture of the chronically mentally ill living in the community. *Journal of Transcultural Nursing, 11*(2), 102–10.

Hinshaw, S. & Cicchetti, D. (2000). Stigma and mental disorder: Conceptions of illness, public attitudes, personal disclosure, and social policy. *Developmental Psychopathology*, 12(4), 555–98.

Holland, A.C. (1996). The mental health of single homeless people in Northhampton hostels. *Public Health*, 110(5), 299–303.

Huxley, P. (1993). Location and stigma: A survey of community attitudes to mental illness. Part 1: Enlightenment and stigma. *Journal of Mental Health*, 2(1), 73–80.

Hyler S., Gabbard G. & Schneider I. (1991). Homicidal maniacs and narcissistic parasites: Stigmatisation of mentally ill persons in the movies. *Hospital and Community Psychiatry*, 42(10), 1044–48.

Knox, J. (1964). *Myth and truth.* Charlottesville: Union Press of Virginia.

Laudet, A., Magura, S., Vogel, H. & Knight, E. (2002). Interest in and obstacles to pursuing work among unemployed dually diagnosed individuals. *Substance Use and Misuse*, 37(2), 145–70.

Link, B., Struening, E., Neese-Todd, S., Asmussen, S. & Phelen, J. (2001). Stigma as a barrier to recovery: The consequences of stigma for the self-esteem of people with mental illnesses. *Psychiatric Services*, 52(12), 1621–26.

Lukoff, D. (1985). The diagnosis of mystical experiences with psychotic features. *Journal of Transpersonal Psychology*, 17(2), 155–81.

Lyons, M. & Ziviani, J. (1995). Stereotypes, stigma, and mental illness: Learning from fieldwork experiences. *American Journal of Occupational Therapy*, 49, 1002–08.

Mann, C. & Himelein, M. (2004). Factors associated with stigmatization of persons with mental illness. *Psychiatric Services*, 55, 185–87.

Mechanic, D. & Aiken, L. (1987). Improving the care of patients with chronic mental illness. *New England Journal of Medicine*, 317(26), 1634–38.

Merves, R. (1992). Homeless women: Beyond the bag lady myth. In M. Robertson & M. Greenblat (Eds.), *Homelessness: A national perspective.* New York: Plenum.

Morgan, K. (2000). *Myth and philosophy from the Presocrates to Plato.* Cambridge: Cambridge University Press.

Nelson, G., Hall, B. & Forchuk, C. (2003). Current and preferred housing of psychiatric consumer/survivors. *Canadian Journal of Community Mental Health*, 22(1), 5–19.

Nelson, G., Hall, B. & Walsh-Bowers., R. (1998). The relationship between housing characteristics, emotional well-being, and the personal empowerment of psychiatric consumer/survivors. *Community Mental Health Journal*, 34, 57–69.

Newman, S. (1994). The housing and neighborhood conditions of persons with severe mental illness. *Hospital and Community Psychiatry*, 45, 338–43.

NorthEast Ohio Consumer Quality Review Team. (1999). Stigma and the consumer: Unraveling stereotypes. www.neoappcare.org/stigma2.html.

Penn, D., Kommana, S., Mansfield, M. & Link, B. (1999). Dispelling the stigma of schizophrenia: II. The impact of information on dangerousness. *Schizophrenia Bulletin*, 25(3), 437–46.

Piat, M. (2000). The NIMBY phenomenon: Community residents' concerns about housing for deinstitutionalized people. *Health and Social Work*, 25(2), 127–38.

Scheid-Cook, T. (1988). Mitigating organizational contradictions: The role of mediating myths. *Journal of Applied Behavioral Science*, 24(2), 161–71.

Schulze, B. & Angermeyer, M. (2003). Subjective experiences of stigma: Schizophrenic patients, their relatives, and mental health professionals. *Social Science and Medicine*, 56(2), 299–312.

SEARCH Conference. (2002). London, Ontario.

SEARCH Conference. (2003). London, Ontario.

Segal, S. & Moyles, E. (1979). Management style and institutional dependency in sheltered care. *Social Psychiatry*, 14, 159–65.

Silverman, J. (1967). Shamans and acute schizophrenia. *American Anthropologist*, 69(1), 21–31.

Stoecker, R. (1997). Are academics irrelevant? Roles for scholars in participatory research. Presented at the American Sociological Society Annual Meetings. http://uac.rdp.utoledo.edu/comm-org/papers98/pr.htm.

Szasz, T. (1961). *The myth of mental illness*. New York: Harper & Row.

Thames Valley District Health Council. (1997). *Mental health reform implementation planning needs assessment*. London: Thames Valley District Health Council.

Torrey, E.F. (1994). Violent behaviour by individuals with serious mental illness. *Hospital and Community Psychiatry*, 45(7), 653–62.

Underhill, C. (2002). Mental health and development: From the local to the global —the involvement of mentally ill people in the developmental process. *Asia Pacific Disability Rehabilitation Journal* (January), 82–91.

Wahl, O. (1999). Mental health consumers' experience of stigma. *Schizophrenia Bulletin*, 25(3), 467–78.

Ward-Griffin, C., Schofield, R., Vos, S. & Coatsworth-Puspoky, R. (2005). Canadian families caring for members with mental illness: A vicious cycle. *Journal of Family Nursing*, 11(2), 140–61.

Zapf, P.A., Roesch, R. & Hart, S.D. (1996). An examination of the relationship of homeless to mental disorder, criminal behaviour, and health care in a pretrial jail population. *Canadian Journal of Psychiatry*, 41(7), 435–40.

Zima, B.T., Wells, K.B., Benjamin, B. & Duan, N. (1996). Mental health problems among homeless mothers: Relationship to service use and child mental health problems. *Archives of General Psychiatry*, 53(4), 332–38.

Chapter 7

"IT'S IMPORTANT TO BE PROUD OF THE PLACE YOU LIVE IN": HOUSING PROBLEMS AND PREFERENCES OF MENTAL HEALTH CONSUMER-SURVIVORS

Cheryl Forchuk, Geoffrey Nelson, and G. Brent Hall

1. INTRODUCTION

Deinstitutionalization, health system restructuring, and a move to supported community living for people with severe mental illness have created the necessity for a comprehensive understanding of existing needs, gaps, and barriers to acquiring and maintaining housing. The issues related to mental health and housing are varied and complex. Research has shown that people with severe mental illness are at risk of losing their housing, living in substandard housing that is not aligned with their preferences, or being placed in inappropriate housing (Goering et al., 2002; Nelson, Hall & Forchuk, 2003; Rochefort, 1993). We believe that it is important to understand housing and mental health issues from the perspective of mental health consumer-survivors.

Researchers have collaborated with community members and mental health consumer-survivors to conduct surveys of survivor preferences for and barriers to obtaining housing and supports (Friedrich et al., 1999; Goering, Paduchak & Durbin, 1990; Goldfinger & Schutt, 1996; Massey & Wu, 1993; Minsky, Riesser & Duffy, 1995; Rogers et al., 1994; Schutt & Goldfinger, 1996; Tanzman, 1993). These surveys provide a great breadth of information about consumer-survivors' preferences for housing and support, with several consistent findings emerging. First, most consumer-survivors prefer to live in their own homes or apartments rather than in other forms of housing offered by social services. Second, consumer-survivors generally want staff support to help them deal with a variety of day-to-day challenges of living independently in the community, and they want control over staff support. For example, consumer-survivors do not want live-in staff, but staff who are on call and who can provide support when needed. Third, the barriers to obtaining their own housing are primarily financial. Most members of this group cannot afford market rents because of dire poverty.

An alternative research approach to understanding consumer-survivor preferences for housing and support involves qualitative data. Qualitative interviews have the potential to provide more depth to understanding people's lived experiences, needs, and preferences, as well as a richer understanding of their life contexts (Patton, 2002). While there have been a few studies that have used qualitative methods to evaluate different types of housing for consumers (Boydell & Everett, 1992; McCarthy & Nelson, 1993; Parkinson & Nelson, 2003; Walker & Seasons, 2002), there have been very few needs assessment studies with consumer-survivors conducted in Canada that have examined their housing and community experiences (Herman & Smith, 1989; Lord, Schnarr & Hutchison, 1987; Morrell-Bellai, Goering & Boydell, 2000). Some of the themes that have emerged from these studies are consistent with the quantitative research—namely, lack of support, both formal services and informal support networks, the stigma of mental illness labels, poverty and unemployment, and living in poor-quality housing. One substantive limitation of these qualitative studies is that they have not examined consumer-survivors' preferences for housing and support.

In June to August of 2001, the Ministry of Health and Long-Term Care asked district health councils (DHCs) in Ontario, forerunners of the current local health integration networks (LHINs), to conduct focus group meetings with mental health consumer-survivors and their families to identify important housing-related issues. Data were collected with the objective of informing preparation of a comprehensive mental health housing policy and an integrated approach to delivering housing for the range of people with serious mental illness. The Thames Valley DHC, the Essex Kent Lambton DHC, the Grey Bruce Huron Perth DHC, and the Waterloo Region Wellington Dufferin DHC partnered with the

Community-University Research Alliance (CURA) on Mental Health and Housing to assist with data collection and analysis. Two guiding research questions were addressed in this qualitative needs assessment, namely: What issues of concern do mental health consumer-survivors have about their current housing situation? What preferences do they have related to housing?

2. RESULTS

A number of interconnected themes are summarized in Table 7.1. The themes were analyzed from the perspectives of the two research questions and therefore broadly grouped under the themes of concerns and preferences and desires. A number of issues were raised that superficially appeared to go beyond the issues of housing. The mental health consumer-survivors' perspective was that these broader issues, such as societal oppression and available supports, were directly related to their ability to obtain and keep housing.

Oppression

The primary concerns raised were issues related to oppression, including stigma, discrimination, being labelled, and being treated differently. Survivors identified stigma as a ubiquitous deleterious influence in their lives. They experienced stigma when dealing with public sector bureaucracies, health care professionals, private landlords, and employment situations. Quotes from participants that exemplify this theme included the following:

> "If you're a psych patient in [city name], they have you on record in the computers when and if you come into emergency. So as they type you on record into the computer, your name comes up. So if a person comes into emergency with a broken arm or whatever, they must see the crisis team first even when their ailment is physical."

> "Low labels are pinned on you. 'That one is on welfare! She's wearing Goodwill clothing.'"

> "They don't believe anxiety is a problem since you're not bleeding."

> "A [potential landlord] said, 'I want someone stable.' I think he saw [name of mental health agency] on call display."

Table 7.1: Themes from Consumer Focus Groups

Domain	Problems/Concerns	Preferences/Desires
Oppression	• stigma, discrimination, labelling, being treated differently	• acceptance • advocacy
Social networks and social supports	• landlords' lack of attention to needs (e.g., repairs) and their ability to evict residents • having to choose between housing that emphasizes support and independence • loneliness and dependence • isolation	• education of consumer-survivors regarding their rights as tenants, education of landlords • finding an equal balance between support and independence • need more social interaction and contact, peer support, drop-in settings
Housing	• lack of affordable and desirable housing • homelessness or precarious housing situation, frequent moves • undesirable housing, poor quality, too small, lack of privacy, restrictive rules, poor neighbourhoods • gender and child issues, changing family situations in conflict with rules about the number of rooms allowed, the rate of subsidy, access to child care, safety for women and children • victimization, break-ins, stealing by others in residence, proximity to sex and drug trade, fear of sexual abuse or re-abuse	• want a home that is stable, desirable, and affordable • desirable housing in a small setting, privacy (own room), modern facility that allows pets • collective decision making • freedom to make choices • choice over gender of living companions • a safe place that is appropriate for children • safety and security, a lock on the door
Poverty and finances	• poverty, low income, disability program difficulties	• need more financial support, especially regarding access to desirable housing
Accessing services	• lack of crisis support in independent living • transportation, accessibility of programs • inaccessibility of medical and mental health services • having to move to get needed services	• want around-the-clock support to be available, drop-in services too • affordable transportation • more readily available support services • getting the right services in the right place

The participants said they wanted acceptance and advocacy. For example:

"Remove labels given to people."

"No matter what the client's problem is, there is no reason not to treat everyone with respect."

"We give back by volunteering in the community. Be my voice."

Social Networks and Social Support

Issues related to social networks and social supports were raised as instrumental to securing and maintaining desirable housing. Problems related to landlords were particularly highlighted. Participants often described landlords as being inattentive to their needs. For example, repairs were often delayed after being reported. Participants were very concerned about the perceived power of landlords and feared being evicted. This created a sense of vulnerability since it was feared that if their housing was lost, it would not be easy to replace it. As a result, participants often remained silent and did not complain about their concerns. Examples of these concerns included the following:

"I don't complain [to the landlord] because I don't want to lose the apartment. I'm not going to bug him about it because I like the apartment."

"Do your chores. Don't cause problems."

In describing their preferences, other consumer-survivors focused on the importance of educating consumer-survivors regarding their rights as tenants, as well as the importance of educating landlords. For example:

"People don't know their rights."

"Landlords should have to take a course once a year or something, telling them what to do [their obligations]."

Study participants described dilemmas related to housing and available supports. Often the housing they desired and the support they perceived that they needed were not located in the same place. A dilemma that was expressed concerned whether consumer-survivors should live where they want, or get the services they need. There was often a struggle with having to choose between support and independence or between loneliness and dependence. One participant noted: "I'm torn. I like my independence, but I like the company too."

This quote also highlights the fact that the key supports desired would address a sense of isolation and loneliness. This was echoed by many participants. For example:

"I'm a very lonely person and I'm gonna have to deal with that."

"What do you do alone when you don't like TV?"

Participants wanted to have both support and independence rather than one exclusive of the other. For example, consumer-survivors wanted to have support available around the clock, but not physically present when not needed. This was expressed in the following quote: "We want people to come, but we want them to leave."

Participants wanted services that emphasized social interaction and the development of social networks. Consumer-survivors described a variety of supports, such as peers, employment, family, friends, and professionals as essential components of a support network. Consumer-survivor organizations, peer support, and drop-in centres were all seen as examples of services that can specifically address the issues of isolation and loneliness. For example:

"I want to be part of what everyone else has to do. By myself, I drive myself crazy."

"If this peer support thing comes through, I think it will work."

Housing

Concerns were expressed regarding the lack of affordable and desirable housing. Participants wishing independent living had great difficulty finding desirable housing that they could afford. For example:

"Why [city name] has such horrible housing available I don't know."

"If you spend five years on the list for geared-to-income housing, you may as well say it doesn't exist."

The difficulty in finding affordable housing created a sense of vulnerability among participants. They described themselves as at risk for homelessness or enduring precarious housing situations. Many described frequent moves in the search to find something both affordable and desirable. Comments included:

"Most of us are one paycheque away from being on the streets."

"Got kicked out of residence in the middle of winter and had to sleep in a car [for] two to three nights."

"I could not believe that me, of all people, could be homeless."

However, as desirable housing typically was unaffordable, participants described the undesirable housing that they could obtain. They described their housing as often being of poor quality, too small, and lacking privacy. In group situations, there were often restrictive rules. Participants complained of being forced to live in poor neighbourhoods. Since there were so few affordable options, participants felt they had no choice about where to live.

The challenges were even greater when children were involved as the rules within the public assistance programs create additional difficulties. For example, the number of rooms allowed depended on the number of children. However, with access being lost or gained, or adolescents moving between home and other settings, the number of children was not a constant. One woman described having to move three times in one year as her teenage daughter kept moving back and forth between parents. Further, locations where housing was available were sometimes not near available daycare, and safety was a major concern for participants. Many felt they were potential victims for predators, and several settings were not perceived to be safe for women or children. When living independently, consumer-survivors were often located in neighbourhoods that had frequent break-ins. When they lived in group-living situations, they described stealing by other people in the residence. The neighbourhoods they were placed in were in close proximity to drug and sex trades. Women participants often had a fear of sexual abuse or re-abuse due to the neighbourhood's perceived lack of safety. Women who had been sexually abused in the past were often not comfortable in settings that included men.

"Being on the third floor of a complex with no elevator … is not practical with two infants, and the presence of a child molester in the same building."

"A [woman's] house has been broken into three times. Crime is a problem in the lodge—lots of pilfering."

Participants wanted a home that is stable, desirable, and affordable. There was a strong preference for independent and supported apartments.

"There is some nice geared-to-income housing here if you can just get into it."

"[Housing agency] is probably the best you can get because it's modern housing."

"We need supportive apartment units."

"A perfect place would be my own apartment."

Desirable housing was consistently described. Participants preferred small settings rather than those where large numbers of people reside. They wanted privacy, which included their own room and modern facilities. It was very important to many that pets were allowed. In group-living situations, they wanted collective decision making, while having the freedom to make their own choices, such as choice over the gender of living companions. For families it was important to have a safe place that is appropriate for children. Sample participants' comments relating to this theme included:

"It's important to be proud of the place you live in."

"Some people need a garden."

"I've got a perfect place ... own room, goldfish in room, television in room, can use phone.... I can do everything except smoke."

"[We] need choice because everyone has different preferences."

"I feel there should be one house with all women, one [for] men, and two that are mixed."

Participants wanted the very basic needs of safety and security met. For many this was symbolized by the simple ability to be able to lock the door. For example:

"I think it's a safe place [has a lock on the door]."

"I double-check that the door is locked and my roommate triple-checks."

Poverty and Finances

Participants' choices were limited due to lack of finances as many were on government disability support programs. Some were on general welfare programs (Ontario Works), while a few were employed. In Ontario, the provincial disability support has not increased for a decade, and the housing allowance is far below market housing values. If a person is on general welfare, the level of support is even lower. This financial gap limited the choices available to participants. For example:

> "Try living on $300 a month. Half my rent comes out of that."

> "Try to save, say, $1,500 for first and last month's rent, to try to move—impossible. Those places where first and last month are not required are usually dumps."

In addition to the obvious preference for increased levels of support, participants also described the need for easier access to the higher-paying disability support in order to access housing. For example:

> "[I] need easier access to disability. I can't work, but I was turned down for [provincial disability income support] because I wasn't severe enough."

> "Some people wait one to two years to get on disability [income support]."

Accessing Services

The issues of housing and ability to access services were seen as interwoven. Keeping housing was seen as related to continued access to supportive services. As well, one's current address could affect which services could be accessed. Participants identified specific service gaps. A major problem was the lack of crisis support in independent living. Many felt that they had to give up their supports in order to live independently. For example:

> "I would have been okay if someone had visited me, but they didn't and I was alone. This led to some trouble with the law. The whole thing could have been avoided if someone had just come over."

Frequent problems with lack of transportation and accessibility were primarily identified by the focus groups that were held in the smaller rural communities. This could lead to a situation where participants from rural communities had to move in order to get needed services. Once again the dilemma appeared to be either to live where one wanted or get the services one needed:

"Low-income housing is not centrally located, and shops and services are inaccessible. This is especially problematic for the elderly who cannot walk as far. There is no public transportation in [a rural community]. Grocery stores are on opposite ends of town and the very edges of town. Cabs are too expensive, and [provincial disability support] does not allow for transportation."

"Why should we have to travel an hour to [a larger city] to see a doctor? How are you going to get there?"

"I lived in a bachelor apartment. I was happy, but it was so far. For 19 months I walked the hills. No buses went out that far. Moved. Really enjoyed living there, but there was no transportation."

The perceived inaccessibility of medical and mental health services was shared by the rural and urban groups. Many described long waits or long waiting lists. For example:

"I waited seven hours once, suffering from a panic attack in emerg."

"There aren't enough doctors and psychiatrists, and the government has limits on the number of visits, so the consumers are actually referred to us [survivor initiative]."

"Waiting lists are false hopes."

Participants had specific suggestions that would help address the accessibility of services. An affordable public transportation system or access to other more affordable forms of transportation were important to many. They wanted around-the-clock support available to them on their request. This help could be something accessed by telephone rather than in close physical proximity. Further, they wanted supports that could be accessed on a drop-in basis rather than requiring referrals and waiting lists. Support services need to be more readily available and to be personal from someone they trusted. They wanted to get the right services in the right place. For example:

"I'm getting help. I have an excellent aftercare worker and doctor."

"I need someone to walk me through things. My worker does."

"To get growth, one must go back to one's roots, to their hometown. One must then seek services there. Get help. Get an apartment, learn to cook, etc. You have to go where you feel comfortable."

3. DISCUSSION AND IMPLICATIONS

Some of this study's findings reaffirm existing qualitative and quantitative research (Friedrich et al., 1999; Walker & Seasons, 2002). While the same general issue of housing suitability is at the heart of our discussion, this study evokes not only the actual voices of mental health consumer-survivors to express their concerns, it also provides a powerful complement to previous research as it systematically reviews and presents consumer-survivors' preferences for housing and support. The participants have not only described issues and concerns that are relevant to them, but also what they see as some potential solutions. Moreover, the findings from this qualitative research provide more depth and texture to the experiences and desires of mental health consumer-survivors than is the case with existing quantitative survey research on consumer-survivors' preferences (Tanzman, 1993).

The participants in the study expressed a consistent preference for independent living arrangements such as supportive apartments, and the issues of oppression/stigma and poverty were pervasive. Consistent with other previous first-person accounts (Capponi, 1992), detailed information about the kinds of supports were provided, including advocacy, various forms of social supports through government and community-based agencies, and better access to services, that would assist consumer- survivors to achieve their desired housing. Consumer-survivors wanted ready access to help, but did not want live-in, 24-hour support, which they perceived to be invasive and inconsistent with "normal" living. Further, the dilemma of either having the supports they need or living where they want adds an additional dimension of coping that cannot easily be resolved as the housing choice constraints are such that achieving adequate supports *and* choice of residential location together is often unfeasible.

A basic sense of both general life and residential satisfaction for any individual or household stems from living in a preferred location, subject to affordability constraints, having fundamental independence in daily living, and, for mental health consumer-survivors, having access to the supports they feel that they need. In contrast, consumer-survivors have been forced to regard these dimensions of residential satisfaction as competing and choose between them, thereby diminishing their overall life satisfaction. Linking supports to a person's address tends to perpetuate this dilemma rather than solve it (Parkinson & Nelson, 2003) as appropriate supports for an individual living in an inappropriate residence fulfills only part of the individual's life satisfaction needs.

Addressing transportation issues is essential to improve access to services such as health care. In particular, survivors residing in rural areas of southwestern Ontario often commented that they had to decide between living in their (preferred) home community or living somewhere where they could have ready access to appropriate services. Again, this reflects a dilemma of living that creates a fundamental dislocation between the comfort of choosing somewhere preferred and comfortable or somewhere that may not be preferred and uncomfortable, solely for the purposes of service accessibility.

While there are clearly preferences and constraints that affect residential decision making for all individuals and households, the choice set for mental health consumer-survivors is so constrained that inevitably at least one aspect, and often more, of fundamental importance for leading a balanced and fulfilling life has to be sacrificed to find somewhere to live. While solutions to these issues are not immediately apparent, discussion of them with consumer-survivors prior to and during discharge planning, and promoting their fulfillment through ongoing community care, are centrally important.

Issues of oppression and poverty were raised by numerous individuals in the focus group discussions, which is quite consistent with what consumer-survivors have been saying for some time (Capponi, 1992). These issues are systemic and, as such, they require systemic responses. Reducing the influence of stigma in the experience of people with a severe mental illness will enhance their quality of life satisfaction across multiple domains, including housing, employment, and utilization of supports. However, this is a long-standing problem that is not easily addressed by anything other than a systemic response. Many problems that participants raised were related to financial issues, often stemming from the Ontario

Disability Support Program. As noted earlier, this provincial income support had not been increased for a decade while the cost of living has steadily increased, with housing costs having increased considerably.

4. CONCLUSIONS

This qualitative research adds to the largely quantitative literature on housing needs and preferences among those who have experienced a severe psychiatric illness. The preference for independent housing with adequate supports was reaffirmed. Similarly, the ongoing changes related to stigma and discrimination were consistently described by participants. Using the voices of focus group participants as a form of resonance for the housing problem, it was possible to distill elements of need and preference that are relatively easily resolved through effective policy formulation and a commitment to addressing needs by provincial governments across Canada.

Mental health consumer-survivors face many housing challenges. Some of these challenges, such as not linking services to location, can be addressed by the mental health system. Others, such as transportation and adequate income, will require a broader societal response involving more than provincial government ministries. Health care practitioners can play a leading role in advocating for fundamental changes in how these needs are met. For example, nurses, social workers, and related helping professions can advocate strongly for bringing about the systemic solutions that are needed, including increased funding for income supports and for public awareness campaigns to address discrimination. These needs stem from pre-discharge planning within hospitals and flow outward through post-discharge follow-up and consultation with community advocacy groups, especially within the non-profit housing sector. Advance practice nurses and social workers are frequently involved in both discharge planning and system advocacy. In both these roles an understanding of the complexity of housing issues, including the consumer-survivors' perspective, is essential.

Collectively, as a society, we need to meet the challenge placed before us by one of the participants, who poignantly requested, "Be my voice." Without this avenue of expression, the voices of the many individuals who participated in the focus groups, and indeed those who are similarly affected but did not have the opportunity to participate, remain unspoken and therefore unheard. Also, it is not enough simply to hear the pleas for assistance. Only through action, based on the needs expressed in this chapter, at the policy level and beyond to policy implementation and planning, can the current housing crisis for mental health consumer-survivors begin to be resolved.

REFERENCES

Boydell, K.M. & Everett, B. (1992). What makes a house a home? An evaluation of a supported housing project for individuals with long-term psychiatric backgrounds. *Canadian Journal of Community Mental Health, 10*(1), 109–23.

Capponi, P. (1992). *Upstairs in the crazy house: The life of a psychiatric survivor*. Toronto: Viking.

Friedrich, R.M.; Hollingsworth, B., Hradek, E., Friedrich, H.B. & Culp, K.R. (1999). Family and client perspectives on alternative residential settings for persons with severe mental illness. *Psychiatric Services, 50*, 509–14.

Goering, P., Paduchak, D. & Durbin, J. (1990). Housing homeless women: A consumer preference study. *Hospital and Community Psychiatry, 41*, 790–94.

Goering, P., Tolomiczenko, G.S., Sheldon, T., Boydell, K. & Wasylenki, D. (2002). Characteristics of persons who are homeless for the first time. *Psychiatric Services, 53*, 1472–74.

Goldfinger, S.M. & Schutt, R.K. (1996). Comparison of clinicians' housing recommendations and preferences of homeless mentally ill persons. *Psychiatric Services, 47*, 413–15.

Herman, N.J. & Smith, C.M. (1989). Mental hospital depopulation in Canada: Patient perspectives. *Canadian Journal of Psychiatry, 34*, 386–91.

Lord, J., Schnarr, A. & Hutchison, P. (1987). The voice of the people: Qualitative research and the needs of consumers. *Canadian Journal of Community Mental Health, 6*(2), 25–36.

Massey, O.T. & Wu, L. (1993). Important characteristics of independent housing for people with mental illness: Perspectives of case managers and consumers. *Psychosocial Rehabilitation Journal, 17*, 81–92.

McCarthy, J. & Nelson, G. (1993). An evaluation of supportive housing: Qualitative and quantitative perspectives. *Canadian Journal of Community Mental Health, 12*(1), 157–75.

Minsky, S., Riesser, G.G. & Duffy, M. (1995). The eye of the beholder: Housing preferences of inpatients and their treatment teams. *Psychiatric Services, 46*, 173–76.

Morrell-Bellai, T., Goering, P. & Boydell, K. (2000). Becoming and remaining homeless: A qualitative investigation. *Issues in Mental Health Nursing, 21*, 581–604.

Nelson, G., Hall, B. & Forchuk, C. (2003). Current and preferred housing of psychiatric consumer/survivors. *Canadian Journal of Community Mental Health, 22*(1), 5–19.

Parkinson, S. & Nelson, G. (2003). Consumer/survivor stories of empowerment and recovery in the context of supported housing. *International Journal of Psychosocial Rehabilitation, 7,* 103–118.

Patton, M.Q. (2002). *Qualitative research and evaluation methods,* 3rd ed. Thousand Oaks: Sage.

Rochefort, D.A. (1993). *From poorhouses to homelessness: Policy analysis and mental health care.* Westport: Auburn House.

Rogers, E.S., Danley, K.S., Anthony, W.A., Martin, R. & Walsh, D. (1994). The residential needs and preferences of persons with serious mental illness: A comparison of consumers and family members. *Journal of Mental Health Administration, 21,* 42–51.

Schutt, R.K. & Goldfinger, S.M. (1996). Housing preferences and perceptions of health and functioning among homeless mentally ill persons. *Psychiatric Services, 4,* 381–86.

Tanzman, B. (1993). An overview of surveys of mental health consumers' preferences for housing and support services. *Hospital and Community Psychiatry, 44,* 450–55.

Walker, R. & Seasons, M. (2002). Supported housing for people with serious mental illness: Resident perspectives on housing. *Canadian Journal of Community Mental Health, 21*(1), 137–51.

Chapter 8

CURRENT AND PREFERRED HOUSING OF MENTAL HEALTH CONSUMER-SURVIVORS

Geoffrey Nelson, G. Brent Hall, and Cheryl Forchuk

1. INTRODUCTION

When the era of deinstitutionalization began in Canada in the 1960s, the main approach to housing people with serious mental illness in the community was custodial housing (Parkinson, Nelson, & Horgan, 1999; Trainor et al, 1993). Custodial housing usually consists of large, congregate facilities, mini-institutions in the community, operated by private landlords for profit. These settings, which include lodging homes and single-room occupancy hotels, typically provide custodial care rather than active rehabilitation programs. After the formation of the Community Mental Health Branch of the Ministry of Health and Long-Term Care in Ontario in 1976, the provincial government began to provide funding for non-profit community mental health and housing agencies to develop supportive housing as an alternative to custodial housing. In supportive housing, staff provides support or rehabilitation in a variety of different types of housing, including halfway houses, group homes, and supervised apartments. In some communities, supportive housing programs were initially organized along a residential continuum, ranging from high-support group settings to lower-support apartments (Ridgway & Zipple, 1990). For example, the Supportive Housing Coalition of Toronto, which created 800 units of supportive housing during the 1980s, initially emphasized group homes, organized according to levels of support (Trainor et al., 1987; Trainor et al., 1993). The idea underlying this approach was to match the needs of the consumer with the appropriate housing type and amount of support.

By the late 1980s, problems with supportive housing and the residential continuum approach were recognized. These problems included the fact that mental health consumer-survivors do not have choice over where they live or with whom they live; they are often concentrated in one setting, thus inhibiting rather than promoting community integration; and they may be forced to move into a less supportive residential setting when they show improvement, thus disrupting relationships that they have developed with living companions and staff (Hogan & Carling, 1992; Ridgway & Zipple, 1990). Such forced relocation can have the effect of disassembling social networks, which other research has shown to be centrally important in facilitating the adaptation of mental health consumer-survivors to life in the community (Hall & Nelson, 1996; Nelson et al., 1992).

It was in this context that Paul Carling and colleagues introduced the concept of "supported housing," which had already taken root in the fields of developmental and physical disabilities under the rubric of "independent living," to the field of mental health as a response to deficiencies in the alternatives that were available (Carling, 1995; Hogan & Carling, 1992; Ridgway & Zipple, 1990). There are three key principles of supported housing. One is that mental health consumer-survivors should have choice and control over where they live and with whom they live. In this regard, the supported housing approach works from a disability rights perspective rather than a medical model. Second, supported housing emphasizes community integration. Rather than creating separate facilities for people with mental health issues, the supported housing approach advocates integration into housing that is available to anyone in a community. Third, to have realistic choices about housing, the supported housing approach recognizes that mental health consumer-survivors need financial and social support to enable them to operate in a normal housing market context. The goal of supported housing is to help individuals "choose, get, and keep" the type of housing that they want. The third of these principles poses a significant practical barrier to achieving the implementation of supported housing in many communities.

In the 1990s, some mental health housing organizations in Ontario began to shift their orientation from that of supportive housing to the supported housing philosophy (Lord et al., 1998; Pyke & Lowe, 1996). Today supportive and supported approaches have been blended in many community mental health housing agencies in Ontario. While housing programs continue to have congregate or group-living settings, most do not employ a levels system or have time limits on residency, and some programs do not have staff specifically attached to the setting. Rather, staff members work with individuals, whatever their place of residence. Also, many housing agencies have developed individual apartments, some of which are scattered and some of which are concentrated in one apartment block, and provide portable staff support to residents of these apartments. Consumer choice and portable support services are the common elements of these different types of housing. Moreover, this mix of types of housing is supported by research that has found positive impacts for both supportive and supported housing on the well-being of consumer-survivors (Goering & colleagues, 1997; Parkinson et al., 1999).

An important component of the supported housing approach has been research on consumer preferences for housing and support. Tanzman (1993) reviewed the findings of 26 of these studies. She reported that consumers consistently said that they wanted to live in their own apartment or house, preferred to live alone or with a spouse/partner or friend rather than other mental health consumer-survivors, to have staff support available as needed, and to have access to material and financial supports, such as rent subsidies, telephone, and transportation. Research published since Tanzman's review has yielded similar results (Friedrich et al., 1999; Goldfinger & Schutt, 1996; Massey & Wu, 1993; Minsky, Riesser & Duffy, 1995; Rogers et al., 1994; Schutt & Goldfinger, 1996). This research has also demonstrated that consumers prefer more independent housing than what treatment staff (Goldfinger & Schutt, 1996; Massey & Wu, 1993; Minsky et al., 1995; Schutt & Goldfinger, 1996) or family members recommend for them (Friedrich et al., 1999; Rogers et al., 1994).

One of the limitations of the existing literature on consumer preferences for housing and support is that few studies have compared where consumers currently live with where they would like to live. One exception to this is a study conducted in Iowa City by Friedrich et al. (1999). They compared the housing preferences of consumer-survivors currently living in three types of settings: (1) congregate facilities with on-site support; (2) supported housing with on-site visits; and (3) apartments or houses with no on-site staff. In each type of setting, the majority of consumer-survivors indicated that they were currently living in the type of housing that they preferred.

Another issue that has not received much attention is how consumers' satisfaction with housing is related to current or preferred housing. Lehman, Possidente, and Hawker (1986) and Lehman, Slaughter, and Myers (1991) reported that consumers living in hospitals or custodial housing had lower levels of housing satisfaction than those living in supportive housing settings. Similar ratings of satisfaction with different types of supportive housing were found in a study by Hanrahan, Luchins, Savage, and Goldman (2001). In an Australian study, Horan, Muller, Winocur, and Barling (2001) compared the satisfaction of mental health consumer-survivors diagnosed with schizophrenia living in either boarding homes or hostels. The boarding homes in this study more closely resemble what we would call group homes in Canada; they are large houses with private bedrooms and more personal space, and residents are actively involved in meal preparation. Hostels, on the other hand, more closely resemble Canadian boarding homes; they are large facilities, they lack privacy and personal space, and staff provide meals, dispense medications, and dole out spending money. They found that residents of boarding homes had significantly higher scores than residents of hostels on general life satisfaction and satisfaction with their living situation. Overall, these findings indicate that consumers who live in supportive housing report higher levels of life satisfaction than consumers living in hospital or custodial housing.

One other important limitation of extant research is that with the exception of one study of the housing preferences of homeless women in Toronto (Goering, Paduchak & Durbin, 1990), the vast majority of the research on consumer preferences for housing has been conducted in the United States. The policy context and political climate of the U.S. have historically been quite different from that of Canada in general. Thus, the extent to which studies in the U.S. can be generalized to Canada is unknown. In the U.S., there is a federal government policy whereby people with serious mental illness can apply to the Department of Housing and Urban Development for Section 8 certificates, which enable low-income individuals to rent market housing at an affordable rate. This policy is congruent with the supported housing approach as it provides consumers with choice about where they want to live, avoids congregate living facilities, and substantially removes or reduces financial barriers to accessing "normal" housing in the community.

In contrast, Canada has no such social policy. Moreover, the federal and Ontario provincial governments have retreated in the past two decades from their role in supporting social housing for low-income citizens (Hulchanski, 1998; Shapcott, 2001). Since 1980, when nearly 25,000 units of affordable housing were created nationwide, there has been a steady decline in government-funded social housing.

From 1994 to 2000, fewer than 1,000 new units of social housing were created per year across Canada. Only recently in Ontario have the consequences of the lack of a national or provincial housing policy and funding for affordable housing for mental health consumer-survivors been recognized. Since 2000, the Ontario government created 3,500 units of supportive and supported housing under the Phase I and Phase II Mental Health Homelessness Initiative.

In this study we were interested in knowing not only if housing satisfaction was related to the current housing of mental health consumer-survivors, but also whether or not there was a discrepancy between where consumers are currently living relative to where they want to live. We expect that those who are living in their preferred type of housing should have higher levels of housing satisfaction than those not living in their preferred housing type.

Four specific objectives were addressed:

1. a comparison of consumer-survivor preferences for housing with their current living situation
2. an examination of housing satisfaction by type of housing
3. a comparison of housing satisfaction of those living in their preferred type of housing with those not living in their preferred type of housing
4. an illustration of a participatory action research approach to the study of consumer-survivors' preferences for housing and supports

2. METHODOLOGY

The sample for this research was drawn from community-based housing that included 18 homes for special care; three temporary; 18 supportive housing units; and 78 independent living settings. Sample quotas were set according to the proportion of beds/units per housing type relative to all beds. The number of people to include in the sample from independent housing was calculated by asking two community mental health agencies for the number of clients that they served. Numbered lists of participants from the Homes for Special Care, shelters, and supportive housing programs constituted the sampling frame for participants from these three types of settings. Participants were randomly selected from these lists until the quota for each setting was achieved. In case of refusal, a substitute was selected for inclusion from the same type of housing. Signs advertising the study were posted in community agencies to recruit participants from those living independently. For some of the types of housing (shelter, independent living), fewer potential women participants were available than hoped, so all potential women participants were included. Only seven people who were invited refused to participate in the study. The reasons for refusal were related to concerns about the length of the interview.

To assess preferences for housing, living companions, and supports, the short version of the Consumer Housing Preference Survey Instrument was used (Tanzman, 1990). The survey instrument, which has been used in numerous studies (e.g., Tanzman, 1993), includes questions about demographic information, current housing, preferred housing, preferred living companions, and the supports needed. The format for most of the items is that of fixed-choice alternatives, which yield categorical data. For example, the question used to assess preferred living situation is "Ideally, what kind of place would you like to live in?" Consumers respond to this question by choosing one of 11 fixed-choice options (e.g., in a group home run by a community mental health centre, in an apartment, in my family's home, in a shelter) or by indicating some other choice. In addition to these fixed-choice questions, there are also a few open-ended questions (e.g., "What is it about that place that would be most important to you?" "What kinds of supports or services do you think you might need in order to be able to live where you want?").

Housing history was measured through a housing history form developed for this study. All moves within the past five years were listed by participants. Participants reported the length of time spent in each residence and whether the move was a desired or undesired change. Finally, a three-item measure of satisfaction with living situation ($\alpha = .81$), taken from the Lehman Quality of Life scale was used (Lehman et al., 1994). Scores on individual items ranged from 1 ("terrible") to 7 ("delighted").

As can be seen in Table 8.1, participants living in different types of housing differ with respect to demographic background and psychiatric history. While the participants did not differ significantly in terms of age, those living in shelters changed residences the most within the past five years, while those living in supportive housing report the fewest number of residential changes. There are proportionately more women than men living in homes for special care or in their own apartment or house, while men predominate in shelters and supportive housing. Those living in their own apartments or houses are more likely to be married or to have been married at some point and are least likely to be employed. Participants who live in supportive housing and in their own apartments or houses have the highest levels of education, and those living in supportive housing are most likely to be employed full-time or part-time. Those

Table 8.1: Comparison of Residents of Different Types of Housing on Demographic Variables and Measures of Psychological Functioning

Demographic Variables and Psychiatric History	Homes for Special Care	Shelter	Supportive Housing	Own Apartment/ House	Statistic
Demographic variables					
Age	43.1 (12.5)	41.3 (11.7)	41.1 (14.1)	38.6 (13.4)	not significant
Number of housing moves in past 5 years	2.2 (4.1)	3.4 (4.5)	0.8 (1.4)	2.4 (3.0)	$F(3,279) = 4.4$[a]
Gender					$\chi^2(3) = 19.5$[a]
Men	38 (42%)	54 (66%)	25 (60%)	27 (35%)	
Women	53 (58%)	28 (34%)	17 (40%)	51 (65%)	
Marital status					$\chi^2(6) = 18.5$[a]
Married/widowed	7 (8%)	4 (5%)	1 (2%)	12 (15%)	
Separated/divorced	17 (19%)	21 (26%)	11 (26%)	29 (37%)	
Single/never married	67 (73%)	57 (69%)	30 (72%)	37 (48%)	
Education					$\chi^2(6) = 30.5$[a]
University or college	13 (14%)	14 (17%)	13 (30%)	30 (38%)	
High school	53 (58%)	60 (73%)	25 (60%)	42 (54%)	
Elementary school	25 (28%)	8 (10%)	4 (10%)	6 (8%)	
Employment status					$\chi^2(6) = 16.5$[a]
Employed part-time or full-time	19 (21%)	13 (16%)	13 (31%)	6 (8%)	
Not employed	72 (79%)	67 (84%)	29 (69%)	72 (92%)	
Psychiatric history					
Primary psychiatric diagnosis (self-reported)					$\chi^2(9) = 58.4$[a]
Schizophrenia	51 (56%)	9 (11%)	20 (48%)	26 (33%)	
Mood disorder	15 (17%)	40 (49%)	9 (21%)	29 (37%)	
Other	20 (22%)	19 (23%)	13 (31%)	20 (26%)	
Unknown	5 (5%)	14 (17%)	0 (0%)	3 (4%)	
Currently taking psychiatric medication					$\chi^2(3) = 48.1$[a]
Yes	85 (93%)	46 (56%)	40 (95%)	66 (85%)	
No	6 (7%)	36 (44%)	2 (5%)	12 (15%)	

[a] $p < .01$. Note that for age and the number of housing moves, means and standard deviations are reported, while for the categorical variables, frequencies and percentages are reported.

living in homes for special care and supportive housing are most likely to have a self-reported primary diagnosis of schizophrenia. Those living in shelters are most likely to have a primary diagnosis of mood disorder and not to be taking psychiatric medication.

3. FINDINGS

Comparison of Housing Preferences with Current Living Situation

A total of 238 (79.3%) of the sample stated that they prefer to live in their own apartment or house (see Table 8.2). Across all different types of current housing, living in an apartment or house is the clear preference. In response to an open-ended question about the most important qualities of their preferred living situation, the qualities most often mentioned by participants are privacy, freedom, independence, and ownership. Other important qualities mentioned are safety and security, having more space, cleanliness, peace and quiet, access to public transportation and services, comfort, decent furnishings and appliances, and having a yard or garden. A few participants also indicated that they want a place suitable for children or one in which they could have a pet. Nearly half of the sample (46.5%) indicated that they prefer to live alone, with the remainder preferring to live with friends (21%), other mental health consumer-survivors (23%), or family or spouse (17%).

Table 8.2: Current Housing by Preferred Housing

Preferred Housing	Current Housing					Total— Preferred Housing
	Homes for Special Care	Shelter	Supportive Housing	Own Apartment/ House	Other (transitional housing, AIDS home)	
Homes for special care	28		2			30 (10.0%)
Shelter		1				1 (0.3%)
Supportive housing	8		10	1		19 (6.3%)
Own apartment/ house	51	78	28	74	7	238 (79.3%)
Other	4	3	2	3		12 (4.0%)
Total—current housing	91 (30.3%)	82 (27.3%)	42 (14.0%)	78 (26.0%)	7 (2.3%)	300 (100%)

Many of the most important supports needed to obtain preferred housing are tangible in nature: transportation (83%), more income/benefits (82%), a telephone (82%), money for a security deposit (78%), and help getting benefits (74%) (Table 8.3). Access to staff support around the clock was also deemed important by a majority of respondents (70%). The most difficult areas for which more support is needed pertain to emotional upsets and budgeting (Table 8.4).

Table 8.3: Supports Needed to Obtain Preferred Housing

Type of Support Needed	n (%)
Transportation	250 (83.3%)
More income/benefits	247 (82.3%)
Telephone	245 (81.7%)
Money for deposit	234 (78.0%)
Help getting benefits	222 (74.0%)
Being able to reach staff by telephone at any time of the day or night	211 (70.3%)
Help finding a place to live	192 (64.0%)
Household supplies	186 (62.0%)
Furniture	182 (60.7%)
Being able to ask staff to come to my home at any time of the day or night	176 (58.7%)
Roommates or housemates	118 (39.3%)
Having staff regularly coming to my home during the day	100 (33.3%)
Help in finding roommates or housemates	58 (19.3%)
Having staff live with me	31 (10.3%)

Table 8.4: Areas of Difficulty and Help Needed

Area of Difficulty	A Lot of Help Needed n (%)	Some Help Needed n (%)	No Help Needed n (%)
Dealing with emotional upsets	72 (24.2%)	152 (51.0%)	74 (24.8%)
Budgeting money	63 (21.0%)	115 (38.3%)	122 (40.7%)
Avoiding emotional upsets	60 (20.0%)	144 (48.0%)	96 (32.0%)
Managing medications	37 (12.5%)	72 (24.3%)	187 (63.2%)
Making friends	31 (10.4%)	65 (21.7%)	203 (67.9%)
Cooking	25 (8.3%)	67 (22.3%)	208 (69.3%)
Getting along with others	22 (7.3%)	78 (26.0%)	200 (66.7%)
Keeping the house clean	21 (7.0%)	82 (27.3%)	197 (65.7%)
Shopping	18 (6.0%)	98 (32.7%)	184 (61.3%)
Laundry	12 (4.0%)	45 (15.0%)	243 (81.0%)

When comparing participants' preferred housing with their current housing, it was found that a total of 113 people (37.7%) in the sample (those in the diagonal cells of Table 8.2) are currently living in their preferred housing type. Thus, the majority of participants are not living in the type of housing that they prefer. This discrepancy is magnified by the fact that only one of the 82 people currently residing in a shelter prefers to live there. Nevertheless, the majority of participants living in homes for special care and supportive housing also want to live in their own apartments. It is also important to note that while 37.7 percent of the sample live in their preferred type of housing, this does not mean that people are living in housing that they are comfortable with. In other words, a person may be living in an apartment and wish to live in an apartment, but that person may or may not find the particular apartment he or she is living in to be satisfactory.

Satisfaction with Living Situation by Type of Housing

The residents of the four main types of housing (those living in housing categorized as "other" were excluded from this analysis, n = 7) were compared on the three-item measure of satisfaction with living situation (Lehman et al., 1994). Participants living in shelters have a lower mean score (3.2, standard deviation (SD) = 1.3) than participants living in homes for special care (4.8, SD = 1.3), supportive housing (5.1, SD = 1.4), or their own house/apartment (5.0, SD = 1.1). A comparison was used to test the difference in scores between participants living in shelters and those living in all of the other three types of housing. This comparison was statistically significant: $t(291) = 10.58$, $p < .001$. To determine the magnitude of this difference, an effect size (ES) was calculated by subtracting the mean of shelter group from the mean of the other three groups combined and dividing by the pooled SD. The ES was found to be 1.3, which, according to Cohen (1988), is a very large effect size in social and health science research. Hence, on average, the satisfaction with living situation for those living in shelters is 1.3 standard deviations lower than those living in other types of housing.

Satisfaction with Living Situation by Living in Preferred Housing

Scores on housing satisfaction with living situation measured for the two groups were also compared, study participants who were living in their preferred type of housing (those on the diagonal in Table 8.2) versus those not living in their preferred type of housing (those off the diagonal in Table 8.2). Those living in the type of housing they preferred had a significantly higher mean score on satisfaction with living situation (5.2, SD = 1.1) than those not living in their preferred housing

$(4.0, SD = 1.5)$, $t(298) = 7.1$, $p < .001$. The Effect Size for this difference was found to be .9, which is also a large effect size (Cohen, 1988).

4. DISCUSSION AND IMPLICATIONS FOR ACTION

There were four objectives in this research: (1) to compare consumer-survivors' preferences for housing with their current living situation; (2) to examine housing satisfaction by type of housing; (3) to compare the housing satisfaction of those living in their preferred type of housing; and (4) to illustrate the value of a participatory action research approach to the study of consumer preferences for housing and supports.

With respect to the initial objective, the results were consistent with previous studies that found that individuals who have been diagnosed with psychiatric illnesses, like most other people, prefer to live in their own house or apartment (Friedrich et al., 1999; Rogers et al., 1994; Tanzman, 1993). This was the first large-scale study of consumer-survivors' preferences for housing in Canada, and it was discovered that Canadian mental health consumer-survivors, like their counterparts in the United States, prefer independent living.

The results of this study also extend previous research by showing that preferences for independent housing options are consistent across a variety of different types of current housing situations. Friedrich et al. (1999) found that participants in their study in Iowa tended to prefer the types of housing in which they were currently residing. Our findings stand in sharp contrast: nearly 80 percent of the participants, including those living in large congregate facilities, shelters, and supportive housing, want to live in their own house or apartment. It is unclear why the findings from the Friedrich study are inconsistent with those of this study and the many other studies of consumer preferences (Tanzman, 1993), which show that people want to live independently, not in the types of housing in which they currently reside.

As in previous studies (e.g., Tanzman, 1993), we also found that the majority of participants identified numerous barriers to obtaining the type of housing they prefer and supports that they wish to have available to them. For the most part, the barriers to independent living are, not surprisingly, financial. The list of concrete supports required to achieve preferred housing reflects concerns about poverty and isolation. Transportation was the most prevalent need even though London, the study site, has a well-developed public transportation system. Similarly, over 80 percent of respondents indicated the need for a telephone. Clearly, if consumer-survivors' budgets are so constrained that they can't afford to take a bus or have a telephone, then it is likely that many other basic resources will be equally inaccessible. Greater financial benefits to access independent living were also underscored by participants (see Table 8.3). These financial concerns reflect the inadequacy of current social policies in Ontario for disadvantaged, low-income people, including those who have experienced mental illness.

As for the "support" component of supported housing, participants noted the need for staff support to help them deal with a variety of day-to-day challenges for living independently in the community. Participants did not want the intrusiveness of live-in staff, but they did want to be able to access staff support at any time of the day or night. In particular, participants noted the need for help in dealing with emotional upsets. Having support staff available to help handle difficult situations as they arise is important for ensuring that consumers can maintain their housing and quality of life in the community (Parkinson et al., 1999).

Regarding the second objective, we found that participants who lived in shelters had much lower levels of housing satisfaction compared with participants living in all of the other types of housing. While previous research has examined satisfaction and quality of life of mental health consumer-survivors residing in different types of housing (Lehman et al., 1986; 1991), no previous research has compared the housing satisfaction of people living in shelters with people living in other types of housing. There is sometimes a public myth that individuals in shelters or on the street live there because that is where they want to be. It is important to note that in this study, not only are levels of housing satisfaction low for those living in shelters, but only one individual in this sample actually wanted to live in the shelter system. Clearly, shelters are not an appropriate solution to the housing challenges faced by mental health consumer-survivors, and proffering this type of housing as a viable form of community living does not have support from this group.

With respect to the third objective, we found that those living in their preferred housing choice had much higher levels of quality of life related to housing compared with people who were not living in their preferred type of housing. Srebnik, Livingston, Gordon, and King (1995) found that the more control mental health consumer-survivors have over their housing, the higher their level of housing satisfaction, residential stability, and psychological well-being. These findings suggest the need for the development of more independent living arrangements than are currently available in communities such as London, Ontario. This finding is also supported in qualitative focus group workshops conducted with mental health consumer-survivors from the CURA research program, in which individuals have stated that they sometimes have to make a choice between the services they want or the housing they want (see Chapter 7). Clearly, with increased opportunities for independent living, mental health consumer-survivors should also have ongoing access to supportive mental health services that are available.

The final objective of this study was to illustrate the value of a participatory action research approach to the study of consumer-survivors' preferences for housing and supports. The preference survey reported in this chapter, along with focus groups with mental health consumer-survivors and family members previously discussed in this section of the book, were the first steps in a participatory action research process designed to enhance the capacity of the London community to meet the needs of mental health consumer-survivors. The research has not only documented the need for independent living, but has also raised the awareness of the community about this issue. Service providers at the local level and policy-makers at the local, provincial, and federal levels of government need to understand consumer-survivors' preferences and the concrete needs necessary to facilitate independent living for this group.

REFERENCES

Carling, P.J. (1995). *Return to community: Building support systems for people with psychiatric disabilities.* New York: Guilford Press.

Cohen, J. (1988). *Statistical power analysis for the behavioral sciences*, 2nd ed. Hillsdale: Erlbaum.

Friedrich, R.M., Hollingsworth, B., Hradek, E., Friedrich, H.B. & Culp, K.R. (1999). Family and client perspectives on alternative residential settings for persons with severe mental illness. *Psychiatric Services, 50,* 509–14.

Goering, P. & colleagues. (1997). *Review of best practices in mental health reform.* Ottawa: Minister of Public Works and Government Services Canada.

Goering, P., Paduchak, D. & Durbin, J. (1990). Housing homeless women: A consumer preference study. *Hospital and Community Psychiatry, 41,* 790–94.

Goldfinger, S.M. & Schutt, R.K. (1996). Comparison of clinicians' housing recommendations and preferences of homeless mentally ill persons. *Psychiatric Services, 47,* 413–15.

Hall, G.B. & Nelson, G. (1996). Social networks, social support, and the adaptation of psychiatric consumer/survivors. *Social Science and Medicine, 43,* 1743–54.

Hanrahan, P., Luchins, D.J., Savage, C. & Goldman, H.H. (2001). Housing satisfaction and service use by mentally ill persons in community integrated living arrangements. *Psychiatric Services, 52,* 1206–09.

Hogan, M.F. & Carling, P.J. (1992). Normal housing: A key element of a supported housing approach for people with psychiatric disabilities. *Community Mental Health Journal, 28,* 215–26.

Horan, M.E., Muller, J.J., Winocur, S. & Barling, N. (2001). Quality of life in boarding houses and hostels: A residents' perspective. *Community Mental Health Journal, 37,* 323–34.

Hulchanski, D. (1998). *Homelessness in Canada: 1998 report to the United Nations.* Available from www.tdrc.net/.

Lehman, A.F., Possidente, S. & Hawker, F. (1986). The quality of life of chronic patients in a state hospital and in community residences. *Hospital and Community Psychiatry, 37,* 901–07.

Lehman, A.F., Postrado, L., Roth, D., McNary, S. & Goldman, H. (1994). An evaluation of continuity of care, case management, and client outcomes in the Robert Wood Johnson program on chronic mental illness. *Millbank Quarterly, 72,* 105–22.

Lehman, A.F., Slaughter, J.G. & Myers, C.P. (1991). Quality of life in alternative residential settings. *Psychiatric Quarterly, 62,* 35–49.

Lord, J., Ochocka, J., Czarny, W. & MacGillivary, H. (1998). Analysis of change within a mental health organization: A participatory process. *Psychiatric Rehabilitation Journal, 21,* 327–39.

Massey, O.T. & Wu, L. (1993). Important characteristics of independent housing for people with mental illness: Perspectives of case managers and consumers. *Psychosocial Rehabilitation Journal, 17,* 81–92.

Minsky, S., Riesser, G.G. & Duffy, M. (1995). The eye of the beholder: Housing preferences of inpatients and their treatment teams. *Psychiatric Services, 46,* 173–76.

Nelson, G., Hall, G.B., Squire, D. & Walsh, R. (1992). Social network transactions among ex-psychiatric patients residing in supportive apartments, group homes, or board-and-care homes. *Social Science and Medicine, 34,* 433–45.

Nelson, G., Ochocka, J., Griffin, K. & Lord, J. (1998). "Nothing about me, without me": participatory action research with self-help/mutual aid organizations for psychiatric consumer/survivors. American Journal of Community Psychology, 26, 881–912.

Parkinson, S., Nelson, G. & Horgan, S. (1999). From housing to homes: A review of the literature on housing approaches for psychiatric consumer/survivors. *Canadian Journal of Community Mental Health, 18*(1), 145–64.

Pyke, J. & Lowe, J. (1996). Supporting people, not structures: Changes in the provision of housing support. *Psychiatric Rehabilitation Journal, 19,* 5–12.

Ridgway, P. & Zipple, A.M. (1990). The paradigm shift in residential services: From the linear continuum to supported housing approach. *Psychosocial Rehabilitation Journal, 13*(4), 11–31.

Rogers, E.S., Danley, K.S., Anthony, W.A., Martin, R. & Walsh, D. (1994). The residential needs and preferences of persons with serious mental illness: A comparison of consumers and family members. *The Journal of Mental Health Administration, 21,* 42–51.

Schutt, R.K. & Goldfinger, S.M. (1996). Housing preferences and perceptions of health and functioning among homeless mentally ill persons. *Psychiatric Services, 47,* 381–86.

Shapcott, M. (2001). *Housing, homelessness, poverty—and free trade in Canada.* Available from http://www.tdrc.net/.

Srebnik, D., Livingston, J., Gordon, L. & King, D. (1995). Housing choice and community success for individuals with serious and persistent mental illness. *Community Mental Health Journal, 31,* 139–52.

Tanzman, B. (1990). *Consumer housing preference survey—short version.* Available from the Centre for Community Change International, www.cccinternational.com/catalog/ins01.htm.

Tanzman, B. (1993). An overview of surveys of mental health consumers' preferences for housing and support services. *Hospital and Community Psychiatry, 44,* 450–55.

Trainor, J., Lurie, S., Ballantyne, R. & Long, D. (1987). The supportive housing coalition: A model for advocacy and program development. *Canadian Journal of Community Mental Health, 6*(2), 93–106.

Trainor, J.N., Morrell-Bellai, T.L., Ballantyne, R. & Boydell, K.M. (1993). Housing for people with mental illness: A comparison of models and an examination of the growth of alternative housing. *Canadian Journal of Psychiatry, 38,* 494–501.

Section III

INTRODUCTION: HOMELESSNESS AND ITS PREVENTION

Section III introduces four distinct contributions on prevention in the arena of homelessness. In Chapter 9 Schofield, Forchuk, Jensen, and Brown present their findings relating to the "Perceptions of Health and Health Service Utilization among Homeless and Housed Mental Health Consumer-Survivors." They discuss the fact that homelessness has a direct impact on health, with homeless individuals reporting several significant barriers to accessing health care. Although research exists regarding the utilization of health services for homeless and housed mental health consumer-survivors, little was known about the perceived health and service utilization of these two groups prior to this work. Key findings include significant differences in the characteristics of each population, their use of health services, and their perceptions of health.

Haldenby, Berman, and Forchuk introduce the reader to issues pertaining to "Homelessness and Health in Adolescents" in Chapter 10. Despite an abundance of resources, many of the world's wealthiest nations have large homeless populations.

People at all stages of development are affected by this problem, but adolescents who are homeless face a unique set of challenges. In this chapter a critical narrative perspective is employed to examine the experiences of homeless adolescents, with particular attention focused on the role of gender and public policy, health experiences and perceptions, and barriers to health care services. Six girls and seven boys participated in semi-structured dialogic interviews. Their stories revealed that living without a home had a substantial impact on their health and wellness. The findings from this study support the need for health care professionals to work in collaboration with homeless youth so that more effective and sensitive care for their unique health needs can be provided. Haldenby was one of the many graduate students who benefited academically and professionally through the CURA, and this chapter is a summary of her master's thesis.

Chapters 11 and 12 look at the extremely pertinent and vexing issue of individuals who are released from a hospital to no fixed address in the community. In Chapter 11, Forchuk, Russell, Kingston-MacClure, Turner, and Dill discover how frequently people were discharged from psychiatric wards to shelters or the street in London, Ontario. They utilized a range of data sources to determine instances of discharges to shelters or the street. Data were analyzed to determine the number of moves occurring between hospital and shelter to no fixed address in the community. All data sets revealed that the problem of discharge to shelters or the street occurred regularly, though all data sources used were also most likely underestimating the extent of the problem. Policies that contribute to this ongoing problem, which extends well beyond London and Ontario, include income-support policies, the reduction in psychiatric hospital beds, and the lack of community supports. Without recognition, this problem is at risk of remaining invisible with no further improvements to the situation. As a result of this finding, Forchuk, Kingston-MacClure, Van Beers, Smith, Csiernik, Hoch, and Jensen undertook "An Intervention to Prevent Homelessness among Individuals Discharged from Psychiatric Wards to Shelters and 'No Fixed Address'" (Chapter 12).

Using the shelter data, which revealed that discharges from psychiatric facilities to shelters or the street occurred at least 194 times in 2002 in London, Ontario, an intervention was developed and tested to prevent homelessness associated with discharge directly to no fixed address. A total of 14 participants at risk of being discharged without housing were enrolled, with half randomized into the intervention group. The intervention group was provided with immediate assistance in accessing housing and assistance in paying their first and last month's rent. The control group received the usual care. Data were collected from participants prior to discharge and at three and six months post-discharge. It was discovered that all of the individuals who had become part of the intervention group were able to maintain permanent housing after three and six months, while all but one individual in the control group remained homeless after three and six months. That one exception joined the sex trade in order to avoid homelessness. The results of this pilot were so dramatic that randomizing to the control group was discontinued. Chapter 12 concludes with a discussion outlining how systemic improvements can prevent homelessness for individuals being discharged from psychiatric wards.

The final chapter of Section III is entitled "Using Electronic Patient Records in Mental Health Care to Capture Housing and Homelessness Information of Mental Health Consumer-Survivors." Richard Booth writes that homelessness among people with psychiatric illness is at an all-time high in Canada. Many explanations for this phenomenon exist, including the incidence of discharge from in-patient hospital directly into the streets or shelter system. With little known about this unseen social issue afflicting many mental health consumers, Chapter 13 provides recommendations for using electronic patient records (EPRs) as a conduit to capture housing and homelessness-related information as a means of prevention. With the increased use of EPRs in the Canadian health care system, the research and clinical benefits of this technology have only recently begun to be realized in mental health care and can become another tool in minimizing issues related to mental health and homeless. An interesting point about Booth's chapter is that this was originally done as one component of a graduate-level interprofessional course on housing and mental health developed from the CURA. The final assignment was to be a paper that could also be submitted for publication. This thoughtful paper was in turn published in a journal and has now become a chapter in this book.

Section III as a whole emphasizes the importance of assessing specific situations and subgroups in relation to homelessness, and underscores the importance of not seeing the "homeless" as a homogeneous group. Without comprehensive assessment and sufficient data, issues risk becoming invisible and it becomes difficult to develop and test appropriate interventions.

Chapter 9

PERCEPTIONS OF HEALTH AND HEALTH SERVICE UTILIZATION AMONG HOMELESS AND HOUSED MENTAL HEALTH CONSUMER-SURVIVORS

Ruth Schofield, Cheryl Forchuk, Elsabeth Jensen, and Stephanie Brown

1. INTRODUCTION

Homelessness has a direct impact on health (Frankish, Hwang & Quantz, 2005). Homelessness is most commonly defined as living on the streets, in public places, or in shelter-type accommodations (Tsemberis, Gulcur & Nakae, 2004). Previous literature indicates that homelessness affects the physical health of individuals by creating and complicating physical illness such as musculoskeletal disorders (Perkins, Tryssenaar & Moland, 1998). In addition, homelessness exposes shelter users to tuberculosis, human immunodeficiency virus/acquired immunodeficiency syndrome, and influenza, and complicates the management of diabetes and asthma (O'Connell, 2004). However, it is important to note that many risk factors associated with homelessness, such as poverty and substance abuse, are also strong independent risk factors for ill health (Frankish et al., 2005).

In addition to increased health risks, increased mortality rates have been observed in the homeless population. Hwang (2000) conducted a cohort study of 8,933 men who used homeless shelters in Toronto, Ontario, and found that those who used homeless shelters experienced significantly higher rates of mortality compared with Toronto's general population. Similarly, Cheung and Hwang (2004) conducted a cohort study with 1,981 women who used homeless shelters in Toronto and found that they too experienced significant excess mortality compared with women in the general population.

Mental health problems, such as schizophrenia and mood disorders, are common among homeless individuals (Toro et al., 1995). In a secondary analysis of 300 shelter users in Toronto, Eynan, Langley, Tolomiczenko et al. (2002) found that 61.3 percent of the sample reported suicidal ideation and 34.4 percent reported having attempted suicide in their lifetime, with a larger proportion of women reporting both ideation and attempts as compared with men. However, Sullivan, Burnam, and Koegel (2000) note that although mental health issues may play a role in initiating homelessness, it is unlikely that they comprise a sufficient risk factor for homelessness. Forchuk, Ward-Griffin, Csiernik, and Turner (2006) suggest that it is the societal response to mental illness, rather than the mental illness itself, that puts mental health care consumers at risk of homelessness.

To further compound the mental and physical health issues experienced by homeless mental health consumer-survivors, research indicates that these individuals report several barriers to accessing health care. In a survey of homeless shelter users in Thunder Bay, Ontario, individuals reported having difficulty in accessing care when needed and being refused care when requested (Perkins et al., 1998). In addition, homeless mental health consumer-survivors interviewed in a qualitative study indicated that they experienced multiple conflicts with professionals and low levels of trust in services, a consequence of frequently experiencing a discrepancy between expectations and service provision (Bhui, Shanahan & Harding, 2006).

An additional barrier to accessing health care includes the priority that individuals ascribe to health care needs. Qualitative research on health among homeless mental health consumer-survivors indicates that individuals attribute low priority to mental health and higher priority to their physical health problems (Bhui et al., 2006). Moreover, O'Connell (2004: 1251) comments: "The relentless immediacy of the daily struggle for safe shelter and a warm meal relegates health needs to a distant priority." Therefore, although physical health may be viewed as a greater priority than mental health, the attainment of basic physical needs outweighs the motivation to seek health services owing to compromised living conditions. Thus, exploration of comparisons between health service utilization of housed and homeless mental health consumer-survivors is warranted.

A paucity of research has compared health outcomes across various living environments. In a random sample of 55 homeless and 85 housed American individuals, those who were homeless were found not to differ from the housed on diagnosis of severe mental illness or physical health symptoms (Toro et al., 1995). Similarly, a cross-sectional survey of 373 economically marginalized homeless and housed American individuals revealed no differences between groups with respect to physical health. However, this study revealed that significantly more homeless individuals accessed health care services, particularly acute care services, as compared with those who were housed (O'Toole et al., 1999). Although these studies compared health among individuals with various housing situations, the samples did not consist uniquely of mental health consumer-survivors.

Limited mental health research has investigated differences in health-related variables of homeless and housed individuals. For example, an American retrospective study (Martinez & Burt, 2006) of 236 adult homeless mental health consumer-survivors with a concurrent disorder reported that the provision of supportive housing resulted in a reduced total number of hospitalizations, as well as a decreased average number of admissions per individual. Moreover, data from a mental health service database of 10,340 mental health consumer-survivors in San Diego, California, indicated that the homeless population was more likely to use emergency-type services, such as the emergency psychiatric unit, than those who were housed (Folsom et al., 2005). Thus, the findings of comparative research are not consistent and highlight the need for further investigation regarding variations in health outcomes between homeless and housed mental health consumer-survivors.

In addition, the lack of consistent correspondence between objective measures of health and service utilization warrants further examination. Individuals' subjective perception of health may contribute to this discrepancy. Mental health research has indicated that perceptions of health can be influenced by severity of symptoms. For example, Gregor, Zvolensky, and Yartz (2005) found that in a sample of 39 individuals with a diagnosis of panic disorder, those with greater symptom severity were more likely to have negative perceptions of their health. In addition, research indicates that perceptions of health vary among the homeless population. A study by Nyamathi et al. (2004) with a sample of 331 homeless individuals in the United States indicated that those who were military veterans perceived their health as less favourable than those who were non-veterans. Although limited research on perception of health in general is available, there is a particular gap in the literature regarding the differences in perceptions of health among housed and homeless mental health consumer-survivors. Thus, the objective of this study was to determine whether or not differences exist between the utilization of health services and the perceptions of health among these two groups.

2. METHOD

The current study consisted of a secondary analysis of quantitative data collected from the Community-University Research Alliance on Mental Health and Housing. A survey design was used to determine the type of housing that works best for different individuals. The structured interview included multiple instruments that examined issues related to housing, demographics, quality of life, severity of psychiatric symptomatology, and the utilization of health and social services. Interviewers consisted of research staff, primarily composed of undergraduate and graduate students.

Data were collected from 300 mental health consumer-survivors living in the London, Ontario, community in 2001, 2002, and 2003. In these years of data collection, the sample was stratified by both gender (male/female) and housing type (homeless shelter/group living/independent living). Individuals participated only once per year; however, they were encouraged to participate in subsequent years. The 2004 sample consisted of 267 individuals, and this sample consisted primarily of repeat interviews and an additional sample from the homeless population. Individuals in group homes were randomized and approached regarding their participation. Those in shelters or on the streets were approached on random days. Individuals living independently could not be randomized so were recruited through direct communication with social service and housing providers, informative posters located in various community locations, and word-of-mouth through the community of mental health consumer-survivors.

3. RESULTS

Characteristics of the Sample
Chi-square analysis[1] revealed a significant difference between homeless and housed mental health consumer-survivors with respect to gender across all four years of data collection with significantly more homeless individuals being male and thus more housed individuals being female. Although gender differences were observed,

Table 9.1: Characteristics of the Sample

Characteristics of the Sample	Percentage of Sample	2001 (n = 300)		2002 (n = 300)		2003 (n = 300)		2004 (n = 267)	
		Homeless	Housed	Homeless	Housed	Homeless	Housed	Homeless	Housed
Gender[a]	Male	65.9	44.0	62.1	44.6	62.0	45.2	73.1	46.0
	Female	34.1	56.0	37.9	55.4	38.0	54.8	26.9	54.0
Marital status	Single/never married	65.9	61.5	65.5	61.5	63.0	57.7	66.3	62.6
	Separated/divorced	25.6	27.5	28.7	29.1	31.5	31.3	27.9	26.4
	Widowed	2.4	5.5	3.4	2.8	2.2	5.8	3.8	4.9
	Married/common law	6.1	5.5	2.3	6.6	3.3	5.3	1.0	6.1
Education	Less than grade school	2.4	1.8	1.1	0.9	1.1	1.0	1.9	3.8
	Grade school	54.9	48.6	58.6	46.9	56.0	44.6	46.2	39.0
	High school	35.4	35.3	26.4	34.1	28.6	34.8	32.7	37.7
	Community college/university	7.3	14.2	13.8	18.0	14.3	19.6	19.2	19.5
Psychiatric diagnosis[b]	Schizophrenia	14.6	54.1	16.1	54.9	16.3	57.2	15.7	55.8
	Mood	47.6	22.5	49.4	21.6	48.9	25.5	45.1	22.1
	Anxiety	8.5	9.6	13.8	8.9	10.9	6.7	12.7	8.0
	Other	9.8	9.2	5.8	7.0	9.8	6.7	7.8	6.1
	Unknown	19.5	4.6	14.9	7.5	14.1	3.9	18.6	8.0

[a] Significant differences across all 4 years at $P < 0.01$.
[b] Significant differences across all 4 years at $P < 0.001$.

homeless and housed mental health consumer-survivors were not found to differ with respect to marital status nor highest level of education in any of the four years of data collection (Table 9.1).

In addition, Chi-square analysis indicated that primary psychiatric diagnoses differ significantly between homeless and housed mental health consumer-survivors in all four years of data collection. Tests of two proportions indicated that housed individuals reported a diagnosis of schizophrenia more frequently than homeless mental health consumer-survivors across all four years, and that homeless individuals reported a diagnosis of a mood disorder more frequently than housed mental health consumer-survivors across the entire period of the study.[2] Finally, significant differences in age were found between homeless and housed mental health consumer-survivors, with homeless individuals reporting a younger mean age across all four years as compared with housed individuals.[3] The overall average age of homeless mental health consumer-survivors was 35.0 ± 12.8 years (n = 363), and the overall average age of housed individuals was 45.9 ± 11.0 years (n = 802).

Results of comparisons of the severity of psychiatric symptomatology and level of functioning between homeless and housed mental health consumer-survivors can be found in Table 9.2. Results of inferential statistics on variables regarding the severity of psychiatric symptomatology indicated no difference between homeless and housed mental health consumer-survivors' emotional withdrawal or attention problems in any of the four years of data collection.[4]

In one year of data collection, specifically 2001, housed mental health consumer-survivors were found to display greater problem severity than homeless individuals with respect to thought processes, interpersonal issues, medical illness, and overall degree of problem severity. In two years of data collection, specifically 2003 and 2004, homeless mental health consumer-survivors were rated as experiencing greater problem severity than their housed counterparts with respect to anxiety, hyperaffect, suicide/danger to self, resistiveness, and security/management issues.[5]

Homeless and housed mental health consumer-survivors differed significantly across three years of data collection with regard to their degree of cognitive problems, self-care, family issues, and role performance.[6] Role performance was not consistent across the three years in which there were found to be significant differences between homeless and housed mental health consumer-survivors. Homeless individuals were found to display greater problem severity on this item than housed individuals in 2003, $t(298) = -3.1$, $P < 0.01$, and 2004, $t(265) = -3.7$, $P < 0.001$; however, housed individuals received greater problem severity scores than the homeless in 2001, $t(298) = 2.6$, $P < 0.01$. Finally, homeless mental health consumer-survivors were consistently found to have greater problem severity as compared

Table 9.2: Problem Severity and Level (M ± SD) of Functioning Variables for Homeless and Housed Mental Health Consumer-Survivors

			Year of Data Collection						
		2001		2002		2003		2004	
	CCAR Variables	Homeless	Housed	Homeless	Housed	Homeless	Housed	Homeless	Housed
Problem severity	Emotional withdrawal	2.4 ± 1.5	2.1 ± 1.4	1.9 ± 1.2	1.9 ± 1.2	2.6 ± 1.4	2.5 ± 1.5	2.5 ± 1.3	2.4 ± 1.3
	Depression[a]	3.2 ± 1.3	2.9 ± 1.6	3.3 ± 1.8	2.7 ± 1.4	3.4 ± 1.6	2.9 ± 1.7	3.6 ± 1.5	2.8 ± 1.5
	Anxiety[b]	3.1 ± 1.6	2.9 ± 1.5	3.1 ± 1.5	2.8 ± 1.4	3.2 ± 1.8	2.6 ± 1.5	3.2 ± 1.6	2.8 ± 1.6
	Hyperaffect[b]	1.7 ± 1.1	1.9 ± 1.3	1.9 ± 1.2	1.7 ± 1.0	2.1 ± 1.2	1.8 ± 1.1	2.1 ± 1.4	1.6 ± 1.0
	Attention problems	2.9 ± 1.5	2.9 ± 1.5	2.4 ± 1.4	2.5 ± 1.3	2.9 ± 1.5	2.9 ± 1.5	3.0 ± 1.5	3.0 ± 1.4
	Suicide/danger to self[a]	2.0 ± 1.1	1.8 ± 1.0	2.1 ± 1.2	1.9 ± 1.1	2.1 ± 1.3	1.7 ± 1.0	2.4 ± 1.3	1.8 ± 1.0
	Thought processes[c]	1.7 ± 1.2	2.6 ± 1.7	2.0 ± 1.5	2.3 ± 1.4	2.4 ± 1.6	2.4 ± 1.5	2.6 ± 1.6	2.8 ± 1.7
	Cognitive problems[d]	1.3 ± 0.8	2.0 ± 1.4	1.3 ± 0.9	1.7 ± 1.1	1.9 ± 1.2	2.0 ± 1.2	1.8 ± 1.0	2.5 ± 1.5
	Self-care/basic needs[e]	2.5 ± 1.5	2.8 ± 1.8	3.4 ± 1.4	2.6 ± 1.4	3.6 ± 1.5	2.5 ± 1.2	3.7 ± 1.3	2.6 ± 1.3
	Resistiveness[b]	1.7 ± 1.1	1.5 ± 0.9	1.7 ± 1.0	1.7 ± 1.0	2.4 ± 1.5	1.9 ± 1.1	2.2 ± 1.4	1.7 ± 1.0
	Aggressiveness[a]	2.2 ± 1.7	1.5 ± 1.0	1.8 ± 1.4	1.4 ± 0.9	2.1 ± 1.6	1.5 ± 1.0	2.4 ± 1.8	1.5 ± 1.2
	Antisocial[a]	1.8 ± 1.4	1.2 ± 0.5	1.4 ± 0.9	1.2 ± 0.4	2.0 ± 1.5	1.2 ± 0.7	2.0 ± 1.4	1.2 ± 0.6
	Legal problems[a]	1.8 ± 1.5	1.2 ± 0.8	1.7 ± 1.2	1.2 ± 0.6	1.6 ± 1.2	1.1 ± 0.5	2.0 ± 1.7	1.1 ± 0.6
	Violence[a]	1.6 ± 1.3	1.1 ± 0.5	1.4 ± 1.1	1.1 ± 0.4	1.7 ± 1.4	1.2 ± 0.6	1.9 ± 1.5	1.1 ± 0.6
	Family issues[f]	2.1 ± 1.6	1.6 ± 1.3	1.6 ± 1.2	1.4 ± 0.8	2.2 ± 1.5	1.6 ± 1.2	2.0 ± 1.7	1.4 ± 1.0
	Family problems with[a]	2.8 ± 1.9	2.1 ± 1.7	2.2 ± 1.6	1.8 ± 1.2	2.4 ± 1.6	1.8 ± 1.3	2.4 ± 1.8	1.8 ± 1.3
	Interpersonal issues[c]	2.2 ± 1.3	2.8 ± 1.7	2.4 ± 1.6	2.5 ± 1.3	2.6 ± 1.5	2.5 ± 1.2	2.6 ± 1.5	2.6 ± 1.4
	Role performance[f]	2.7 ± 1.6	3.3 ± 1.8	2.9 ± 1.2	2.9 ± 1.4	3.4 ± 1.5	2.8 ± 1.4	3.1 ± 1.5	2.5 ± 1.2
	Substance abuse[a]	2.8 ± 1.4	1.9 ± 1.0	2.6 ± 1.5	1.9 ± 0.9	3.1 ± 1.6	1.9 ± 1.0	3.1 ± 1.3	1.9 ± 1.0
	Medical illness[c]	2.2 ± 1.3	2.6 ± 1.5	2.4 ± 1.4	2.4 ± 1.4	2.4 ± 1.5	2.3 ± 1.3	2.6 ± 1.7	2.8 ± 1.7
	Security issues[b]	1.4 ± 1.0	1.3 ± 0.9	1.4 ± 1.0	1.4 ± 1.0	1.6 ± 1.3	1.4 ± 0.9	2.0 ± 1.5	1.2 ± 0.7
	Overall[c]	3.8 ± 1.2	4.2 ± 1.2	4.0 ± 1.2	3.7 ± 1.1	4.2 ± 1.3	4.0 ± 1.2	4.6 ± 1.1	4.3 ± 1.1

Table 9.2: continued

	Year of Data Collection							
CCAR Variables	2001		2002		2003		2004	
	Homeless	Housed	Homeless	Housed	Homeless	Housed	Homeless	Housed
Societal/role[e]	5.2 ± 1.0	5.0 ± 1.0	5.7 ± 0.8	5.1 ± 0.9	5.8 ± 1.0	5.0 ± 1.1	5.8 ± 1.0	5.0 ± 1.0
Interpersonal	5.2 ± 1.2	5.4 ± 1.2	5.7 ± 1.1	5.5 ± 1.2	5.6 ± 1.3	5.3 ± 1.2	5.6 ± 1.1	5.4 ± 1.2
Daily living[e]	5.6 ± 0.8	5.5 ± 1.0	5.9 ± 0.7	5.4 ± 1.2	6.1 ± 0.9	5.3 ± 1.3	5.9 ± 0.9	5.4 ± 1.1
Physical functioning[c]	2.8 ± 1.9	3.6 ± 1.9	3.2 ± 2.2	3.4 ± 2.2	3.4 ± 2.1	3.6 ± 2.3	3.6 ± 2.5	3.9 ± 2.4
Cognitive/intellectual[c]	4.1 ± 1.3	5.1 ± 1.4	4.6 ± 1.4	4.9 ± 1.4	5.0 ± 1.4	4.9 ± 1.4	5.2 ± 1.3	5.4 ± 1.3
Overall[e]	5.3 ± 0.9	5.4 ± 0.9	5.8 ± 0.9	5.4 ± 1.0	5.9 ± 1.0	5.4 ± 1.0	5.9 ± 0.8	5.6 ± 0.8

Level of functioning

CCAR, Colorado Client Assessment Record.
[a] Significant across all 4 years at P < 0.05.
[b] Significant in 2003 and 2004 at P < 0.05.
[c] Significant in 2001 at P < 0.05.
[d] Significant in 2001, 2002, and 2004 at P < 0.01.
[e] Significant in 2002, 2003, and 2004 at P < 0.05.
[f] Significant in 2001, 2003, and 2004 at P < 0.05.

with housed individuals across all four years of data collection concerning ratings of depression, aggressiveness, anti-social problems, legal problems, violence/danger to others, and substance abuse.[7]

With respect to the level of functioning variables, only interpersonal level of functioning did not differ between groups in any of the four years of data collection. In one year of the study, specifically 2001, homeless individuals were found to have greater levels of functioning as compared with the housed mental health consumer-survivors with respect to physical functioning and cognitive/intellectual functioning. However, across three years of data collection, housed individuals were consistently found to have greater levels of functioning than the homeless in terms of daily living/personal care, societal/role, and current overall level of functioning.[8]

Utilization of Health Services

In 2001, significantly more homeless mental health consumer-survivors reported an admission to hospital in the past month than housed individuals $[\chi^2(1) = 13.1, P < 0.001]$. A comparison between the number of admissions to a provincial psychiatric hospital, the psychiatric ward of a general hospital, and general hospital in the past month was not possible as groups of individuals reporting an admission in 2001 were too small for adequate comparison. Only three people reported an admission to a provincial psychiatric hospital, two of whom were homeless and one of whom was housed. Five homeless individuals reported an admission to a psychiatric ward of a general hospital; however, no housed individuals reported such admissions in the past month. Finally, a total of 11 individuals (five homeless and six housed) reported an admission to a general hospital, stating that they were admitted for such reasons as appendectomy, diabetes complications, flu, removal of gallbladder, knee replacement, injuries resulting from assault, miscarriage, reconstructive surgery, and shortness of breath.

In addition to the greater proportion of homeless individuals reporting an admission to hospital in the past month, homeless individuals in 2001 reported a greater number of psychiatric hospitalizations during the previous two years as compared with those who were housed $[t(95) = -1.9, P < 0.05]$. However, admissions to hospital in the past month and number of psychiatric hospitalizations in the past two years did not significantly differ between homeless and housed mental health consumer-survivors in 2002, 2003, or 2004.[9]

Perceptions of Health

The analysis revealed no significant difference across all four years of data collection between homeless and housed mental health consumer-survivors with respect to their feelings about their physical well-being. However, in 2002 and 2004, a significant difference was observed between homeless and housed individuals' feelings about their health in general, with those who were homeless reporting lower satisfaction than housed individuals. Moreover, homeless and housed mental health consumer-survivors were consistently found to differ significantly with respect to their feelings about their emotional health, with those who were homeless reporting more negative feelings about their emotional well-being as compared with their housed counterparts (Table 9.3).[10]

Table 9.3: Homeless and Housed Mental Health Consumer-Survivors' Perceptions of Health (M ± SD)

		Year of Data Collection							
		2001		2002		2003		2004	
		Homeless	Housed	Homeless	Housed	Homeless	Housed	Homeless	Housed
How do you feel about...	Health in general	4.4 ± 1.6	4.6 ± 1.6	4.0 ± 1.7	4.4 ± 1.5	4.2 ± 1.6	4.5 ± 1.6	3.8 ± 1.6	4.6 ± 1.5
	Physical health[a]	4.0 ± 1.8	4.4 ± 1.6	3.8 ± 1.8	4.2 ± 1.6	4.0 ± 1.7	4.4 ± 1.6	4.2 ± 1.6	4.4 ± 1.7
	Emotional well-being[b]	3.5 ± 1.3	4.5 ± 1.6	3.2 ± 1.5	4.4 ± 1.6	3.8 ± 1.6	4.3 ± 1.6	3.2 ± 1.6	4.4 ± 1.5

[a] Significant in 2002 and 2004 at P < 0.05. [b] Significant across all 4 years at P < 0.05.

4. DISCUSSION

The homeless and the housed represent very different groups of individuals. Those who were homeless tended to be younger, male, and more likely to have a diagnosis of mood disorder. On the other hand, those who were housed were more likely to be older, female, and have a diagnosis of schizophrenia. These findings are consistent with a recent analysis of data from a mental health service database in San Diego by Folson, Hawthorne, Lindamer et al. (2005). The sample consisted of 10,340 individuals (15 percent) who reported being homeless. The homeless individuals were more likely to be younger and male, as compared with the housed. However, individuals with schizophrenia and bipolar disorder had higher rates of homelessness than those with depression, which varies from the results observed in the current analysis.

It should be noted that who is homeless and who is housed is likely dependent on contextual factors and available supports within the specific community. In this sample, people with schizophrenia seemed to have an easier time accessing group homes. Many were housed in the homes for special care (HSC) program, which required prior admission to a tertiary care facility. As that service is more likely to be accessed by people with a diagnosis of schizophrenia, it is not surprising that they were subsequently able to access HSC. Similarly, the increased number of women who found housing was related to easier access to public housing. Individuals who have a history of abuse or domestic violence are fast-tracked and given priority into London's housing program. Without fast-tracking, it can take years to access public housing in this community, which has a waiting list of 5,000 units and only approximately 1,000 units turning over each year. As programs geared to females and individuals diagnosed with schizophrenia have successfully managed to provide housing for mental health consumer-survivors, it is likely that additional housing supports specific to those who concurrently struggle with substance misuse, mood and anxiety disorders, or anti-social personality traits are required to assist in alleviating homelessness. In a different community, with different criteria for housing programs, there may be different demographics.

Homeless individuals display greater problem severity with respect to self-care/basic needs and substance abuse and lower daily living/personal care functioning than housed mental health consumer-survivors. Thus, homeless individuals may be at greater risk for infection and disease than housed individuals, which would be consistent with greater use of health services to address self-care deficits. In addition, homeless individuals also display greater problem severity with respect to resistiveness, anti-social problems, legal issues, and aggressiveness compared with housed mental health consumer-survivors. Consequently, homeless individuals may experience greater personal barriers to accessing health care than housed individuals and justify the need for more non-traditional services, such as a health bus, a mobile service that is common in other health jurisdictions in Ontario.

Homeless individuals were rated as having greater problem severity than housed mental health consumer-survivors across all four years of data analysis regarding depression, aggressiveness, anti-social problems, legal problems, violence/danger to others, family problems, and substance abuse. This is a cluster of problems not unexpected with a marginalized and oppressed group. These problems are often interrelated and difficult to treat in the absence of stable housing. This range of problems indicates the complexity of issues faced by the homeless population.

Those who are homeless seem to have different health needs compared with those who are housed based on differences in age, gender, diagnosis, severity of psychiatric symptomatology, and level of functioning. This implies different policies, and interventions are required for these different groups. Homeless mental health consumer-survivors reported more admissions to hospital for physical conditions in the past month and more psychiatric hospitalizations in the past two years as compared with housed individuals. This is consistent with the literature that the homeless are a less stable group than the housed (O'Toole et al., 1999, Folsom et al., 2005). This finding also corroborates previous findings that homeless mental health consumer-survivors are more comparable with other homeless people than with housed individuals with mental health issues (Sullivan, Burnam & Koegel, 2000). However, this finding was not consistent across all four years of data collection.

It is interesting to note that there was no difference between homeless and housed mental health consumer-survivors with respect to perception of physical health. This may be different from studies that have found increased health challenges among the homeless population. However, it is a subjective perception of health, not an objective rating. Findings more consistent with past studies were that the homeless reported feeling less satisfied with their emotional well-being and their health in general than housed mental health consumer-survivors.

As this study is a secondary analysis, it has the limitations associated with that approach. Instruments may not have been ideal for capturing the variables of interest to the question as they were selected with a different question in mind. Any sources of error in the design and implementation of the original study may not be known. Bias that may have existed in the original study is inherited in a secondary analysis (Polit & Hungler, 1991). In addition, in this secondary analysis, utilization of services was measured, but not barriers to accessing health care.

Further information on barriers would provide additional insight into health care utilization.

In conclusion, individuals who have had a history of psychiatric problems and are homeless have many differences than similar individuals who are housed. Increased problems such as depression, substance abuse, and difficulty with the law highlight the need for multiple system responses to meet complex problems. Consideration of the findings of this study can raise interesting questions: Do individuals who are homeless have more needs because they are homeless? Or, are more vulnerable individuals more likely to become homeless? The variation in many findings from year to year underscores both the constantly changing face of homelessness, as well as the need to look longitudinally at the issues to address this population's unmet needs.

NOTES

1. *Housing status:* 2001: $\chi^2(1) = 11.3$, $P < 0.01$; 2002: $\chi^2(1) = 7.5$, $P < 0.01$; 2003: $\chi^2(1) = 7.2$, $P < 0.01$; 2004: $\chi^2(1) = 18.9$, $P < 0.001$.
   Marital status: 2001: $\chi^2(3) = 1.5$, ns; 2002: $\chi^2(3) = 2.4$, ns; 2003: $\chi^2(3) = 2.6$, ns; 2004: $\chi^2(4) = 6.0$, ns.
   Highest level of education: 2001: $\chi^2(3) = 2.9$, ns; 2002: $\chi^2(3) = 3.5$, ns; 2003: $\chi^2(3) = 3.4$, ns; 2004: $\chi^2(3) = 1.9$, ns.
2. *Primary psychiatric diagnoses:* 2001: $\chi^2(4) = 49.6$, $P < 0.001$; 2002: $\chi^2(4) = 42.6$, $P < 0.001$; 2003: $\chi^2(4) = 46.4$, $P < 0.001$; 2004: $\chi^2(4) = 43.4$, $P < 0.001$.
   Diagnosis of schizophrenia: 2001: $Z = -6.15$, $P < 0.001$; 2002: $Z = -6.15$, $P < 0.001$; 2003: $Z = -6.57$, $P < 0.001$; 2004: $Z = -6.47$, $P < 0.001$.
   Diagnosis of a mood disorder: 2001: $Z = 4.26$, $P < 0.001$; 2002: $Z = 4.78$, $P < 0.001$; 2003: $Z = 3.98$, $P < 0.001$; 2004: $Z = 3.94$, $P < 0.001$.
3. *Age:* 2001: $t(298) = 8.3$, $P < 0.001$; 2002: $t(297) = 5.3$, $P < 0.001$; 2003: $t(297) = 6.0$, $P < 0.001$; 2004: $t(265) = 9.6$, $P < 0.001$].
4. *Emotional withdrawal:* 2001: $t(172) = 1.4$, ns; 2002: $t(298) = 0.2$, ns; 2003: $t(298) = -0.3$, ns; 2004: $t(265) = -1.0$, ns.
   Attention problems: 2001: $t(298) = 0.4$, ns; 2002: $t(298) = 0.7$, ns; 2003: $t(298) = 0.002$, ns; 2004: $t(265) = 0.3$, ns.
5. *Thought processes:* $t(205) = 4.8$, $P < 0.001$.
   Interpersonal issues: $t(190) = 3.0$, $P < 0.01$.
   Medical illness: $t(298) = 2.4$, $P < 0.05$.
   Overall degree of problem severity: $t(296) = 2.8$, $P < 0.01$.

Anxiety: 2003: t(298) = −2.6, P < 0.05; 2004: t(265) = −2.1, P < 0.05.
Hyperaffect: 2003: t(298) = −2.1, P < 0.05; 2004: t(177) = −3.0, P < 0.01.
Suicide/danger to self: 2003: t(140) = −3.0, P < 0.01; 2004: t(171) = −4.1, P < 0.001.
Resistiveness: 2003: t(136) = −2.8, P < 0.01; 2004: t(176) = −2.9, P < 0.01.
Security/management issues: 2003: t(131) = −2.0, P < 0.05; 2004: t(129) = −5.0, P < 0.001.

6. *Cognitive problems:* 2001: t(242) = 4.8, P < 0.001; 2002: t(195) = 3.1, P < 0.01; 2004: t(262) = 4.3, P < 0.001.
   Self-care/basic needs: 2002: t(298) = −4.6, P < 0.001; 2003: t(143) = −6.3, P < 0.001; 2004: t(251) = −7.0, P < 0.001.
   Family issues: 2001: t(125) = −2.0, P < 0.05; 2003: t(147) = −3.1, P < 0.01, 2004: t(153) = −2.8, P < 0.01.

7. *Depression:* 2001: t(169) = −2.0, P < 0.05; 2002: t(133) = −2.9, P < 0.01; 2003: t(298) = −2.3, P < 0.05; 2004: t(265) = −4.2, P < 0.001].
   Aggressiveness: 2001: t(100) = −3.2, P < 0.01; 2002: t(113) = −1.9, P < 0.05; 2003: t(118) = −3.5, P < 0.01; 2004: t(158) = −4.6, P < 0.001].
   Anti-social problems: 2001: t(89) = −4.4, P < 0.001; 2002: t(100) = −2.6, P < 0.05; 2003: t(110) = −4.4, P < 0.001; 2004: t(132) = −5.2, P < 0.001].
   Legal problems: 2001: t(100) = −3.7, P < 0.001; 2002: t(105) = −4.0, P < 0.001; 2003: t(102) = −3.8, P < 0.001; 2004: t(121) = −5.1, P < 0.001].
   Violence/danger to others: 2001: t(88) = −3.2, P < 0.01; 2002: t(96) = −2.3, P < 0.05; 2003: t(107) = −3.4, P < 0.01; 2004: t(122) = −4.8, P < 0.001.
   Family problems: 2001: t(134) = −2.8, P < 0.01; 2002: t(126) = −2.3, P < 0.05; 2003: t(150) = −2.9, P < 0.01; 2004: t(174) = −2.5, P < 0.05].
   Substance abuse: 2001: t(107) = −5.0, P < 0.001; 2002: t(116) = −4.2, P < 0.001; 2003: t(117) = −6.5, P < 0.001; 2004: t(172) = −7.5, P < 0.001.

8. *Interpersonal level of functioning:* 2001: t(298) = 1.3, ns; 2002: t(298) = −1.4, ns; 2003: t(298) = −1.7, ns; 2004: t(265) = −1.1, ns].
   Physical functioning: 2001 t(298) = 3.3, P < 0.01.
   Cognitive/intellectual functioning: 2001 t(298) = 5.3, P < 0.001.
   Daily living/personal care: 2002: t(244) = −4.8, P < 0.001; 2003: t(246) = −6.1, P < 0.001; 2004: t(249) = −4.2, P < 0.001].
   Societal/role: 2002: t(298) = −5.2, P < 0.001; 2003: t(298) = −5.5, P < 0.001; 2004: t(265) = −6.5, P < 0.001].
   Current overall level of functioning: 2002: t(179) = −3.8, P < 0.001; 2003: t(298) = −4.3, P < 0.001; 2004: t(265) = −2.4, P < 0.05.

9. 2002: [$\chi^2(1)$ = 3.6, ns; t(298) = 0.5, ns respectively], 2003: [$\chi^2(1)$ = 0.2, ns; t(297) = −0.1, ns respectively], 2004: [$\chi^2(1)$ = 0.4, ns, t(265) = 0.1, ns].

10. *Physical condition:* 2001: $t(298) = 1.8$, ns; 2002: $t(297) = 1.8$, ns; 2003: $t(296) = 1.7$, ns; 2004: $t(265) = 0.8$, ns].
General health: 2002: $t(296) = 2.2$, $P < 0.05$; 2004: $t(265) = 3.6$, $P < 0.001$].
Emotional health: 2001: $t(298) = 5.2$, $P < 0.001$; 2002: $t(296) = 6.2$, $P < 0.001$; 2003: $t(294) = 2.5$, $P < 0.05$; 2004: $t(264) = 6.4$, $P < 0.001$].

REFERENCES

Bhui, K., Shanahan, L. & Harding, G. (2006). Homelessness and mental illness: A literature review and a qualitative study of perceptions of the adequacy of care. *International Journal of Social Psychiatry 52*, 152–65.

Browne, G.B., Arpin, K., Corey, P., et al. (1990). Individual correlated of health service utilization and the cost of poor adjustment to chronic illness. *Medical Care 28*, 43–58.

Cheung, A.M. & Hwang, S.W. (2004). Risk of death among homeless women: A cohort study and review of the literature. *Canadian Medical Association Journal 70*, 1243–47.

Ellis, R., Wackwitz, J. & Foster, M. (1991). Uses of an empirically derived client topology based on level of functioning: Twelve years of the CCAR. *Journal of Mental Health Administration 18*, 88–100.

Ellis, R., Wackwitz, J. & Foster, M. (1996). *Treatment outcomes using level of functioning and independent measures of change: An alternate approach for measurement of change.* Denver: Decision Support Services, Department of Mental Health.

Eynan, R., Langley, J., Tolomiczenko, G., et al. (2002). The association between homelessness and suicidal ideation and behaviours: Results of a cross-sectional survey. *Suicide and Life-Threatening Behaviour, 32*, 418–27.

Folsom, D.P., Hawthorne, W., Lindamer, L., et al. (2005). Prevalence and risk factors for homelessness and utilization of mental health services among 10,340 patients with serious mental illness in a large public mental health system. *American Journal of Psychiatry, 162*, 370–76.

Forchuk, C., Ward-Griffin, C., Csiernik, R. & Turner, K. (2006). Surviving the tornado of mental illness: Psychiatric survivors' experiences of getting, losing, and keeping housing. *Psychiatric Services 57*, 1–5.

Frankish, C.J., Hwang, S.W. & Quantz, D. (2005). Homelessness and health in Canada: Research lessons and priorities. *Canadian Journal of Public Health 96*, S23–S29.

Gregor, K.L., Zvolensky, M.J. & Yartz, A.R. (2005). Perceived health among individuals with panic disorder: Associations with affective vulnerability and psychiatric disability. *Journal of Nervous and Mental Disease 193*, 697–99.

Hwang, S.W. (2000). Mortality among men using homeless shelters in Toronto, Ontario. *Journal of the American Medical Association 283*, 2152–57.

Lehman, A.F., Postrado, L., Roth, D., et al. (1994). An evaluation of continuity of care, case management, and client outcomes in the Robert Wood Johnson program on chronic mental illness. *Milbank Quarterly 72*, 105–22.

Martinez, T.E. & Burt, M.P. (2006). Impact of permanent supportive housing on the use of acute care health services by homeless adults. *Psychiatric Services 57*, 992–99.

Nyamathi, A., Sands, H., Pattatucci-Aragón, A., et al. (2004). Perception of health status by homeless U.S. veterans. *Family and Community Health, 27*, 65–74.

O'Connell, J.J. (2004). Dying in the shadows: The challenge of providing health care for homeless people. *Canadian Medical Association Journal, 170*, 1251–52.

O'Toole, T.P., Gibbon, J.L., Hanusa, B.H., et al. (1999). Utilization of health care services among subgroups of urban homeless and housed poor. *Journal of Health Politics, Policy, and Law 24*, 91–114.

Perkins, J.M., Tryssenaar, J. & Moland, M.R. (1998). Health and rehabilitation needs of a shelter population. *Canadian Journal of Rehabilitation 11*, 117–22.

Polit, D.F. & Hungler, B.P. (1991). *Nursing research: Principles and methods*, 4th ed. New York: J.B. Lippincott.

Sullivan, G., Burnam, A. & Koegel, P. (2000). Pathways to homelessness among the mentally ill. *Social Psychiatry and Psychiatric Epidemiology, 35*, 444–50.

Toro, P.A., Bellavia, C.W., Daeschler, C.V., et al. (1995). Distinguishing homelessness from poverty: A comparative study. *Journal of Consulting and Clinical Psychology, 63*, 280–89.

Tsemberis, S., Gulcur, L. & Nakae, M. (2004). Housing first, consumer choice, and harm reduction for homeless individuals with a dual diagnosis. *American Journal of Public Health, 94*, 651–56.

Chapter 10

HOMELESSNESS AND HEALTH IN ADOLESCENTS

Amy Haldenby, Helene Berman, and Cheryl Forchuk

1. INTRODUCTION

Many of the world's wealthiest nations have a large homeless population despite an abundance of natural and material resources. Due to the inherently transient nature of homelessness and few agreed-on definitions, it is difficult to obtain an accurate picture of those who are living without a home (Panter-Brick, 2002). However, there is evidence that a significant proportion is made up of adolescents (City of Calgary, 2006). The leader of the New Democratic Party of Canada, Jack Layton (2000), observed that the word "homeless" conjures up powerful images of people who have no roof under which to reside or individuals and families who live in "substandard" housing. However, how the term is defined is rooted in ideology (Ensign, 1998) and can influence who is researched and how the findings are interpreted. For the purposes of this study, homelessness includes individuals who live on the streets, are in the shelter system, or are continuously moving between temporary housing arrangements. Throughout this research the terms "homeless," "street-involved," and "living on the streets" are used interchangeably.

The City of Toronto (1999) report, commissioned by the Mayor's Homelessness Action Task Force, identified youths under the age of 18 as the fastest-growing group of users of emergency hostels. Living without a home, and thus at the margins of society, is thought to create grim consequences for adolescents' health, development, and overall well-being (Panter-Brick, 2002).

2. BACKGROUND AND SIGNIFICANCE

In the past two decades changes in the national economy, including socio-economic restructuring in Canada, have had a substantial impact on adolescents nation-wide (Dematteo et al., 1999). The effects of this restructuring are demonstrated through cuts to social programs and supports, as well as drastic reductions to welfare and unemployment insurance. These factors have led to an increase in the number of youths living in poverty. Although there are many other factors, including various forms of abuse and neglect, that play a role in the homelessness of adolescents (Martijn & Sharpe, 2005), such structural changes are also thought to contribute to the rise of street-involved youths in Canada. There is, however, little knowledge regarding how these social and political factors influence the experience of being without a home.

The gender stratification of contemporary Western society can be characterized by a devaluing of the lives of girls and women (Neysmith, 1995). Consequently, gender is also a powerful shaper of an individual's experiences and can therefore influence how young women and men create different meanings out of similar circumstances. As a result of their lower position in the social hierarchy, it has been suggested that living without a home places adolescent women at a significant disadvantage (Ensign & Panke, 2002). Little research, however, has been conducted to confirm or refute this idea. In the absence of such knowledge, health care professionals are typically limited in their ability to provide care for this population.

It has, however, been well documented that homeless adolescents experience a variety of health-related concerns (Boivin et al., 2005). Despite this fact, many researchers have found that these youths are the least likely to access the available health care services (Barkin et al., 2003; Shiner, 1995). It is therefore crucial for health care providers to better understand both the physical and mental health perceptions and experiences of this group in order to provide more effective approaches to holistic health care.

3. HOMELESS YOUTHS

There is a widely accepted misconception that youths who reside on the streets are there by choice (City of Toronto, 1999). In fact, numerous reports have identified various forms of abuse, including physical, sexual, and emotional, as critical factors that cause young people to flee their homes (Caputo, Weiler & Anderson, 1997; Russell, 1996). It is thought that a comprehensive understanding of homelessness also requires attention to macro-level factors such as poverty, support networks, and employment (Boydell, Goering & Morell-Bellai, 2000; Morrell-Bellai, Goering & Boydell, 2000). In this section of the chapter, the literature that relates to the health of adolescents once they become homeless, and the barriers they face when trying to access health care, will be discussed.

Many adolescents who are homeless experience a range of physical and emotional health problems (Panter-Brick, 2004). Several quantitative studies have shown that this population has a particularly high rate of suicide ideation (Leslie, Stein & Rotheram-Borus, 2002; Rew, Taylor-Seehafer & Fitzgerald, 2001). It is thought that this risk is even more amplified among gay, lesbian, bisexual, and transgendered youths (Cochran et al., 2002; Noell & Ochs, 2001). Homeless youths have a high prevalence of depression and other psychiatric disorders, which in turn are associated with elevated rates of intravenous drug use (Rhode et al., 2001). Substance abuse is also correlated with homelessness among adolescents (Mallett, Rosenthal & Keys, 2005). Homeless youths also suffer from an increased rate of acute and chronic respiratory diseases (Clatts et al., 1998; Hwang, 2001). The increase in respiratory disease might be related to exposure to tuberculosis and influenza (O'Connell, 2004), which can result from staying in crowded quarters such as emergency shelters or squats.

In addition to being at risk for various physical and emotional problems, homeless adolescents are often forced to engage in "survival sex," whereby sexual activity is traded for money, drugs, or shelter (Rew, Chambers & Kulkarni, 2002). As a result, these adolescents might have more sexual partners than the adolescent population in general, which in turn also negatively affects their emotional and physical well-being (Anderson et al., 1996; Clatts et al., 1998). They are also likely to be involved in some form of high-risk sexual activity, such as inconsistent condom use and prostitution (Johnson et al., 1996).

Several large quantitative studies conducted in urban centres in North America have shown that homeless adolescents are at high risk for contracting HIV infection (Dematteo et al., 1999; Walters, 1999). It has been estimated that these youths are six to 12 times more likely to become infected with HIV than any other group of youths (Rotheram-Borus et al., 2003), as well as being more likely to contract chlamydia (Shields et al., 2004).

Many researchers have observed that homeless adolescents are more likely to become victims of many forms of violence than those who are not homeless (Kipke et al., 1997; Whitbeck, Hoyt & Ackley, 1997). Street involvement has also been found to increase the risk of mortality by eight to 11 times that of the general population (Hwang, 2000; Roy et al., 2004).

A number of researchers have also examined the experience of adolescent homelessness (Kidd, 2004; Paradise & Cauce, 2002). In a study of street youths in Brazil, experiences of homelessness varied according to the local context and circumstances (Raffaelli et al., 2000). This finding is important because it highlights the problems inherent in attempts to generalize the experiences of street-involved youths across diverse settings and cultures. Also of interest was Ensign and Bell's (2004) finding that health-seeking behaviours differed by gender. Female youths sought care more often, typically preferred to be accompanied by a friend, and also reported more safety concerns while ill and living on the streets than did their male counterparts.

Although homeless adolescents experience a variety of health-related concerns, they rarely access health care services (Barkin et al., 2003; Shiner, 1995). Some barriers they encounter are fears that they will experience discriminatory attitudes (Gerber, 1997) and be negatively judged by health providers (Ensign, 2001; Reid, Berman & Forchuk, 2005). There is evidence that these concerns among homeless youths are warranted. In research with medical students, more negative attitudes toward homeless people were found at the end of their courses than at the beginning (Masson & Lester, 2003). Among nursing students, care has been denied to homeless clients in certain situations (Zrinyi & Balogh, 2004). It is possible that health professionals' negative attitudes regarding homeless individuals dissuade this population from accessing needed health care, which, in turn, contribute to their poorer level of health.

4. UNIQUE CHALLENGES THAT HOMELESS ADOLESCENT WOMEN FACE

Several investigators have examined the unique challenges that homeless female adolescents face, and have concluded that they are the most vulnerable subculture within the homeless population (Ensign & Panke, 2002). There is some evidence that the nature of victimization while residing on the streets differs for women and men. More specifically, several researchers have observed that women and girls are significantly more likely to be sexually assaulted than are men and boys (Kipke et al., 1997; Rew et al., 2001; Tyler et al., 2001). The detrimental effects that result from such violence include fear, anger, hostility, depression, anxiety, and humiliation (Fontaine & Fletcher, 1999; Hall, 2000; Nehls & Sallmann, 2005). Sexualized violence can also increase the risk of contracting HIV, a problem that is well documented among this subpopulation (Clements et al., 1997; O'Connor, 1998).

Several different investigators (Chen et al., 2004; Harrison, Fulkerson & Beebe, 1997) have also found that a history of childhood sexual abuse increases the risk of substance abuse among homeless youths. As girls are sexually abused with much greater frequency than are boys (Trocme & Wolfe, 2001), homeless adolescent women are thought to be at considerable risk for substance abuse. There are reports that there is a relationship between substance abuse and prostitution among homeless female adolescents, which is thought to have adverse consequences for the women's physical and emotional health (Weber et al., 2004). Finally, there is some evidence that suicide is more prevalent among adolescent homeless women than it is among their male counterparts (Leslie et al., 2002; Molnar et al., 1998). Collectively, these research findings offer compelling documentation that homeless young women are at a substantial health disadvantage.

However, what remains missing from the literature is consideration of the youths' perceptions about homelessness. As well, there are few studies that explore the experiences of homeless adolescents, or the ways in which gender and public policy influence their experiences.

Many researchers have tended to characterize this population as a homogeneous group. In effect, this depiction negates the importance not only of gender but also of race, ability, and the other related social locations and identities. To present a comprehensive analysis, a commentary regarding current policy that affects homeless youths is also required.

5. THE CONTEMPORARY POLICY CONTEXT

Over the past 15 years the Canadian federal government has absolved itself of its responsibility for homelessness by devolving the funding and implementation of most affordable housing programs onto the provinces and territories, which have, in some cases, foisted the responsibility for them onto the municipalities. Each level of government has its own perspective on the issue of homelessness, with little consensus as to possible solutions. Consequently, millions of allocated social housing dollars have been left unspent. With lack of federal leadership, there are limits to what can be accomplished. The failure of the different levels of Canadian government to work as a cohesive whole contributes to an inability to meet the unique housing needs of homeless individuals, including adolescents.

Among the scant social housing programs, only a few have addressed youths as a subpopulation of the homeless, and even fewer have addressed young women in particular. Historically, the Youth Homeless Strategy, which was part of the National Housing Initiative (NHI) established in 1999 by the Liberal government, narrowly focused on adolescents' job training (Government of Canada, 2004). Although employment status contributes to a person's ability to find and maintain housing, this program overlooked major factors that contribute to their homelessness such as poor levels of well-being and lack of affordable housing. All NHI programs have since been dissolved. Currently, there are few remaining policies that relate to housing needs for youth. Of these, the federal government's Shelter Enhancement Program focuses solely on emergency and second-stage housing (Canada Mortgage and Housing Corporation [CMHC], 2007b). Although this type of shelter is needed to initially help those fleeing violent situations, this program fails to address the long-term housing needs of individuals with histories of abuse. Also, individuals who access this program are expected to contribute financially to the operating costs (CMHC, 2007b). With a few exceptions, such as the First Nations Market Housing Fund (CMHC, 2007a), the current government's housing policies fail to consider how a multitude of factors such as poverty, age, ability, race, and gender influence the housing needs of homeless individuals.

These issues and concerns led to a study to explore the experience of homelessness among adolescents. More specifically, the research questions that guided this investigation were:

- How is homelessness experienced by adolescents?
- How does gender shape these experiences?
- How is health perceived and experienced by homeless adolescents, and what are the barriers they encounter with respect to the health care system?
- How does current Canadian policy shape these experiences?

6. METHOD

Design
The selected research design was a critical narrative analysis. This approach integrates key ideas from critical social theory and narrative inquiry. Critical theory

builds on Marxist thought to consider that multiple, often overlapping forms of oppression exist. From an epistemological perspective, knowledge within a critical theory framework is historically constructed and socially situated. Thus, characteristics such as social class, race, age, ability, and gender are considered to be social constructions that afford differing access to power and privilege within our society (Browne, 2000). Depending on one's social location or identity, individuals and groups have unequal ability to participate fully in society. One aim of research that is informed by critical theory is to examine individual experiences, but also to consider how these are shaped by broader social, political, and historical contexts.

As selected study participants were from a group who are often in the margins of society, this research created a "space" for the voices and perspectives of homeless adolescents to be heard. At the same time, their individual, subjective experiences were analyzed with particular attention to the manner by which those experiences are shaped by gender and public policy.

Narrative inquiry is a research method that is highly compatible with critical social theory. Narrative inquiry involves using language as the medium that reflects meanings, which are understood as the groundwork of reality (Riessman, 1993). The participants' stories are rooted in time, place, and personal experience (Lieblich, Tuval-Mashiach & Zilber, 1998; Riessman, 1993), which provide insight into social patterns as they are seen through the lens of an individual (Patton, 2002; Riessman, 1993). In this research the social patterns and culture that were revealed through the individuals' stories can be used to better understand the experiences of living without a home.

Sample

After ethics approval was obtained through the University of Western Ontario's research ethics board, the study participants were recruited from a community centre that works with adolescents who are homeless. This centre is located in the downtown area of a southwestern city in Ontario. Information about the study was provided to the agency staff, who assisted with recruitment by allowing discussion about the study during various youth group meetings. The youths who were interested in participating were asked to contact the researcher by phone or e-mail or in person during a visit to the centre. After meeting the adolescent, the researcher provided a letter of information. The main points of the letter were reviewed at the beginning of the interview, and any questions the participants had were addressed. Informed consent was obtained verbally and in writing at the time of the interview.

All male and female participants had self-identified as being homeless, were able to speak and understand English, and, with one exception, ranged in age from 14 to 19 years. The rationale for the lower age limit is that 14 is the legal age at which individuals can agree to participate in research without parental consent. In recognition of the diversity within the homeless adolescent population, efforts were made to recruit youths from a variety of backgrounds and ethnicities. Thus, one Black male participant who was six months above the specified age range was granted acceptance to participate. All other youths were White.

The total sample consisted of six female and seven male participants. All participants were given the choice of taking part in group or individual interviews. Five of the women and four of the men opted to be interviewed individually. Two group interviews were conducted with one consisting of two adolescent males and the other that consisted of one adolescent male and one adolescent female participant. In both of these interviews the two participants knew one another and considered each other friends. The final decision regarding sample size was determined during the course of the research according to the criterion of saturation (Patton, 2002). Sampling was thus discontinued when no new themes were found to be emerging from the data.

Data Collection Procedures
The individual and group interviews followed a semi-structured format and were dialogic and interactive in nature. Critical theory assumes that the standards of truth are always social (Campbell & Bunting, 1991). Thus, new knowledge is co-constructed between the researcher and the participants. Field notes were taken after the interviews, which assisted the nurse researcher in revising the interview guide as the study progressed and in data analysis (Patton, 2002).

Data Analysis
All interviews were audio-recorded and transcribed verbatim as soon as possible following the interview. Transcripts were reviewed by the interviewer for accuracy. Once transcription was completed, a narrative style of analysis was conducted with the assistance of Atlas-Ti, a qualitative software program. This process involved several readings of the transcripts to capture initial impressions (Lieblich et al., 1998). More focused codes were then developed as ideas surfaced from the narratives. The code list was continuously revised to accommodate new perspectives and to collapse overlapping categories. The focused code list guided the analysis, and more abstract themes evolved from the transcribed stories. Attention was paid to both the content of the story and the way in which it was told (Lieblich et al., 1998).

Zimmerman and West (1987) have argued that society "invisibly" guides people to behave socially within the dichotomous norms of femininity and masculinity. It is therefore thought that gender is embedded in our everyday experiences, which influence how youths create different meanings out of similar circumstances. Social understandings of gender and their influence on the narratives were therefore considered throughout the analysis. Ideas that emerged from the transcripts that did not fit the evolving code list were recognized as important and considered throughout the analysis. In all cases except for the one boy/girl group interview, young women's and young men's transcripts were initially analyzed separately. Finally, dominant themes were identified, and conclusions were made.

7. FINDINGS

All participants appeared eager to share their stories and did so in an insightful way. Five themes emerged from their narratives: (1) the realities of exiting street life; (2) negotiating dangerous terrain; (3) rethinking family; (4) the hazards of being female; and (5) the elusive nature of health and the health care system. As critical research invites reflection on the contextual factors that shape and influence a person's experience, a separate analysis of current Canadian policy was completed. These findings will be addressed in relation to the participants' stories.

"You're Just Stuck": The Realities of Exiting Street Life

Several participants expressed the belief that they were unable to change their current situation and obtain stable housing. Seeing few options, many participants stated that they felt "stuck." As one youth who was living at a shelter at the time of the interview explained:

> "Um, like the fact that I'm just, like, stuck in my life, there's nothing really I could do right now ... well, just, like, stuck in a shelter. I can't really—I don't talk to my dad, so I don't really want to live with him. I don't really want to live with my mom, plus where she lives it's too crowded anyway."

One male participant had received assistance from the Children's Aid Society (CAS) and noted that without their involvement, "then you're just stuck. You got no one to help you out pretty much." Thus, feeling stuck meant perceiving few options and little or no support. It was clear, however, that the youths were dissatisfied with their homeless status and aspired to something better. Often the participants described a strong determination to reach their goals. Throughout their stories, they shared positive images of the future, including their hope that living without a home "does not last a long time." One youth talked about his desire to follow in his brother's footsteps and "try and get college done" and maybe "join the [army] reserves." Recognizing that this would not be easy, he also asserted that he was determined to get himself "off the streets."

Although many comments reflected a desire to bring about change, it was acknowledged that achieving personal goals would be extremely difficult. Many spoke about the desire to get off the streets, but described various barriers that kept them from doing so. The inability to obtain stable employment, education, or training was often mentioned. In one group interview, participants shared that being judged negatively by potential employers because they resided in a shelter could impede finding employment. Another participant, who suffered from chronic fatigue syndrome, explained how her health condition prevented her from finding employment:

> "I'd like to have a job, you know. I'd like to be able to be more independent, but I can't, um, because society doesn't really understand, um, where—they don't understand chronic fatigue. And I mean a job can't be based around how the employee is feeling, you know? They've got to be, you know, if they book you in there, you have to be there, right? And so it's hard. That's tough to deal with."

Feeling misunderstood, judged, and unsupported while attempting to overcome barriers contributed to a belief among many of the youths that they could rely only on themselves, and that reversing their homeless status would be extremely difficult. In summary, many of the participants explained that they felt stuck, and meaningful strategies to end their homelessness seemed elusive. They believed that their efforts were thwarted by barriers over which they had little or no control. They described feeling unsupported and judged, and ultimately began to rely only on themselves to bring about change.

"I Can't Really Feel Safe": Negotiating Dangerous Terrain

Several of the participants discussed the desire to have a place for themselves that was safe and comfortable, a place they could call "home." The living circumstances for the homeless youths in this research varied, but included couch surfing, staying in shelters, and sleeping in parks, stairwells, or abandoned cars. Residing in public spaces often left the youths exposed to violence, which further threatened their sense of safety and affected their emotional well-being. Living in a shelter at the time of the interview, one participant commented:

"I don't know because I can't really feel safe because I'm out here in this world.... You can't really feel safe because you don't know what's going to happen next. You don't know if this drunk is going to come up and punch you in the face for no reason just because he's drunk or if this guy's going to start something with you, and you can't really feel safe there."

Several youths explained that they had been robbed, threatened, and ridiculed or forced to witness physical fights. After being beaten to the point of hospitalization by three older men in a back alley, a male participant commented that he "can't feel safe anymore."

Being exposed to constant threats of violence and with no safe place to go, the youths' daily focus was on meeting their urgent safety and physical needs. Many of the youths chose to tell stories that portrayed them as survivors. The fact that they were living on the streets and still alive was something that they were proud of. The participants told about creative strategies they used in an attempt to feel safe. These included being part of a group, which served as a form of protection while sleeping outside. This peer group would also "help you out" in the event of a fight. Others talked about feeling safer when they were a "one-man army" or when they wore neutral colours so as not to be affiliated with a gang. Carrying a weapon such as a knife and using humour to distract a potential "enemy" were also described as ways to create a sense of safety. Although staying within the confines of the shelter afforded some protection, safety seemed to be an unattainable goal when they lacked places of their own.

"They're in the Same Situation as You": Rethinking Family

A multitude of complex factors combined to contribute to the homelessness among the study participants. Most of the participants had grown up in poverty. Several described various forms of violence, including sexual, emotional, and physical abuse by one or more parent or step-parent that occurred during their childhoods. Others told of emotional abuse by a sibling. Some of the participants explained that problems experienced by their parents, including substance abuse, mental health problems, or unresolved grief, led to their neglect when they were children. One youth had a cognitively impaired sibling who needed full-time care at home, requiring her mother's full attention.

A few participants described their efforts to seek help for the abuse, confiding in an adult or a youth pastor. According to them, their concerns were either perceived to be untrue or trivialized. These responses resulted in feelings of abandonment and betrayal. A young female participant who had fled from her home because of emotional abuse by her parents and sister commented, "I just, um—I find that—I mean I have parents, but in many ways I feel like an orphan."

In addition to feeling betrayed and abandoned by their families, several participants also felt similarly disconnected from their peers. Many youths explained that they felt like outcasts, "being on the bottom of the list," or "the most made fun of person at school." One youth was forced to quit high school while he was homeless because the only shelters were downtown and he could not afford the necessary bus tokens. He commented:

> "I don't really talk to anybody from my high school anymore. Things went sour with a lot of them too, though, eh, because they found out I was living on the streets. If you know anything about high school kids gossiping and like that are talking behind your back, it kind of starts, 'Oh [participant's name] is homeless,' blah, blah, blah, and they all have this, you know, impression of homelessness that, um, that has stuck with them, I guess. It's not exactly the cool thing to be the homeless guy in high school, you know what I mean? They like you more if you're the captain of the football team, I think."

Prior to becoming homeless, he had been well liked by his peers, but subsequently felt like an outcast.

The sense of betrayal and abandonment at both the family and the peer levels led to deeper connections with individuals who shared similar experiences. While living on the streets, all of the participants developed meaningful relationships in which they felt supported, cared for, and protected. Some youths found these relationships to be more "real," as they could empathize with one another and talk about their situations without feeling that they were being judged negatively. After living on the streets, one participant was able to establish meaningful relationships with other homeless youths because, as he stated, "they're in the same situation as you."

Often street culture provided the youths with the "family" that they felt they never had. Close friends were the people in their lives who could be trusted and on whom they could rely. It was stated that friends would not "blow me off like my family did." After being dropped off at a shelter because her father and stepmother couldn't "deal with her," one female participant commented:

> "And when you're homeless too, like you kind of, like, because nobody that's living in a shelter really has, like, close family, it's, like, everyone kind of, like, connects and you find your own group and, like, your own family within that."

All participants desired meaningful relationships. Sharing similar experiences often allowed the youths to feel connected and supported after being abandoned and betrayed by family and peers.

"More Things Can Happen to You": The Hazards of Being Female

Although all of the participants had discussed being exposed to various types of violence while homeless, vulnerability to gender-based violence was particularly pronounced among the female participants. Some told of physical and financial abuse, and one participant was forced to return to living in a shelter after she fled her verbally abusive boyfriend. Other females told about harassment while living on the streets, which is captured in the following comment: "I just feel, like, if you're a girl, like, a lot of the older, sort of weird guys at places like that may hit on you and make you feel strange about yourself." It was also shared that women are more likely to sell their bodies to meet their various needs, one of which was a place to sleep.

Being female meant having more complex health concerns. Money was needed for feminine hygiene products and birth control. Fear of getting pregnant was expressed by several young women. One female participant stated:

> "With a girl, with me being a girl, there's maybe a biased thing just because I am a girl, but there are more things that can happen to you. Like, if you're living on the streets, you have to afford feminine hygiene products. You've got to afford, like, everything that there is to do with that. You've got to worry about if you get pregnant ... and guys don't have to worry about getting pregnant. They don't have to worry about getting their period. They don't have to worry about getting raped in the middle of the night because usually guys—especially guys who live on the street—are tough enough to take care of themselves. There are some girls who can; there are a lot of girls I know who can't."

There was a common perception that young women living on the streets were unable to take care of themselves:

> "I think that sometimes, like, living in the street especially, females need to be a little bit more tough ... because guys think that we're not that tough so if we stand up for ourselves and show them we are, then, like, they're not going to mess with you or whatever."

As a result of this perception, some of the young women felt forced to prove otherwise. To one female participant, it was important that she "not back down when called upon to fight," even if the opponent was male and much larger than she was. Developing a reputation of being tough, in some cases, helped a woman feel safer.

In summary, young female adolescents had a multitude of concerns while living on the streets. They experienced a variety of violence, had complex health concerns, and were viewed as unable to care for themselves. For one participant, being female and homeless equated to feeling "more used than you are appreciated."

"It Takes a Toll on You": The Elusive Nature of Health and the Health Care System

Many youths spoke about the energy and effort that being homeless demands. A young male participant, who fled from a violent home where he was ridiculed and physically abused for being gay, stated that he was "very fatigued all the time, like, not tired, but fatigued, I think, is the right word. I don't know, like, not really tired to go to bed, but you're just, like, exhausted by the littlest thing." Another youth spoke about how fatigue prevented him from "getting stuff accomplished." A few participants felt that no one wanted to talk to them. Many others were depressed, lonely, and ashamed to tell people of their current situation. Describing how he feels about himself, one participant stated:

> "Really, like, insecure and, like, I didn't have, like, very health, like, high self-esteem and, like, I'd always think that, like, people thought I was, like, a bad person and didn't want to, like, hang out with me because of who I was. And, like, I'd just sort of, like, get really depressed and, like, start thinking that everybody hates you, and really they don't. And, like, scared to talk to people because you think that they're not going to want to, like, interact with you, or whatever."

When hurt or ill, several participants indicated that, if necessary, they would access traditional forms of health care, such as emergency rooms and clinics. However, many described obstacles that kept them from doing so. No longer covered by his father's health insurance, one participant was left feeling as though he would have to pay to use Canada's public system. Others noted their inability to afford expensive prescriptions or eye exams. Another youth commented that she "will do anything and everything to stay out of going to a hospital" after she experienced what she considered insensitive care while being hospitalized following the death of her newborn daughter.

Whereas some participants described barriers to care, others claimed there was inadequate support available for them to feel healthy. Feeling healthy involved having access to resources such as a place to have a shower and a safe place to live. Others described health as eating each day, living a low-stress life, and being able to support themselves. It was perceived that there was a tendency for some homeless people to "give up" because they were not initially supported. This idea was captured in the following statement:

> "Yeah, but the way that happened is because no one would help them in the first place. People that need support and they don't have [it], if they would just have that support, they could, like, make a whole world of a difference from turning someone from committing suicide and someone turning into a good citizen and having a job, just because they never had support. And they didn't know where to turn, or what to do, and they got in with the wrong crowd. They needed money for a place to stay, so they started prostituting themselves or selling drugs and end up in jail or whatever, end up robbing houses, blah, blah, blah, and go down the wrong road all because they didn't know where to turn. They had no help."

According to the participants, lack of social support contributed to a more complex situation than they had faced prior to becoming homeless.

A perception among other participants was that homelessness is hidden from society, a perception that made it difficult to access services. It was explained that before becoming homeless, a male participant viewed the shelter system as a service used by "just old people, like old guys." Similarly, a few other participants said that when initially homeless, they were unaware that there were even shelters available, let alone ones that are primarily for youths or women. This lack of knowledge about available services led them to sleep outside, sometimes in the middle of winter. During one pair interview, participants shared that health services were not publicly advertised because of the negative image it would reflect on the government.

Several of the participants spoke about the lack of specific health care services. When reflecting back on her time in a group home, a young female participant commented that the counsellors to whom she had access were not trained "to deal with a lot of stuff." She also noted that she "would have liked to have more actual counselling, like, on a weekly basis to deal with a lot of my stuff." Recognizing that she needed someone to whom she could talk, this young woman observed that there were no appropriate health care services available to her. Another participant had a similar experience. Trying to come to terms with her history of sibling abuse, she found that the violence that she endured was often dismissed as sibling rivalry. She said there were no resources to help her because the seriousness of sibling violence was not recognized. Dealing with her history was described as being "really hard."

Homelessness and the Public Policy Context

Public policy regarding housing shaped the lives of homeless youths in subtle and direct ways. Not having the education or the proper training kept many youths from finding employment. Chronic health problems and feelings of being judged negatively also prevented them from obtaining work. As a result, poverty was central in the lives of virtually all of the participants. Some youths noted that small amounts of money were fairly easy to come by, but having enough money for rent and other necessities was much more difficult. According to one, it was "just that large amounts of money where you could, you know, go get your own place and stuff like that. That's, you know, that's kind of a bit harder to get." Having this "jump start" was seen as a way to get out of their situation.

Several youths spoke about the difficulties of continuing their education while homeless. Not knowing where they were going to sleep at night, feeling insecure, and having no income with which to buy food made regular school attendance extremely difficult. Recently discharged from jail to a shelter, a male participant commented on his frustration of not being able to receive social assistance:

> "No, not really because, like, there's not much you can really do when you're 17 at all. Like, if you're 18, you can get on welfare, like, no big deal, but when you're 17, you have to have, like, the only way you can get on welfare is, like, student welfare and it's, like, too late.... It's too late in, like, the semester to even start school right now."

Not being able to continue their schooling meant that many of the participants were not eligible for social assistance.

8. DISCUSSION

All of the participants created stories that included ideas and issues that were current in their lives. They discussed the desire for a situation that was "better" than the one they currently had. Although their narratives revealed a sense of determination, the youths encountered many barriers, including social policies that were not sensitive to their situations, chronic physical and mental health issues, and perceived judgment of others. These obstacles prevented them from reaching their goals. This analysis shifts the sole blame of a person's homelessness from the individual and captures how public policy contributes to their lack of options. This research challenges the socially accepted idea that homeless youths are "lazy" and cannot be "bothered" to find a job. Exposure to various forms of violence and being forced to focus on their daily survival had detrimental effects on the adolescents' perceptions of their physical and mental health and well-being. As they observed, having a safe and secure place of their own would allow them to redirect their energies to the fulfillment of other goals, such as completing their education or finding employment. This brings attention to the fundamental role that affordable housing plays in the physical and emotional well-being of youths. In addition, in this study, gender was clearly an important context to homelessness, with homeless adolescent females particularly vulnerable to distinct forms of violence. Although many described a range of physical and emotional health problems, the participants generally perceived little available material or emotional support. The accessibility gap between homeless youths and needed health-related services emerged as an important feature in their lives.

Based on the findings from this research, several important implications might be suggested. Of particular importance, this study highlighted the role for agencies working with adolescents experiencing homelessness. Social and health care professionals working with homeless youths have ample opportunity to facilitate group discussions that address their circumstances. Through discussion, social and health care professionals and homeless youths can collaboratively identify solutions to their situations. All care providers can invite homeless youths to join them in lobbying local governments as a way to initiate change. In addition, social and health professionals can encourage adolescents to participate in community-based programs that help raise awareness about homelessness. Professionals can also facilitate peer-led support groups for those who have experienced violence, as well as advocate for ongoing affordable long-term counselling services. They can also work with homeless youths to increase the visibility of homelessness in the school system. This awareness will ultimately help link youths in the process of becoming homeless to the needed social and health-related services.

This study makes it clear that adolescent females have even more complex social and health needs while homeless. To promote the wellness of young homeless women, all social and health care providers should consider the fact that being female places homeless adolescents in a position where they are likely to experience various forms of violence such as sexual assault and harassment. For supportive and effective care to be provided, it is crucial to recognize that these events have detrimental effects on the health and well-being of homeless adolescents. Creating "safe spaces" where homeless youths can talk with one another about the challenges they face, and about violence in particular, is a possible avenue for a health promotion intervention.

With respect to education, inclusion of nursing, medical, and social work curricula related to the needs and challenges of homeless youths is essential. Offering clinical practice opportunities that would afford exposure to this population, and to street culture more broadly, increases the likelihood that health services can be provided in a compassionate and non-judgmental manner.

As well, more research is still needed that will more fully examine the perceptions of homeless youths. To understand how youths perceive their well-being, more effective care programs can be developed and implemented. This study noted an accessibility gap between health care services and those who need them. Research that explores the nature of where adolescents are receiving health-related information would be helpful to better develop care programs. As the health of lesbian, gay, bisexual, and transgendered individuals is generally even poorer than that of other homeless youths (Cochran et al., 2002; Noell & Ochs, 2001), research that considers their perspectives on health is needed to provide effective health care programs. In addition, more research that attempts to create a deeper understanding of how ability and race influence the health and well-being of homeless youths is needed.

Social policies that influence an adolescent's homeless situation extend beyond the urgent need to expand our current affordable housing initiatives. Living on the streets often forces adolescents to focus on daily survival, making it difficult to stay enrolled in school or to maintain a job. It is essential that all social policies consider homeless youths' situations so that those who choose to exit street life have the ability and the resources to do so. Changes to the eligibility criteria for social assistance so that homeless youths would be able to receive support under this initiative are an important policy direction.

There were several limitations with regard to this study. First, despite the researchers' efforts, only one community service was used to recruit participants. As critical research examines a variety of contextual factors, such as race, gender, and socio-economic status, lack of a diverse sample inhibits an understanding of homelessness among these groups. Second, in this study gender was examined as a binary concept. To do so limits the involvement of youths who do not self-identify as either one of the two dominantly accepted gender identities, female and male.

This further limited the ability to understand how various factors such as gender orientation shape the perceptions and experiences of homeless adolescents. The third limitation of this study was the inability to share emerging findings with many of the participants. Due to the transient nature of homeless adolescents' lifestyle, it was difficult to locate many of the youths after the initial interview. Finally, the findings of this research suggest that adolescent males do not experience sexualized violence as do adolescent females, though with the stigma surrounding this issue, some of the male participants might have chosen not to disclose such information.

The findings of this study highlight the experiences of homeless youths and offer insights into the complex nature of homelessness. Extending the issue beyond the individual allows for the consideration of how contextual factors influence the experiences of homeless adolescents. This study draws attention to the fundamental roles that affordable housing policies and gender play in shaping the physical and mental health of homeless adolescents. To recognize an accessibility gap between the current health care services and those who need them, health care professionals can also use the knowledge from this investigation to provide more culturally meaningful and sensitive care to homeless adolescents.

REFERENCES

Anderson, J.E., Cheney, R., Clatts, M., Farugue, S., Kipke, M., Long, A., et al. (1996). HIV risk behavior, street outreach, and condom use in eight high-risk populations. *AIDS Education and Prevention, 8*, 191–204.

Barkin, S.L., Balkrishnan, R., Manuel, J., Anderson, R.M. & Gelberg, L. (2003). Health care utilization among homeless adolescents and young adults. *Journal of Adolescent Health, 32*(4), 253–56.

Boivin, J., Roy, E., Haley, N. & du Fort, G.G. (2005). The health of street youth. *Canadian Journal of Public Health, 96*(6), 432–37.

Boydell, K.M, Goering, P. & Morrell-Bellai, T.L. (2000). Narratives of identity: Re-presentation of self in people who are homeless. *Qualitative Health Research, 10*, 26–38.

Browne, A.J. (2000). The potential contributions of critical social theory to nursing science. *Canadian Journal of Nursing Research, 32*, 35–55.

Campbell, J.C. & Bunting, S. (1991). Voices and paradigm: Perspectives on critical and feminist theory in nursing. *Advances in Nursing Science, 13*(3), 1–15.

Canada Mortgage and Housing Corporation. (2007a). *First Nations housing market fund*. Retrieved July 18, 2007, from www.cmhc-schl.gc.ca/en/ab/

Canada Mortgage and Housing Corporation. (2007b). *Shelter enhancement program.* Retrieved July 19, 2007, from www.cmhc-schl.gc.ca/en/co/prfinas/prfinas_011.cfm

Caputo, T., Weiler, R. & Anderson, J. (1997). *The street lifestyle study.* Ottawa: Health Canada.

Chen, X., Tyler, K.A., Whitbeck, L.B. & Hoyt, D.R. (2004). Early sexual abuse, street adversity, and drug use among female homeless and runaway adolescents in the Midwest. *Journal of Drug Issues, 34*(1), 1–21.

City of Calgary. (2006). *Count of homeless persons in Calgary.* Retrieved January 15, 2007, from www.calgary.ca/docgallery/bu/cns/homelessness/2006_calgary_ homeless_count.pdf#search-%22count%20of%20homeless%20person%20in%20 downtown%20calgary%2

City of Toronto. (1999). *Taking responsibility for homelessness, an action plan for Toronto: Report of the Mayor's Homelessness Task Force.* Toronto: City of Toronto.

Clatts, M.C., Davis, W.R., Sotern, J.L. & Attillasoy, A. (1998). Correlates and distribution of HIV risk behaviors among homeless youths in New York City: Implications for prevention and policy. *Child Welfare, 77,* 195–207.

Clements, K., Gleghorn, A., Garcia, D., Katz, M. & Marx, R. (1997). A risk profile of street youth in Northern California: Implications for gender-specific human immunodeficiency virus prevention. *Journal of Adolescent Health, 20*(5), 343–53.

Cochran, B.N., Stewart, A.J., Ginzler, J.A. & Cauce, A.M. (2002). Challenges faced by homeless sexual minorities: Comparison of gay, lesbian, bisexual, and transgender homeless adolescents with their heterosexual counterparts. *American Journal of Public Health, 92*(5), 773–77.

Dematteo, B.A. Major, C., Block, B., Coates, R., Fearon, M., Goldberg, E., et al. (1999). Toronto street youth and HIV/AIDS: Prevalence, demographics, and risk. *Society for Adolescent Medicine, 25,* 358–66.

Ensign, J. (1998). Health issues of homeless youth. *Journal of Social Distress, 7*(3), 159–74.

Ensign, J. (2001). "Shut up and listen": Feminist health care with out-of-the-mainstream adolescent females. *Issues in Comprehensive Pediatric Nursing, 24,* 71–84.

Ensign, J. & Bell, M. (2004). Illness experiences of homeless youth. *Qualitative Health Research, 14,* 1239–54.

Ensign, J. & Panke, A. (2002). Barriers and bridges to care: Voices of homeless female adolescent youth in Seattle, Washington, U.S.A. *Issues and Innovations in Nursing Practice, 25,* 166–72.

Fontaine, K. & Fletcher, J. (1999). *Mental health nursing.* Menlo Park: Addison Wesley Longman.

Gerber, G.M. (1997). Barriers to health care for street youth. *Journal of Adolescent Health, 21*, 287–90.

Government of Canada. (2004). *NHI programs: Communities taking the lead.* Retrieved March 22, 2006, from www.hrsdc.gc.ca/eng/homelessness/index.shtml

Government of Ontario. (2006). *The Ministry of Community and Social Services.* Retrieved October 29, 2006, from www.mcss.gov.on.ca/mcss/english/pillars/social/programs/ow.htm

Hall, J.M. (2000). Core issues for female child abuse survivors in the recovery from substance misuse. *Qualitative Health Research, 10*, 612–31.

Harrison, P.A., Fulkerson, A. & Beebe, T.J. (1997). Multiple substance use among adolescent physical and sexual abuse victims. *Child Abuse and Neglect, 21*, 529–39.

Hwang, S.W. (2000). Mortality among men using homeless shelters in Toronto, Ontario. *Journal of the American Medical Association, 283*, 2152–57.

Hwang, S.W. (2001). Homelessness and health. *Canadian Medical Association Journal, 164*(2), 229–33.

Johnson, T.P., Aschkenasy, J.R., Herbers, M.R. & Gillenwater, S.A. (1996). Self-reported risk factors for AIDS among homeless youth. *AIDS Education and Prevention, 8*, 308–22.

Kidd, S.A. (2004). "The walls were closing in, and we were trapped": A qualitative analysis of street youth suicide. *Youth & Society, 36*(1), 30–55.

Kipke, M., Simon, T.R., Montgomery, S.B, Unger, J.B. & Iversen, E.F. (1997). Homeless youth and their exposure to and involvement in violence while living on the streets. *Society for Adolescent Medicine, 20*(5), 360–67.

Layton, J. (2000). *Homelessness: The making and unmaking of a crisis.* Toronto: Penguin.

Leslie, M.B., Stein, J.A. & Rotheram-Borus, M.J. (2002). Sex specific predictors of suicidality among runaway youth. *Journal of Clinical Child and Adolescent Psychology, 31*(1), 27–40.

Lieblich, A., Tuval-Mashiach, R. & Zilber, T. (1998). *Narrative research: Reading, analysis, and interpretation.* Thousand Oak: Sage.

Mallett, S., Rosenthal, D. & Keys, D. (2005). Young people, drug use, and family conflict: Pathways into homelessness. *Journal of Adolescence, 28*, 185–99.

Martijn, C. & Sharpe, L. (2005). Pathways to youth homelessness. *Social Science & Medicine, 62*, 1–12.

Masson, N. & Lester, H. (2003). The attitudes of medical students towards homeless people: Does medical school make a difference? *Medical Education, 37*(10), 869–72.

Molnar, B.E., Shade, S.B., Kral, A.H., Booth, R.E. & Watters, J.K. (1998). Suicidal behaviour and sexual/physical abuse among street youth. *Child Abuse & Neglect, 22*(3), 213–22.

Morrell-Bellai, T., Goering, P.N. & Boydell, K.M. (2000). Becoming and remaining homeless: A qualitative investigation. *Issues in Mental Health Nursing, 21,* 581–604.

Nehls, N. & Sallmann, J. (2005). Women living with a history of physical and/or sexual abuse, substance abuse, and mental health problems. *Qualitative Health Research, 15,* 365–81.

Neysmith, S.M. (1995). Feminist methodologies: A consideration of principles and practice for research in gerontology. *Canadian Journal on Aging, 14*(1), 100–18.

Noell, J.W. & Ochs, L.M. (2001). Relationship of sexual orientation to substance use, suicidal ideation, suicide attempts, and other factors in a population of homeless adolescents. *Journal of Adolescent Health, 29,* 31–36.

O'Connell, J.J. (2004). Dying in the shadows: The challenge of providing health care for homeless people. *Canadian Medical Association Journal, 179*(8), 1251–52.

O'Connor, M.L. (1998). Unsafe behaviours place street youth, especially women, at risk of HIV. *Family Planning Perspectives, 30*(1), 50–51.

Panter-Brick, C. (2002). Street children, human rights, and public health: A critique and future directions. *Annual Review of Anthropology, 31,* 147–71.

Panter-Brick, C. (2004). Homelessness, poverty, and risks to health: Beyond at risk categorization of street children. *Children's Geographies, 2*(1), 83–94.

Paradise, M. & Cauce, A.M. (2002). Home street home: The interpersonal dimensions of adolescent homelessness. *Analyses of Social Issues and Public Policy, 2*(1), 223–38.

Patton, M.Q. (2002). *Qualitative research and evaluation methods,* 3rd ed. London: Sage.

Raffaelli, M., Koller, S.H., Reppold, C.T., Kuschick, M.B., Drum, F.M., Bandeira, D.R., et al. (2000). Gender differences in Brazilian street youth's family circumstance and experiences on the streets. *Child Abuse & Neglect, 24*(11), 1431–41.

Reid, S., Berman, H. & Forchuk, C. (2005). Living on the streets in Canada: A feminist narrative study of girls and young women. *Issues in Comprehensive Paediatric Nursing, 28,* 237–56.

Rew, L., Chambers, K.B. & Kulkarni, S. (2002). Planning a sexual health promotion intervention with homeless adolescents. *Nursing Research, 51*(3), 168–74.

Rew, L., Taylor-Seehafer, M. & Fitzgerald, M.L. (2001). Sexual abuse, alcohol and other drug use, and suicidal behaviors in homeless adolescents. *Issues in Comprehensive Pediatric Nursing, 24,* 225–40.

Rhode, P., Noell, J., Ochs, L. & Seeley, J.R. (2001). Depression, suicidal ideation, and STD-related risk in homeless older adolescents. *Journal of Adolescence, 24*(4), 447–60.

Riessman, C.K. (1993). *Narrative analysis.* London: Sage.

Rotheram-Borus, Song, J., Gwadz, M., Lee, M., Rossem, R. & Koopman, C. (2003). Reductions in HIV risk among runaway youth. *Prevention Science, 4*(3), 173–87.

Roy, E., Haley, N., Leclerc, P., Sochanski, B., Boudreau, J. & Boivin, J. (2004). Mortality in a cohort of street youth in Montreal. *Journal of the American Medical Association, 292,* 569–74.

Russell, L.A. (1996). Homeless youth: Child maltreatment and psychological distress. Unpublished doctoral dissertation, University of California, Los Angeles.

Shields, S.A., Wong, T., Mann, J., Jolly, A.M., Haase, D., Mahaffey, S., et al. (2004). Prevalence and correlates of Chlamydia infection in Canadian street youth. *Society of Adolescent Medicine, 34,* 384–90.

Shiner, M. (1995). Adding insult to injury: Homelessness and health services use. *Sociology of Health and Illness, 17*(4), 525–49.

Trocme, N. & Wolfe, D. (2001). *The Canadian incidence study of reported child abuse and neglect.* Retrieved October 29, 2006, from www.phac-aspc.gc.ca/publicat/cissr-ecirc/pdf/cmic_e.pdf

Tyler, K.A., Hoyt, D.R., Whitbeck, L.B. & Les, B. (2001). The effects of a high-risk environment on the sexual victimization of homeless runaway youth. *Violence and Victims, 16*(4), 441–55.

Walters, A.S. (1999). HIV prevention in street youth. *Journal of Adolescent Health, 25,* 187–98.

Weber, A.E., Boivin, J., Blais, L., Haley, N. & Roy, E. (2004). Predictors of initiation into prostitution among female street youths. *Journal of Urban Health, 81*(4), 584–95.

Whitbeck, L.B., Hoyt, D.R. & Ackley, K.A. (1997). Abusive family backgrounds and later victimization among runaway and homeless adolescents. *Journal of Research on Adolescence, 7*(4), 375–92.

Zimmerman, D.H. & West, C. (1987). Doing gender. *Sociologists for Women in Society, 1*(2), 125–51.

Zrinyi, M. & Balogh, Z. (2004). Student nurse attitudes towards homeless clients: A challenge for education and practice. *Nursing Ethics, 11*(4), 334–48.

Chapter 11

FROM PSYCHIATRIC WARD TO THE STREETS AND SHELTERS

Cheryl Forchuk, Gord Russell, Shani Kingston-MacClure, Katherine Turner, and Susan Dill

1. INTRODUCTION

The issue of discharge from hospital ward to shelters or to the streets is rarely discussed in the literature, but all too commonly experienced by individuals with psychiatric disorders. Even well-run shelters are not appropriate places for recovery from mental illnesses as staff–resident ratios are very low. In London, Ontario, the ratio is typically 1:50, with shelter residents often exposed to the drug and sex trades. Residents have little privacy and may need to share bedrooms with upwards of 20 others. Many intrusive questions may be asked publicly on intake, and when shelters are over capacity, as is usually the case year round, many residents end up sleeping in chairs.

The issue of psychiatric illness as a risk for homelessness has frequently been cited in the literature (Cohen & Thompson, 1992; Koegel, Burnam &

Baumohl, 1996; Kuno et al., 2000; Lamb & Bachrach, 2001; Lamb & Lamb, 1990; Robertson, 1992, Sullivan & Burnam, 2000). Goering, Tolomiczenko, Sheldon, Boydell, and Wasylenki (2002) found that 64 percent of first-time shelter users in Toronto had a history of drug abuse, and that 64 percent also had other mental health problems. Similarly, for those who had previously been in shelters, 71 percent had drug abuse histories and 69 percent had other psychiatric problems. However, although mental illness has long been identified as a risk factor for homelessness and unstable housing, our understanding of this pattern continues to evolve. In the early literature, housing problems were related to the illness per se (Drake, Wallach & Hoffman, 1989; Kuno et al., 2000; Lamb & Bachrach, 2001; Lamb & Lamb, 1990, Sullivan & Burnam, 2000). However, social concerns such as poverty and the lack of affordable housing have since been identified as more substantive reasons for the problem (Draine et al., 2002; Drake & Wallach, 1999; Koegel et al., 1996, Kuno et al., 2000, Lamb & Bachrach, 2001; Sullivan et al., 2000).

McChesney (1990) uses the analogy of musical chairs to explain the relationship between poverty and affordable housing and homelessness. If there are more people than there are chairs, when the music stops, some people will be left without chairs. Likewise, if there are more people suffering from poverty than there are affordable homes, when they are discharged from hospitals, some will be left homeless. Using this same analogy, one can imagine that if some of the people have a mental illness among their barriers to obtaining housing, they may be that much less effective in quickly grabbing one of the few homes available when they are discharged.

Although it is well accepted that people with mental illnesses are overrepresented in the homeless population, this is not generally linked to discharge from hospital. The issue of individuals with mental illnesses being discharged directly from a psychiatric ward to a shelter has rarely been examined in the literature, which makes it difficult to ascertain how common this is. In Wong, Culhane, and Kuhn's (1997) examination of factors related to family shelter use in New York City, recent discharge was not mentioned as a contributing factor, though, not surprisingly, 73.6 percent of respondents gave poverty as the reason for being homeless. Stuart and Arboleda-Florez (2000) found that shelter residents in Calgary, Alberta, experienced greater psychiatric symptoms and were more likely to access mental health services. However, the report did not collect information on how many had a recent hospital admission. Double, MacPherson, and Wong (1993) tracked a random sample of 100 people discharged from acute psychiatric wards in Sheffield, England, for five years and found that no one in this group became homeless. Similarly, Leff (1993) reported on 216 patients discharged between 1989 and 1990 in London, England, of whom none were without housing a year after follow-up, while Pickard, Proudfoot, and Wolfson (cited in Leff, 1993) followed a different group of 103 patients discharged from a London, England, hospital and also discovered that none were homeless a year later. These findings were reported at the same time as shelters were reporting increasing numbers of users with psychiatric difficulties. Leff (1993) suggested the issue may be the problem of access to acute hospital services rather than the process after services have been received. In contrast to these British studies, an American study (Olfson, Mechanic, Hansell, Boyer & Walkup, 1999) found that 7.6 percent of 263 patients diagnosed with schizophrenia reported homelessness within three months of discharge in New York City. Again, none of the study's participants are mentioned as being homeless directly after discharge.

However, the press presents a bleaker picture of the issue of discharge from psychiatric wards to shelters or the street. In the Toronto *Globe and Mail*, a 1997 headline read "Shelters forced to care for the mentally ill" (Philp, 1997) and stated that "Psychiatric hospitals discharge patients to the shelter as a matter of course. Shelter staff, as versed as any doctor in Ontario's Mental Health Act, struggle almost daily to have obviously ill individuals admitted to psychiatric wards where a chronic shortage of beds has left psychiatrists reluctant to treat all but the most violent and delusional people." Despite literature to the contrary, one shelter organization in London, England, stated that "many shelter projects report patients discharged from hospital and psychiatric units into bed and breakfast and other poor quality temporary housing" (Diaz, 2000: 7). In the United States the Metropolitan Denver Homeless Initiative (2003) did a one-day point-in-time survey of homeless people on January 27, 2003. They found 31 people had spent the previous night (January 26) in a general hospital and 37 in a psychiatric hospital. While these combined to be less than 1 percent of the total homeless population, it is still a concern that 68 people became homeless literally overnight in only one community after being discharged from health institutions established to care for them.

The period immediately following discharge from shelter has been described as a "critical time" to prevent homelessness (Jones et al., 2003; Susser et al., 1997) and perhaps the period following discharge from a psychiatric ward needs likewise to be considered a "critical time." Thus, the CURA on Mental Health and Housing project sought to determine: How frequently have people been discharged from psychiatric wards to shelters or the street in one year in London, Ontario?

2. METHODOLOGY

The city of London, with its population of 337,300, has three acute-care psychiatric wards within one general hospital and a tertiary psychiatric hospital on two sites, London and St. Thomas, which serve London and the surrounding counties, with administration provided by another general hospital. The psychiatric hospital changed to this new governance in 2001 as part of the province of Ontario's mental health reform plans. This has been accompanied with ongoing reductions in psychiatric beds. All psychiatric admissions are coordinated through one psychiatric emergency department. London has three shelters exclusively for men, five for women, and one facility that accepts both men and women.

This study was descriptive in nature with a number of data sources accessed to determine the number of discharges to shelters or the street. Both the tertiary care facility and general hospital examined their fiscal year discharge databases to determine the extent of the problem. The discharge data did not allow easy extraction of this information. The addresses of known shelters, as well as "no fixed address," needed to be cross-checked with the address on the discharge for each person. The tertiary care system did not allow running more than one variable at a time, which resulted in an inability to determine discharges by gender. Nor would this method include people who did not divulge that they had lost their housing, or those who discovered after discharge that their housing had disappeared. After noting the difficulty in gathering this information retrospectively, the general hospital initiated a prospective project to track the frequency of discharge to "no fixed address" or shelters for future analysis.

Shelters searched their databases for referrals from psychiatric wards and for individuals who reported having been recently discharged from a psychiatric ward. This method was also prone to systematic error. The vast majority of people entering the shelter system state they are there as a self-referral, and many would not share information about a recent psychiatric hospitalization. The shelters also reviewed the specific histories of people who had been discharged in this manner in order to create case studies based on the amalgamation of several similar situations.

3. FINDINGS

All data sets examined revealed that the problem of discharge to shelters or the streets occurred regularly. Not surprisingly, somewhat different numbers emerged

Table 11.1: Discharges to No Fixed Address in 2002 from Psychiatric Wards

Place of discharge	Total number of discharges	Number of discharges to no fixed address	Gender breakdown
Discharges from general hospital	1588	93[1]	53 male, 40 female
psychiatric ward		64[2]	38 male, 26 female
Discharges from psychiatric hospital	1090	74	Unknown
against medical advice		47[3]	Unknown

1 Number includes instances in which individuals were hospitalized and discharged to no fixed address more than once in 2002 (i.e. number includes some of the same individuals more than once).
2 Number refers to separate individuals discharged to no fixed address.
3 Researchers unable to clarify how many of these discharges (n = 47) were the same as the discharges to no fixed address (n = 74).

Table 11.2: Proportion of CURA Respondents Discharged to No Fixed Address from Community Psychiatric Facilities

	People referred	
Type of referral	Total number	Gender breakdown
Referrals to London shelter from London Hospital (12 months)	194	105 male, 89 female
Referrals to St Thomas shelter from St Thomas Hospital (12 months)	17	17 female
Hospital referral to local community mental health agency with no fixed address or at risk for homelessness	37	Unknown

from the various data sets. The data from the hospitals are summarized in tables 11.1 and 11.2 and illustrate that there were at least 167 instances of discharge to "no fixed address" or shelter. As the tertiary care facility staff thought the issue was related to discharge against medical advice, that information is also included. Shelter data revealed similar numbers with a minimum of 194 instances of discharge from psychiatric ward to shelter found to have occurred within the same year. However, due to the confidentiality of files, it was not possible to determine the extent of the overlap between the 167 instances from the hospitals and the 194 cases from the shelters. The independent CURA data indicated that 11.8 percent of the first year and 8.6% of the second year of the cohort had been discharged from a psychiatric ward to a shelter. (Figure 11.1 and 11.2)

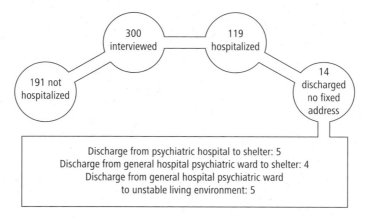

Figure 11.1: Data from 2001 That Display How Many Participants Have Been Interviewed, How Many Were Hospitalized and Discharged to a No Fixed Address

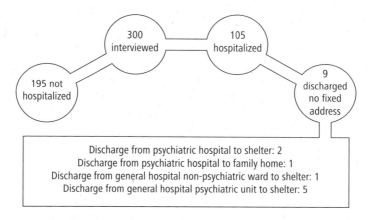

Figure 11.2: Data from 2002 That Display How Many Participants Have Been Interviewed, How Many Were Hospitalized and Discharged to a No Fixed Address

4. CASE STUDIES

In addition to the quantitative data collected, case studies were developed from composites of situations in order to illustrate typical scenarios of the consequences of homelessness. The first scenario was developed by shelter staff.

Dara

Dara is a young, large, and unkempt-looking woman who arrived at a shelter from hospital after fleeing a situation of abuse. Dara reported that over the past few years, the situation with her trustees had become unbearable. They controlled her finances, her comings and goings, and her access to the telephone. They also controlled her access to food and to outside contacts. Her trustees live in the same building as Dara and have access to her apartment at any time. She requested help in finding a new residence.

Dara has a list of psychiatric medications that she says help her with the "voices" and anxiety. She indicated that she took her medications regularly. On the day of admission to shelter at 3:20 a.m., Dara had an episode of shortness of breath, chest pain, and rapid heart rhythm. Staff was unsure if there was an outstanding medical issue with her and an ambulance was called. Dara was discharged from emergency within six hours, though she received no follow-up information. She stated that the doctor told her to come back if she had another "seizure." Shelter staff believed that the incident was a panic attack, which is common in victims of abuse. It should be noted that there was no nursing or medical staff employed at that shelter at that time, although a public health nurse visited weekly.

After the first week in shelter, Dara decided that she had not heard the voices in a few days and thought that she did not need her medications any longer, so she stopped taking her medications against the advice of staff and soon began to experience "episodes." During one of these, she fell to the floor, and stated that she was unable to walk. The fall was not witnessed; however, staff observed her walking unassisted before the ambulance arrived.

Dara did not qualify for special priority status (SPS) with housing because the person who abused her was not an intimate partner or family member. The usual wait for housing with SPS is approximately three weeks, and without SPS the wait typically takes months, which is well beyond the 42-day maximum length of stay in shelter. As well, once a unit becomes available, then affordability becomes a problem.

During the next two and one half weeks, the ambulance was called on seven different occasions for Dara. There were two calls to police and four to the mental health crisis team to assess her. The symptoms that Dara presents are slightly different each time, and on two occasions staff felt that a taxi to the hospital was sufficiently safe and that an ambulance was not needed. On one occasion, Dara had another shelter resident call 911 for her to secure an ambulance without staff knowledge.

On each and every occasion Dara was discharged from emergency and returned to the shelter with no follow-up information. On the final visit to hospital emergency, the discharge was delayed, forcing the shelter to release the shelter bed to another family in need. When Dara was discharged from emergency, the shelter staff arranged a transfer to another shelter as no alternative housing had been found during Dara's 42-day stay.

Mr. J.

The case of Mr. J. was developed by hospital staff. Mr. J., a retired 35-year-old single man, lived alone in a one-bedroom apartment. Over the past year, the landlord had received numerous complaints about Mr. J. from other tenants. Mr. J. had approached other tenants yelling obscenities and making inappropriate comments. He had neglected his personal hygiene and his dirty, dishevelled appearance, and the odour emanating from his apartment, had upset other tenants. Most recently, Mr. J. believed that people were after him, and they were trying to "set him up," and he had begun to make threats to numerous tenants. The landlord had begun eviction proceedings, which further upset Mr. J., and the police were called following an incident when Mr. J. trashed his apartment. The police brought him to the hospital's emergency department, where he underwent a psychiatric assessment.

Mr. J. was admitted to the acute-care adult mental health program of his local hospital on an involuntary basis for 72 hours to allow for further assessment. The symptoms of his illness prevented him from having any insight into his illness; in fact, he believed that he was not ill and that the hospital staff was working in collusion with everyone else who were trying to "set him up." Discharge planning began immediately, but was hindered by Mr. J.'s refusal to sign releases allowing hospital staff to speak to his landlord or to his family and friends because of his paranoia. As a result, the discharge planner was unaware that he was being evicted from his apartment.

Mr. J. was started on medications immediately upon hospitalization and responded well. At the end of the 72-hour period, he was no longer considered a threat to himself or others and he became a voluntary patient. Although he had stabilized quickly, Mr. J.'s symptoms of paranoia still persisted, and believing he was well, he insisted on signing himself out of hospital against medical advice before the discharge planner could obtain releases to speak to the landlord to ascertain the details of his housing and psychiatric follow-up.

Mr. J. returned to his apartment and discovered that the period to appeal the eviction notice had expired and he no longer had an apartment to return to. Consequently, he showed up at the local shelter, an option that, other than the streets, was his only perceived choice at that time. However, the shelter atmosphere only exacerbated his illness.

5. IMPLICATIONS FOR PRACTICE

Health care practitioners need to recognize that a shelter is not an appropriate "address" for discharging individuals recovering from mental illness. A number of systems issues, including a decrease in available affordable housing, a decrease in psychiatric hospital beds, and a shortened length of psychiatric stay, have all contributed to this problem.

Finding appropriate housing and avoiding a potential eviction require time. If assessment of the stability of the current housing situation does not occur on admission, there may not be sufficient time to avert a housing crisis for the individual when he or she is discharged. If housing has been lost prior to admission, plans need to be quickly instituted to find alternate housing. This may include the need to secure adequate income support. If the current housing is unsafe, alternate housing needs to be found. Unsafe housing may include violence in the home, structural safety concerns, or unsafe neighbourhoods. For example, individuals who are struggling with recovery from substance abuse should not return to a hotel room where alcohol is sold downstairs as the primary business venture. Where there is stable housing, the ability to maintain the housing over the course of the hospitalization needs to be considered. Questions such as how the rent will be paid need to be addressed. Figure 11.3 illustrates some potential questions to consider in assessing housing stability. Without careful consideration of housing stability, the gains made during a hospitalization may be quickly lost after discharge.

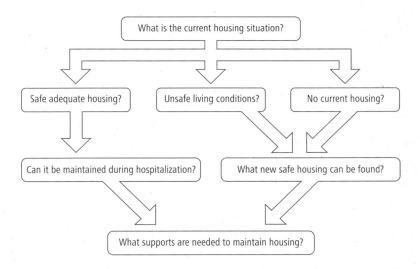

Figure 11.3: Considerations for Avoiding Discharge to Shelter or to the Streets

6. DISCUSSION

Discharge from psychiatric wards to shelters or the streets is a real problem. Even from the conservative estimates, which are prone to underreporting, it would have occurred at least 194 times in London in 2002 alone. Based upon this initial assessment, several suggestions are already evident.

Hospitals and shelters need to systematically collect data on the issue of discharge to shelter or the streets. Without this information, the problem is at risk of remaining invisible and no steps to improve the situation will occur. The issue is not a simple matter of poor discharge planning on the part of the hospital. The issue is far more systematic. The average length of stay has shortened and the available affordable housing market is diminished. Sometimes the only way to admit the next patient, who is often in crisis, is to discharge one who is psychiatrically stable, even if appropriate housing has not been obtained. Hospital staff need to assess the housing situation immediately on admission to have a chance of making appropriate arrangements if a change is required on discharge. Hospital staff and community workers also must openly acknowledge that this problem exists and to lobby for the appropriate housing and service resources to prevent this unacceptable situation. No person discharged from a psychiatric ward should be sent to a shelter or the streets as a discharge plan unless this is his or her wish. As only one in 300 people interviewed by the CURA stated the shelter was a desired housing arrangement (Nelson, Hall & Forchuk, 2003), it can be assumed that rarely would the consumer find this arrangement acceptable.

REFERENCES

Cohen, C.I. & Thompson, K.S. (1992). Homeless mentally ill or mentally ill homeless? *American Journal of Psychiatry, 169,* 816–23.

Diaz, R. (2000). *Mental health and homelessness.* Shelter, London. Retrieved November 19, 2005, from www.shelter.org.uk .

Double, D., MacPherson, R. & Wong, W. (1993). Tracing patients from acute psychiatric wards. *Journal of the Royal Society of Medicine, 86,* 533–34.

Draine, J., Salzer, M., Culhane, D. & Hadley, T. (2002). Role of social disadvantage in crime, joblessness, and homelessness among persons with serious mental illness. *Psychiatric Services, 53,* 565–73.

Drake, R.E. & Wallach, M.A. (1999). Homelessness and mental illness: A story of failure. *Psychiatric Services, 50,* 589.

Drake, R.E., Wallach, M.A. & Hoffman, J.S. (1989) Housing instability and homelessness among aftercare patients of an urban state hospital. *Hospital and Community Psychiatry, 40,* 46–51.

Goering, P., Tolomiczenko, G., Sheldon, T., Boydell, K. & Wasylenki, D. (2002). Characteristics of persons who are homeless for the first time. *Psychiatric Services, 53,* 1472–74.

Jones, K., Colson, P.W., Holter, M.C., Lin, S., Valencia, E., Susser, E. & Wyatt, R.J. (2003). Cost-effectiveness of critical time intervention to reduce homelessness among persons with mental illness. *Psychiatric Services, 54,* 884–90.

Koegel, P., Burnam, M.A. & Baumohl, J. (1996) The causes of homelessness. In J. Baumohl (Ed.), Homelessness in America. pp. 24–33. Phoenix: Oryx.

Kuno, E., Rothbard, A.B., Averyt, J. & Culhane, D. (2000). Homelessness among persons with serious mental illness in an enhanced community-based mental health system. *Psychiatric Services, 51,* 1012–16.

Lamb, R.L. & Bachrach, L.L. (2001). Some perspectives on deinstitutionalization. *Psychiatric Services, 52,* 1039–45.

Lamb, H. & Lamb, D. (1990). Factors contributing to homelessness among the chronically and severely mentally ill. *Hospital and Community Psychiatry, 41,* 301–05.

Leff, J. (1993). All the homeless people—where do they all come from? *British Medical Journal, 306,* 669–70.

McChesney, K.Y. (1990). Family homelessness: A systematic problem. *Journal of Social Issues, 46,* 191–205.

Metropolitan Denver Homeless Initiative. (2003). Homelessness in the Denver Metropolitan Area. *Point-in-Time Survey.* Denver: Metropolitan Denver Homeless Initiative.

Nelson, G., Hall, B. & Forchuk, C. (2003). Current and preferred housing of psychiatric consumer/survivors. *Canadian Journal of Community Mental Health, 22*(1), 5–19.

Olfson, M., Mechanic, D., Hansell, S., Boyer, C. & Walkup, J. (1999). Prediction of homelessness within three months of discharge among inpatients with schizophrenia. *Psychiatric Services, 50,* 667–73.

Philp, M. (1997). Shelters forced to care for mentally ill. *The Globe and Mail.* Retrieved November 5, 2004, from csf.colorado.edu/forums/homeless/oct97/0027.html.

Robertson, M. (1992). The prevalence of mental disorder among homeless people. In R. Jahiel (Ed.), *Homelessness: A prevention-oriented approach.* 57–86. Baltimore: Johns Hopkins University Press.

Stuart, H. & Arboleda-Florez, J. (2000). Homeless shelter users in the post deinstitutionalization era. *Canadian Journal of Psychiatry, 45,* 55–62.

Sullivan, G. & Burnam, K.P. (2000). Pathways to homelessness among the mentally ill. *Social Psychiatry Psychiatric Epidemiology, 35,* 444–50.

Susser, E., Valencia, E., Conover, S., Felix, A., Tsai, W.Y. & Wyatt, R.J. (1997). Preventing recurrent homelessness among mentally ill men: A "critical time" intervention after discharge from a shelter. *American Journal of Public Health, 87,* 256–62.

Wong, Y., Culhane, D. & Kuhn, R. (1997). Predictors of exit and reentry among family shelter users in New York City. *Social Service Review, 9,* 441–62.

Chapter 12

AN INTERVENTION TO PREVENT HOMELESSNESS AMONG INDIVIDUALS DISCHARGED FROM PSYCHIATRIC WARDS TO SHELTERS AND "NO FIXED ADDRESS"

Cheryl Forchuk, Shani Kingston-MacClure, Michele Van Beers, Cheryl Smith, Rick Csiernik, Jeffrey S. Hoch, and Elsabeth Jensen

1. INTRODUCTION

In recent decades, the trend in mental health has been toward "dehospitalization" (Sussman, 1998). During the last 30 years, mental health policy within the province of Ontario has led to hospital bed closures and poorly planned discharge of individuals into the community with support services that lack funding (Lightman, 1997). It is well accepted that people with mental illness are overrepresented in the homeless population (Eynan et al., 2002, Steinhaus, Harley & Rogers, 2004); however, this is not generally linked to discharge from hospital. People living on the streets or in shelters are at an increased risk of contracting medical illnesses, such as tuberculosis or HIV infection, or becoming a victim of assault or rape (Frankish, Hwang & Quantz, 2005).

Mental illness has long been identified as a risk factor for homelessness and unstable housing (Drake, Wallach & Hoffman, 1989; Lamb & Lamb, 1990). Olfson,

Mechanic, Hansell et al. (1999) identified specific issues related to individuals with schizophrenia and schizoaffective disorder (n = 263) that contributed to short-term homelessness in the United States, namely, substance abuse, persistent symptoms related to the individual's mental illness, and poor ratings on global functioning. However, other literature suggests additional risk factors for homelessness. In Switzerland, Lauber, Lay, and Rossler (2006) conducted a study to identify characteristics of psychiatric in-patients who were at risk for homelessness at the time of discharge. Data collected from a psychiatric patient case register identified the individuals who had the greatest risk as those who had no stable housing before admission, had low clinical improvement during hospital stay, received less therapeutic measures, were discharged early, and received no care after discharge. The authors concluded that health care teams should address the problem of patients who are identified as without stable housing by immediately initiating the discharge plan on the day of the patient's admission. Kuno, Rothbard, Averyt et al. (2000) studied the community mental health system to examine homelessness of mentally ill people in the United States and recommended the establishment of emotional support during transition to help ensure stable housing.

The simple lack of affordable housing has also been identified as the source of homelessness rather than any mental health or other form of illness per se (Draine et al., 2002; Drake & Wallach, 1999; Koegel, Burnam & Baumohl, 1996; Forchuk et al., 2006). In Norway, a high-income society with a strong social welfare emphasis, it has been suggested that individuals with schizophrenia who are given the necessary economical practical support may live in the community with low incidences of homelessness (Melle et al., 2000). Similarly, a variety of studies from the United States have indicated that housing assistance and support have encouraged stable housing and prevented homelessness and admission to psychiatric institutions (Goldfinger et al., 1999; Shern et al., 1997). Housing assistance offered in these studies were either independent, staffed group, or community housing. Participants in a narrative study from Canada indicated that supportive housing brought more stability and a positive sense to their lives, improved relationships, and improved their well-being through access to useful resources (Nelson et al., 2005). Although housing is well accepted as a socio-economic determinant of health in Canada (Raphael, 2004), there has been inadequate research on these systemic issues. One such deficit is the benefit of health interventions versus those providing stable and affordable housing to vulnerable groups, such as those with mental illness (Dunn et al., 2006).

Within the United Kingdom, Trieman, Leff, and Glover (1999) conducted a study to assess the resettlement of patients discharged from psychiatric settings.

Patients who stayed in hospital for a least one year were followed for five years from the point of discharge into the community. At discharge these patients received housing and community supports to assist with resettlement into the community. Of the 523 participants, 469 (89.6 percent) remained housed within the community five years after discharge from hospital. Conclusions drawn from this study indicate that a solid infrastructure and a comprehensive care plan provide patients with adequate means to resettle successfully.

Another study within the United Kingdom examined the effect of a 12-bed in-patient unit specifically for mentally ill homeless people (Killaspy et al., 2004). In this 12-month prospective controlled design study, patients were either admitted into the designated unit (intervention) or general psychiatric units (control). The intervention group received carefully coordinated plans of discharge. The intervention group was able to engage with community services more successfully and had better medication compliance compared with the control group. However, no differences were found between the two groups with regard to stable housing. The researchers attributed this result to characteristic differences between the two groups, including the longer history of homelessness of people within the intervention group. In a similar attempt to prevent recurrent homelessness in the United States, Susser Valencia, Conover et al. (1997) tested an intervention called the critical time intervention (CTI). CTI, lasting approximately nine months, consisted of two major components: the establishment of formal and informal relationships, and a personal support within the community during the adjustment period after hospital discharge. Ninety-six men who entered into community housing from shelter were recruited into this study, randomized, and followed for 18 months. Results from this study indicated a reduction in average nights of homelessness between the intervention and control group. These findings further suggest that support during the "critical" transition may prevent homelessness.

2. LOCAL FREQUENCY AND UNDERSTANDING OF DISCHARGE TO HOMELESSNESS

The issue of discharge from the psychiatric ward to shelters, or the street, is difficult to access or to track, but the CURA on Mental Health and Housing was able to collect data on this phenomenon. This CURA study examined how frequently people were discharged from psychiatric wards to shelters or the street in London, Ontario. Investigation of the data from various sources, including hospitals and shelters, revealed that discharge to "no fixed address," meaning either homeless shelters or to the street, occurred regularly. In fact, of the 2,678 total discharges from general hospital psychiatric wards and tertiary care psychiatric hospital wards in 2002, at least 167 discharges were to no fixed address. Data collected directly from the shelters in London indicated 194 instances within the same time period. Analysis of files to determine the overlap between the two reporting sites was restricted because of confidentiality. In examining the different sources of data, it was concluded that within one year, discharge to no fixed address occurred at least 194 times (Forchuk et al., 2006; see also Chapter 11).

Preventing homelessness in patients discharged from psychiatric wards is a real need. The issue appears, however, not to be merely a simple matter of poor discharge planning on the part of hospitals and health care staff. It is far more systemic and multifaceted as there are multiple factors affecting the quality and effectiveness of discharge planning for people hospitalized for treatment of mental illness. These include both individual issues and systemic issues.

Affordability has been recognized as one of the three main housing needs in Canada (Steele, 1998). Two main contributors to a lack of affordability that have been identified in the literature include the inflation of housing costs and the government's low priority of social support services because of balancing deficits with demands for tax cutbacks (Bunting, Walks & Filion, 2004). Currently in Ontario there is a limited supply of affordable housing, which presents a challenge for individuals who are low-income earners. With a shortage of affordable housing, the client may need help in finding suitable accommodation, and will need to move quickly to pay rental fees when an appropriate place is found. Often individuals are forced to live with others, go to the shelters, or, if no other options exist, go to the streets. Tragically, these people are at risk of falling victim to the sex and/or the drug trade, and other unsafe occupations to establish and maintain housing. These individual and systemic issues are relevant to mental health professionals as they illustrate the complexities and hardships of clients that may not be so clearly presented on hospital admission, but are crucial at time of discharge. When mental health care professionals are aware of system issues impacting vulnerable populations, they must act as advocates for change to practices within the health care system and so assist in reducing negative outcomes for consumers.

3. A PILOT STUDY TO PREVENT HOMELESSNESS

The purpose of this pilot study was to do preliminary testing on an intervention to prevent homelessness following a psychiatric admission. The assistance was two-pronged in order to address systemic issues:

1. Assistance and advocacy in finding affordable housing through the auspices of a community housing advocate from the Canadian Mental Health Association (CMHA) who came to the ward immediately when the patient at risk of discharge to no fixed address was randomized to the intervention group. Special funding allowed an additional CMHA part-time employee to be hired for this purpose. Normally, because of high caseload and backlog, approximately half the referred patients are discharged before the housing advocate has an opportunity to meet with them.
2. A streamlined process of obtaining community start-up funds that would cover first and last months' rent. For the purposes of this study, processes were changed so that managers at both Ontario Works and Ontario Disability Support Program were able to fast-track the application for intervention participants.

This pilot project was a collaborative effort among hospital, community, and university partners. The income support providers were Ontario Works and Ontario Disability Support Program. The CURA on Mental Health and Housing and the CMHA were research and support providers. The aim of this pilot test was to utilize the strengths of this alliance to help alleviate some of the coordination barriers by locating and securing housing for patients discharged from psychiatric wards.

4. METHODS

The study employed a randomized control design to evaluate the effectiveness of the new approach. Participants who were at risk of being discharged to no fixed address were enrolled in the study and completed an initial interview in hospital. At the end of the interview, they chose an envelope that determined whether they would be in the intervention or the control group. All participants were randomly selected using this envelope method to avoid selection bias. Those in the intervention group received assistance in finding housing (housing advocate plus fast-tracked income support) while those in the control group received the usual care. Usual care did not include direct and immediate assistance with housing, but did include referral to social work for housing support if requested by the health care team during in-patient stay.

Participants were recruited from an acute care psychiatric ward within a general hospital (n = 12) and a tertiary care psychiatric hospital (n = 2). These sites provide all the psychiatric in-patient services for London, Ontario. A total of 14 participants (nine men and five women) were eligible and completed all phases of the study with regard to the primary outcome of current housing. Participants were equally divided with seven in the intervention group and seven in the control group. Characteristics, including the participants' age, primary diagnoses, marital status, and length of hospital stay, are summarized in Table 12.1. The control and intervention group participants were similar at the period of enrolment, thus additional variables were not controlled for during the analysis.

Table 12.1: Participant Characteristics

Characteristics	Control (n = 7)	Intervention (n = 7)
Female	2	3
Male	5	4
Age—mean years (SD)	31 (13.4)	35 (15.2)
Age range	18–52	21–63
Length of admission—mean weeks (SD)	1.67 (0.7)	3.36 (5.6)
Marital status		
Single/never married	4	5
Separated/divorced	2	2
Married/common-law	1	0
Primary diagnosis (self-reported)		
Schizophrenia	2	3
Mood disorder	2	4
Anxiety disorder	2	0
Other	1	0

SD = standard deviation

It was hypothesized that participants receiving the intervention would be more likely to obtain and maintain housing than those in the control group. It was further hypothesized that the intervention group would have less utilization of hospital services after discharge and maintain a higher level of functioning and quality of life compared with the control group.

Participants in this study were interviewed before being discharged from hospital, and then again three months and six months after discharge. Each interview lasted approximately one hour. Questions included current services being used, housing preferences, satisfaction with life, and current severity of illness. On completion of each interview each participant received $20 compensation for his or her time, effort, and travel expenses. As participants were at risk of homelessness, there was a possibility that they might be difficult to locate after discharge. Participants were asked to identify approximately five people who could be contacted to help locate them for future interviews.

Participants who had no address to go to after the hospitalization had to meet several other criteria before being enrolled in the study. Participation inclusion criteria included being between 18 and 75 years of age; having a diagnosis of serious mental illness, such as schizophrenia or major mood disorder, with stabilized symptoms at hospitalization; a secured source of income; the ability to live independently as assessed at admission; a length of hospitalization of less than 12 months; and interest in private sector housing. Exclusion criteria included refusing treatment recommendations, discharging against medical advice, having a history of drug or alcohol abuse within the past three months, or having a history of violence. It was the original intent to collect pilot data on 20 participants to do preliminary testing of the intervention and to determine the sample size required for a full investigation. However, data collection was stopped after 14 subjects were enrolled as the results were already statistically significant, and it appeared the participants in the control group were being seriously disadvantaged by usual care.

Ethical procedures and practices were followed in accordance with National Homelessness Initiative, Ethical Guidelines for Conducting Research Involving Homeless People (2004). Ethics approval was received from the University of Western Ontario Ethics Review Board to conduct this pilot project. This approval covered the hospital sites through their affiliation with the university. Written consent was obtained from all participants, and privacy and confidentiality were maintained.

5. FINDINGS

Descriptive analysis was done on all variables. Differences between the mean scores of the intervention and control groups were determined using t-tests on continuous data (e.g., age) and chi-square for categorical data (e.g., housed/homeless). There were no statistically significant differences at baseline. With regard to the primary outcome measure, the pilot revealed that all individuals in the intervention group attained independent housing prior to or within two days of discharge and maintained housing when interviewed at the three- and six-month intervals. All but one individual in the control group did not attain housing and remained homeless at the three- and six-month intervals (Table 12.2). The exception joined the sex trade to avoid homelessness. The results of this pilot investigation were so dramatic that randomizing to the control group stopped and plans began to routinely implement the intervention.

When working with individuals in the intervention group, an average of two to three hours of advocacy work was needed to prevent homelessness after discharge. During this time, the advocate would assist the person in finding housing and with communicating with potential landlords.

Table 12.2: Significance of Intervention

Achieved Housing	Intervention		
	Yes	No	Total
No	0	6	6
Yes	7	1	8
Total	7	7	14

Pearson chi2(1) = 10.5000 Pr = 0.001
Likelihood-ratio chi2(1) = 13.3798 Pr = 0.000
Cramér's V = −0.8660
gamma = −1.0000 ASE = 0.000
Kendall's tau-b = −0.8660 ASE = 0.120
Fisher's exact = 0.005

6. IMPLICATIONS

Ultimately, hospital recidivism and homelessness were prevented in this participant group by helping these patients at a crucial transition period from hospital into the community. The results of this pilot study support findings from both Goldfinger et al. (1999) and Shern et al. (1997), and indicate that very simple policy changes are sufficient to prevent homelessness in this population. Nurses, social workers, and other allied health care providers within in-patient mental health care settings play a vital role in advocating for such improvements in policy. The findings indicate that systemic problems, such as difficulty accessing funds in a timely fashion, contribute to the homelessness in this population. This echoes the earlier contention of Forchuk, Ward-Griffin, Csiernik, and Turner (2006), who used an analogy of a tornado to describe the experiences of psychiatric survivors losing housing. In that paper (see Chapter 4), the tornado was described as the societal response to mental illness. Although the primary outcome measure of this study has significant implications for current practice, further research is needed to acknowledge the effect on hospital costs and individual perceived quality of life. Forchuk, Russell, Kingston-MacClure, Turner, and Dill (2006) concluded that approximately 194 individuals, on entry to shelter, reported direct discharge from a psychiatric setting in London, Ontario, in 2002. This would indicate that the recruitment for this pilot could have reached over 90 participants within a six-month period. However, the inclusion criteria for this study purposely selected individuals who could be classified as the "healthier" at risk of homelessness group, such as those without a history of substance abuse, recent housing loss, and who had stable income supports. The findings would suggest that if even these participants could not escape homelessness, more vulnerable, less stable participants would certainly have had difficulty doing so. Instead, this study demonstrated that a simple policy change could produce dramatic results in the housing status of mentally ill people at risk of homelessness.

There are several limitations that are inherently present in a pilot study. It is important to acknowledge that this study utilizes a small sample size specific to a particular population only, and thus will have difficulty generalizing to the overall population. However, the sample was randomized and data do provide new knowledge, which has the potential to contribute to mental health care within in-patient settings. The findings also reinforce the necessity of continued research into development and implementation of homelessness intervention programs for mentally ill people at risk of homelessness. The results from this pilot project provide a glimpse of some of the complex underlying issues and needs related to housing in this population while offering a potential solution as opposed to a temporary fix for the problem.

Discharge from psychiatric wards to shelters or the street is a significant social problem. Neglecting to address this issue poses a risk of prolonged homelessness. This pilot project provided participants with immediate support and assistance in obtaining housing on discharge from a psychiatric hospitalization. This intervention was found to be effective for participants randomized into the intervention group as they were able to maintain housing at the three- and six-month follow-up intervals. There is a great need for systemic solutions related to income support and assistance in finding housing to prevent homelessness among people being discharged from psychiatric wards. As demonstrated in this pilot project, policies related to housing and community start-up costs have the potential to provide timely assistance in finding housing for people who have been psychiatrically admitted to hospital and thus reduce homelessness.

REFERENCES

Bartsch, D.A., Shern, D.L., Coen, A.S., et al. (1995) Service needs, receipt, and outcomes for types of clients with serious and persistent mental illness. *Journal of Mental Health Administration, 22,* 388–402.

Browne, G., Arpin, K., Corey, P., et al. (1990) Individual correlates of health services utilization and the cost of poor adjustment to chronic illness. *Medical Care, 28,* 43–58.

Bunting, T., Walks, R.A. & Filion, P. (2004) The uneven geography of housing affordability stress in Canadian metropolitan areas. *Housing Studies, 19,* 361–93.

Draine, J., Salzer, M., Culhane, D., et al. (2002) Role of social disadvantage in crime, joblessness, and homelessness among persons with serious mental illness. *Psychiatric Services, 53,* 565–73.

Drake, R.E. & Wallach, M.A. (1999). Homelessness and mental illness: A story of failure. *Psychiatric Services, 50,* 589.

Drake, R.E., Wallach, M.A. & Hoffman, J.S. (1989) Housing instability and homelessness among aftercare patients of an urban state hospital. *Hospital and Community Psychiatry, 40,* 46–51.

Dunn, J.R., Hayes, M.V., Hulchanski, D.J., Hwang, S. & Potvin, L. (2006) Housing as a socio-economic determinant of health. *Canadian Journal of Public Health, 97,* 11–15.

Eynan, R., Langley, J., Tolomiczenko, G., et al. (2002) The association between homelessness and suicidal ideation and behaviours: Results of a cross-sectional survey. *Suicide and Life-Threatening Behavior, 32,* 418–27.

Forchuk, C., Russell, G., Kingston-MacClure, S., Turner, K. & Dill, S. (2006) From psychiatric ward to streets and shelters. *Journal of Psychiatric and Mental Health Nursing, 13,* 301–08.

Forchuk, C., Ward-Griffin, C., Csiernik, R., & Turner, K. (2006) Surviving the tornado of mental illness: Psychiatric survivors' experiences of getting, losing, and keeping housing. *Psychiatric Services, 57,* 558–62.

Frankish, C.J., Hwang, S.W. & Quantz, D. (2005) Homeless and health in Canada: Research lessons and priorities. *Canadian Journal of Public Health, 96* (Supplement 2), S23–S29.

Goldfinger, S.M., Schutt, R.K., Tolomiczenko, G.S., et al. (1999) Housing placement and subsequent days homeless among formerly homeless adults with mental illness. *Psychiatric Services, 50,* 674–79.

Herman, S. & Mowbray, C. (1991) Client topology based on functional assessment level assessments: Utility for service planning & monitoring. *Journal of Mental Health Administration, 18,* 101–15.

Killaspy, H., Ritchie, W., Greer, E., et al. (2004) Treating the homeless mentally ill: Does a designated inpatient facility improve outcome? *Journal of Mental Health, 13,* 593–99.

Koegel, P., Burnam, M.A. & Baumohl, J. (1996) The causes of homelessness. In J. Baumohl (Ed.), *Homelessness in America* (pp. 24–31). Phoenix: Oryx.

Kuno, E., Rothbard, A., Averyt, J., et al. (2000) Homelessness among persons with serious mental illness in an enhanced community-based mental health system. *Psychiatric Services, 51,* 1012–16.

Lamb, H. & Lamb, D. (1990) Factors contributing to homelessness among the chronically and severely mentally ill. *Hospital and Community Psychiatry, 41,* 301–05.

Lauber, C., Lay, B. & Rossler, W. (2006) Homeless people at disadvantage in mental health services. *European Archives of Psychiatry and Clinic Neruoscience, 256,* 138–45.

Lehman, A.F., Postrado, L.T., Roth, D., et al. (1994) An evaluation of continuity of care, case management, and client outcomes in the Robert Wood Johnson Program on chronic mental illness. *Milbank Quarterly, 72,* 105–22.

Lightman, S. (1997) Discharge planning and community housing in Ontario. *Discharge Planning and Community Housing in Ontario, 25,* 63–75.

Melle, I., Friis, S., Hauff, E., et al. (2000) Social functioning of patients with schizophrenia in high-income welfare societies. *Psychiatric Services, 51,* 223–28.

National Homeless Initiative (2004). Ethical guidelines for conducting research involving homeless people. Ottawa: Government of Canada.

Nelson, G., Clarke, J., Febbraro, A., et al. (2005) A narrative approach to the evaluation of supportive housing: stories of homeless people who have experienced serious mental illness. *Psychiatric Rehabilitation Journal, 29,* 98–104.

Olfson, M., Mechanic, D., Hansell, S., et al. (1999) Prediction of homelessness with three months of discharge among inpatients with schizophrenia. *Psychiatric Services, 50,* 667–73.

Raphael, D. (2004). *Social determinants of health: Canadian perspectives.* Toronto: Canadian Scholars' Press Inc.

Shern, D.L., Felton, C.J., Hough, R.L., et al. (1997) Housing outcomes for homeless adults with mental illness: Results from the second-round McKinney program. *Psychiatric Services, 48,* 239–41.

Steele, M. (1998) Canadian housing allowances inside and outside the welfare system. *Canadian Public Policy, 24,* 209–32.

Steinhaus, D.A., Harley, D.A. & Rogers, J. (2004) Homelessness and people with affective disorders and other mental illnesses. *Journal of Applied Rehabilitation Counseling, 35,* 36–40.

Susser, E., Valencia, E., Conover, S., et al. (1997) Preventing recurrent homelessness among mentally ill men: A "critical time" intervention after discharge from shelter. *American Journal of Public Health, 87,* 256–62.

Sussman, S. (1998) The first asylums in Canada: A response to neglectful community care and current trends. *Canadian Journal of Psychiatry, 43,* 260–64.

Trieman, N., Leff, J. & Glover, G. (1999) Outcome of long stay psychiatric patients resettled in the community: Prospective cohort study. *British Medical Journal, 319,* 13–16.

Chapter 13

USING ELECTRONIC PATIENT RECORDS IN MENTAL HEALTH CARE TO CAPTURE HOUSING AND HOMELESSNESS INFORMATION OF MENTAL HEALTH CONSUMER-SURVIVORS

Richard G. Booth

1. INTRODUCTION

Homelessness among people with psychiatric illness remains a complex social issue for mental health providers. On any given day in Canada, a country of 32 million people, it has been estimated that over 100,000 people are living on the streets, in emergency shelters, or in acutely substandard housing (Statistics Canada, 2005). Of this population, a significant percentage of these people suffer from a severe mental illness.

As a multifaceted issue, the causes of homelessness among individuals with mental illness have been widely debated (Folsom & Jeste, 2002). Deinstitutionalization, unstable housing, poor discharge planning and community follow-up, lack of affordable housing, and biased economic forces have all been purported as possible contributors to the current homelessness issue (Folsom & Jeste, 2002; Forchuk et al., 2006; Susser et al., 1997). There is also good empirical evidence in the literature suggesting that severe mental illness is a contributing risk factor in becoming homeless (Caton, 1995; Folsom & Jeste, 2002).

Unfortunately, gaps in the literature pertaining to mental health and housing are considerable. Even with the high percentage of homeless individuals suffering from a mental illness, there seems to be a significant lack of research and statistics capturing the true extent of this issue. With the continued push for deinstitutionalization in mental health care, it is vital to keep accurate records outlining the disposition of consumer-survivors after in-patient discharge. Currently, little is known about where consumer-survivors are discharged in the community, let alone their housing status or its stability. As a determinant of health, housing should be a significant component of the admission and discharge planning for in-patients. Regardless, every year, thousands of consumer-survivors are discharged into unstable housing conditions or to the streets. As an invisible phenomenon, the event of being discharged directly from hospital into a homeless situation must be prevented.

However, with so little known about the rates, statistics, and demographics of people discharged from hospitals to the streets, it is difficult to create recommendations to assist in housing this vulnerable population adequately. It has been reported that the immediate month after discharge from in-patient services into community living is a critical time for recovery (Susser et al., 1997). The discontinuity after discharge into the community places an enormous strain on already fragile relationships among individuals, family, and outpatient health providers. Without adequate community housing after discharge, there is a significant risk that some mental health consumer-survivors will become chronically homeless or reliant on in-patient admission as a means of housing.

2. ELECTRONIC PATIENT RECORDS IN MENTAL HEALTH CARE

With the downsizing of in-patient beds, current emphasis has been on refining the existing psychiatric services to make them as efficient as possible. One purported solution is the use of electronic patient records (EPR) to streamline information and expedite record keeping for hospital in-patients. As a national initiative in Canada, the introduction of EPRs into clinical care has been seen as a required development for the evolution of the health system. Accordingly, vast quantities of resources have been dedicated to creating and testing this type of technology to support clinical record keeping (Health Canada 2001; 2002; 2003).

As Freedman (2003) states, the use of information technology to support psychiatry is a natural partnership because of the specialty's focus on information itself, rather than intricate diagnostic technologies or procedures found in other specialties. Therefore, Freedman suggests that including EPR in psychiatry has the potential to positively transform the specialty by allowing clinicians to capture core consumer-related information along with the ability to couple this data with research and treatment guidelines. Regardless, the integration of EPRs into mental health care has been slow to occur. Similarly, examples of EPRs shown in the literature tend to be stand-alone applications that lack integration with other larger and more widely used platforms found in general medical hospitals.

As a result of the specific information that clinicians require in order to be effective in their roles, care must be taken in designing EPRs for mental health. This chapter is unable to cover all the areas in need of modification for applicability in mental health settings. Thus, its focus will be on the need for an EPR to have the capability to systematically collect information pertaining to discharge and housing issues of mental health consumer-survivors.

3. HOMELESSNESS IN MENTAL HEALTH POPULATIONS

Forchuk, Russell, Kingston-MacClure, Turner, and Dill (2006) reported that the topic of discharge from hospital directly to an emergency shelter or the streets is an area that has been neglected in the literature. Although some authors (Belcher & First, 1988; Killaspy et al., 2004) indirectly linked it as a possible causative factor in homelessness, much of the literature focused on housing and homelessness of people with mental illness seems to negate the true frequency of such events (Olfson et al., 1999). In a large study conducted in the San Diego County area, Folsom, Hawthorne, Lindamer, Gilmer, Bailey, Golsham et al. (2005) reported that 1,569 (15 percent) of 10,340 patients with serious mental illness experienced some period of homelessness over a 12-month follow-up. Similarly, homeless patients were 10 times more likely to use crisis services and four times more likely to require in-patient hospitalization or access to the emergency psychiatric units than their housed counterparts.

Similarly, Kuno, Rothbard, Averyt, and Culhane (2000) discovered that 104 (24 percent) of 438 people with severe mental illness in the Philadelphia area became homeless after hospitalization in an acute psychiatric care facility. The authors tracked clients through their community care over four years and found that the community outpatient mental health treatment was not sufficient to prevent 11 percent of the sample population from becoming homeless.

Susser et al. (1997) found that utilizing "critical time" interventions immediately after discharge from a hospital institution into the community assisted in reducing the number of patients who became homeless. Conducted in New York City, the study involved randomly assigning a sample of 96 men to receive either critical-time interventions that focused on providing specialized supports to the client in the immediate months after discharge, or standard community services that were currently in place. Over the two-year period, 8% of the men who had received the critical-time interventions became homeless in comparison to 23 percent who received standard community services.

Killaspy et al. (2004), concerned about the increased health morbidity of patients returning to the streets after psychiatric in-patient discharge in the London boroughs of Camden and Islington, United Kingdom, conducted a study to capture the effect that in-patient treatment had on discharge outcomes. They found that a specialized in-patient unit designed to provide coordinated discharge planning for homeless populations was not significantly more effective at reducing homelessness than was a control unit, though there may have been some selection bias toward the treatment group, where typically the population was more chronically homeless than the population admitted to the control unit. Finally, Trieman, Leff, and Glover (1999) conducted a prospective cohort study on a sample of 523 patients who had spent over a year in hospital prior to discharge in the North East Thames Regional Health Authority, United Kingdom. As part of the resettlement strategy, they attempted to provide patients with accommodations and community supports to meet their long-term needs. Over the five-year follow-up period, the authors determined that 201 (38%) patients were readmitted to a hospital at least once. The authors also concluded that less than 1% of the original sample became chronically homeless. Equally, a significant cross-section of patients were found to be living in either staffed residential homes or independent apartments (90%) at the end of the study. This outcome provides good empirical evidence supporting the effectiveness of providing comprehensive psychiatric care to help sustain mental health consumer-survivors in the community.

Overall, little directly translatable information was found pertaining to discharge from hospital to no fixed address. Although the literature does not explicitly outline the extent of the issue, it can be inferred that a significant portion of mental health consumer-survivors are either discharged to the street or become homeless soon after discharge. The Forchuk et al. (2006) study conducted in London (see also Chapter 11) determined that at least 194 (11.6%) of 1,588 consumer-survivors discharged over a one-year period from in-patient admissions were discharged directly to a shelter or the streets. The estimate of 194 individuals discharged into unstable housing arrangements was noted to be conservative as retrospective data collection methods were hampered by difficulties in capturing discharge information from the various hospital and shelter databases. It was also reported that many of the hospital databases failed to include if consumer-survivors' housing arrangements were retracted soon after discharge. Equally, the majority of shelter users reported themselves as self-referred and would not disclose a recent hospital discharge.

4. ELECTRONIC PATIENT RECORDS AND HOMELESSNESS

Forchuk et al.'s (2006) difficulty in capturing information pertaining to consumer-survivors discharged into unstable housing is not surprising given the fragmented record and database systems that currently connect mental health providers. The use of electronic patient records in psychiatry is still a relatively new concept in both the practice and academic literature. Freedman (2003) asserts that psychiatrists have been slower than other physicians to adopt computerized documentation systems. Similarly, the nursing and related allied health professionals' literature is almost completely devoid of articles pertaining to EPRs to assist client care in the mental health specialty.

Over the last decade there has been much interest in moving to an electronic documentation system to support and improve the longitudinal medical records of clients. According to Young, Mintz, Cohen, and Chinman (2004), in severe mental illnesses like schizophrenia, up-to-date information is pertinent for optimal treatment and recovery. Similarly, like all chronic illnesses, both consumer-specific and scientific information are needed to assist the interdisciplinary team in treatment protocols. Unfortunately, as Cradock, Young, and Sullivan (2001) discovered in a review of paper-based records of mental health consumer-survivors, medical records generally fail to capture the true extent of symptom and medication side effects that are actually displayed during clinical assessment. By re-examining the fundamental principles underlying the development of electronic records, it may be possible to improve the quality of information recorded in EPRs by attending to the interface's structural ability to assist clinicians in recording and retrieving pertinent clinical information for use in patient care (Rector, Nowlan & Kay, 1991).

Well-designed EPR systems also may be of great value for clinical research. Young et al. (2004) and Cradock et al. (2001) have both reported that a significant barrier to utilizing research findings to improve practice stems from the systemic lack of aggregate, quality data captured in consumer documentation. As a neglected asset of computerized documentation seldom mentioned in the academic literature, EPRs can expedite information collection, epidemiological research, and assist national health agencies in creating registers of diseases and treatments (Powell & Buchan, 2005; Rector, Nowlan & Kay, 1991). Therefore, it is important during the creation and implementation of EPRs that emphasis be placed upon creating documentation packages that capture not only the medical details of consumer-survivors, but also index their vast longitudinal social and demographic information. Young et al. (2004) describe eight key "psychiatric vital signs" that should be included in any EPR system designed for psychiatric care. They include: (1) measures of patient symptoms, including psychosis, behaviour, and suicidality; (2) medication side effects; (3) medication compliance; (4) medical issues; (5) potential addiction and substance abuse information; (6) family/caregiver contacts and information; (7) presence of recent stressors; and (8) housing status.

Accordingly, any EPR serving a mental health population should create features in the platform to allow a health provider to accurately track and document housing-related issues. Housing status should be interlinked with both admission and discharge planning to ensure that efforts can be made to prevent consumer-survivors from losing accommodations due to a hospital admission. Equally, closely tied to housing stability are income and financial determinants. For many chronic mental health consumer-survivors, government social supports generally make up a large portion of their monthly income. With the convoluted regulations and guidelines regarding funding and eligibility (see Chapter 3), EPRs could be programmed with decision-support features to flag potential individuals who are at increased risk of losing a source of government income due to regulatory deadlines or prolonged in-patient admissions. Clinical decision-support systems are commonly found in computerized physician order entry systems and have been shown to substantially reduce medication administration errors in general medical hospitals (Kaushal, Shojania & Bates, 2003). By incorporating similar decision-support systems into EPRs for mental health consumer-survivors, clinicians could be alerted to deadlines in governmental funding policies and upcoming rental payments for consumer-survivors.

EPRs also should have the ability, due to their programming and database structure, to capture both generic and specific cumulative data. Unlike paper-based discharge notes written for specific clients, the pooling of electronic discharge information into demographic and occurrence data could be valuable to researchers and policy-makers attempting to gauge the housing options and outpatient care needs of mental health consumer-survivors. For instance, the outcomes of many community housing placements for consumer-survivors tend to become lost in the handwritten notes of their medical records. By creating EPRs with specific criteria to capture and summarize information about housing stability for specific consumer-survivors, recommendations for appropriate future housing placements could be made.

Similarly, the gulf in the continuum of care between the hospital and community could be better managed if the EPR system used by hospitals allowed off-site access to community care clinicians. With newer encryption Internet technologies, EPRs can offer off-site access to approved clinicians through a secured Internet connection. This improved access to members in the circle of care can facilitate information transfer and keep current records within a centralized database.

Information flow for clinicians is important in order to ensure that evidence-based decisions are made in a timely and accurate fashion. Future EPR solutions for mental health care should have the ability to be teamed with data warehouses of resource information to assist clinicians and consumer-survivors. Blackburn (2001) has noted that mental health providers require a wide range of information because of the complexity of consumer-survivors' lives and their illnesses. Clinicians arranging housing options for consumer-survivors often require a breadth of information ranging from government policies and housing regulations to external funding agencies and community supports. By ensuring that these types of pertinent municipal and provincial information are easily accessible to clinicians, more time can be spent ensuring that the consumer-survivors' needs are met in the community.

5. BARRIERS AND ETHICAL ISSUES OF EPRS IN MENTAL HEALTH CARE

Although a well-implemented EPR system may have many benefits, the contentious topics of cost, user uptake, security, and privacy must still be considered. In order to operate a successful EPR in practice, a significant financial investment in software, hardware, and technical support personnel is required. To date, only a handful of cost-benefit analysis studies have been conducted on the implementation of EPRs in health care. The results of these studies are varied, showing both financial net gains and losses depending on the assumptions factored into the calculations (Kaufman, 2005). User uptake has also been historically cited as a barrier to the implementation of EPR systems (Blakely, Smith & Swenson, 2004; Dansky et al., 1999). Regardless, with the steady flow of Internet-savvy health professionals and digital natives entering the workforce, resistance to information technology in health care will decline in the future (Richards, 2001). However, privacy and security concerns still surround the usage of EPRs in health care. As Barrows and Clayton (1996) reported, it is essential to implement a cohesive information security policy that is policed to ensure that vulnerabilities and infractions are detected and addressed. Having a secure EPR system is not only important for legal and litigation considerations, but also for ethical reasons. The consequence of unwanted disclosure of personal information has the potential to create economic, social, and even psychological harm for some individuals (Gostin, 1997).

Although an in-depth analysis of EPR barriers and ethical considerations goes beyond the intended scope of this chapter, it is important to realize the ethical and financial realities of using electronic record technology in health care. Equally, these hurdles should not be seen as static barriers but as areas for future discussion and collaboration among the parties involved in mental health care. As a health system that purports itself to be client-centred, the development of EPRs for mental health could be the ideal fulcrum by which to demonstrate this commitment to consumer-survivors, the public, and health professionals.

6. CONCLUSIONS

Using EPRs to track and assess the housing of mental health consumer-survivors is not a cure for the current shortage of affordable housing or the issue of consumer-survivors discharged into uncertain housing conditions. With the emphasis upon deinstitutionalizing mental health consumer-survivors into the community, further research will be required to shed light on the housing needs of this population. EPRs specifically designed to capture and synthesize housing information will no doubt assist the research and policy agendas of many academics and front-line clinicians. Only through this proactive approach in utilizing EPRs can a sizable quantity and quality of information about mental health consumer-survivors and their housing be collected in a timely fashion.

Although this chapter has only briefly touched upon some of the possible recommendations in EPR design for mental health consumer-survivors and their housing, three conclusions are evident from this work. First, mental health requires an EPR that can be adapted to not only capture information about the medical and psychiatric status of a consumer-survivor but also the rich social information of an individual. Included in the social information should be a well-developed section pertaining to housing status. Second, EPRs should not be seen just as a replacement for handwritten chart notes. EPRs should be created with the intent of streamlining information and making it accessible for clinical work and with the summation capabilities necessary for clinical research. Finally, EPRs should be a way of assisting communication among agencies in the continuum of care. The housing of mental health consumer-survivors can be a complex task requiring communication and information sharing among numerous clinicians and agencies. EPRs may be a way of organizing and expediting communication to assist consumer-survivors in finding and maintaining housing after discharge from hospital.

As electronic health innovations begin to markedly shape the face of health care, the specialty of mental health must also begin to embrace technology in support of client care. Without further emphasis on developing EPRs with the capability to capture information pertinent to the mental health discipline, there is a significant chance that EPRs will not be utilized to their fullest potential.

REFERENCES

Barrows, R. & Clayton, P. (1996). Privacy, confidentiality, and electronic medical records. *Journal of the American Medical Informatics Association, 3*(2), 139–48.

Belcher, J. & First, R. (1988). The homeless mentally ill: Barriers to effective service delivery. *The Journal of Applied Social Sciences, 12*(1), 62–78.

Blackburn, N. (2001). Building bridges: Towards integrated library and information services for mental health and social care. *Health Information and Libraries Journal, 18*, 203–12.

Blakely, T., Smith, K. & Swenson, M. (2004). The electronic record as infrastructure. *Psychiatric Rehabilitation Journal, 27*(3), 271–74.

Caton, C. (1995). Mental health service use among homeless and never-homeless men with schizophrenia. *Psychiatric Services, 46*(11), 1139–43.

Cradock, J., Young, A. & Sullivan, G. (2001). The accuracy of medical documentation in schizophrenia. *The Journal of Behavioral Health Services & Research, 28*(4), 456–65.

Dansky, K., Gamm, L., Vasey, J. & Barsukiewicz, C. (1999). Electronic medical records: Are physicians ready? *Journal of Healthcare Management, 44*(6), 440–54.

Folsom, D., Hawthorne, W., Lindamer, L., Gilmer, T., Bailey, A., Golsham, S., Garcia, P., Unutzer, J., Hough, R. & Jeste, D. (2005). Prevalence and risk factors for homelessness and utilization of mental health services among 10,340 patients with serious mental illness in a large public mental health system. *American Journal of Psychiatry, 162*(2), 370–76.

Folsom, D. & Jeste, D. (2002). Schizophrenia in homeless persons: A systematic review of the literature. *Acta Psychiatrica Scandinavica, 105*, 404–13.

Forchuk, C., Russell, G., Kingston-MacClure, S., Turner, K. & Dill, S. (2006). From psychiatric ward to the streets and shelters. *Journal of Psychiatric & Mental Health Nursing, 13*(3), 301–08.

Freedman, J. (2003). The role of information technology in evidence-based practice. *Psychiatric Clinics of North America, 26*, 833–50.

Gostin, L. (1997). Health care information and the protection of personal privacy: Ethical and legal considerations. *Annals of Internal Medicine, 127*(8), 683–90.

Health Canada. (2001). Toward electronic health records. Ottawa: Health Canada.

Health Canada (2002). Telehealth and electronic health record: a guide to sustainability. Ottawa: Health Canada.

Health Canada. (2003). Toward an evaluation framework for electronic health records. Ottawa: Health Canada.

Kaufman, K. (2005). Problems with the electronic medical record in clinical psychiatry: A hidden cost. *Journal of Psychiatric Practice, 11*(3), 200–03.

Kaushal, R., Shojania, K. & Bates, D. (2003). Effects of computerized physician order entry and clinical decision supports systems on medication safety. *Archives of Internal Medicine, 163*, 1409–16.

Killaspy, H., Ritchie, W., Greer, E. & Robertson, M. (2004). Treating the homeless mentally ill: Does a designated inpatient facility improve outcome? *Journal of Mental Health, 13*(6), 593–99.

Kuno, E., Rothbard, A., Averyt, J. & Culhane, D. (2000). Homelessness among persons with serious mental illness in an enhanced community-based mental health system. *Psychiatric Services, 51*(8), 1012–16.

Olfson, M., Mechanic, D., Hansell, S., Boyer, C. & Walkup, J. (1999). Prediction of homelessness with three months of discharge among inpatients with schizophrenia. *Psychiatric Services, 50*(5), 667–73.

Powell, J. & Buchan, I. (2005). Electronic health records should support clinical research. *Journal of Medical Internet Research, 7*(1), e4.

Rector, A., Nowlan, W. & Kay, S. (1991). Foundations for an electronic medical record. *Methods of Information in Medicine, 30*, 179–86.

Richards, J. (2001). Nursing in a digital age. *Nursing Economics, 19*(1), 6–12.

Statistics Canada. (2001). Census: analysis series. Collective dwellings. Catalogue no. 96F0030XIE2001009. Ottawa. Statistics Canada.

Susser, E., Valencia, E., Conover, S., Felix, A., Tsai, W. & Wyatt, R. (1997). Preventing recurrent homelessness among mentally ill men: A "critical time" intervention after discharge from a shelter. *American Journal of Public Health, 87*(2), 256–62.

Trieman, N., Leff, J. & Glover, G. (1999) Outcome of long stay psychiatric patients resettled in the community: Prospective cohort study. *British Medical Journal, 319*, 13–16.

Young, A., Mintz, J., Cohen, A. & Chinman, M. (2004). A network-based system to improve care for schizophrenia: The medical informatics network tool (MINT). *Journal of the American Medical Informatics Association, 11*(5), 358–67.

Section IV

INTRODUCTION: ADDITIONAL CHALLENGES

The homeless population is not homogeneous, nor are consumer-survivors who are homeless. Housing issues related to mental health and homelessness are intricate and multifaceted, leading to even more challenges for those working in this field, particularly for those experiencing this intersection of issues. This fourth section of the book explores some of the additional complexities that must be considered when intersecting oppressions arise. Issues of diversity, coming from a rural community without services, concerns related to sex, gender, displacement, and addiction are the specific additional complexities examined, though there are many others beyond these that are just as significant and worthy of future exploration.

Chapter 14, Berman, Gorlick, Csiernik, Ray, Forchuk, and Jensen's work, "The Changing Face of Diversity in the Context of Homelessness," begins this fourth section. The authors contextualize the concept of diversity and then discuss homelessness and mental illness with specific attention to homelessness among newcomer populations, youth, and the elderly. The research for this chapter was conducted using critical ethnographic and participatory action research approaches. Its findings thus led to a different orientation to diversity, underscored by the lack of diversity in the population studied when it came to race and ethnicity and also to socio-economic status, for the key unifying attribute of participants was their poverty. Insights gained regarding diversity pertained to the decontextualization of family life, the fluid nature of homelessness, and conflicts brought on by the generation gap in the homeless population. This distinct conceptualization of diversity moves our thinking beyond the traditional framework associated with this idea not only with the population but with all groups whom we too easily label and stereotype.

Chapter 15 explores rural mental health, a much under-examined issue. Forchuk, Montgomery, Berman, Ward-Griffin, Csiernik, Gorlick, Jensen, and Riesterer all contributed to this secondary data analysis based on the CURA data collected between 2001 and 2006. In "Gaining Ground, Losing Ground: The Paradoxes of Rural Homelessness," rural clients, family members, and community mental health workers all describe their efforts to secure health services and housing as a dynamic process of both gaining and losing ground. Movement toward recovery for rural-based mental health consumer-survivors is challenged by the lack of resources, health and social services, with the most significant issue, not surprisingly, being insufficient and inadequate housing. In their search for services, clients and, at times, their entire families, uprooted themselves to relocate to nearby urban areas. Relocation, however, did not always address health, financial, employment, and, critically, housing needs. Moving to an urban centre also had a propensity to threaten both the consumer-survivors' and families' sense of security as it reduced their access to previously established rural social connections and a much more familiar and often less stressful lifestyle. Gaining ground through relocation was particularly impeded when clients relied on urban homeless shelter services.

A theme touched on in several previous chapters is the difference between men and women in this practice and policy arena. Chapter 16, "Exploring Differences between Community-Based Women and Men with a History of Mental Illness," by Forchuk, Jensen, Csiernik, Ward-Griffin, Ray, Montgomery, and Wan, is a much more focused discussion of this topic. What is particularly interesting is that there is still relatively little understood concerning the role of sex with regard to people with a history of mental illness residing in the community. This chapter, using all five years of the CURA data, explores quantitative differences with regard to health status, psychiatric history, levels of functioning, personal strengths and resources, and severity of illness. Results indicate that more women than men were housed, more women than men with mental illness were coupled, while men had fewer social supports and greater substance abuse issues than did women. These findings suggest that health services within the community must consider these sex differences if they wish to properly assist Canadian individuals diagnosed with mental illnesses.

In Chapter 17, Berman, Alvernaz, Mulcahy, Forchuk, Edmunds, Haldendy, and Lopez discuss uprootedness and displacement in their critical narrative study of three specific groups of girls: homeless, Aboriginal, and newcomers to Canada. Uprootedness and displacement are a common part of everyday life for millions of girls and young women throughout the world. While much of the discourse concerning uprootedness and displacement has centred on movement from one country to another, these issues are also a reality for many within Canada. Notably, a steadily growing population of homeless and Aboriginal girls have also experienced uprootedness and dislocation from home, community, and, in some cases, family. For many of these girls and young women, multiple forms of individual and systemic violence are central features of their lives. The primary purpose of this critical narrative study was to examine how uprootedness and displacement have shaped mental health and well-being among these three specific groups. In-depth narrative interviews conducted with 19 girls from southwestern Ontario revealed that although there is much diversity within and between these groups, uprootedness and displacement create social boundaries and profound experiences of disconnections in relations for all of them. Barriers to establishing and re-establishing social connections generate dangerous spaces within interlocking systems of oppression such as races, sex, and age. However, in negotiating new spaces, there is the potential for forming and re-forming alliances where sources of support hold the promise of hope. Within these spaces of hope and pathways of engagement, connections offer a renewed sense of belonging and well-being. The findings highlight the relevance of uprootedness in girls' lives, provide beginning directions for designing gender-specific and culturally meaningful interventions, and comprise a substantial contribution to the growing body of research related to girls and young women.

The final chapter of Section IV, "Is Substance Abuse Even an Issue? Perceptions of Male and Female Community-Based Mental Health Consumer-Survivors," is a contribution by co-editor Rick Csiernik. Despite our increasing knowledge of the complexity of concurrent disorders, the majority of research has involved either institutionalized or specific clinical populations, and there have been limited opportunities to directly examine issues at the community level, particularly if there are any differences between women and men. Building on Chapter 16, differences between male and female respondents were examined and found to exist in terms of family substance abuse, social supports, and problematic parental substance abuse. While the overall level of functioning was similar for both sexes, men reported more problems with substance use, while women reported a greater overall problem severity. The most surprising outcome, particularly considering the numerous references made in previous chapters to addiction issues, was the lack of importance of substance abuse issues in respondents' lives. The findings again support the fact that specific services by sex are required for this population, though the likelihood of attending such programs would be greatly enhanced if rudimentary income and housing needs were first addressed.

Chapter 14

THE CHANGING FACE OF DIVERSITY IN THE CONTEXT OF HOMELESSNESS

Helene Berman, Carolyne Gorlick,
Rick Csiernik, Susan L. Ray,
Cheryl Forchuk, Elsabeth Jensen,
and Fatmeh Al-Zoubi

1. INTRODUCTION

The face of homelessness has changed dramatically over the past decade. Once stereotypically believed to be a problem of hobos, winos, and mildly deranged men, it is now widely recognized that homelessness is a grim reality for many sectors, including women and children, those with and without families, the young, old, and older, as well as people from all races and ethnicities. Despite the abundance of Canada's resources, a growing cadre of people who had once considered themselves to be safely ensconced within the "middle class" are finding themselves without safe, stable, or affordable housing. With these changes, the old stereotypes are being replaced with new stereotypes, which include high school dropouts, bag ladies, aggressive panhandlers, and people who engage in violence, crime, promiscuity, and profanity. Together, the stereotypes comprise an image of "social undesirability." As Sev'er (2002) has observed, the new images and stereotypes contribute to a "depersonalized other" whom those of privilege learn to dislike, dismiss, avoid, and reject. Rather than being seen as victims of circumstances that they are powerless to change, the new homeless are blamed for their inability to obtain housing, swept off the streets, and locked out of the parks while governments continue to seek new ways to criminalize what they do.

The changing face of homelessness also implies new pathways to homelessness (Sullivan, Burham & Koegel, 2000). For some, homelessness is a temporary, episodic situation, perhaps associated with a particular crisis or circumstance; for many, however, it is a chronic, persistent, and pervasive feature of their everyday lives. At the broader social/structural level, growing numbers of people in Canada are living in poverty (Frankish, Hwang & Quantz, 2005), unable to find stable employment with sufficient wages to match housing costs. Amid tenuous and uncertain circumstances, many are ultimately forced out of existing housing arrangements.

Efforts to clearly establish the nature and prevalence of homelessness in Canada are complicated by a lack of agreed-upon definitions, the challenges associated with identifying homeless people, the transient nature of homelessness, and well-founded suspicions regarding participation in surveys and other research methodologies. Understanding the social and historical context of homelessness requires consideration of changing policies and political/economic landscapes. The current homeless situation in Canada, and in Ontario more specifically, cannot be fully understood without some consideration of two overarching political and ideological realities: first, the Conservative political landscape that characterized the province of Ontario throughout the 1990s and that continued into the new millennium; and second, the neo-liberal framework of multiculturalism. With respect to the former, significant policy changes during the 1990s resulted in the devolution of social housing or the downloading of social housing onto inadequately resourced municipalities. This change, in conjunction with welfare cuts, lack of affordable child care, multiple barriers to health care, insufficient social benefits, and steadily shrinking social safety nets, contributed to a steadily growing "homeless problem."

At the same time, Canada has become markedly more diverse, with approximately 250,000 new immigrants and refugees entering Canada each year (Statistics Canada, 2007). Although many of these newcomers arrive in Canada with a reasonably high health status, ensured through stringent health selection processes, several studies have shown a decline in their health status as a result of social exclusion (Galabuzi, 2004; Hyman, 2001; Noh et al., 1999). Whether this decline may be directly attributed to racism has not been firmly established. However, there is growing evidence that processes of exclusion, including racism and discrimination, place racialized groups at higher risk for mental health problems (Anderson, 2000; Beiser, 1988; Dossa, 2004; Jiwani, 2006). Combined with material and emotional losses, the erosion of familiar support networks, and changing gendered roles and expectations, all of which are common aspects of post-migration experiences, the increased potential for downward economic mobility, the "racialization of poverty," and the increased likelihood of homelessness becomes clear.

As one of the few countries in the world to have a formal *Multiculturalism Act*, Canada is often applauded as a humanitarian nation, where newcomers are welcome and discrimination prohibited. In reality, discourses on multiculturalism and diversity may mask or obscure discriminatory and racist practices that, in effect, deny access to housing by those who are marked as "Other." As used here, the notion of "othering" refers to a process whereby people are marked as different or "lesser than" by virtue of their social identity: race, gender, class, sexual orientation, ability. Within the context of our research, "Other" refers to those who have not been accorded civil, political, or social rights, including housing, to which they are entitled.

Based on these ideas, a critical ethnographic study was conducted to examine the particular challenges, intersecting vulnerabilities, and strengths faced by diverse groups of homeless people living in southwestern Ontario. In this chapter, we examine the "changing face" of homelessness, with particular attention to the notion of diversity. As discourses of diversity in Canada are underpinned by the assumptions and ideology of multiculturalism, we interrogate this framework and consider its implications with respect to homelessness. The current research will be discussed, incorporating the perspectives from both consumer-survivors and service providers. Lastly, we propose implications for health and social service professionals, policy-makers, and program developers.

2. REVIEW OF CURRENT KNOWLEDGE

In recent years, a growing number of researchers have examined the issue of homelessness using various perspectives and methodologies. While this scholarly literature has yielded new understandings regarding the problem as it exists in Canada, few researchers have attended to the issue of diversity in the context of homelessness. Instead, "the homeless" tend to be conceptualized as a relatively homogeneous group. When diversity is taken into consideration, it is most commonly conceptualized as a proxy for race or ethnicity. In order to understand the issues and challenges faced by diverse populations, we extend our search beyond Canada and look to the research that has been conducted globally with particular attention to immigrants and refugees, youth, and the elderly.

Homelessness and the Experience of Mental Illness

Researchers from virtually every continent have consistently found that people with mental health problems are overrepresented in the homeless population. In a study of Toronto shelters, Goering, Tolomiczenko, Sheldon, Boydell, and Wasylenki (2002) found that 64 percent of first-time shelter users and 69 percent of repeat users had at least one type of psychiatric problem. Similar findings have been found in other countries. For example, in a German study, Fichter, Quadflieg, Koniarczyk, Greifenhagen, Wolz, Koegel, and Wittchen (1999) reported that 94.5 percent of the homeless men in Munich had at least one DIS/DSM-III Axis I psychiatric diagnosis. A Danish study found 82 percent of homeless individuals had a mental illness (Thomsen et al., 2000). Haugland, Siegel, Hopper, and Alexander (1997) reported that in New York State, 72 percent of the homeless people studied had an addiction, with 21 percent diagnosed with various types of mental illnesses. They also found that those with mental illness remained homeless twice as long as others without mental illness. In Brazil, a study of 83 homeless individuals found that all but one had a psychiatric problem (Heckert et al., 1999).

Although mental illness has long been identified as a risk factor for homelessness and unstable housing, our understanding of this pattern is evolving. Early studies identified this phenomenon as related to the illness per se (Drake, Wallach & Hoffman, 1989; Lamb & Lamb, 1990), but more recently poverty and the lack of affordable housing have been identified as sources of the problem (Draine et al., 2002; Drake & Wallach, 1999; Koegel, Burnam & Baumohl, 1996). People with mental illness can be considered members of an oppressed group who suffer stigma and discrimination, which, in turn, can limit their access to housing and employment. Negative attitudes, including discrimination from family, co-workers, their community, and even health care providers, have been described (Geller, 2001; Drake & Wallach, 1999; Wahl, 1999).

Homelessness and Newcomer Populations

Research interest in homelessness among diverse populations within the Canadian context has been limited. In a sample of residents in Toronto shelters, Goering et al. (2002) found that 32 percent of first-time shelter users and 24 percent of repeat shelter users were non-Caucasian. In the United States, several studies have reported differences with regard to race and/or gender. For example, Warren and colleagues (1992) concluded that minority women were particularly vulnerable to homelessness because they experienced increased poverty levels and were often single mothers. They also found that of all minority women experiencing homelessness, African-American women were the most vulnerable to physical and psychological illness. In that study, 75 percent of the respondents had psychological assessment scores that indicated the need for additional testing.

Netto (2006) has observed that immigrants, refugees, and ethnic minorities face unique structural or institutional barriers that affect their housing options. Lack of affordable housing, along with declining income and low levels of social assistance provided to refugees, converge to make acceptable housing difficult, if not impossible, to obtain (Dunn et al., 2006; Fiedler, Schuurman & Hyndman, 2006). In Canada, homelessness has been described as a particular problem in the Greater Vancouver area, where high numbers of immigrants arrive annually. Unable to obtain suitable employment, many face "downward mobility" (Anderson, 2000) and find themselves living at or below the poverty level. It has been suggested that homelessness among these groups is often "hidden," characterized by involuntary "doubling-up" or shared accommodations, and/or unsustainable rent burdens (Fiedler et al., 2006; Turnbull & Podymow, 2002).

In one study conducted in Scotland to explore causes of homelessness among different ethnic groups and patterns of access and use of relevant services, Netto (2006) found that homelessness among Black and other ethnic minority groups typically results from leaving the home of a friend or relative, with nearly one-third reporting that they had lost their last home in this way. The homeless participants in Netto's research also reported that discriminatory policies and procedures for the allocation of social housing compounded the challenge in obtaining satisfactory housing. Netto noted that newcomer populations rarely used the homelessness services of mainstream agencies. While the reasons were not explicitly addressed, newcomers' reluctance or inability to use the existing services constitutes a substantial obstacle to achieving any meaningful solutions.

Homelessness among Youth

In recent years, there has been some evidence to suggest that youth may be particularly vulnerable to the problem of homelessness, and that homelessness among young people is on the rise. Several researchers have reported a range of complex and interrelated circumstances that contribute to homelessness among adolescents and young adults. Family interactions that are characterized by violence, verbal put-downs, and other forms of demeaning behaviour have been described as factors that often influence the decision to "run away" from home (Haldenby, Berman & Forchuk, 2007; O'Dwyer, 1997; Robert, Pauze & Fournier, 2005).

Academic difficulties have been noted by some researchers. In a study conducted with 69 youth at a drop-in centre in Toronto, it was found that the majority had dropped out of high school, had encounters with the criminal justice system, and had used at least one kind of drug in the past 12 months (Cameron et al., 2004). According to Kidd and Davidson (2006), a prior history of parental criminality, domestic violence, and substance abuse increased the risk of youth homelessness. Similar findings were reported in a multi-state study conducted in Missouri, Iowa, Nebraska, and Kansas (Whitbeck & Hoyt, 2000), which also described both positive and negative outcomes when youth rely on peers for social support.

Investigating the causal pathways to youth homelessness in Australia, Martijn and Sharp (2006) observed the occurrence of past trauma among 50 percent of the homeless youth and an increase in the number of psychological diagnoses. These researchers also noted that criminal behaviour, including substance abuse, did not precede homelessness, but occurred once "on the streets." The failure of mainstream programs such as child welfare, juvenile corrections, and mental health services to adequately protect youth was also cited as an implicating factor.

Several researchers have observed a range of adverse health consequences associated with homelessness among youth. According to a report by the National Alliance to End Homelessness (2007), between 40 percent and 60 percent experienced physical abuse, and between 17 percent and 35 percent experienced sexual abuse. In interviews conducted with homeless youth from an affluent Toronto suburb, a substantial number had been imprisoned, experienced physical abuse, and exhibited depressive symptomatology and suicidal ideation (Cameron et al., 2004).

Living in shelters or on the street without support exposes youth to considerable risk for physical and sexual assault, hunger, anxiety disorders, depression, post-traumatic stress disorder, and suicide (Antoniades & Tarasuk, 1998; Boivin et al., 2005; Haldenby et al., 2007; Flick, 2007; Kidd & Davidson, 2006; O'Dwyer, 1997). In addition, homeless youth are more likely to become involved in prostitution, illegal and dangerous behaviours, and to be drug abusers (Kemp, Neale & Robertson, 2006; Kidd & Davidson, 2006). While homeless youth appear to be at considerable risk for various health challenges, several researchers have described numerous systemic barriers faced by this group in their efforts to obtain satisfactory health services. According to Ensign and Bell (2004), homeless youth under age 18 are often denied health care at hospitals because of their underage status, while youth over age 18 find it difficult to obtain stable housing because of health care expenses. Reid, Berman, and Forchuk (2005) reported that homeless youth are often reluctant to seek health care because they encounter negative and demeaning stereotypic attitudes from health care providers.

Much of the research related to homeless youth has tended to depict this population as a relatively homogeneous group, with little attention to the role of gender and the particular challenges faced by homeless girls and young women. Exceptions are studies conducted by Haldenby, Berman, and Forchuk (2007) and Berman, Alvernaz Mulcahy, Forchuk, Edmunds, Haldenby, and Lopez (2009), who described the heightened risks of violence faced by girls and young women who are living on the streets. Similar findings were reported by Ensign and Bell (2004), who noted that most homeless female youth who took part in their ethnographic study reported fears about their safety. In addition, those who were living on the streets reported more illnesses related to substance use and greater reliance on emergency departments for health care than did clinic-based youth (Ensign & Bell, 2004).

Homelessness and the Elderly

With respect to the elderly, poverty, deinstitutionalization, and lack of affordable housing have been reported as the three main causes of homelessness (Stergiopoulous & Hermann, 2003). While research related to homelessness among this population is sparse, the findings suggest that lack of safe and affordable housing, declining physical health, mental health problems, disrupted relationships, violence, and abuse all play a role (Hightower, Hightower & Smith, 2003; Stergiopoulous & Hermann, 2003). In addition, the death of a spouse, social isolation, discrimination, or lack of knowledge about benefits and services can compound the risk of homelessness (Hecht & Coyle, 2001; Tully & Jacobson, 1994). In a study undertaken in the Lower Mainland in British Columbia, Hightower and colleagues conducted focus groups and interviews with seniors, health providers, social and municipal planners, and representatives from other advocacy and community-serving agencies. Findings revealed that almost 20,000 seniors in households were "at risk" by this definition—8,245 aged 55–64, and 11,240 who were 65 or older.

Diversity and Policy

Although cultural issues are largely national, there is no national housing policy, national mental health policy, or national family policy. Without a national effort to coordinate and develop responses to housing, mental health, and families, each of the three policy areas struggles to innovate at the provincial/territorial level and ultimately the community level. Subsequently when successful and proven programs occur, there is often a time constraint to disseminate information and initiate implementation of similar programs in other jurisdictions. More specifically, the mandate to provide safe and affordable housing for everyone encompasses federal, provincial, and municipal sectors, with a growing trend to download responsibility to the local level. The lack of affordable housing is particularly problematic for mental health consumer-survivors because governments across Canada have pursued a policy of deinstitutionalization while changes in the social and affordable housing landscape were occurring. The lack of a national family policy underscores the significance of housing and mental health policy, ensuring that homeless families and those who support them will find the pathways out of homelessness formidable, confusing, uncompromising, and, for many, unreachable. Thus, putting the responsibility of understanding the complex problems on individuals rather than focusing on the inadequacies of the social, political, and economic system is unlikely to resolve matters. It is noteworthy that Rosenheck and Lam (1997) examined variation in service use among individuals who were both homeless and experiencing mental illness. They found that individual client characteristics explained only 2–3 percent of the variation, while the differences between communities were much more significant.

While the current knowledge suggests that homelessness may be experienced differently by virtue of one's social location and identity, little research has been conducted to examine this idea. In response to this knowledge gap, a critical ethnographic study was carried out in southwestern Ontario. The overall purpose of this research was to explore the intersecting vulnerabilities among individuals who are homeless and have psychiatric challenges, and who are differently situated with respect to race, class, age, gender, sexual orientation, and ability.

3. THEORETICAL AND METHODOLOGICAL UNDERPINNINGS

Critical ethnography and participatory action research (PAR) provided the theoretical and methodological framework for this study. Ethnography is the method of choice when seeking to make explicit what is implicit in a culture (Germain, 1993). Traditionally ethnographers collect data from detailed observations in the field and from unstructured interviews (Atkinson & Hammersley, 1994; Leininger, 1985). While all ethnographers share an interest in culture, there are different types of ethnography. Quantz (1992) describes critical ethnography as a form of ethnography in which the researcher attempts to re-present the "culture" of people living in asymmetrical power relations. Derived from ideas associated with Critical Social Theory, a critical ethnographic approach facilitates the description and analysis of cultural assumptions that inhibit, repress, and constrain (Thomas, 1993). It challenges repressive cultural definitions and offers to engage in positive social change (Denzin & Lincoln, 1994; Thomas, 1993). Thus, it is a method that is used to describe not only what is, but what could be.

Participatory action research (PAR) is a broad methodology that has been understood and implemented in vastly different ways, with respect to both the degree and nature of "participation." As used in the current research, the notion of PAR was derived from ideas and principles of Paulo Freire (1970), who emphasized the notion of research as praxis, or the combination of research, action, and change. Integral to this notion of PAR, it is generally agreed that for research to contribute to meaningful change, it must have meaning to those whom the research claims to be about. Consistent with this idea, the research team comprised community and academic researchers. Some members of the team were affiliated in various ways—as volunteers, staff, and/or board members—with the agencies that were included in the research. The long-standing relationships that have been established and nurtured over years of working together on past research, policy initiatives, and community engagement facilitated trust in the research process, the team, and the recruitment of participants. More importantly, the participatory nature of the project ensured ongoing collaboration throughout all stages of the project, from the conceptualization and design of the study to the dissemination of findings. This type of collaboration is particularly important as it helps to ensure that the study findings will have meaning and relevance in the lives of those who are homeless. Moreover, because the homeless population in general has largely been marginalized, exploited, and silenced, the research team paid particular attention to the development of research approaches that would not contribute to further marginalization or exploitation. While an aim of research derived from critical social theory is empowerment and change (Berman, Ford-Gilboe & Campbell, 1998), we take a modest stance in this regard. Rather than claiming responsibility for anyone's empowerment, one aim of our research was to contribute to new understandings and insights for the researchers and participants, referred to by Freire as *conscientizacao*. Through the creation of research "spaces" that allow and encourage individuals to critically reflect upon the circumstances of their lives, to "name their reality," and to consider strategies to change that reality, it is thought that new understandings evolve, thus enhancing the likelihood for social action and change.

4. METHODS

Based on these ideas, focus groups were conducted in a flexible manner, with questions designed to encourage dialogue, reflection, and critique on the part of all participants, including the group facilitators. All participants received a participant fee, and food was provided during the focus group. Prior to the start of the group, the facilitator reviewed the letter of information that participants were previously given, addressed their questions, and obtained consent from those who agreed to participate.

Focus groups were conducted over approximately a one-year period with consumer-survivors and service providers from an array of community agencies and shelters that provide services to those who are homeless. As defined here, the term "homeless" was used broadly and included those who self-identified as homeless and typically consisted of individuals who had no fixed address, lived on the streets, and/or couch surfed. While some of these agencies offer services to particular subgroups—for example, one participating organization was dedicated to meeting the needs of homeless Aboriginal peoples—most do not specify particular target populations beyond the broad category of homelessness.

The criterion of saturation was used to guide decisions regarding the final sample size. Consistent with most qualitative research designs, data were collected and analyzed simultaneously, and data collection was discontinued when no new themes emerged from the data. The final sample consisted of seven focus groups with consumer-survivors, and eight focus groups with service providers. Most of the focus groups consisted of approximately 10–12 participants, although some contained as few as three and as many as 15 participants. The interview guide was a semi-structured format that allowed us to explore with the consumer-survivor participants the circumstances that led to their current homelessness; the feelings associated with homelessness; family situations; the barriers they encountered in their efforts to obtain stable housing, including discrimination and other forms of exclusion; the nature of support (material, financial, and/or emotional) that they received; and how they envisioned their housing circumstances five years from the time of the focus groups. As well, participants were asked what would have been helpful that they perhaps did not receive, thereby inviting critical dialogue and reflection. The focus groups for service providers were similarly conducted in an interactive manner. Questions posed to this group concerned the nature of the services they provided, descriptions of the population served, perceived barriers to effective service delivery, policies and approaches regarding service delivery to diverse populations, and perceived gaps or constraints in achieving their agency objectives.

The southwestern Ontario community where the research was conducted has a growing ethnoculturally diverse population, with newcomers from Central and South America, Eastern Europe, the Middle East, and Southeast Asian communities. However, the study sample did not reflect this diversity, an issue that we consider later in this chapter. Rather, diversity in the current study sample was evident with respect to age, gender, and family structure. The constant among all groups was chronic, pervasive, and enduring poverty and a profound sense of pessimism—at times cynicism—about the possibility that this could change.

Data were analyzed using the typology method, which is a systematic method for classifying similar events, actions, objects, people, and places into discrete groupings (Berg, 2004). The analysis was, in essence, an iterative process of critical reflection, tentative identification of key themes, and returning to the data to ensure that there were no leftover data that did not fit. Thomas (1993) describes "de-familiarization" as a process of taking the obvious—namely, the data themselves and preliminary typologies—and stepping back to look at it and analyze it in a fresh and critical light. It is also described as a process of decoding and de-analyzing to ensure that all possible connotations and analyses have been considered in light of the context and culture of the participants and the researchers. As critical ethnography is first and foremost a critical endeavour, the study must be looked at for its potential to effect change. This reflection may enlighten the researchers to change that has already occurred at the level of the individual, or at the broader social, structural, organizational, and/or policy level.

5. FINDINGS

All of the participants described multiple challenges and difficulties they faced regarding homelessness. However, the most consistent issue that was articulated repeatedly by virtually all participants was poverty. All other concerns were deemed secondary to, and of lesser importance than, the dire financial circumstances that profoundly shaped their everyday lives. Other key themes that emerged from the data concerned the decontextualization of family life, the fluid nature of homelessness, the younger versus the older generation of homeless, and the hidden homeless.

The Centrality of Poverty

From the perspective of the participants, poverty is the central construct that shapes the lives of homeless individuals. Embedded within this "narrative" is not their diversity but their core commonality. They become "Othered," not so much by ethnicity/race, gender, age, or other markers of "difference" but by the pervasive, persistent, and pernicious experience of "being poor." They consistently described, in powerful and profound ways, the chronic and enduring nature of poverty and typically saw few solutions. Moreover, poverty was viewed as the root cause of all other problems commonly associated with homelessness. While homelessness was associated with multiple challenges, including compromised nutrition, lack of social supports, physical and emotional health problems, and numerous barriers encountered in their efforts to seek services, at the heart of all these difficulties is poverty. In essence, the participants described a cascading chain of events that were all attributed to chronic poverty and a very real perception that they had few options, choices, or alternatives. The interconnectedness between poverty and social isolation was poignantly described by one participant, who stated:

> "... I got friends who invite me over to go somewhere for I don't know on the weekend. And it's, like, I'm embarrassed because I have to say 'No, um, I got other plans.' I lie because I don't have the money to pay for whatever it is, so ... or, well, you have a dinner with them, eh? It's like, well, I don't have $20 to throw in for a barbecue for the weekend type of thing.... So like I said, it all boils down to having like a little extra money just to do something, you know, like a social activity with friends or a club or something."

As this comment reveals, the inability to provide a small amount of cash for a social gathering precludes the opportunity to be with friends, thereby cutting off a potentially important source of support.

Several participants stated that they are not able to provide first and last months' rent to landlords, noting that the public assistance they receive is inadequate, and asserting that landlords are inflexible with respect to this requirement. As one study participant said, "The majority of time they want first and last [months' rent] and I mean the majority of people are on social assistance and they give you what $520 to live off of, you know. They don't give you first and last ..., you know, so I mean it's hard...." Another elaborated on this idea:

> "They don't even want to compromise, like, when you suggest it, 'No, sorry, you got to give me the whole money or nothing.' And that's not right. We're in a shelter. How are you going to come up with, like, $300 or $600 or whatever you owe? Plus then you have to have first and last months' rent. Then you have to have money for the hook-up for your hydro and stuff, plus moving expenses and stuff. Everything's so expensive nowadays, like, you just can't do all that at once."

Frequently, the inability to provide first and last months' rent resulted in a range of alternative, temporary, and inadequate housing "solutions." One participant stayed in a motel until the money ran out, at which time she then went to a shelter.

Most participants believed that they encountered subtle and explicit forms of discrimination because they were poor. In some instances, the discrimination was difficult to locate, taking the form of condescending looks and demeaning attitudes. At other times, discrimination was manifested more overtly in the form of hostile remarks or exclusionary behaviours. For example, "What I find is there's a lot of snickering, there's a lot of looking down. Even if, um, basically it's just when you walk in, people have judged you already, even before you open your mouth."

A commonly heard theme from all participants was the cyclical and spiralling nature of poverty. While being poor is in and of itself a hardship, several participants told of the chain of adverse events that often unfolds. As one female participant explained, sometimes she is "lucky" to get a bus pass, but this might have to be sold for money to phone the doctor, or so she can do the laundry. Similar scenarios were recounted by many of the participants.

The feeling that they are caught in a catch-22 situation with few ways out, and the profound sense of frustration, was evident in this woman's comments:

> "I don't feel like I'm heard anymore. I feel like all I am is a number to the government, and no matter what I try to do to not become a number anymore, they blackball you. If you go and get a job while you're on assistance, they take it off your $1,000. How are you supposed to get ahead when you are not even off the system—when you are making it harder for me than it already is?"

Poverty was thus a defining feature of everyday life among the study participants, with adverse consequences that affected the participants' physical and emotional well-being. Service providers seemed acutely aware of the effects of poverty, and expressed their frustration at their inability to provide meaningful, long-term support. While they recognized that their interventions alleviated short-term challenges, they typically viewed these as limited and temporary strategies that rarely resulted in sustainable structural change that would ultimately create more equitable relationships. The inadequacy of current social assistance benefits was clearly articulated by one service provider, who said:

> "There has to be a huge policy change in the way our social services are … delivered for people. People cannot survive on Ontario Works and ODSP, and we are forcing people into poverty and homelessness, and then if they do end

up in a shelter, then it's trying to find affordable housing is impossible. So it's the lack of affordable housing. Even if there was enough affordable housing for everybody who is on Ontario Works and ODSP today, they still wouldn't be able to survive on that amount of money and to feed their kids and themselves."

The service providers seemed keenly aware of poverty as the fundamental inequality in the lives of those who were homeless. However, among this group, there appeared to be a willingness to overlook poverty as the problem was too large to address. Instead, under their respective agency mandates, they turned their attention to seeking short-term and temporary ways to improve the lives of those who are homeless. Policies have not been created in Canada specifically for the homeless family. Policies have been strung together with gaps and overlaps, weighed down by inconsistencies and the lack of political will for a coordinated change at federal, provincial, and community levels.

The Decontextualization of Family Life

Contrary to prevailing stereotypes, a growing number of today's homeless comprise various family constellations, including mother-headed single-parent families, youth, elderly, as well as two-parent families that may or may not include children. In addition, refugee and immigrant families are becoming part of Canada's homeless family population. Newcomer families sometimes expect that they will receive support from established members or families of their ethnic or racial communities. This is not always the case. As one service provider observed:

> "Cultural clash [exists] with refugees or immigrants coming into Canada, coming into their own community here, which has already, to some extent, been assimilated…. The cultural community is always changing."

For some newcomers, the ethnic or racial community in place functions as a protector from loss of employment, downward income mobility and loss of housing. For other newcomers, the protective element of their community is less accessible. Once out of the shelter system, newcomer individuals and families become increasingly isolated, cutting themselves off or being cut off from their racial or ethnic community, which may further stigmatize them. A service provider offered an example of losing these social networks:

> "We have a number of clients where the women are experiencing postpartum depression. Was it because of the trauma of leaving their country and coming

to Canada? Is it the result of being isolated from those female family members that would have provided so much support? Within their own cultural community, the understanding of postpartum depression may not be relevant. You know, 'Get over it, you're fine. Your life is good. What is wrong with you? Why are you crying all the time?' So we're getting a lot of women coming in ... feeling like they have absolutely nobody."

Decontextualization of family life for newcomers, as well as for those born in Canada, contributes to individual and family social isolation. This new sense of place is formalized and institutionalized by policies, rules, and regulations that do not recognize the complex and ever-changing intersecting vulnerabilities that newcomers face on a daily basis. From the study's population there is a perception among those homeless, and among service providers, that the programs and services established for those who are homeless are antithetical to family life.

The very nature of shelter living is mutually incompatible with the daily existence of being in a family. Parenting becomes one element of family life that is more visible, monitored, and responded to in a homeless shelter. A service provider at a shelter noted:

> "I think that the greatest thing I hear from the parents is their inability to manage their children because they are in this group setting and other people are managing their children.... You kind of feel as a parent [that] you're under the microscope of every other parent who's in that setting and every staff member who might be making a judgment on how good or not so good of a parent you are."

Other perceived vulnerabilities are also visible in the shelter, as a service provider observed:

> "If you are in a shelter, parenting is not your priority ... if there are difficulties in parenting, addictions issues, mental health issues, and all the rest. You can't hide from that in a shelter!"

In sum, those in shelters likened their lives to being in a "fishbowl." The complete absence of private spaces meant that every parenting decision and interaction was observed and scrutinized by everyone around them. In some instances, women were forced to live apart from their partners because there were no suitable shelters to accommodate couples. A few noted that, while they had temporary shelter, their husbands were on the streets, living in cars, or couch surfing. As one woman told us, "Right now he's [my husband's] couch surfing for a month until we can find somewhere to stay. There's nowhere else to go for him."

While most homeless families have little idea of housing policy and program pathways, refugee and immigrant families are often further constrained by a limited ability to speak either one of Canada's official languages and lack information about service delivery programs and rules. Service providers agreed that there is a need to wrap services around families rather than have families independently, and in isolation, seek a complex path to available services and accessible resources. What also frequently adds to the difficulty is the contrary and contradictory nature of related and necessary programs. Thus, intersecting vulnerabilities experienced by individuals and families are reinforced by the inconsistent and conflicting nature of some programs and policies affecting the homeless. In the following quote, a service provider comments on the manner in which sometimes contradictory, vague, and uncoordinated requirements of various governmental ministries affect families:

> "The Ministry of Community and Social Services might demand that a form be filled out by someone in health. If you don't have a family doctor, you don't have anyone to fill out your forms, then you don't get your Ontario Works and then you don't get your drug card, and then it snowballs and it becomes very difficult when physicians aren't accepting new patients..... People are marginalized through no fault of their own. They really can't get into the system without some of these vital little links."

Programming emphasis continues to be on the individual rather than the family unit. One repercussion of this is a neglect of the needs of children who are homeless or who are part of a homeless family. When a family is homeless, typically there are enforced separations and child welfare often becomes involved, so the familial role becomes subverted and redefined.

Focusing on individual rather than familial needs as a program response is also evident at the agency level, as well as at the broad social and policy levels. The net result is that homelessness further erodes any possibility of a fruitful and cohesive family life. In the words of one mother:

> "I am having a very hard time with housing. I can't afford to live. Okay, according to [child protection services] I have to have a one bedroom in order to have my kids do home visits, but [with] the income that I'm bringing, I can't

even get a bachelor. To get into housing, me and my husband—sorry, me and my ex-husband—we shared a place and he went out drinking for two months on the rent, which I didn't know about. So I had the rears [I was in arrears]. Well, I have to pay $900 before I can even get accepted into housing, but I'm a high priority. So, in order for me to even get housing that I'd be able to afford and have that bedroom for my children, I will have to pay that off. So, and they won't even accept where I would pay an extra $50 or $60 a month to pay it off on top of my rent. And that is a problem because now I'm looking at a place that I don't even know what it is going to look like. I'm not even supposed to go past $335. Am I supposed to live in a room and never have my kids back? Screw that. I'm fighting for my kids and I'm not letting them go, but I'm in a situation where it's a no-win."

Similar concerns were shared by other mothers who participated in this study. One spoke about the discrimination she experienced because she has teenaged children:

"Even though my kids are good … they think all the teenagers are bad.… A lot of places I went to, [as] soon as they found out I had teenagers, they did not want me."

In sum, lack of privacy, time constraints, social boundaries, as well as significant interventions at the individual, family, service provider, and institutional level, move a family in a diametrically and fundamentally opposite path from what constitutes "being home."

The Fluid Nature of Homelessness

Homelessness is not a static condition for the study's participants as they were typically constantly "on the move." Their ideas of home ranged from sleeping rough, to couch surfing, to living in shelters.

"It's a place you call home … until you try to get back on your feet, but I find that with myself … you keep trying and trying, but then I just fall right back down.…"

This transience left them continually striving to connect with people and programs. The connections that they were able to establish tended to be tenuous and were easily broken. Loneliness was a powerful constant in most of the participants' lives.

> "I think there needs to be more housing for women who are dealing with the, um, loneliness part. Some women, basically, cannot live alone.... There's no place for them to go. Where do they go?"

Thus, it is not surprising that family life is incongruent for most.

Service providers also commented on revolving door situations where the same homeless individuals keep utilizing the same services, and this is accompanied by a perception that the uphill struggle to access housing is getting steeper. Both service providers and homeless participants felt they were running as fast as possible to respond, but were not able to keep up with the changing nature of homelessness and the lack of response immediacy.

The Younger versus the Older Generation of Homeless

The increasing rise of homeless adolescents and young adults has created tensions among the homeless population in the shelter system. Many of the participants expressed dissatisfaction with mixing the younger generation with the older generation of homeless. One participant clearly articulated the tension created:

> "And the main thing about this place—I'm going to tell you straight up right now—they should not have kids in here. They should not have women mixed up with the men, and they should have them separate.... We're adults here, okay? I mean I don't have to listen to some snot-nose little brat screaming at this girlfriend and telling her all kinds of names and all this stuff.... We're supposed to take a back seat to these kids; they're out front all the time.... I've seen them sitting right beside a garbage can and throw a friggin' can across the road."

Another participant reflected the youth's difficulties with the older generation of homeless:

> "Yeah, there's a lot of soap opera that goes on ... especially the older guys who had a lifetime of probably, you know, drugs...."

One possible solution suggested by several of the adult participants was to separate the youth from the adults by placing them in their own building. The generational context of homelessness adds a new dimension and new challenges that have not been addressed.

6. DISCUSSION

In our study, specifically designed to explore issues of diversity, almost every participant was of European ancestry, and it was also a "White" population who was using services provided for the homeless. The literature indicates that this is not who the population is, yet these are the individuals who attended focus groups and whom service providers indicated were using their services. The "why" merits speculation and attention. Does the face of homelessness change once we move from the major metropolitan Canadian communities of Toronto, Vancouver, and Montreal, or are racialized and other minority populations avoiding the use of the services provided?

Among the possible explanations for the demographic of our study was that London and communities like it still have relatively small newcomer populations and do not have the historical and generational context that might lead to homelessness of visible minority populations. Also, if there are issues of homelessness in ethnoculturally diverse groups, they may seek assistance within their own communities and not utilize mainstream established agency resources. So, then, where are the hidden homeless, and why do racialized minority homeless groups avoid using established mainstream agencies?

The incongruities that arose from this study's findings necessitate examining the issue of diversity and difference among homeless individuals in terms of intersecting inequalities. People's identities are multiple and cannot be understood by one demographic marker alone, such as age but not ethnicity, or class but not race. Intersecting vulnerabilities were evident among all participants. This process is one where individuals become marked as different, as the Other, such that their differences prolong their homelessness. While service organizations that participated in the study had addressed the issue of cultural sensitivity among their staff, their mandated approaches largely continued to mask structural inequalities with their emphasis focused mostly on the individual taking all the risks. Social service and health care practice must recognize that the bifurcation of policy intentions and implementation realities continues to trap individuals and families as well as service providers in a never-ending context that lessens possibilities of escaping homelessness.

The lack of found racial differences also speaks to our use of language. A focus on culture or ethnicity as euphemisms for "diversity" detracts attention from social, economic, and political factors that exclude and trivialize the concerns of those who are marked as "different" be they racialized minorities, impoverished individuals, members of the gay/lesbian/bisexual/transexual community, or those with physical or mental challenges. Sensitivity to diversity cannot be translated solely into food and dance. Genuine efforts to be inclusive will require attention to unequal relations of power that determine one's status and how resources are distributed. Discourses on multiculturalism and diversity may mask or obscure discriminatory practices that deny housing to those who are marked as "Other."

REFERENCES

Anderson, J.M. (2000). Gender, "race," poverty, health, and discourses of health reform in the context of globalization: A postcolonial feminist perspective in policy research. *Nursing Inquiry*, 7(4), 220–29.

Antoniades, M. & Tarasuk, V. (1998). A survey of food problems experienced by Toronto street youth. *Canadian Journal of Public Health*, 89(6), 371–75.

Atkinson, P. & Hammersley, M. (1994). Ethnography and participant observation. In N.K. Denzin & Y.S. Lincoln (Eds.), *Handbook of qualitative research* (pp. 248–61). Thousand Oaks: Sage Publications.

Beiser, M. (1988). *After the door has opened: Canadian Task Force on Mental Health Issues Affecting Immigrants and Refugees*. Ottawa: Multiculturalism and Citizenship.

Berg, B. (2004). *Qualitative research methods for the social sciences*, 5th ed. Boston: Allyn and Bacon.

Berman, H., Alvernaz Mulcahy, G., Forchuk, C., Edmunds, K., Haldenby, A. & Lopez, R. (2009). Uprooted and displaced: A critical narrative study of homeless, Aboriginal, and newcomer girls in Canada. *Issues in Mental Health Nursing*, 30(7), 418–30.

Berman, H., Ford-Gilboe, M. & Campbell, J.C. (1998). Combining stories and numbers: A methodological approach for a critical nursing science. *Advances in Nursing Science*, 21(1), 1–15.

Boivin, J.F., Roy, E., Haley, N. & Galbaud du Fort, G. (2005). The health of street youth. *Canadian Journal of Public Health*, 96(6), 432–37.

Cameron, K.N., Racine, Y., Offord, D.R. & Cairney, J. (2004). Youth at risk of homelessness in an affluent Toronto suburb. *Canadian Journal of Public Health*, 95(5), 352–56.

Denzin, N. & Lincoln, Y. (Eds.). (1994). *Handbook of qualitative research*. Thousand Oaks: Sage Publications.

Dossa, P. (2004). *Politics and poetics of migration: Narratives of Iranian women from the diaspora*. Toronto: Canadian Scholars' Press Inc.

Draine, J., Salzer, M., Culhane, D. & Hadley, T. (2002). Role of social disadvantage in crime, joblessness, and homelessness among persons with serious mental illness. *Psychiatric Services, 53,* 565–73.

Drake, R.E., McHugo, G.J., Bedout, R.R., Becker, D.R., Marris, M., Bond, G.R. & Quimby, E. (1999). A randomized clinical trial of supported employment for inner-city patients with severe mental disorders. *Archives of General Psychiatry, 56,* 627–633.

Drake, R.E. & Wallach, M.A. (1999). Homelessness and mental illness: A story of failure. *Psychiatric Services, 50,* 589.

Drake, R., Wallach, M. & Hoffman, J. (1989). Housing instability and homelessness among aftercare patients of an urban state hospital. *Hospital and Community Psychiatry 40,* 46–51.

Dunn, J.R., Hayes, M.V., Hulchanski, J.D., Hwang, S. & Potvin, L. (2006). Housing as a socio-economic determinant of health. *Canadian Journal of Public Health, 97,* S11–S15.

Ensign, J. & Bell, M. (2004). Illness experiences of homeless youth. *Qualitative Health Research, 14*(9), 1239–54.

Fichter, M., Quadflieg, N., Koniarczyk, M., Greifenhagen, A., Wolz, J., Koegel, P. & Wittchen, H.U. (1999). Mental illness in homeless men and women in Munich. *Psychiatric Practice, 26*(2), 76–84.

Fiedler, R., Schuurman, N. & Hyndman, J. (2006). Hidden homelessness: An-indicator-based approach for examining the geographies of recent immigrants at risk of homelessness in Greater Vancouver. *Cities, 23*(3), 205–16.

Flick, U. (2007). Homelessness and health: Challenges for health psychology. *Journal of Health Psychology, 12*(5), 691–95.

Frankish, C.J., Hwang, S.W. & Quantz, D. (2005). Homelessness and health in Canada: Research lessons and priorities. *Canadian Journal of Public Health, 96*(Supplement 2), 23–29.

Freire, P. (1970). *Pedagogy of the oppressed.* New York: Seabury Press.

Galabuzi, G.E. (2004). Social exclusion. In D. Raphael (Ed.), *Social determinants of health: Canadian perspectives.* Toronto: Canadian Scholars' Press Inc.

Geller, J.L. (2001). Taking issue: Ain't no such thing as a schizophrenic. *Psychiatric Services, 52*(6), 715.

Germain, C. (1993). Ethnography: The method. In P.L. Munhall & C.O. Boyd (Eds.), *Nursing research: A qualitative perspective,* 2nd ed. (pp. 237–68). Norwalk: Appleton-Century-Crofts.

Goering, P., Tolomiczenko, G., Sheldon, T., Boydell, K. & Wasylenki, D. (2002). Characteristics of persons who are homeless for the first time. *Psychiatric Services, 53,* 1472–74.

Haldenby, A., Berman, H. & Forchuk, C. (2007). Homelessness and health in adolescents: A critical narrative analysis. *Qualitative Health Research, 17*(9), 1232–44.

Haugland, G., Siegel, C., Hopper, K. & Alexander, M.J. (1997). Mental illness among homeless individuals in a suburban county. *Psychiatric Services, 48*(4), 504–09.

Hecht, L. & Coyle, B. (2001). Elderly homeless: A comparison of older and younger adult emergency shelter seekers in Bakersfield, California. *American Behavioral Scientist, 45*(1), 66–79.

Heckert, U., Andrade, L., Alves, M.J. & Martins, C. (1999). Lifetime prevalence of mental disorders among homeless people in a southeast city in Brazil. *European Archives of Psychiatry Clinical Neuroscience, 249*(3), 150–55.

Hightower, H.C., Hightower, J. & Smith, M.J. (2003). *Out of Sight, Out of Mind: The Plight of Seniors and Homelessness.* New Westminster: Seniors Housing Information Program.

Hyman, I. (2001). *Immigration and health.* Health Canada Working Paper Series, no. 01-05. Ottawa: Health Canada.

Jiwani, Y. (2006). *Discourses of denial: Mediations of race, gender, and violence.* Vancouver/Toronto: UBC Press.

Kemp, P.A., Neale, J. & Robertson, M. (2006). Homelessness among problem drug users: Prevalence, risk factors, and trigger events. *Health and Social Care in the Community, 14*(4), 319–28.

Kidd, S.A. & Davidson, L. (2006). Youth homelessness: A call for partnerships between research and policy. *Canadian Journal of Public Health, 97*(6), 445–47.

Koegel, P., Burnam, M. & Baumohl, J. (1996). The causes of homelessness. In J. Baumohl (Ed.), *Homelessness in America.* 24–33. Phoenix: Oryx.

Lamb, R.L. & Lamb, D. (1990). Factors contributing to homelessness among the chronically and severely mentally ill. *Hospital and Community Psychiatry, 41*, 301–05.

Leininger, M.M. (1985). Ethnography and ethnonursing: Models and modes of qualitative data analysis. In M.M. Leininger (Ed.), *Qualitative research methods in nursing.* 73–117. Orlando: Grune and Stratton.

Martijn, C. & Sharp, L. (2006). Pathways to youth homelessness. *Social Science & Medicine, 62*, 1–12.

National Alliance to End Homelessness. (2007). *Youth homelessness.* Fact checker series. Retrieved June 2008, from www.endhomelessness.org.

National Law Center on Homelessness and Poverty. (2002). *National mental health information* center. Available at mentalhealth.samhsa.gov/cmhs/Homelessness/.

Netto, G. (2006). Vulnerability to homelessness, use of services, and homelessness prevention in Black and minority ethnic communities. *Housing Studies, 21*(4), 581–603.

Noh, S., Beiser, M., Kaspar, V., Hou, F. & Rumens, J. (1999). Perceived racial discrimination, discrimination, and coping: A study of South East Asian refugees in Canada. *Journal of Health and Social Behaviour, 40,* 193–207.

O'Dwyer, B. (1997). Pathways to homelessness: A comparison of gender and schizophrenia in inner-Sydney. *Australian Geographical Studies,* 35(3), 294–307.

Quantz, R.A. (1992). On critical ethnography (with some postmodern considerations). In M.D. LeCompte, W.L. Milroy & J. Preissle (Eds.), *The handbook of qualitative research in education.* 447–505. California: Academic Press Inc.

Reid, S., Berman, H. & Forchuk, C. (2005). Living on the streets in Canada: A feminist narrative study of girls and young women. *Issues in Comprehensive Pediatric Nursing, 28,* 237–56.

Robert, M., Pauze, R. & Fournier, L. (2005). Factors associated with homelessness of adolescents under supervision of the youth protection system. *Journal of Adolescence, 28,* 215–30.

Rosenheck, R. & Lam, J.A. (1997). Individuals and community-level variation in intensity and diversity of service utilization by homeless persons with serious mental illness. *Journal of Nervous and Mental Disorders, 185,* 633–38.

Sev'er, A. (2002). Flight of abused women, plight of Canadian shelters: Another road to homelessness. *Journal of Social Distress and the Homeless,* 11(4), 307–24.

Statistics Canada (2007). Longitudinal survey of immigrants to Canada. Ottawa: Statistics Canada.

Stergiopoulous, V. & Hermann, N. (2003). Old and homeless: A review and survey of older adults who use shelters in an urban setting. *Canadian Journal of Psychiatry,* 48(5), 374–80.

Sullivan, G., Burnam, A. & Koegel, P. (2000). Pathways to homelessness among the mentally ill. *Social Psychiatry and Psychiatric Epidemiology, 35,* 444–50.

Thomas, J. (1993). *Doing critical ethnography. Qualitative research methods,* vol. 26. Newbury Park: Sage Publications.

Thomsen, R.L., Balsløv, K.D., Benjaminsen, S.E. & Petersen, P. (2000). Homeless persons residing in shelters in the county of Funen I. Psychological characteristics and need of treatment. *Ugeskr Laeger,* 162(9), 1205–10.

Tully, C. & Jacobson, S. (1994). Homeless elderly: America's forgotten population. *Journal of Gerontological Social Work,* 22(3–4), 61–81.

Turnbull, J. & Podymow, T. (2002). The health consequences of poverty in Canada. *Canadian Journal of Public Health,* 93(6), 405–406.

Wahl, O. (1999). Mental health consumers' experience of stigma. *Schizophrenia Bulletin,* 25(3), 467–78.

Warren, B.J., Menke, E.M., Clement, J. & Wagner, J. (1992). The mental health of African-American and Caucasian-American women who are homeless. *Journal of Psychosocial Nursing and Mental Health Services, 30*(11), 27–30.

Whitbeck, L.B., Hoyt, D.R. (2000). Abuse, support, depression among homeless and runaway adolescents. *Journal of Health and Social Behaviour, 41*(4), 408–20.

Chapter 15

GAINING GROUND, LOSING GROUND: THE PARADOXES OF RURAL HOMELESSNESS

Cheryl Forchuk, Phyllis Montgomery, Helene Berman, Catherine Ward-Griffin, Rick Csiernik, Carolyne Gorlick, Elsabeth Jensen, and Patrick Riesterer

1. INTRODUCTION

A recent Canada-wide estimate reports that 6 million or 19 percent of Canadians live in rural areas (Statistics Canada, 2008). In contrast to their urban counterparts, rural Canadians have poorer health status, engage in higher economic and lifestyle risk behaviours, attain lower educational levels, and have less socio-economic resources (Canadian Population Health Initiative, 2006). Despite variations among provinces with respect to urban–rural income differences, in 2000, rural annual income was approximately 20 percent less than that of urban populations (Statistics Canada, 2004). People diagnosed with enduring mental illness are a lower income rural subpopulation. Single adults relying on Ontario Disability Support receive "a mere 63 per cent of the poverty line" (Stapleton, 2010). Low income does not cause mental illness, but vulnerable people are at greater risk of "drifting" to even lower levels of the socio-economic strata (Hurst, 2007; Wilton, 2004). Unable to pay for their basic needs such as shelter, these individuals' risk for homelessness increases.

"Degrees of destitution" (Speak, 2004) may not be apparent to outsiders since rurality's density and distance can distort the nature and magnitude of poverty. By association, rural homelessness is also hidden from public and policy decision makers. Living in inadequate accommodations or with violent others, staying temporarily with friends or relatives, and seeking non-local services contributes to the invisibility of rural homelessness in Canada (Burns, Bruce & Marlin, 2003), as well as internationally (Milbourne & Cloke, 2006). Recent Canadian studies seeking to better understand rural homelessness among people with mental illness have reported lack of housing accessibility, adequacy, and affordability as substantive issues (Bruce, 2003; Canadian Institute for Health Information, 2008; Skott-Myhre, Raby & Nikolaou, 2008).

In addition to housing needs, people with mental illness have unique health service needs. However, a review of the international literature on rural mental health found that the rates of psychiatric illness were consistently undetermined (Philo, Parr & Burns, 2003). The combination of lack of continuity of services, inaccessibility, distances to travel, absence of readily available transportation, and attrition of health care professionals exacerbate stress and reduce the abilities of this population to secure adequate income and housing (Canadian Mental Health Association, 2005; Moore & Skaburskis, 2004; Philo et al., 2003). Rural people with mental health issues have needs similar to those of urban-residing consumer-survivors, but integrating mental health and social services in rural areas has been a challenge throughout Canada.

This chapter examines rural homelessness and health services experienced by mental health consumer-survivors, their families, and community mental health workers. The findings contribute to the small body of Canadian research in this area and have the potential to inform efforts to address homelessness among this vulnerable rural population.

2. METHOD

The design is a secondary analysis of data based upon the original CURA on Mental Health and Housing data collected from 2001 to 2006. In addition, focus group data from another study on crisis services (Forchuk et al., 2009) that encompassed rural areas was included to further expand on the CURA data, leading to an additional 20 focus groups during 2006–07. The sample for this secondary analysis included informants who identified themselves as "rural" residents at the time of the interview, or who had previously lived in a rural area. They were not asked to specifically disclose their rural home community. There were five groups of informants: (1) service providers, (2) consumer-survivors, (3) peer support workers, (4) consumer-survivors who are now successfully living in the community and who provided help to other consumer-survivors as they attempt to reintegrate into the community themselves, and (5) "family" members, mostly mothers and fathers of consumer-survivors, though spouses, siblings, and some children also took part in the discussions. Aside from the service providers group, most of the participants came from a lower socio-economic stratum.

The data analysis team consisted of several members of the original study group, along with some additional researchers with interest in and knowledge of rural mental health. Analysis involved reading all of the initial transcripts to find references to rural experiences. Once relevant data were identified, content analysis—a systematic process of coding and grouping qualitative data to identify discernable patterns or themes (DeSanits & Ugarriza, 2000; Hsieh & Shannon, 2005; Morgan, 1993)—was undertaken. This process involved several researchers independently reading the transcripts to code data. More focused codes were then developed as patterns were identified in the data. The code list was continuously revised to accommodate new perspectives and to collapse overlapping groups of data. The focused code list guided the analysis, and more abstract themes evolved from the transcribed data.

3. FINDINGS

Participants described a dialectical theme of gaining and losing ground constituted by a complex interplay of health, place, social, and service processes. Efforts of community integration and, for some, reintegration were necessary for desired health outcomes. Rural attributes, however, challenged clients', families', and community mental health workers' efforts to establish or maintain health and to secure adequate housing. Gaining ground was described as having physical, social, and service supports that enabled participants to live in a preferred, familiar, socially connected, rural setting. In contrast, losing ground referred to having limited choices and opportunities and being viewed by others as "a hick from the sticks," vulnerable and dependent. Participants described gaining and losing ground in the following areas: (1) social ties; (2) mental health and social services; (3) transportation; and (4) relocation.

Social Ties

Participants often described their physical and social geographies in ideal terms: "peaceful," "tranquil," "tight-knit," "full of relaxing recreational options." Rural places provided them with a sense of security and belonging. As one participant stated, "Everyone has their place in the social fabric, even if you're only a second cousin." Receiving or attending to the needs of a rural person diagnosed with some form of mental illness, however, altered participants' perceptions of the value of "close-knit" social connections. Consumer-survivors, families, and service providers spoke about the size of the community, noting that "everybody knew everyone else's business." Consumer-survivors who "fell in with a bad crowd" shared the stress of stigmatization as well as discrimination. Their stress was especially heightened when the conflict involved social service providers. Such strained relationships negatively influenced their abilities to secure supports and services. To cope, some consumer-survivors made the choice to relocate to an urban area. Lack of support and resources often led to homelessness and uncertainty about their future. For example:

> "I couldn't live there. I was ashamed of myself, so I moved to ... I'd say a bigger city, where there were more people. I guess I figured ... I could hide or something. I had a car so I slept in the car so I wouldn't have to pay rent. That way my money would go farther and I was trying to figure out where [I] was going."

Some family members also perceived and experienced social exclusion because of their association and relationship with a mental health consumer-survivor.

Mental Health and Social Services

Numerous factors contributed to the inaccessibility of mental health services in rural areas, including shortages of primary care workers or specialists, insufficient support and service programs, lack of trusting relationships with health care workers, overburdened health care providers, long waiting lists, and lack of transportation to and from services.

Some individuals tried to gain ground by relying on the private sector for mental health services, including counsellors, psychologists, and psychiatrists, when available. However, even these services were limited and the cost of these services was a barrier for many people living with mental illness. Without access to support or services, consumer-survivors were put at risk of relapse. One study participant shared his perception of current services in his rural community:

> "There are no external options. There used to be a private psychiatrist, so if for some reason a person did not qualify for adult mental health services or they were kicked out for whatever reason are ineligible for it, there was at least a private site that you could access and still maintain psychiatric services."

Without many external options, trust in the health care worker's ability was critical. Lack of trust often contributed to their sense of powerlessness. One consumer-survivor explained:

> "The fact that there is a monopoly in the area relating to a psychiatric clinical support, that's not criticism, that's just the way it is.... It's like there is a monopoly on psychiatric services and if that psychiatric service has made a decision on somebody, you know, like any monopoly, you're kinda stuck going, 'Well, now what?'"

The emphasis within rural mental health care services on crisis intervention as opposed to prevention or rehabilitation has fuelled negative outcomes for both mental health consumer-survivors and the system. Since only limited treatment is available, there is an increased likelihood that consumer-survivors and their families will experience crises. Moreover, crisis services also face severe shortages. In some communities, crisis services were available only during typical business hours, and even fewer resources were available on evenings and weekends. While consumer-survivors waited for service, they contacted crisis lines only to get no answer, so they had no option other than to leave messages on answering machines. They often had to wait hours or even days until someone was able to return their call. For those without access to a phone, as was often the case among the homeless or those with limited income, crisis services were not able to return their calls. These consumer-survivors were forced to try again or to seek relief from other services. One study participant reported on the crisis services available in her community:

> "Maybe four days then and if they have a holiday, then they are off the Wednesday and that gives you Thursday, Friday, and Saturday to have your nervous breakdown. I mean, you know, 'cause you have to call crisis on the weekend and who wants to do that? I'm making a joke of it, but it's not funny."

Professional and crisis-line volunteers reported similar concerns; these service providers have all recognized that the system is "very reactive and not proactive."

The structure of current mental health care services, as well as a lack of human resources, contributed to many providers feeling overwhelmed.

Without crisis support, many consumer-survivors lost ground; prolonged crisis often led to a decrease in functioning and eviction became a potential reality. Those who had difficulty accessing crisis services often engaged in risky behaviours and/or found themselves homeless before they could access the services they needed. One consumer stated, "You have to throw a brick through a window to get shelter."

Some individuals tried to gain ground by entering the legal system to access services. Such actions reflect the consumer-survivors' frustration and desperate need for services. If consumer-survivors "can't get the help they need" when they need it, a "vicious circle" develops and consumers end up shuffling between the legal and health care systems. Some professionals believed that if the mental health services were more accessible, consumer-survivors "wouldn't have to resort to violence."

Even when consumer-survivors were able to access crisis services without resorting to criminal or violent behaviour, this process was still perceived as challenging. If a doctor was not available for a psychiatric assessment, the consumer-survivor was required to go to a major city even if he or she did not need a bed. Arriving at crisis services only to be denied services created anger and frustration for the consumer-survivors, their families, and workers. Several people shared stories of being "turned away" after long waits. One mother, who was also a peer support worker, explained her wait with her daughter when she required emergency services for her psychosis:

> "We've had to sit there and wait and wait and wait and then they give her a high dose of some sort of a needle in order to put her to sleep so that she won't cause any more trouble. She still lays there and waits and waits. It has been very, very frustrating when you're trying to be there and be a comfort and a calming influence, and you're just sitting there."

The lack of resources made voluntary admissions very rare. In most cases, consumer-survivors could receive psychiatric care only involuntarily. In many rural areas, being admitted because a person was deemed to be a danger to himself or herself or to others became a precondition for access to any psychiatric services.

Vulnerability to illness placed individuals at serious risk of homelessness. In rural areas, there are far fewer resources to prevent and manage homelessness and few emergency shelters or crisis beds available. Therefore, in search of housing, consumer-survivors moved frequently and were forced to live a nomadic lifestyle. Relocation was necessary as some perceived that they "[wore] out their welcome" and others needed to flee from abuse, creditors, family, the law, or their "own personal demons." Many simply needed access to services.

While they waited anywhere from "five to six years" for housing, consumer-survivors often tried to avoid losing ground by relying on their families' help. Without family and timely housing supports, consumers felt their only choice was to return to unhealthy or unsafe environments. Moving in and out of shelters became the strategy to maintain a sense of safety. Lack of housing and support services contributed to consumer-survivors losing ground as they became "stuck," "hopeless," or "cycled in and out of services." As one person put it:

> "Couch surfing becomes a way of life due to limited housing options, lack of support services, long waiting lists, lack of affordable housing, and low income. Such temporary fixes in order to keep a roof over your head and away from unsafe situations impedes having a life."

Consumer-survivors and their families often perceived that they have no adequate housing options within their community. Many possible accommodations, such as geared-to-income housing or group homes, are often assessed as substandard quality due to disrepair or location in unsafe neighbourhoods. For some individuals with mental health issues, their only choice was to reside in retirement and nursing homes. For places without assertive community treatment (ACT) teams, long-term care far from home was the only option consumer-survivors had for gaining ground unless family members felt they could care for the individual themselves.

Consumer-survivors, families, or workers did not perceive simply increasing the number of available accommodations as an adequate solution. Housing was conceived as a mediator for health. If services are not responsive and sensitive to the consumer-survivors' needs and abilities, securing permanent housing and attaining recovery are unlikely. One mental health worker explained:

> "If we set up housing, a huge apartment building, and said, 'Everybody who's homeless or going to be, come and see us—we've got a place for you.' Within two months, a lot of those people will be homeless again because the cause of their homelessness was never addressed. You have to address the basic problem, and every person is different—why they're homeless."

To address lack of formal services, rural networks designed creative solutions. Local grassroots organizations and informal volunteers provided housing and other services to consumer-survivors. The rural communities represented in this study relied heavily on donations of funding and housing space rather than funded shelters and community agencies. For example, a local church generously provided space for community groups. However, this generosity resulted in scheduling conflicts with other events. In another community, a 24-hour, consumer-survivor-run drop-in-centre offering a few beds and a kitchen provided a valuable resource for individuals at immediate risk of homelessness. Volunteers even opened up their homes as emergency shelters and initiated consumer-survivor groups, providing a place to meet.

Transportation

Transportation was a frequent concern for consumer-survivors, family members, and service providers. Transportation plays a key role in people's ability to gain or lose ground. Transportation was more than a means to get from one place to another; it was an aspect of making and maintaining connections, becoming integrated into communities, and adhering to treatment regimens. It was also a necessary safety strategy for rural women living in abusive situations. Many consumer-survivors wanted to gain ground by becoming involved in support groups. However, without adequate transportation, many lost ground instead. Often people who had a mental illness, but no transportation, became isolated, despondent, and subsequently relapsed. Consumer-survivors and workers often spoke of their frustrations about how much time they had to spend travelling. Longer distances were particularly onerous if consumer-survivors relied on others for transportation or if the weather was poor for driving.

Available transportation was described in terms of "lucky," "too expensive," or "non-reimbursable from Ontario Works and Ontario Disability." Several communities had no public transit available and therefore consumer-survivors had to rely on family, friends, or neighbours. If their situation was perceived as a crisis, they often relied on police services while others resorted to hitchhiking. One individual shared her story about the dangers associated with a lack of transportation:

> "I hitchhiked home [from the hospital] 'cause I don't have any family.… Oh yeah, and it was very scary as an older woman. But the other guy [the driver], he says, 'Don't worry, honey.' He says, 'You come from the hospital?' I said 'Yeah.' … Well, I tell you I was scared even though the man had a cross dangling [from his mirror]. I was still very scared."

Relocation

A number of rural residents and their families reported trying to gain ground by relocating to secure mental health services, housing, or safety. One woman shared her reason for relocation:

> "I, uh, I couldn't, like, abuse was, ran through the house, so I couldn't take it no more. So, I finally stood up for myself and I went and told somebody and I was taken out of the house and sent to another place and then, like, foster homes. And then just kept on running away and doing all that, and then just continued on from there."

Participants regularly discussed the fact that they were faced with the choice of either moving away from home or living without proper access to the services they required. However, relocation for the sake of "a new life" involved additional risks, including isolation and lack of urban preparedness. Unfortunately, these risks often resulted in people losing ground rather than gaining ground.

Often it was a health care worker's recommendation that led individuals to relocate from a rural to an urban community. Many consumer-survivors could be "processed" for either psychiatric services or housing only if they were situated in an urban environment. Many individuals lamented the fact that they had to move. Often families moved with consumer-survivors for support. Although one mother recognized her daughter's need for services, relocation threatened her daughter's quality of life:

> "They want to send [my daughter] to [a city]. I said, 'Over my dead body' because she needs to stay home, she needs her family, friends, church, and community. I'm over 70. I visit her every day or every other day. It's a grave concern, you know, when you have someone who [says] there's no place for her."

Some consumer-survivors were forced to stay in the city because life on the streets had resulted in legal problems. Others were forced to relocate to meet agency requirements, and many individuals relocated to escape abuse. If people decided to relocate, they risked losing the support of their rural community's large, informal network. The anonymity of the city was viewed as both the proverbial blessing and curse. The city presented many opportunities that were unavailable in smaller towns, such as more services, employment, housing, and education. As well, many people relocated from rural communities to urban centres in order to access shelters. While these opportunities could often be extremely beneficial, they could also be very dangerous, especially for people from small towns who were unaware of the realities of shelter life. Participants claimed that shelters house dangerous fellow residents, and are riddled with thieves, violence, and drugs. Many participants who relocated from rural areas expressed their surprise at what they found in the urban centres. Moving in and out of shelters became their strategy for maintaining a sense of safety. Some former rural residents even expressed a preference for living on the streets, where they felt safer than in the shelters, for which they had originally moved to access. Unfortunately, once people moved to the city and took up residence in the shelter system, they were "bounced" from one shelter to another.

4. DISCUSSION

The findings suggest that the inaccessibility of housing and the inadequacy of mental health supports in rural communities undermined people's efforts to improve their health and living conditions. Ensuring that those living in rural communities have better access to health and housing services may not only allow them to remain in their home communities, it may help prevent them from becoming homeless in the first place. As well, given the connection between the lack of access to services and the lack of transportation, mobile services may be an effective solution (Forchuk et al., 2009). Agencies serving rural communities may need to look at creating their own mini public transit systems. For example, providing a hospital van may be one way to simultaneously address service and transportation issues in rural communities. Finally, shifting the responsibility for the administration of social housing back to the province would address the issue of some communities' inability to afford public housing due to their small municipal tax base. Based upon the project's findings, implementing these few changes would likely help rural residents living with mental health issues gain more ground than they lose.

Many consumer-survivors found that they were losing more ground than they were gaining over time. The limited services offered to those with mental health issues tended to focus on crisis rather than on prevention. When mental health crises were left unmanaged, many individuals were unable to handle the situation and often ended up homeless as a result. Further exacerbating the problem was the fact that most rural communities had few, if any, shelters or affordable transport to services available for these individuals to utilize. While the community tried to supplement these supports through volunteerism, the needs of the rural homeless population were far too high for the supply to meet the demand. There simply were not enough volunteers and service providers available within these rural communities to help everyone in need. Those who were unable to access the services they required often moved to the city; however, many of these individuals were unable to adjust to city life and found themselves homeless. Once they moved into urban homeless shelters, they found it very difficult to get out again. Despite consumer-survivors' and their families' attempts to seek help, they often experienced frustration in the face of inaccessible or inadequate services.

However, it would be misleading and unfair to report that all the rural individuals at risk of homelessness were forced to relocate to urban environments due to lack of choices. Individuals in rural areas were not passive victims of forces beyond their control. They utilized many innovative strategies in an effort to stay in their rural communities—to stay home. Families often went to great lengths to keep their loved ones in their rural homes. A number of individuals opened their homes to those in need and became peer support workers. Others resorted to living in tents, makeshift cabins, and abandoned cars. Some hitchhiked from one rural community to another. While they were often forced to move to urban environments, some returned to their rural roots once they regained some degree of stability in their lives. Nevertheless, many former rural residents were uprooted by their experiences with mental illness and the inadequate services available in their rural hometowns.

Gaining ground and losing ground were not exclusive categories. Rather, the homeless people who took part in this study spoke about times during which they felt they were overcoming the challenges of their everyday lives, during which they were gaining ground. At the same time, however, the same individuals spoke about periods of setbacks, frustration with an unsupportive social system, and forced relocation from rural to urban settings. In this respect, they felt they were losing ground. While clearly the participants demonstrated a great deal of strength and resilience in the face of adversity, the balance was heavily tipped toward the very real sense that they were losing more ground than they were gaining.

REFERENCES

Bruce, D. (2003). *Housing needs of low-income people living in rural areas.* Ottawa: Canadian Mortgage and Housing Corporation. Retrieved November 6, 2008, from www03.cmhc-schl.gc.ca/b2c/b2c/init.do?language=en&shop=Z01EN&areaID=0000000123&productID=00000001230000000002.

Burns, A., Bruce, D. & Marlin, A. (2003) *Rural poverty discussion paper. Rural and small town programme.* Retrieved November 6, 2006, from www.rural.gc.ca/researchreports/pov/poverty-pauvrete_e.phtml.

Canadian Institute for Health Information. (2008). *Mental health and homelessness.* Ottawa: Canadian Institute for Health Information. -Retrieved November 6, 2008, from intraspec.ca/mental_health_report_aug22_2007_e.pdf.

Canadian Mental Health Association. (2005). A "house" in the country. *Network Magazine, 21*(1), 19–20.

Canadian Population Health Initiative. (2006). *How healthy are rural Canadians? An assessment of their health status and health determinants.* Ottawa: Public Health Agency of Canada. Retrieved November 6, 2008, from www.phac-aspc.gc.ca/publicat/rural06/pdf/rural_canadians_2006_report_e.pdf.

DeSanits, L. & Ugarriza, D.N. (2000). The concept of theme as used in qualitative nursing research. *Western Journal of Nursing Research, 22,* 351–72.

Forchuk, C., Jensen, E., Martin, M.L. & Csiernik, R. (2009). *Crisis services: A comparative approach to evaluation.* Toronto: Ontario Mental Health Foundation.

Hsieh, H.-F. & Shannon, S.E. (2005). Three approaches to qualitative content analysis. *Qualitative Health Research, 15*(9), 1277–88.

Hurst, C. (2007) *Social inequality: Forms, causes, and consequences.* Boston: Pearson Education Inc.

Milbourne, P. & Cloke, P. (2006). *International perspectives on rural homelessness.* London: Routledge.

Moore, E. & Skaburskis, A. (2004). Canada's increasing housing affordability burdens. *Housing Studies, 19*(3), 395–413.

Morgan, D.L. (1993). Qualitative content analysis: A guide to paths not taken. *Qualitative Health Research, 3*(1), 112–21.

Philo, C., Parr, H. & Burns, N. (2003). Rural madness: A geographical reading and critique of the rural mental health literature. *Journal of Rural Studies, 19,* 259–81.

Skott-Myhre, H., Raby, R. & Nikolaou, J (2008). Towards a delivery system of services for rural homeless youth: A literature review and case study. *Child Youth Care Forum 37,* 87–102.

Speak, S. (2004). Degrees of destitution: A typology of homelessness in developing countries. *Housing Studies, 19*(3), 465–82.

Statistics Canada. (2004). Study: Rural–urban income gap. *The Daily.* Retrieved November 6, 2008 from www.statcan.ca/Daily/English/041223/d041223b.htm.

Statistics Canada. (2008). Study: Canada's rural demography. *The Daily.* Retrieved November 6, 2008, from www.statcan.ca/Daily/English/081104/d081104a.htm.

Stapleton, J. (2010). With the recent increase in Ontario's minimum wage the gap between the welfare rate is as wide as it was during the Depression. *The Mark*. Retrieved October 26, 2010, from www.themarknews.com/articles/1240-backtoscratch.

Wilton, R. (2004). Putting policy into practice? Poverty and people with serious mental illness. *Social Science and Medicine, 58*, 25–39.

Chapter 16

EXPLORING DIFFERENCES BETWEEN COMMUNITY-BASED WOMEN AND MEN WITH A HISTORY OF MENTAL ILLNESS

Cheryl Forchuk, Elsabeth Jensen, Rick Csiernik, Catherine Ward-Griffin, Susan L. Ray, Phyllis Montgomery, and Linda Wan

1. INTRODUCTION

Historically, the mental health care system operated as if people with mental illness were a genderless group with uniform needs. In 1981, Test and Berlin wrote that "[t]here appears to be a pervasive lack of research, thought, or sensitivity to gender-related issues" (1981: 136) in relation to people living with chronic mental illness. During the past two decades, clinicians and researchers have increasingly become aware that being male or female influences a person's stress responsiveness, symptom presentation, course of illness, treatment response, and access to and use of mental health services (Kawa et al., 2005; Kornstein & Clayton, 2002; Lubotsky Levin, Blanch & Jennings, 1998; Test, Burke & Wallisch, 1990; Young, Korszun & Altemus, 2002).

Sex and gender are distinct concepts. Sex refers to biological characteristics, such as hormones, pharmacokinetics, and neuroendocrine and neurotransmitter pathways, while gender encompasses the socially constructed roles and relationships that society attributes to being male or female (Health Canada, 2003). These terms, however, are often confused with each other and used inappropriately in mental health research, contributing to erroneous statements about gender differences in mental illness (Nasser, Walders & Jenkins, 2002). The mental health status of women and men involves more than just biology; it includes gender attitudes, behaviours, and socio-cultural roles and relationships, especially in view of expanding community mental health services. Gender/sex-based sensitive health research investigates the manner in which sex interacts with gender to create health and living conditions. It also examines problems that are more unique, prevalent, and serious, or for which there are distinct risk factors for women than for men (Health Canada, 2003). There is limited research relating to sex and gender and its effects on health, particularly in the field of community mental health. Among the most distinct differences are that women are twice as likely to have a diagnosed mood disorder and are more likely to suffer depressive episodes (Scheibe et al., 2003; Steiner, Dunn & Born, 2003); men with schizophrenia are more likely to commit suicide and stay longer in a psychiatric institution (Brunette & Drake, 1998; Castle, McGrath & Kulkarni, 2000; Seeman & Fitzgerald, 2000); while women with co-current disorders are at greater risk for secondary health problems like sexually transmitted diseases (RachBeisel, Scott & Dixon, 1999). Therefore, it is essential to take sex and gender into account when generating meaningful knowledge that enhances the health of both women and men.

Due to these differences in relation to mental illness, it is not surprising that research also suggests there is a relationship between sex/gender and outpatient mental health service use (Rhodes et al., 2002; Yaeger et al., 2006). While much research has been conducted to uncover sex/gender differences in individuals with mental illnesses, several authors (Ad Hoc Working Group on Women, Mental Health, Mental Illness, and Addictions, 2006; Freeman, Arnold & McElroy, 2002; Lubotsky et al., 1998; Women's Issues in Mental Health Task Force, 1996; World Health Organization, 2000) suggest that even more research is needed to fully understand differences with respect to risk factors and to ensure that mental health programs adequately and effectively cater to both men's and women's unique needs.

To date, there is a limited amount of research relating specifically to sex and gender and its effects on health, particularly in community mental health. As well, little research has been conducted on gender or sex differences among Canadians with mental illnesses, particularly Canadians within the community rather than in an institution. To strengthen policies and services to better meet men and women's needs, gender- and sex-based analyses are critical (Health Canada, 2003). Thus, this chapter aims to provide additional information pertaining to the differences and the similarities between women and men who are experiencing or who have survived mood, psychotic, and/or psychoactive substance-use disorders. This secondary analysis looked to corroborate previous research on gender/sex differences and to discover any other differences that may be present specifically between community-based Canadian men and women with mental illness.

2. METHOD

Secondary analysis was undertaken of data collected through five consecutive years (2001–06) from the CURA study on Mental Health and Housing. The Research Ethics Board at the University of Western Ontario reviewed the study proposal and gave ethics approval (Review ethics number 03896E).

In the primary study, the total interview sample size was 1,503 community clients. Of these, the data reflects 887 separate individuals who completed quantitative questionnaires during the five-year study period. All of them were located in London, Ontario, and its catchment area. All participants had at least a one-year history of mental illness, were 16 years of age or older, and provided informed consent. Some participants were included in more than one year of the study; however, if repeated participants were not found, they were replaced with new participants of the same sex and housing arrangement. All participants who took part in the study were offered the chance to participate in the following year. The samples were stratified by sex (female or male) and housing type (homeless shelter, group living, independent living). All participants received an honorarium of $20 for each data collection session. The in-depth quantitative interviews included demographic utilization of current health and social services, housing preferences, life satisfaction, income history, and severity of mental illness. Pearson chi-square analyses were performed on all categorical variables, while independent sample t-tests (two-tailed) were done on all continuous variables. Other analyses that were done were frequencies, means, and standard deviations. A significant level of alpha .05 was used to determine statistical significance. All analyses were carried out in *Statistical Analysis: Statistical Package for the Social Sciences Version 14.0*. If an item was left blank, it was dropped from the analysis.

3. RESULTS

Sample

Over the five years of data collection, the women's average age ranged from 42.2 to 43.6, while the men's average age ranged from 40.2 to 45.2. The average age of onset of a mental illness for both genders was in the low twenties. Women's average onset ranged from 21.2 to 22.6, whereas men's ranged from 20.6 to 23.6. Thus, there were no significant differences in these variables (Table 16.1).

Table 16.1: Average Age and Average Age of Onset of a Mental Illness

	Year 1	Year 2	Year 3	Year 4	Year 5
Average age	41.21	40.96	43.26	43.17	43.9
Average age: Males	40.21	41.32	42.96	45.2	44.73
Average age: Females	42.2	42.97	43.57	43.17	42.94
Average age of onset	21.24	22.7	22.4	21.21	22.85
Age onset: Males	20.61	22.67	22.2	21.32	23.6
Age onset: Females	21.91	21.66	22.6	21.21	21.92

Table 16.2: Percentage of Highest Level of Education (CCAR) among Women and Men

	2001		2002		2003		2004		2005	
	Male	Female	Male	Female	Male	Female	Male	Female	Male	Female
No formal schooling	0.7	0	0.7	1.3	2	0	0	0	0.5	0
Elementary school or less	10	14.7	7.4	12	12.8	12.8	14.9	12.4	10.4	13.7
Some high school	41.3	37.3	39.9	37.3	38.9	33.1	29.2	31.9	34.6	35.3
Completed high school	20	24.7	20.9	22	23.5	23.6	23	24.7	25.3	24.8
Some college or university	17.3	7.3	13.5	8.7	10.7	9.5	29.2	31	11.5	9.2
Completed college/university	9.3	14	14.9	16.7	11.4	18.2	0	0.9	17.6	16.3
Other	2	1.3	2.7	2	0.7	2.7	1.9	0.9	0	7
χ^2	27.309		3.97		7.96		2.451		3.328	

Note: No significant differences among all five years.

Demographics

The demographic characteristics were stable from year to year. In the years 2001–04, more women than men claimed to have completed high school and college or university. However, there were no significant differences in education status between women and men across all five years of data collection (Table 16.2).

For marital status, more men than women were single, while more women were married or separated. Significant differences for the single/never married category between men and women were found in 2001, 2003, 2004, and 2005 (Table 16.3).

Table 16.3: Percentage of Marital Status (CCAR) among Women and Men

	2001*		2002		2003*		2004**		2005***	
	Male	Female	Male	Female	Male	Female	Male	Female	Male	Female
Single/never married	78	50.7	65.8	62.3	72.2	47	75.2	51.3	68.1	52.6
Married	3.3	6	2.7	6	2.6	6	2.6	5.3	3.8	8.4
Separated	4.7	14	10.1	11.3	6.6	17.4	9.2	15.9	7.1	12.3
Divorced	21.3	12.7	18.1	16.6	17.2	20.8	11.1	20.4	17	22.7
Widowed	1.3	8	3.4	4	1.3	8.7	2	7.1	3.8	3.9
χ^2	27.309		2.286		26.024		17.228		10	

* Significant difference at $p < .001$. ** Significant difference at $p < .01$. *** Significant difference at $p < .05$.

Psychiatric Diagnoses/History

More women identified a mood disorder as their primary psychiatric diagnosis whereas more men identified schizophrenia or a substance-related disorder as their primary psychiatric diagnosis. More women than men reported they had been diagnosed with post-traumatic stress disorder (PTSD). Therefore, significant differences exist between women and men across the first four years, 2001, 2002, 2003, and 2004 (Table 16.4).

However, inconsistent results were obtained regarding admissions to a provincial psychiatric hospital. In some years, men had a higher average number of admissions than women, while in other years the opposite was true. Significant sex differences are present only in 2002.[1] For all years except 2002 and 2003, men had a higher average number of admissions to a general psychiatric ward. This number of admissions was significantly different between women and men for 2003.[2] In some years, more women than men were admitted to a general hospital, while in other years more men than women had admissions to a general hospital. Thus, no overall significant differences between men and women were found.

Table 16.4: Percentage of Primary Psychiatric Diagnosis (CCAR) among Women and Men

	2001		2002		2003*		2004**		2005	
	Male	Female	Male	Female	Male	Female	Male	Female	Male	Female
Developmental handicap	2.7	4	2	3.3	1.3	1.3	2	1	0.5	0.6
Disorder of childhood/adolescence	2	2.7	2	1.3	1.3	1.3	2	1	0	0.6
Substance-related disorder	0.7	0	0.7	0	0	0	0	0	2.2	0.6
Schizophrenia	50	34.7	53	35.1	49.7	35.6	44.3	35.2	40.7	26.6
Mood disorder	27.3	32	24.8	33.1	27.2	39.6	32.9	28.6	34.1	40.9
Anxiety disorder	6	3.3	4	4	4	2.7	5.4	5.7	6.6	6.5
Organic disorder	0	1.3	0	0	0	0	0	0	0	0
Personality disorder	0.7	3.3	2.7	2.6	2	5.4	2.7	5.7	3.3	3.2
Other	2	2	0	0.7	4.6	1.3	0	2.9	3.3	4.5
Unknown	7.3	8.7	9.4	9.3	9.3	5.4	10.1	13.3	8.8	11
PTSD	1.3	8	1.3	10.6	0.7	7.4	0.7	6.7	0.5	5.2
χ^2	19.378		22.593		22.429		15.807		15.879	

* Significant difference at $p < .01$.   ** Significant difference at $p < .05$.

Only in 2002 was there a statistical difference related to addiction. The significant difference between women and men found was about whether or not they were dependent on psychoactive drugs.[3] In all five years more men claimed to be dependent on a psychoactive drug. Men scoring 2 or higher on the substance abuse rating had a consistent higher mean score of approximately 3 in comparison to women. A score of 2 to 3 indicates occasional or mild functioning difficulties due to substance abuse and a weak control with respect to one or more substances. Significant sex differences existed from 2001–04[4] (see also Chapter 17).

Levels of Functioning

No differences in interpersonal, societal role, and physical domains of functioning were observed. Nevertheless, significant sex differences did exist for areas of functioning in cognition, daily care, and current overall level of functioning. In 2002,

2004, and 2005 men had a higher average score than women for level of cognitive functioning. Significant differences were revealed only in 2002.[5] The average score for level of functioning for daily care was similar between women and men, ranging from 5.4 to 5.8. Significant sex differences were reported only in 2005.[6]

Personal Strengths and Resources

In terms of current overall strengths and resources, women's average score ranged from 4.7 to 5.1, while the men's range was greater: 4.9 to 5.3. The difference across the five years between sexes was not significant. Results related to social support showed that men had fewer support people in their lives than women. Mothers and friends were the most common primary support people for both sexes. Significant differences were evident only in 2003 as to whether support people were present or not: $\chi^2(1, 300) = 5.33, p < .05$. There were also significant differences between sexes in who the primary support person was in three years of the study (2001, 2004, and 2005), with women more likely to have a partner as their support person.[7]

Severity of Illness

Statistical analysis indicated that women had a higher average score for overall degree of problem severity. Women had a mean score ranging from 3.9 to 4.4, while men had a mean score ranging from 4.9 to 5.3. A score of 4 to 5 means moderately high to average overall level of functioning as most people of the same age, sex, and subculture. However, this was not statistically significant across the five years.

Housing

There were significant differences between women and men who were housed and homeless[8] throughout all five years of the study.

4. DISCUSSION

The differences found between women and men with respect to diagnoses in such areas as mood disorder and schizophrenia are consistent with other studies (Allan & Martin, 2004; Anthony, Warner & Kessler, 1994; Diaz-Granados & Stewart, 2006; Kirkbride et al., 2006; Scheibe, et al, 2003; Steiner, Dunn & Born, 2003; Thorup et al., 2007; Weissman & Klerman, 1977; Weissman et al., 1984). Corroborating previous Canadian research (Rhodes et al., 2002), this study found that men were more likely to have substance abuse issues correlating with their mental health issues. A particularly important finding was that men were more dependent than women on psychoactive drugs in all five years of the study. However, most importantly, this finding suggests it is essential that Canadian service providers pay particularly close attention to substance abuse issues when treating men with a history of mental illness (Kimberly & Osmond, 2003).

As well, this study found that women are more likely to suffer from post-traumatic stress disorder, which reiterates previous research suggesting that women with mental illness are more likely than men to have a history of abuse and/or childhood trauma (Becker et al., 2005; Calvete & Cardenoso, 2005; Gearon & Rachbeisel, 2002). Histories of trauma among homeless women suggest the importance of women-only shelters for safety and privacy. Studies have illustrated that social support reduces the potential harmful impact of trauma and offers a moderate reduction in PTSD symptomology (Bal et al., 2005; Brewin, Andrews & Valentine, 2000; Ozer et al., 2003). Specialized services enhancing social support specifically for women with PTSD are needed to mediate trauma's harmful effects. As well, further research is needed to examine how homelessness increases women's exposure to trauma. For example, crowded shelters, substandard housing, and lack of personal safety, as well as access to specialized programs, need to be assessed for their potential impact on the incidence of PTSD among women and children.

This study's finding that more women than men are coupled is also supported by other studies (Test et al., 1990; Brunette & Drake, 1998). Overall, this study's results suggested that more women than men had social support people. Findings in 2001, 2004, and 2005 revealed significant differences between who men and women identified as their primary support person. Relational skills are an important part of being a member of a human community. Lack of relational skills can prevent individuals from finding and maintaining suitable housing that meets their needs. Health care professionals need to be sensitive to this population's need for support in developing relational skills and building social circles. Men are more likely to need support in building interpersonal skills in order to develop adequate social support systems, so specialized treatment within the community catering specifically to this population is needed.

One of this study's most important findings was a correlation between sex and homelessness. Previous gender analysis research has shown that women without housing will form relationships with men to avoid being in a shelter, although these relationships may be abusive (Bridgman, 2003; Novac, Brown & Bourbonnais, 1996). Passaro (1996) suggests that homelessness and gender stereotypes intersect to perpetuate a pattern of women learning to work through the system by appearing docile, compliant, and worthy in order to spend less time being homeless. Even though women had a higher, though not statistically significant, average score for overall degree of problem severity, and even though men scored higher in cognitive, daily care, and current overall level of functioning, women were still more likely than men to be housed and have a stronger support system. Men are generally more likely than women to be homeless (Usall et al., 2001), and this sample indicates that this general finding is also applicable to Canada's population of individuals with mental illness. Strategies specifically targeting men with mental illness are necessary to prevent homelessness for this population. Other research (Goldfinger et al., 1999; Shern et al., 1997) indicates having proper support can help prevent homelessness in people with mental health issues. However, more research must still be conducted to explore whether women's stronger support systems have contributed to the fact that they are more likely to remain housed.

As well, regardless of the differences and similarities between sexes, the large number of homeless individuals with mental illnesses is indicative of an underlying issue. According to the data, poverty and the lack of affordable housing for the population of community-based consumers of psychiatric services is a substantial problem in need of immediate attention. The fact that this study found men with mental illness consistently had less social support and were much more likely to be homeless cannot be ignored. It indicates there is a strong need for services catering specifically to men with mental illness to ensure that they receive enough social and housing support. Social support levels were also low overall, emphasizing the importance of assessing, augmenting, and creating specialized social support approaches for both men and women, including suitable levels of supportive housing.

Many of the findings were inconsistent from year to year. For example, there were no consistent results found relating to average mean scores of the various areas of level of functioning. In some years, women obtained a higher average score than men and vice versa. There were also year-to-year differences related to use of various services. This variation from year to year illustrates the importance of looking at utilization over several years rather than at a single cross-sectional sample.

Addressing questions through secondary analysis creates limitations in any study. Standard limitations include the following: the instruments may not be the best for capturing the phenomenon of interest; sources of error in the design and implementation of the original study may not be known; and any existing bias from the original study is inherited in a secondary analysis (Polit-O'Hara & Hungler, 1991). For this secondary analysis, however, these limitations were minimized by confidence in the instruments and because the majority of the authors also participated in the primary investigation. Although this study revealed some differences between Canadian men and women, more research is still needed to better understand the influence of sex and gender on mental health. As the identification of health advantage and health risk factors are influenced by social environments, researchers need to look at how social networks of men and women with a history of mental illness can be examined through qualitative methods such as in-depth interviews and focus groups.

In this study, new enrolments occurred each year and some participants repeated the interviewing process from year to year. Consequently, approximately half of the sample was consistent from year to year, while the other half changed. Due to repeated community sampling and the group's transient nature, we reported separate cross-sectional samples. This also has the advantage of seeing which findings are consistent over time.

5. CONCLUSION

This study's examination of differences between Canadian men and women with mental illness revealed some findings that are consistent with the previous literature: women are more likely to have a mood disorder and experience PTSD; men are more likely to experience schizophrenia and addiction; and men are more likely to be homeless and living alone. Some findings, such as use of services, varied from year to year. This highlights the need to look at these issues longitudinally rather than simply cross-sectionally. Although affordable and safe housing seems to be an obvious intervention, it will not be sufficient without a better understanding of how best to support the unique needs of women and men to help them maintain their functioning and quality of life. Since this study's findings corroborate other research and suggest that sex differences are also prevalent in Canadians with mental illnesses, it is essential to conduct more research so that health communities can adjust their treatments and services to properly meet men and women's separate mental health needs. Narrowly viewed, these findings address the interrelationships between attributes of individual mental illness and homelessness. From a wider social lens, however, findings suggest a pattern of structural violence, lack of a safety net, and poverty that lead to the oppression of this population.

NOTES

1. $t(150) = -2.49$, $SEM = .016$, $p < .01$
2. , $t(293) = -1.023$, $SEM = .020$, $p < .05$ and 2005, $t(250) = 1.326$, $SEM = 0.016$, $p < .01$

3. $\chi^2(1, 300) = 8.711, p < .01$
4. 2001 $(t(186) = 3.99, SEM = .139, p < .001)$; 2002 $(t(194) = 3.05, SEM = .140, p < .01)$; 2003 $(t(195) = 3.92, SEM = .161, p < .001)$, and 2004 $(t(197) = 2.85, SEM = .151, p < .01)$
5. $t(296) = 2.27, SEM = .160, p < .05$, and 2003, $t(288) = -1.57, SEM = .161, p < .05$
6. $t(301) = .475, SEM = .097, p < .05$
7. 2001, $\chi^2(15, 300) = 25.35, p < .05$; 2004, $\chi^2(14, 267) = 35.17, p < .01$, and 2005, $\chi^2(12, 209) = 27.69, p < .01$,
8. 2001, $\chi^2(1, 300) = 11.35, p < .01$; 2002, $\chi^2(1, 300) = 7.54, p < .01$); 2003, $\chi^2(1, 300) = 7.17, p < .01$; and 2004, $\chi^2(1, 300) = 23.33, p < .001$.

REFERENCES

Ad Hoc Working Group on Women, Mental Health, Mental Illness, and Addictions. (2006). *Women, mental health, and mental illness and addiction in Canada: An overview.* Canadian Women's Health Network. Retrieved December 4, 2006, from www.cwhn.ca.

Allan, R. & Martin, C.R. (2004). Are there gender differences in affective disturbance in schizophrenia? *Clinical Effectiveness in Nursing, 8,* 140–42.

Anthony, J.C., Warner, L.A. & Kessler, R.C. (1994). Comparative epidemiology of dependence on tobacco, alcohol, controlled substances, and inhalants: Basic findings from the National Comorbidity Survey. *Experimental and Clinical Psychopharmacology,* 2(3), 244–68.

Bal, S., De Bourdeaudhuij, I., Crombez, G. & Van Oost, P. (2005). Predictors of trauma symptomatology in sexually abused adolescents: A 6-month follow-up study. *Journal of Interpersonal Violence,* 20(11), 1390–1405.

Becker, M.A., Noether, C.D., Larson, M.J., Gatz, M., Brown, V. & Hechman, J. (2005). Characteristics of women engaged in treatment for trauma and co-occurring disorders: Findings from a national multisite study. *Journal of Community Psychology,* 33(4), 429–43.

Brewin, C.R., Andrews, B. & Valentine, J.D. (2000). Meta-analysis of risk factors for posttraumatic stress disorder in trauma-exposed adults. *Journal of Consulting and Clinical Psychology,* 68(5), 748–66.

Bridgman, R. (2003). *Safe haven: The story of a shelter for homeless women.* Toronto: University of Toronto Press.

Brunette, M. & Drake, R.E. (1998). Gender differences in homeless persons with schizophrenia and substance abuse. *Community Mental Health Journal,* 34(6), 627–42.

Calvete, E. & Cardenoso, O. (2005). Gender differences in cognitive vulnerability to depression and behaviour problems in adolescents. *Journal of Abnormal Child Psychology, 33*(2), 179–92.

Castle, D.J., McGrath, J. & Kulkarni, J. (2000). *Women and schizophrenia.* Cambridge: Cambridge University Press.

Diaz-Granados, N. & Stewart, D.E. (2006). *A literature review on depression among women: Focusing on Ontario.* Toronto: University Health Network Women's Health Program.

Duran, B., Malcoe, L.H., Sanders, M., Waitzkin, H., Skipper, B. & Yager, J. (2004). Child maltreatment prevalence and mental disorders outcomes among American Indian women in primary care. *Child Abuse & Neglect, 28*(2), 131–45.

Freeman, M.P., Arnold, L.M. & McElroy, S.L. (2002). Bipolar Disorder. In S.M. Kornstein & A.H. Clayton (Eds.), *Women's mental health: A comprehensive textbook* (pp. 166–81). New York: The Guilford Press.

Gearon, J.S. & Rachbeisel, J.A. (2002). Schizophrenia. In S.G. Kornstein & A.H. Clayton (Eds.), *Women's mental health: A comprehensive textbook* (pp. 182–94). New York: The Guilford Press.

Goldfinger, S.M., Schutt, R.K., Tolomiczenko, G.S., Seidman, L., Penk, W.E., Turner, W. & Caplan, B. (1999). Housing placement and subsequent days homeless among formerly homeless adults with mental illness. *Psychiatric Services, 50*(5), 674–79.

Health Canada. (2003). *Exploring concepts of gender and health.* Ottawa: Health Canada.

Kawa, I., Carter, J.D., Joyce, P.R., Doughty, C.J., Frampton, C.M., Wells, J.E., Walsh, A.E.S. & Olds, R.J. (2005). Gender differences in bipolar disorder: Age of onset, course, comorbidity, and symptom presentation. *Bipolar Disorders, 7,* 119–25.

Kendall-Tackett, K. (2002). The health effects of childhood abuse: Four pathways by which abuse can influence health. *Child Abuse and Neglect, 6–7,* 715–30.

Kimberly, D. & Osmond, M. (2003). Concurrent disorders and social work intervention. In R. Csiernik & W.S. Rowe (Eds.), *Responding to the oppression of addiction.* 227–248. Toronto: Canadian Scholars' Press Inc.

Kirkbride, J.B., Fearon, P., Morgan, C., Dazzan, P., Morgan, K., Tarrant, J., et al. (2006). Heterogeneity in incidence rates of schizophrenia and other psychotic syndromes: Findings from the 3-center ÆSOP study. *Archives of General Psychiatry 63*(3), 250–58.

Kornstein, S.M. & Clayton, A.H. (2002). *Women's mental health: A comprehensive textbook.* New York: The Guilford Press.

Lubotsky Levin, B., Blanch, A.K. & Jennings, A. (1998). *Women's mental health services: A public health perspective.* Thousand Oaks: Sage Publications, Inc.

Nasser, E.H., Walders, N. & Jenkins, H.J. (2002). The experience of schizophrenia: What's gender got to do with it? A critical review of the current status of research on schizophrenia. *Schizophrenia Bulletin, 28*(2), 351–62.

Novac, S., Brown, J. & Bourbonnais, C. (1996). *No room of her own: A literature review on women and homelessness.* Ottawa: Canada Mortgage and Housing Corporation.

Ozer, E.J., Best, S.R., Lipsey, T.L. & Weiss, D.S. (2003). Predictors of posttraumatic stress disorder and symptoms in adults: A meta-analysis. *Psychological Bulletin,* 129(1), 52–73.

Passaro, Joanne. 1996. *The unequal homeless: Men on the streets, women in their place.* New York: Routledge.

Polit-O'Hara, D. & Hungler, B.P. (1991). *Nursing research: Principles and methods.* Baltimore, Maryland: Lippincott, Williams & Wilkins Publisher.

Rachbeisel, J., Scott, J. & Dixon, L. (1999). Co-occurring severe mental illness and substance use disorders: A review of recent research. *Psychiatric Services,* 50(11), 1427–34.

Rhodes, A.E., Goering, P.N., To, T. & Williams, J.I. (2002). Gender and outpatient mental health service use. *Social Science & Medicine,* 54(2002), 1–10.

Scheibe, S., Preuschhof, C; Bagby, R. (2003). Are there gender differences in major depression and its response to antidepressants? *Journal of Affective Disorders,* 75C31, 223–235.

Seeman, M.V. & Fitzgerald, P. (2000) Women and schizophrenia: Clinical aspects. In D.J. Castle, J. McGrath & J. Kulkarni (Eds.), *Women and schizophrenia.* 35–50. Cambridge: Cambridge University Press.

Shern, D.L., Felton, C.J., Hough, R.L., Lehman, A.F., Goldfinger, S., Valencia, E., Dennis, D., Straw, R. & Wood, P.A. (1997). Housing outcomes for homeless adults with mental illness: Results from the second-round McKinney program. *Psychiatric Services,* 48, 239–41.

Simpson, T.L. (2003). Childhood sexual abuse, PTSD, and the functional roles of alcohol use among women drinkers. *Substance Use and Misuse,* 38(2), 249–70.

Steiner, M., Dunn, E. & Born, L. (2003). Hormones and mood: From menarche to menopause and beyond. *Journal of Affective Disorders,* 74(1), 67–83.

Test, M.A. & Berlin, S.B. (1981). Issues of special concern to chronically mentally ill women. *Professional Psychology,* 12(1), 136–45.

Test, M.A., Burke, S.S. & Wallisch, L.S. (1990). Gender differences of young adults with schizophrenia disorders in community care. *Schizophrenia Bulletin,* 16(2), 331–44.

Thorup, A., Waltoft, B.M., Pedersen, C.B., Mortensen, P.B. & Nordentoft, M. (2007). Young males have a higher risk of developing schizophrenia: A Danish register study. *Psychological Medicine,* 37(4), 479–84.

Twamley, E.W., Jeste, D.V. & Lehman, A.F. (2003). Vocational rehabilitation in schizophrenia and other psychotic disorders: A literature review and meta-analysis of randomized controlled trials. *Journal of Nervous and Mental Disease,* 191(8), 515–23.

Usall, J., Araya, S., Ochoa, S., Busquets, E., Gost, A. & Marquez, M. (2001). Gender differences in a sample of schizophrenic outpatients. *Comprehensive Psychiatry, 42*(4), 301–05.

Usall, J., Ochoa, S., Araya, S., Marquez, A. & NEDES Group. (2003). Gender difference and outcome in schizophrenia: A 2-year follow-up in a large community sample. *European Psychiatry, 18*(2003), 282–84.

Weissman, M.M. & Klerman, G.L. (1977). Sex differences and the epidemiology of depression. *Archives of General Psychiatry, 34*(1), 98–111.

Weissman, M.M., Leaf, P.J., Holzer, C.E., Myers, J.K. & Tischler, G.L. (1984). The epidemiology of depression: An update on sex differences in rates. *Journal of Affective Disorders, 7*(3–4), 179–88.

Women's Issues in Mental Health Task Force. (1996). *Policy consultation document respecting women's issues in mental health.* Toronto: Canadian Mental Health Association, Ontario Division.

World Health Organization. (2000). *Women's mental health: An evidenced-based review.* Retrieved May 8, 2006, from whqlibdoc.who.int/hq/2000/WHO_MSD_ MDP_ 00.1.pdf.

Yaeger, D., Himmelfarb, N., Cammack, A. & Mintz, J. (2006). DSM-IV diagnosed posttraumatic stress disorder in women veterans with and without military sexual trauma. *Journal of General Internal Medicine, 21*(s3), S65–S69.

Young, E.A., Korszun, A. & Altemus, M. (2002). Sex differences in neuroendocrine and neurotransmitter systems. In S.G. Kornstein & A.H. Clayton (Eds.), *Women's mental health: A comprehensive textbook* (pp. 3–30). New York: The Guilford Press.

Chapter 17

UPROOTED AND DISPLACED: A CRITICAL NARRATIVE STUDY OF HOMELESS, ABORIGINAL, AND NEWCOMER GIRLS IN CANADA

Helene Berman, Gloria Alvernaz Mulcahy, Cheryl Forchuk, Kathy Edmunds, Amy Haldenby, and Raquel Lopez

1. INTRODUCTION

Uprooting and displacement are a common part of everyday life for millions of girls throughout the world. Canadians typically understand such experiences as occurring "elsewhere," in nations where war, human rights abuses, and civil unrest prevail. As a result, little attention has been paid to uprooting and displacement among those who reside within Canada. In recent years, researchers have examined the importance of community, belonging, and citizenship in the lives of girls and young women in Canada (Berman & Jiwani, 2002; Downe, 2006; Gonick, 2003; Haldenby, Berman & Forchuk, 2007; Khanlou et al., 2002; Lee, 2006). However, this body of work remains sparse, and little scholarly inquiry has been undertaken to explore the meaning of uprooting and displacement in girls' lives, including how the experience of these events and the meanings attached to them have influenced girls' sense of well-being. This chapter examines uprooting and displacement among three groups of girls and young women in Canada who have been displaced from their homes, families, countries, and/or communities: (1) immigrant and refugee girls; (2) homeless girls; and (3) Aboriginal girls. Findings from a recent study will be presented, with particular attention to the intersections of race, space, gender, and class. Strategies that girls and young women use to overcome, resist, and challenge the relational disconnection from peers, family members, school, and community, which typically accompany uprooting, will be examined. Lastly, the way in which experiences of uprootedness are commonly shaped by violence in the lives of girls and young women will be considered.

2. BACKGROUND AND SIGNIFICANCE

Apfelbaum (2000) has stated that we live in an "era of uprooting." During the last decade, global conflict, religious, ethnic and racial persecution, tyranny, war, and economic uncertainty have all combined to leave no continent without immigrants and refugees. Although numbers vary, and depend on the source and one's definition, it is clear that large portions of humanity are on the move. To put this phenomenon into perspective, when the United Nations High Commissioner for Refugees was first established in 1951, there were 1.5 million refugees; today it is estimated that there are close to 32 million refugees, displaced people, and asylum seekers worldwide (UNHCR, 2008). Current Canadian policy is to admit approximately 220,000 newcomers each year. About 24 percent of these are under the age of 16, and approximately one in 10 girls is under 15 years of age (Berman & Jiwani, 2008).

Much of the discourse concerning uprooting and displacement has centred on movement from one country to another. However, uprooting from homes and/ or communities is also a reality for many within Canada's borders, particularly among homeless girls and Aboriginal girls. Although the experiences of these groups differ in many respects, all have endured the loss of what they have known as "home." For some, this loss is accompanied by shattered or culturally eradicated communities. While it would seem plausible that dislocation has adverse consequences for girls, little research has been conducted to either confirm or refute this assertion. Moreover, little is understood about the intersecting influences of uprooting, emotional well-being, and other forms of oppression, including poverty, violence, and racism, in girls' lives.

3. CONCEPTUALIZING UPROOTEDNESS

In one of the most insightful writings related to uprooting and displacement, Malkki (1995) examined the issue of displacement and exile among Hutu refugees who fled "selective genocide" in Burundi in 1972. In this "ethnography of displacement," Malkki challenged the "a priori" assumption that "the refugee experience" is, by necessity, accompanied by loss of culture, identity, and habits. As common notions of culture are biased "toward rooting rather than travel" (Clifford, 1988: 338), it is generally assumed that violated, broken roots are tantamount to a fractured cultural identity, a "damaged" nationality, and are incongruous with the health of individuals, families, and communities. The "territorializing, grounding metaphors of identity—roots, soil, trees, seeds—are replaced, or 'washed away', in tides, streams, rivers, waves, and so forth" (Malkki, 1995: 15). These fluid names for the uprooted convey and reinforce widespread understandings about home and homeland, identity and nationality. Uprootedness, from this perspective, may be understood as one of the most profound of human tragedies. Malkki, however, insists that we look beyond the notion of displacement solely as a human tragedy to gain insight into the lived meanings that displacement and uprooting have for particular groups. With respect to the refugees from Burundi who were the focus of Malkki's research, the experience of exile did not erode the collective identity shared by the refugees. Rather, the refugees located their identities within their very displacement. Malkki cautions, however, that this was not the case for all refugees and that for others, relationships between roots and identity were differently constituted.

A similar perspective was articulated by Naficy (1993), who examined the situation of Iranian immigrants and refugees after they fled to the United States. Naficy discussed "liminality," a concept that has received considerable attention in the field of medical anthropology and that refers to a "betwixt-and-between" stage. According to Naficy, uprootedness is often accompanied by feelings of pain and paralysis, especially when the migration is a result of tragedy or political circumstances beyond one's control. At the same time, however, Naficy observed that "liminality ... also positions the exiles to reterritorialize, or build, themselves anew" (1993: 86). Thus, liminality is not only characterized by a sense of transition, but also a presiding *communitas* that develops among those who find themselves sharing a temporary liminal space (Turner, 1969).

According to Malkki and Naficy, uprooting and displacement can have different meanings for individuals and groups, depending on the social, cultural, and political contexts in which uprooting is experienced. Similarly, the ways in which mental health is shaped by uprootedness and displacement are likely to be highly variable. Thus, our research examined the lived experiences of displacement, highlighting not only those structural forces that marginalize and subordinate girls who are homeless, Aboriginal, or new to Canada, but also their sense of agency. Looking at their lives in the context of displacement directs attention to the effects of isolation and the disruption of social ties, and an examination of how girls actively engage in strategies to create a sense of self and belonging.

4. CURRENT KNOWLEDGE AND UNDERSTANDINGS

A number of researchers have documented a range of mental health problems associated with individuals who have been uprooted and/or displaced and have recognized the specific vulnerabilities of particular subgroups within the larger population. However, the vast majority of this literature concerns adults and, to a lesser extent, "children and youth." Few Canadian studies have focused exclusively on girls, uprooting, and mental health. Perhaps the most extensive research focused on girls in Canada has been undertaken by the Alliance of Canadian Researchers on Violence (Berman & Jiwani, 2002). This national consortium of community and academic researchers used a range of innovative methodologies to explore how violence becomes "normalized" in the lives of a diverse group of girls and young women, including Aboriginal and newcomer girls.

Immigrant and Refugee Girls

Between 2001 and 2006, approximately 128,000 immigrant and refugee children and youth under the age of 15 were admitted to Canada. Of these, about one-half were female (Statistics Canada, 2008). A review of the literature reveals few Canadian studies examining the realities and experiences of racialized girls from immigrant and refugee families. During the past decade, however, this trend has begun to shift (Berman & Jiwani, 2008; Bourne, McCoy & Smith, 1998; Handa, 1997; Jiwani, 2006; Lee, 2006; Matthews, 1997).

Jiwani spoke about the "intersecting vulnerabilities" experienced by racialized immigrant and refugee girls of colour. According to Jiwani, through processes of socialization, racialized girls who are marked as different by virtue of their skin colour or religious/cultural differences are Othered and, in essence, devalued. Lee has similarly examined the situation of girls of colour in Victoria, British Columbia, demonstrating how "ideologies of whiteness" (p. 106) effectively silence girls' expressions of identity, reinforcing their exclusion and marginalization.

Several researchers have revealed that girls from racialized immigrant cultures experience dissatisfaction with, and strain from, the normative values imposed by their own cultures (Miller, 1995; Rosenthal, Ranieri & Klimidi, 1996). The contextual factors influencing and shaping this dissatisfaction tend not to be examined in structural terms—that is, as arising from the subordinate position of the cultural group in relation to the dominant society, and/or the construction of racialized communities as "deviant others" (Handa, 1997; Razack, 1998). Exceptions to this trend are found in American studies, which focus on the differential rates of violence against Afro-American girls and women (Kenny, Reinholtz & Angelini, 1997; Wyatt & Riederle, 1994), and studies examining girls at risk who come from a variety of different cultural backgrounds (Joe & Chesney-Lind, 1995; Razack, 1998).

Homeless Girls

Due to the lack of data on homelessness, both globally and nationally (Haldenby, Berman & Forchuk, 2007), and the lack of an agreed-upon definition of homelessness (Kelly & Caputo, 2001), it is impossible to determine the precise number of girls who are homeless. However, there is evidence that the number of those who are without safe and adequate housing in Canada has increased during the past two decades (Novac et al., 2002; Hulchanski, 2004; Shapcott, 2004).

Several studies conducted in the United States and Canada have documented the intense stress and uncertainty in the lives of homeless children and the adverse effects of homelessness on their health, development, academic success, and behaviour (Boivin et al., 2005; Ensign & Bell, 2004; Herth, 1998; Miller et al., 2004). Reports suggest that homeless children have twice the rates of acute and chronic physical disorders as compared to the general population and other children living in poverty, and that these children experience psychological, emotional, and developmental problems, as well as learning problems (DiBiase & Waddell, 1995; Rohde et al., 2001; Rotheram-Borus, 2003; Shields et al., 2004). Several researchers have reported that many homeless youth have either directly experienced or witnessed violence in their homes and communities (Novac et al., 2002; Kipke et al., 1997; Trocme & Wolfe, 2001; Tyler, Hoyt & Whitbeck, 2000). For many adolescents who are homeless either by choice and/or necessity, a distinction that is often impossible to make, life on the streets may be a means to escape what they consider to be intolerable conditions at home (Hyde, 2005; Rew, Taylor-Seehafer & Fitzgerald, 2001).

The dominant discourse on homelessness continues to characterize this population as poor, lazy, mentally deficient, middle-aged, and male (Csiernik, Forchuk, Speechley, Ward-Griffin, 2007; Reid, Berman & Forchuk, 2005). Alternatively, homelessness has been brought to the public imagination as the "street child" who resides in so-called "underdeveloped" nations in other parts of the world (Boyden, 1997; Panter-Brick, 2002; Stephens, 1995). One result of this persistent mythology is that little research has been conducted with homeless adolescent girls, and their unique needs and challenges have been largely overlooked.

Aboriginal Girls

While considerable research has been conducted with Aboriginal peoples in general, very few studies have focused specifically on Aboriginal youth, and even fewer have concerned the lives of Aboriginal girls and young women (Downe, 2006). Thus, there are significant gaps in our current understanding of how Aboriginal girls fare within the larger context of uprooting and displacement. Where girls are included in research, they are rarely portrayed as agents of knowledge. More commonly, they are included as "objects of study" in analyses of on- and off-reserve violence (Long, 1995), residential school abuse (Miller, 1997), community displacement (Fournier & Crey, 1997), young offenders (Aboriginal Corrections Policy Unit, 2002; Cabrera, 1995; Moyer, 2000), motherhood and mothering (Fiske, 1993; Lavell-Harvard, 2006), and cultural identities (Anderson, 2000; Carter, 1997). A number of clinically based studies in the United States and, to a lesser extent, Canada have explored various health-related conditions among Aboriginal youth: psychiatric disorders and social role adaptation (Beiser et al., 1993; Gotowiec & Beiser, 1994; Zvolensky et al., 2001); alcohol and drug addiction and abuse (Beauvais et al., 2002; Herman-Stahl & Chong, 2002; Novins, Beals & Mitchell, 2001); nutrition and eating disorders (Croll et al., 2002; Story, Stevens, Evans, Cornell, Juhaeri, Gittelsohn et al., 2001), as well as HIV/AIDS and sexually transmitted infections (Craib et al., 2003; Heath et al., 1999; Mill, 2000; Tyndall, Currie, Spittal, Li, Wood, O'Shaughnessy et al., 2003). Fetal alcohol syndrome has received particular attention (Golden, 1999; May & Hymbaugh, 1989; Williams & Gloster, 1999), as has suicide (Garroutte et al., 2003; Gartrell, Jarvis & Derkson, 1993; Johnson & Tomren, 1999; Wissow et al., 2001).

Aboriginal girls are seven times more likely than non-Aboriginal girls in Canada to commit suicide (Statistics Canada, 2000) just as they are more likely to witness and experience violence in their homes. In Canada, as well as in the United States, Aboriginal children are more likely than African-American,

African-Canadian, or White students to experience race-based violence in schools (Public Agenda On-line, 2003). Among Aboriginal adult women, there is evidence that those who report greater vulnerability to violence similarly report more mental health problems, including depression and addiction (Waldram, Herring & Young, 1997).

4. THEORETICAL AND METHODOLOGICAL UNDERPINNINGS

The theoretical and methodological underpinnings of the current research are derived from critical social theory (CST), intersectionality theory, and narrative inquiry. From a critical perspective, knowledge is grounded in politics with the insistence that social phenomena be related to the historical whole, and to the structural context in which they are situated (Lather, 1991). Closely linked to, and compatible with, CST is intersectionality theory. Although the term was first articulated by Crenshaw in the 1990s, Black feminist scholar Patricia Hill Collins (1991) had previously written about the interlocking "matrices of domination" to describe the multiple and intersecting inequalities, derived from race, gender, class, and ability, that shape the lives of women (Crenshaw, 1997). An intersectional analysis directs attention away from an exclusive focus on individual stories and experiences to consideration of larger systemic and structural inequalities. By locating the issue of uprooting and displacement within a political and social context, critical theory can provide a practical and relevant framework for understanding the lived experiences of girls while simultaneously seeking strategies to challenge oppressive circumstances in their lives.

Although narrative inquiry embraces many theoretical approaches, several assumptions are shared. One of these is a consensus as to the pervasive nature of stories and storytelling. Humans are storytelling beings who, individually and socially, lead storied lives. While narratives may take many forms, they generally consist of stories that include a chronological ordering of events and an effort to bring coherence to those events. Van Maanen (1988) spoke about "critical tales," or the use of narrative approaches within a critical framework. The interest in such tales is to shed light on larger social, political, symbolic, or economic issues. Thus, in telling stories about their experiences and the ways in which these experiences, in turn, shape their sense of well-being, girls may communicate not only their perceptions about what happened to them, but also the social, economic, and political meanings of those events.

5. RESEARCH METHODS

This study was conducted in a southwestern Ontario community where the researchers have well-established relationships with leaders from each of the study populations. Based on community and academic partnerships, each stage of the research was designed and carried out in collaboration with those who work most closely with the study population. The sample consisted of 19 participants and included six Aboriginal girls, six homeless girls, and seven newcomer girls, aged 14–19. During face-to-face dialogic interviews, we examined the various discursive means and strategies whereby uprooting and displacement are defined, experienced, and reproduced over time in different social contexts and examined how, in turn, these experiences affect girls and young women. Consistent with the theoretical assumptions, one research goal is the development of knowledge in ways that have potential for emancipation and empowerment. A central aspect of the study design was, therefore, the use of dialogic and reflective techniques in which respondents became actively involved in the construction and validation of meaning (Maguire, 1987). An interview guide was used flexibly, with probes to encourage dialogue, critical reflection, and elaboration of responses. Narrative interviewing requires an open-ended structure that allows the participants to direct the flow and focus of the conversation. While the research team established the context for the interview, offering overall direction and providing affirming feedback, the participants took the lead, making associations among concepts as they understood these.

Information about the study was provided to potential participants by counsellors within the partner agencies. Girls who expressed interest contacted the researchers either by phone or e-mail at which time the study was described in more detail. Since not all of the girls who had experienced uprooting and displacement have been associated with community organizations, we also advertised the study in places that girls frequent, such as shopping malls and community centres.

All participants were given the choice of being interviewed alone or in a small group consisting of two to four girls. The rationale for this option was the potential power of group interviews to provide a context in which individuals are able to analyze the struggles they have encountered and the challenges they have faced, to simultaneously "collectivize" their experiences, and develop a sense of empowerment as they begin to see the possibilities for change. It was then the task of the researchers to analyze these references systematically within an "overall narrative frame" (Borland, 1991: 63).

Interviews were transcribed verbatim and analyzed using techniques appropriate to the analysis of narrative data. While content and semantic analyses were drawn upon to some extent (Becker, Beyene & Ken, 2000; Greenlagh, 2001), the main analytical technique was narrative analysis. This process involves breaking the narrative down into "idea units," or clauses in the interview transcript, which are numerically coded. Common themes were then determined from these units and collated. The product of the analysis is a "core narrative" (Garro, 2003) and accompanying themes. Initially, data from Aboriginal, homeless, and newcomer girls were analyzed separately. A comparison of themes across and within the three groups of participants was then conducted, revealing areas of convergence and divergence, as well as an overall mapping of how girls and young women relate their experiences of displacement and uprooting with overall well-being.

Diversity within groups was anticipated and factored into the research. As the experiences of newcomer groups vary by class, conditions of migration, size of community in Canada, and accessibility in terms of language skills and accreditation, and other less tangible factors, we sought to recruit individuals from different backgrounds and who represented communities that are both well established and recent in Canada. Similarly, there is no single, homogeneous homeless population of girls or one distinct Aboriginal community. Rather, there are important dynamics and distinctions that occur across and within the study populations. Attention to the ways in which the participating girls' narratives reference these dynamics was necessary and enriched our understanding of displacement and uprooting in the context of their lives. Recruitment of Aboriginal participants was therefore not restricted to any one nation, nor was homelessness defined by those in particular geographic locations, or urban or rural settings. This diversity was viewed as a strength of the study and is reflected in the analysis.

Approval to conduct the study was obtained from the university's Human Subjects Review Board. Although participation in research for youth under the age of 18 typically requires parental consent, we successfully petitioned the Review Board to waive this requirement. Our rationale was twofold. First, from a pragmatic perspective, obtaining parental approval was not feasible for many in the research, particularly for homeless girls who were estranged from their families. Second, from a philosophical, political, and human rights perspective, the requirement for parental consent would have precluded participation among some of the most vulnerable and marginalized girls whose voices have historically been silenced and excluded from research. A letter of information was developed for parents, but their consent was not required. Consistent with provincial and professional regulations, the girls were told in advance that if they disclosed violence that was currently occurring, we would be required to report this information to the appropriate agency.

6. FINDINGS AND DISCUSSION

The findings presented here are a co-constructed account that privileges the voices of participants, but also recognizes the authors' position and power in selecting, presenting, and interpreting the participants' experiences. We integrate the voices of Aboriginal, homeless, and newcomer girls throughout the results, not in an effort to suggest more "sameness" than in fact exists, but in an attempt to convey the essences of uprooting and displacement. Woven throughout the participants' narratives are philosophical fragments and analyses written by the research team and based on our theoretical sensitivity both in the nascent field of girl studies and in authoring this manuscript. This integration of findings and the discussion is intended to present a cohesive depiction of the girls' stories and experiences. All names are pseudonyms, most chosen by the participants.

At the Heart of the Story
Girls who have experienced uprooting and displacement exist as bodies marked by gender, race, and class, moving through liminal spaces, seeking connections and reconnections. It is in these liminal spaces where they occupy the position of "other." However, it is here that they also learn new ways of being, connecting, and belonging. Their lives on the fringes and in the margins are thus shaped by prevailing and interlocking structures of domination. Through these structures, they strive to develop a sense of self that is strong and resilient, that fosters a sense of agency, and that can counter the hopelessness, despair, and pessimism that often seem so pervasive.

This "core narrative" implies that uprooting and displacement are accompanied by multiple tensions and contradictions, and that these arise from, and are manifested in, individual, social, cultural, and political domains. Moreover, the core narrative reflects the idea that space is a social construction (Kawash, 1998), that identity and space are intertwined, that because of uprooting and displacement, girls exist in marginalized spaces where disconnections from important people and places occur. Barriers that arise from interlocking systems of oppression and other forms of social exclusion—including racism, classism, negative stereotyping, and legacies of colonialism—limit the ability of girls to (re)establish connections and, ultimately, generate *dangerous spaces*. Through processes of resistance and negotiation of new *spaces of hope*, girls may find *spaces of belonging*, where sources of support are found and alliances formed. We refer to this process as *pathways of engagement* and throughout the remainder of this section, will elaborate on these ideas.

Experiences of Uprooting

All of the girls who participated in this research experienced some form of uprooting and displacement from their homes, families, and/or communities. For some, uprooting was a single event, as was the case for most of the newcomer girls, who described uprooting in the context of migration from their countries of origin, namely, Saudi Arabia (two), Somalia (two), Korea (one), Iran (one), and Iraq (one). Six were Muslim, and one converted to Christianity from Buddhism. For all of these girls, the move to Canada necessitated leaving behind extended family members, friends, and a country they knew and loved. Although the route to Canada was a somewhat circuitous one for this group, with all except one residing temporarily in at least one other country before arriving in Canada, they experienced relative geographic stability after resettlement.

In contrast, the Aboriginal girls and homeless girls described uprooting as a pervasive and recurrent feature of their lives. The Aboriginal girls spoke about frequent family moves throughout much of their childhood, with some recalling that they had moved as many as three or four times per year. One of the girls told of living in one location for two years, but this was atypical. In some cases, there was frequent movement between the urban setting and the reserve; for others, the moves occurred within different parts of the same city or between neighbouring communities. More than one-half of this group had extended family and friends living on the reserve from whom they felt estranged while living in the city. Two Aboriginal girls who were sisters explained that their father had been "adopted out" to a non-Aboriginal family when he was a young child. These girls explained that their family had essentially lost all connections to the Aboriginal community in general and to the reserve in particular. However, one of the sisters described a great deal of inner tension, ambiguity, and dissonance regarding her Aboriginal roots and identity. This sibling actively sought out Aboriginal peers and engaged in Aboriginal-related activities at her school. In contrast, her older sister did not establish relationships within the Aboriginal community. Most noted that everyday family life included violence, neglect, substance abuse, and chronic poverty.

At the time of the interviews, the girls who were homeless described an assortment of "accommodations," which included living on the streets, couch surfing, staying in shelters, or temporarily residing with their mothers and/or boyfriends, or some combination of these. All of these girls spoke of difficult childhoods and chaotic homes where interactions were often characterized by physical, sexual, and emotional violence against their mothers and themselves. In addition, they told of sibling abuse, mental illness of one or both parents, chronic poverty, and substance abuse, including the drug-related deaths of two parents. Like the Aboriginal girls, moves for the homeless girls within and between cities were frequent throughout their childhoods.

Displacement and Disconnection in Dangerous Spaces

Inherent in the narratives shared by girls from all three study populations was a profound sense of disconnection from family, culture, and/or community. Together, these contributed to a dissonance with respect to space, place, and identity. The girls repeatedly described feelings of "being different," of not belonging, of being outside and on the fringes. While they weren't always clear precisely what they were excluded from, there was a strong perception that there was some larger community to which they didn't belong. They lived their lives on the periphery, in liminal spaces, where they felt marginalized and devalued.

All six of the Aboriginal girls who took part in the study spoke of the disruptions and disconnections they had suffered in relationships with school friends and with extended family members that, in their opinion, were compounded by the frequent moves. This brief exchange during an interview with one of the Aboriginal girls, who was describing what "home" meant to her, illustrates this sense of disconnection:

> *Participant:* I'm not really sure. Just a place where it's a roof over your head, I don't know.
> *Interviewer:* How do you feel when you talk about the word "home"?
> *Participant:* None really. None.
> *Interviewer:* Any good feelings like happy, or any bad feelings like sad when you think of home?
> *Participant:* Um ... happy.
> *Interviewer:* What kinds of things make you happy about home?
> *Participant:* My bed. [laughs]

In this excerpt, the notion of home is more about having a bed and a place to sleep, rather than a place where relationships are formed, emotional warmth is experienced, or connections with important others are fostered. While this participant stated that home makes her "happy," the sense of happiness was derived from the knowledge that she would have a place to sleep, and that home would ensure a modicum of physical comfort.

For some of the Aboriginal girls, there were ambiguous and contradictory emotions regarding their sense of space and place. Cynthia, 18 years old, was the mother of three young children, all of whom had been placed in "protective custody." She had also been in custody, commonly referred to as being "in care," during much of her own childhood, growing up in a home where everyday life included exposure to drugs, violence, and poverty. Until age 13, Cynthia lived on the reserve, moving frequently and ultimately attending eight different elementary schools. Throughout her teen years, she moved numerous times from the reserve to the city and back. At the time of the interview, Cynthia had just moved into a shelter after leaving her common-law partner, a man who had been physically abusive and against whom a restraining order had been issued. Cynthia's ambivalence about her "community" was reflected in her comments about life in the city and on the reserve. On the one hand, the reserve represented a space of belonging. In Cynthia's words, "I liked living on the reserve. I think of home as being on the reserve with my family." On the other hand, the reserve simultaneously evoked painful associations and represented a space of danger.

> "Right now... I like my community [reserve], but there is too much gossip. Like people, they just talk shit on the reserve, so they never, like, really help me.... I think I'd rather be in the city because, um, most of the things I need to do are already up here."

While moving to the city resulted in separation from her family, who remained on the reserve, she added that life on the reserve meant "moving into drugs and violence." Hopeful that she will be able to create a home for herself and her children, she stated, "I'm just trying to establish my own home for me and my kids, so that's the big thing I think about."

Disconnection and alienation also stemmed from an awareness of themselves as "different," which typically related to how the girls looked, spoke, dressed, or other less tangible markers of difference. The spaces the girls occupied were shaped by deeply entrenched understandings as to where they did and did not belong, understandings that were intricately linked to relations of power, class, and well-established social hierarchies. The inability to move freely across social boundaries and spaces is reflected in the words of another Aboriginal girl, who stated, "I don't really associate with friends, like, I don't have some friends here because I've learned in the past couple of years not to make friends."

The newcomer girls had a very clear sense of space and astute perceptions as to which spaces were welcoming and, conversely, those where they were not welcome. These girls typically described multiple losses associated with migration—loss of family and friends, loss of cultural familiarity and belonging. On arrival in Canada, they felt disconnection as they resettled, usually in highly demarcated multicultural enclaves within a predominantly White city. These enclaves are symbolic of Canada's commitment to multiculturalism, and are often "celebrated" as evidence of Canada's receptivity to newcomers. While these newcomer communities afford a sense of belonging and may contribute to stronger family bonds, these spaces were often characterized by widespread "downward mobility" and financial challenges. Moreover, they served as constant reminders to the girls that there is a larger society to which they do not belong, and in which they do not feel welcome. This idea was evident in the words of Chan-sook from Korea:

"… without any reason I just don't want to talk to anyone. I think it's because sometimes I feel really lonely and even though I live here with my friends, new friends here, but sometimes I really miss—I don't miss Korea, but I sometimes regret coming here, you know what I mean?"

For the homeless girls, uprooting commonly began long before they began to define themselves as "homeless." These girls spoke repeatedly about histories of violence, substance abuse, poverty, and mental illness. Frequent relocations were the norm, and notions of community and belonging were elusive. In a somewhat ironic and paradoxical twist, homelessness afforded some the stability and at least some sense of safety, which were so markedly absent during their childhoods. As Chelsea stated:

"I'm really glad that I'm not living with either of my parents anymore because it means that, yeah, I might move a couple of more times, but at least it's in my control. I know where I'm gonna be, and I don't have to move, you know? I mean who knows how many more times my mom's going to move."

Implicit in Chelsea's comments is the suggestion that stability may have little to do with physical space. Rather, stability is derived from feeling grounded and connected to others.

While homelessness was associated with a sense of freedom from families that were described as oppressive, abusive, and controlling, the girls did not appear to be intentionally severing connections with their families, at least not entirely.

CHAPTER 17

Some maintained family contact while living on the streets, but they welcomed the emotional and physical distance, which they considered to be a positive aspect of displacement. Amanda attributed leaving home to an ultimatum from a stepmother with whom she did not get along.

> "I was a really angry child, I guess, like, after my mom passed away. I never got, like, counselling or anything and I just, like, pretty much I just, like, hated everyone.... I just wanted to die. And then, I don't know, my dad started dating again and the woman who is my stepmother now moved in to my house when I was, like 15, and we just, like, I just despised her and then we just got into confrontations all the time, so she basically told my dad it was either, like, me or her, and she wanted to be a part of the family and I really didn't. So they just kind of dropped me off at the shelter one day.... After my stepmother moved in, like, I didn't feel wanted at all, right? Which is what made me want to leave, like, I think you need to feel wanted, especially when you're a teenager and depressed or, like, angry. You just need to feel like you're wanted somewhere and feel comfortable and I just never felt that really."

Whether the girls who were homeless had left home by choice or were forced to leave was not always apparent. More often, the "decision" to leave was imposed on them, as was the case with Amanda. Homelessness for these girls was neither sudden nor unexpected, but seemed like a logical next step in a life fraught with experiences of abuse and feelings of rejection. In essence, the disconnections experienced by this group had begun prior to becoming homeless, and it was during their days, weeks, and months of living on the streets that they began to create a new sense of family and belonging, both of which had been so profoundly lacking throughout much of their lives.

Life on the streets was also fraught with risk and danger. According to the girls, violence was commonplace, theft was routine, and drugs were readily available. All of these placed the homeless girls at considerable risk for physical health problems, including sexually transmitted diseases, unwanted pregnancy, and nutritional deficiencies. One of the homeless girls spoke about homelessness as follows:

> "I hate moving from one place to another, never knowing where you're going to be the next day, never knowing that—especially if you're out actually sleeping on the street and you fall asleep—that's like entrusting the people of the city not to come up and harm you. I am petrified of people. I don't like a lot of people, like, I don't like the idea of falling asleep and having someone come

up and find me and I have something on me, like, I have smokes on me that I need or something, and that I'll have, like, no smokes left because they'll rob me or they'll hurt me or they could take advantage of me. And I'm just little me. I can do some stuff, but I'm just little me."

Tenuous Connections amid Spaces of Hope

The ability of newcomer girls to speak at least one of Canada's two official languages, English or French, enhanced the possibilities for movement in and out of marginalized spaces, the communities that are inhabited primarily by other newcomer families. However, the desire to move out of these spaces was continually weighed against an equally compelling desire to remain in these spaces, where they generally felt accepted, where they were unlikely to encounter subtle or explicit forms of racism, and where they derived some solace in their connections to history, culture, and heritage. From the girls' vantage point, these were welcoming spaces that offered hope, encouragement, and a sense of solidarity with others in similar circumstances.

"Like, in our neighbourhood there's [sic] so many Somalis and they all came from Somalia. They came to my country so I feel like I'm happy to have them here. And other people, well, I don't know. They're mostly friends. I feel like I'm home in here too…. Sometimes we go together every Friday at night, sort of like I'm in Africa."

Several newcomer girls who were interviewed together similarly commented about feeling accepted in the community where they and their families have resettled.

"I met lots of Arab people over here because I'm from the Middle East. And I feel I'm more connected to them, like, because, you know, they speak the same language I speak, so, like, really that's talk with our mother language. So it's kind of nice, like, to practise it so we don't forget it. But I feel really more connected to, like, people from our country.

Another participant added:

"I feel the same thing actually because now even my friends at school notice that I really like to be with Arab people because I feel like I belong—like we all belong to the same place…. So, like, when we talk together, we're, like, get each other like that, so it is, like, easier, I guess. And I have, like, a Korean friend and she is, like, very nice too and I feel like she is new too, so it's like—I don't know. But I really like—because I am from—like, you feel that you belong there more, like, than—than the Canadian community."

Even in their schools, where they felt relatively safe and secure, the notion of space was clearly delineated, with several girls describing places where they "hung out" together, sections of the gym or cafeteria, apart from "the others."

While the idea that connections were vitally important was heard repeatedly, many simultaneously expressed some concern regarding what they perceived as the tenuousness of these connections. According to Lynette, one of the homeless girls, "and then you always know that once you're on top and everything is going good, everything is just going to crash and turn into shit again. Like, that's just life really, so I don't know. I just felt more comfortable down there—rock bottom—I think."

Frequently, the homeless girls described the connections that were established as being explicitly related to the shared sense of abandonment and betrayal by family. Also evident in their comments was a depiction of themselves as "outcasts."

"I think a lot of people down here—I mean I talk about family … with my close friends, but it's not something that we talk about openly with everybody down here, you know. Sometimes we do, but we don't really—I think I've noticed down here, like, people don't tend to tell the whole world down here. You tell your closest friends and you talk with your close friends about it and stuff, and sometimes you'll share it with everybody, but everyone down here has had different experiences and everyone's been betrayed in some sort of way. I think there's that understanding of, um, being kind of being betrayed and abandoned. I think a lot of people down here have had that feeling, so I think that's largely where we connect—our different experiences where we're kind of outcast from the society. And, yeah, things like that. Yeah."

Several Aboriginal girls explained that efforts to sustain connections with people, particularly those on the reserve, were often thwarted by lack of money or other material resources. Shauna spoke about the difficulties of keeping up past relationships because without money—all of which was used for food and rent—she was unable to purchase a phone card. Thus, structural barriers, such as poverty and limited access to resources, were key factors in determining their capacity to establish and maintain meaningful connections.

While most girls viewed community as something positive, and demonstrated the ability to create at least some semblance of a community for themselves, this was not always the case. Linda, an Aboriginal girl, was 15 years old and pregnant at the time she was interviewed. She had moved with her mother many times throughout her life, attending numerous different schools. Her desire to establish connections seemed rather limited, at least based on her comments and outward demeanour, and she had difficulty articulating what "community" meant to her. Linda did not appear to invest heavily in her physical space, has never had any meaningful say over when or where she would move next, or where "home" would be. Her relationships with her mother, her boyfriend, and her "unborn child," were the stability points in her life, although all of these were tenuous and dependent on factors over which she had little control.

Linda's repeated displacements contributed to a lack of insight about the meaning of community—what it is or could be—for herself and her family. In her words, community is about a "roof over my head, a bed, a place for my things—books and stuff." Moreover, community is comprised of "whoever is around where you live," but generally entails little emotional connection or investment.

Negotiating Spaces of Belonging

Liminal and marginalized spaces are not readily categorized as positive or negative, good or bad. While liminal spaces may be construed as places of danger, under some conditions, liminality may offer a "space of belonging." For many, life in the margins represented a welcoming space. For example, the sense of community and belonging for newcomer girls was derived from being among others of similar ethnocultural backgrounds as themselves. Within the multicultural enclaves—the spaces that they were essentially forced to occupy—isolation and marginalization were reinforced and sustained through raced, gendered, and classed determinations regarding movement in and out of these socially constructed spaces. Individuals within these communities, many of whom are unable to speak either of Canada's official languages, are literally silenced in the most profound way possible. For girls who are able to speak English or French, there is greater ability to move in and out of these liminal spaces, but racism and other forms of social exclusion pervade all aspects of their lives and limit such movement.

For the homeless group, homelessness represented an end to the oppressive and dangerous circumstances of their homes, an escape from what they considered to be a horrendous situation, and hope for "something better." In essence, homelessness afforded a sense of control that they had not been able to attain when living with their families. As one stated:

CHAPTER 17

"I'm kind of establishing who I am right now. Now that I'm out on my own, although I still have some current issues to deal with like family issues, I'm more—I'm able to deal with the past and to start sorting through all of what happened when I was growing up and that."

The notion of "home" for those who were homeless was typically understood and experienced as a place of violence and alienation. United in their collective experiences of marginalization and isolation, they achieved a sense of belonging and purpose. This seemingly contradictory idea was heard often in the girls' voices and stories as they spoke about connections and disconnections, belonging and exclusion, balance and imbalance, cohesion and fragmentation. It was in the liminal spaces where they often felt accepted and gained a greater sense of connection to their history, culture, and heritage. The (re)creation of family was described by Amber, one of the homeless girls:

"And I've got a street family, like, I've got close friends that I would help out or they would help me out. A street family is, you know, there's people that I've helped out. Some stay with us once in a while and we help them out. And they don't bring drugs or alcohol into our home. And we're just—you know, they help us out with food or we help them out with whatever. You know, I help people out with cigarettes and just, uh, they help me, you know? We just look out for each other. I just, um—I find that—I mean I have parents, but in many ways I feel like an orphan."

As these comments reveal, the "street family" replaced traditional understandings about family. It was with this group that the homeless girls derived a sense of comfort, safety, security, and belonging. Although Amber noted that she has parents, she still felt "like an orphan." Homelessness also afforded some an opportunity to reflect philosophically on their purpose and place in this world, and to gain insights into themselves, evident in the words of Miranda, who poignantly stated:

"Well, like, it sucks. Like, I would have liked to be able to stay in one place, in a stable environment, but at the same time I also think that if I didn't go through it, like, I wouldn't be who I am."

The bonds and new notions of family and community that arose out of shared experiences were reflected in the words of Dakota, who was homeless, "couch surfing" with friends:

"We all kind of understand where we've been and, you know, if a person wants to talk, then you talk, but if they just want to be left alone, you can tell. And I don't know, I think I noticed it more at first, you know? I've been here for, you know, probably five or six months and now I don't—I don't notice the language as much. But, um, I definitely notice, like, when you first come down here, like, there's a big culture shock when you first get into it, especially like me. I've been—I mean I grew up as a P.K., a pastor's kid. So, like, going from, you know, P.K. and hanging out with, like, 'goody-goody two shoes' to hanging out with street kids is a pretty big shock. So, yeah, it's just a huge difference. Like, it's a majorly different culture and that, and people don't realize that.... And everyone's—everyone's, like, down here there's, like, there's codes and everything, you know? It's all street codes, you know, like everyone knows. You just know when to leave a person alone and all this stuff, you know?"

Through their collective experiences of uprooting and displacement, the girls described new spaces of hope and encouragement, spaces where they could join with others who understood their experiences, where they could collectivize their struggles, and celebrate their accomplishments. Despite their awareness about potential dangers on the streets, on reserves, and in their communities, these "spaces of hope" were where commonplace notions of family were re-evaluated and a sense of community was created, often for the first time.

Among the Aboriginal girls, three of the five explicitly stated that uprooting did not have an impact on their lives. Interestingly, the two sisters who commented that uprooting did affect them came from relatively stable families from whom they received emotional support and at least some degree of economic security. One of these sisters identified strongly with her Native background, even though many aspects of her heritage were unknown due to her father's "adoption out." This individual had an extensive social network, was active in extracurricular activities, and had high educational aspirations that included attending university and the desire to become a neurologist, influenced by her own negative experiences with the health care system as a result of epilepsy.

In contrast, another one of the Aboriginal girls told of very different experiences and perspectives with respect to uprooting, disconnection, and her sense of space/identity. This girl was pregnant at the time of the interview and gave birth during the course of the research. She had run away when she was 13, and described few examples of engagement or connection outside of her relationships with her mother and her mother's boyfriend. Although she stated that uprooting had little effect on her, this young woman was unable to describe any type of emotional connectedness, did not engage in school, and maintained that she had no meaningful or satisfying social life. Pregnancy evoked a new sense of attachment and importance, unlike anything she had experienced previously.

The negotiation of spaces of belonging for newcomer girls typically entailed creating conditions that would allow them to fulfill hopes and dreams in Canada. Often linked to ideals about peace and social justice, these girls talked about the need to overcome barriers such as language, racism, achieving academic success, and "adaptation" to the new spaces they inhabit. While disconnections were a prevalent theme imbedded in the girls' stories, they simultaneously spoke about connections and the creation of spaces of belonging. Thus, the ideas of connection and disconnection cannot be understood in a linear manner, but exist in a dialectical relationship to one another.

7. CONCLUSION

The girls who participated in this study openly shared their thoughts and feelings, the challenges they faced, and the barriers they encountered with respect to uprooting and displacement. In the process, they revealed much about strength, courage, and hope. The capacity of these girls and young women to reconnect in spaces where they felt a sense of belonging was influenced, in part, by the social, economic, and emotional resources that were available to them.

Girls who have been uprooted from their homes, families, and communities are forced to reside in "liminal spaces," which Razack (2002) referred to as "the border between civilized and primitive space" (p. 13). These spaces are not neutral places, but are defined by, and sustained through, unequal, deeply hierarchical power relations that are based on history, economics, politics, and culture. Whether these spaces are the urban slums of inner cities, the multicultural enclaves situated within predominantly White settler communities or the "Indian" reserves, movement in and out of these spaces is highly regulated and controlled. Further, movement is influenced by social locations and identities and is, at once, raced, gendered, and classed. Frequently, life in liminal spaces is accompanied by danger and necessitates the negotiation of dangerous terrain.

Upon resettlement in Canada, the newcomer girls in this research all lived in a publicly subsidized housing community with a large newcomer population. The idea of resettling newcomers in communities with other newcomers is largely heralded as an example of Canada's tolerance and acceptance as a means of preserving "cultural practices," and as an example of the benefits of multiculturalism. Interestingly, there is little mention of race within this discourse. Instead, culture becomes the proxy for race. As Jiwani (2006) has observed, racial differences become encoded as cultural differences, and race itself is culturalized.

Regulatory practices such as admission criteria, legislation concerning crime and deviance, social practices, and stereotypical judgments about people of colour and the homeless are some of the ways in which particular groups are constructed, and social spaces defined and restricted within the Canadian landscape. Through these processes, girls derive a sense of identity, of who they are in this world, and where they do and don't belong. And through these processes, they also learn about privilege and place, about who is valued and who is not. At times, we were struck by seemingly contradictory comments regarding disconnections and the idea of finding connections in liminal spaces. These seemingly contradictory comments reflect the ambiguity and inner tension that many girls who have been uprooted and displaced experience. In this context, the notion of "nested identities" discussed by the Aboriginal scholar Gerald Alfred (1995) has a great deal of relevance. Developed in relation to Mohawk identity, the idea of nested identities implies that identities are not clearly delineated; rather, they are "nested" in social, historical, and political contexts.

This research contributes theoretically and methodologically to the burgeoning literature on the gendered effects of structural violence and displacement. As the girls' narratives are grounded in "institutional landscapes" (Saris, 1995: 67), they reveal processes of power, vulnerability, and violation. The narrative themes imbedded in the girls' stories reveal insights into marginalized spaces where disconnections occur in relations with self/other, friends, family, school, and community.

As a result of downward mobility and poverty, language barriers, racism, and discrimination, newcomer communities often become marginalized spaces where the inhabitants are largely excluded from the privileges commonly afforded to those from the dominant culture (Anisef, Kilbride & Khattar, 2003). Similar patterns of exclusion were experienced by homeless and Aboriginal girls. While experiences of displacement and uprooting may be characterized by personal violations of security, opportunity, home, and identity, these experiences also reflect the vulnerable and subordinated social positions and locations of the uprooted.

The findings of this research have important implications for mental health practitioners who work with girls and young women. Most importantly, girls need "safe spaces" where they can talk openly and honestly about their experiences, where they can contemplate the ways in which uprootedness has affected their sense of belonging and overall well-being. Aside from the literature dealing with health and poverty, few studies have addressed dislocation or uprooting as a form of systemic, institutional, or structural violence. In her classic study of child death in an impoverished *barrio* in Brazil, Scheper-Hughes (1992) examined how the structural violence of racism and poverty, the presiding fear of state-sanctioned slaughter of squatter settlers, and sexism undermine women's health and maternal practice. The narratives of the women in Scheper-Hughes's study repeatedly revealed links among structural violence, individual assault, child mortality, and ill health. With respect to Aboriginal, newcomer, and homeless girls, forced migration, displacement, and uprooting constitute specific forms of violence that jeopardize, in fundamental ways, their sense of self, belonging, and space. That so many showed a capacity to negotiate new spaces of hope and belonging, despite dwelling within what Sibley refers to as a "landscape of exclusion," is a testament to their strength, resilience, and sense of agency.

REFERENCES

Aboriginal Corrections Policy Unit. (2002). *Choices and consequences: Offenders as a resource for crime prevention*. Ottawa: Aboriginal Corrections Policy Unit of Canada.

Alfred, G. (1995). *Heeding the voices of our ancestors: Kahnawake Mohawk politics and the rise of native nationalism*. Toronto: Oxford University Press.

Anderson, K. (2000). *A recognition of being: Reconstructing Native womanhood*. Toronto: Second Story Press.

Anisef, P., Kilbride, K.M. & Khattar, R. (2003). The needs of newcomer youth and emerging "best practices" to meet those needs. In P. Anisef & K.M. Kilbride (Eds.), *Managing two worlds: The experiences and concerns of immigrant youth in Ontario* (pp. 196–234). Toronto: Canadian Scholars' Press Inc.

Apfelbaum, E.R. (2000). And now what, after such tribulations? Memory and dislocation in the era of uprooting. *American Psychologist, 55*, 1008–13.

Beauvais, F., Wayman, J.C., Jumper-Thurman, P., Plested, B. & Helm, H. (2002). Inhalant abuse among American Indian, Mexican American, and non-Latino White adolescents. *American Journal of Drug and Alcohol Abuse, 28*(1), 171–87.

Becker, G., Beyene, Y. & Ken, P. (2000). Health, welfare reform, and narratives of uncertainty among Cambodian refugees. *Culture, Medicine, and Psychiatry, 24*, 139–63.

Beiser, M., Lancee, W., Gotowiec, A., Sack, W. & Redshirt, R. (1993). Measuring self-perceived role competence among First Nations and Non-Native children. *Canadian Journal of Psychiatry, 38*, 412–19.

Berman, H. (2000). The relevance of narrative research with children who witness war and children who witness woman abuse. *Journal of Aggression, Maltreatment, and Trauma, 3*(1), 107–25.

Berman, H. (2003). Getting critical with children: Empowering approaches with a disempowered group. *Advances in Nursing Science, 26,* 102–13.

Berman, H. & Jiwani, Y. (Eds.). (2002). *In the best interests of the girl child.* London: The Alliance of Five Research Centres on Violence.

Berman, H. & Jiwani, Y. (2008). Newcomer girls in Canada: Implications for interventions by mental health professionals. In S. Guruge & E. Collins (Eds.), *Working with immigrant and refugee women: Guidelines for mental health professionals* (pp. 137–56). Toronto: Centre for Addiction and Mental Health.

Boivin, J., Roy, E., Haley, N. & du Fort, G.G. (2005). The health of street youth. *Canadian Journal of Public Health, 96*(6), 432–37.

Borland, K. (1991). "That's not what I said": Interpretive conflict in oral narrative research. In Sherna B. Gluck & Daphne Patai (Eds.), *Women's words: The feminist practice of oral history* (pp. 63–75). New York: Routledge.

Bourne, P., McCoy, L. & Smith, D. (1998). Girls and schooling: Their own critique. *Resources for Feminist Research, 26*(Spring, 1/2), 58–68.

Boyden, J. (1997). Childhood and the policy makers: A comparative perspective on the globalization of childhood. In A. James & A. Prout (Eds.), *Constructing and reconstructing childhood* (pp. 190–215). London: Falmer Press.

Cabrera, N.J. (1995). Violence by and against children in Canada. In J. Ross (Ed.), *Violence in Canada: Sociopolitical perspectives* (pp. 126–52). New York: Oxford University Press.

Carter, S. (1997). *Capturing women: The manipulation of cultural imagery in Canada's prairie west.* Montreal: McGill-Queen's University Press.

Clifford, J. (1988). *The predicament of culture: Twentieth century ethnography, literature, and art.* Cambridge: Harvard University Press.

Collins, P.H. (1991). *Black feminist thought: Knowledge, consciousness, and the politics of empowerment.* New York: Routledge.

Craib, K.J., Spittal, P.M., Wood, E., Laliberte, N., Hogg, R.S., Li, K., Heath, K., Tyndall, M.W., O'Shaughnessy, M.V. & Schechter, M.T. (2003). Risk factors for elevated HIV incidence among Aboriginal injection drug users in Vancouver. *Canadian Medical Association Journal, 168*(1), 19–24.

Crenshaw, K. (1997). Resisting whiteness' rhetorical silence. *Western Journal of Communication, 61*(3), 253–278.

Croll, J., Neumark-Sztainer, D., Story, M. & Ireland, M. (2002). Prevalence and risk and protective factors related to disordered eating behaviors among adolescents: Relationship to gender and ethnicity. *Journal of Adolescent Health, 31*(2), 166–75.

Csiernik, R., Forchuk, C., Speechley, M. & Ward-Griffin, C. (2007). De 'myth' ifying mental health – Findings from a Community University Research Alliance (CURA)," *Critical Social Work, 8*(1) (2007), pp. 1–15.

DiBiase, R. & Waddell, S. (1995). Some effects of homelessness on the psychological functioning of preschoolers. *Journal of Abnormal Child Psychology, 23,* 783–92.

Dossa, P. (2001). Narrative mediation of conventional and new paradigms of "mental health": Reading the stories of immigrant Iranian women. In P. Dossa (Ed.), *Research on immigration and integration in the metropolis.* 21–28. Vancouver: Vancouver Centre of Excellence.

Downe, P. (2006). Aboriginal girls in Canada : Living histories of dislocation, exploitation, and strength. In Y. Jiwani, C. Steenbergen & C. Mitchell (Eds.), *Girlhood: Redefining the limits* (pp. 1–14). Montreal: Black Rose Books.

Ensign, J. (2001). "Shut up and listen": Feminist health care with out-of-the-mainstream adolescent females. *Issues in Comprehensive Pediatric Nursing, 24*(1), 71–84.

Ensign, J. & Bell, M. (2004). Illness experiences of homeless youth. *Qualitative Health Research, 14*(9), 1239–54.

Ensign, J. & Panke, A. (2002). Barriers and bridges to care: Voices of homeless female adolescent youth in Seattle, Washington, U.S.A. *Journal of Advanced Nursing, 37*(2), 166–72.

Fiske, J. (1993) Child of the state, mother of the nation: Aboriginal women and the ideology of motherhood. *Cutlure, 13*(1), 17–35.

Fournier, S. & Crey, E. (1997). *Stolen from our embrace: The abduction of First Nations children and the restoration of Aboriginal communities.* Vancouver: Douglas & McIntyre.

Garro, L.C. (2003). Narrating troubling experiences. *Transcultural Psychiatry, 40*(1), 5–43.

Garroutte, E.M., Goldberg, J., Beals, J., Herrell, R. & Manson, S.M. (2003). Spirituality and attempted suicide among American Indians. *Social Science and Medicine, 56*(7), 1571–79.

Gartrell, J.W., Jarvis, G.K. & Derksen, L. (1993). Suicidality among adolescent Alberta Indians. *Suicide and Life-Threatening Behavior, 23,* 366–73.

Goldberg, D. (1993). *Racist culture: Philosophy and the politics of meaning.* Oxford: Blackwell Publishers.

Golden, J. (1999). "An argument that goes back to the womb": The demedicalization of fetal alcohol syndrome, 1973–1992. *Journal of Social History, 33*(2), 269–98.

Gonick, M. (2003). *Between femininities: Ambivalence, identity, and the education of girls.* Albany: State University of New York Press.

Gotowiec, A. & Beiser, M. (1994). Aboriginal children's mental health: Unique challenges. *Canada's Mental Health* (Winter), 7–11.

Greenlagh, S. (2001). *Under the medical gaze: Facts and fictions of chronic pain.* Berkeley: University of California Press.

Haldenby, A.M., Berman, H. & Forchuk, C. (2007). Homelessness and health in adolescents. *Qualitative Health Research, 17,* 1232–44.

Handa, A. (1997). Caught between omissions: Exploring "culture conflict" among second-generation South Asian women in Canada. Unpublished doctoral dissertation, University of Toronto.

Heath, K.V., Cornelisse, P.G., Strathdee, S.A., Palepu, A., Miller, M.L., Schechter, M.T., O'Shaughnessy, M.V. & Hogg, R.S. (1999). HIV-associated risk factors among young Canadian Aboriginal and non-Aboriginal men who have sex with men. *International Journal of STD and AIDS, 10*(9), 582–87.

Herman-Stahl, M. & Chong, J. (2002). Substance abuse prevalence and treatment utilization among American Indians residing on-reservation. *American Indian and Alaska Native Mental Health Research, 10*(3), 1–23.

Herth, K. (1998). Hope as seen through the eyes of homeless children. *Journal of Advanced Nursing, 28,* 1053–62.

Hulchanski, J.D. (2004). How did we get there? The evolution of Canada's "exclusionary" housing system. In J.D. Hulchanski & M. Shapcott (Eds.), *Finding room: Policy options for a Canadian rental housing strategy*. Toronto: University of Toronto Press.

Hyde, J. (2005). From home to street: Understanding young people's transitions into homelessness. *Journal of Adolescence, 25,* 171–83.

Jiwani, Y. (2006). *Discourses of denial.* Vancouver: University of British Columbia Press.

Joe, K. & Chesney-Lind, M. (1995). "Just every mother's angel": An analysis of gender and ethnic variations in youth gang membership. *Gender & Society, 9*(4), 408–31.

Johnson, T. & Tomren, H. (1999). Helplessness, hopelessness, and despair: Identifying the precursors to Indian youth suicide. *American Indian Culture and Research Journal, 23*(3), 287–301.

Jones, P.S. & Meleis, A.I. (1993). Health is empowerment. *Advances in Nursing Science, 15*(3), 1–14.

Kawash, S. (1998). The homeless body. *Public Culture, 10*(2), 319–39.

Kelly, K. & Caputo, T. (2001). Responding to youth at risk: An overview of recent research in English Canada. In M. Gauthier & D. Pacom (Eds.), *Spotlight on ... Canadian youth research* (pp. 39–52). Quebec: Les Presses de l'Université Laval.

Kenny, J.W., Reinholtz, C. & Angelini, P. (1997). Ethnic differences in childhood and adolescent sexual abuse and teenage pregnancy. *Journal of Adolescent Health, 21*(1), 3–10.

Khanlou, N., Beiser, M., Cole, E., Freire, M., Hyman, I. & Kilbride, K.M. (2002). *Mental health promotion among newcomer female youth: Post-migration experiences and self-esteem.* Ottawa: Status of Women Canada.

Kipke, M.D., Simon, T.R., Montgomery, S.B., Unger, J.B. & Iverson, E.F. (1997). Homeless youth and their exposure to and involvement in violence while living on the streets. *Journal of Adolescent Health, 20,* 360–67.

Lather, P. (1991). *Getting smart: Feminist research and pedagogy with/in the postmodern.* New York: Routledge, Chapman & Hall.

Lavell-Harvard, D. (2006). *Until our hearts are on the ground: Aboriginal mothering, oppression, resistance, and rebirth.* Toronto: Demeter Press.

Lee, J. (2006). Locality, participatory action research, and racialized girls' struggles for citizenship. In Y. Jiwani, C. Steenbergen & C. Mitchell (Eds.), *Girlhood: Redefining the limits* (pp. 89–108). Montreal: Black Rose Books.

Long, D.A. (1995). On violence and healing: Aboriginal experiences, 1960–1993. In Jeffrey Ross (Ed.), *Violence in Canada: Sociopolitical perspectives* (pp. 40–77). New York: Oxford University Press.

Maguire, P. (1987). *Doing participatory research: A feminist approach.* Amherst: University of Massachusetts, Center for International Education.

Malkki, L.H. (1995). *Purity and exile: Violence, memory, and national cosmology among Hutu refugees in Tanzania.* Chicago: University of Chicago Press.

Matthews, J.M. (1997). A Vietnamese flag and a bowl of Australian flowers: Recomposing racism and sexism. *Gender, Place, and Culture, 4*(1), 5–18.

May, P.A. & Hymbaugh, K.J. (1989). A macro-level fetal alcohol syndrome prevention program for Native Americans and Alaska natives: Description and evaluation. *Journal of Studies on Alcohol, 50,* 508–18.

Mill, J.E. (2000). Describing an explanatory model of HIV/AIDS among Aboriginal women. *Holistic Nursing Practice, 15*(1), 42–56.

Miller, B.D. (1995). Precepts and practices: Researching identity formation among Indian Hindu adolescents in the United States. *New Directions for Child Development, 67,* 71–85.

Miller, J.R. (1997). *Shingwauk's vision: A history of Native residential schools.* Toronto: University of Toronto Press.

Miller, P., Donahue, P., Este, D. & Hofer, M. (2004). Experiences of being homeless or at risk of being homeless among Canadian youths. *Adolescence, 39*(156), 735–55.

Moyer, S. (2000). Race, gender and homicide: Comparisons between Aboriginals and other Canadians. In Ruth M. Mann (Ed.), *Juvenile crime and delinquency: A turn of the century reader* (pp. 303–20). Toronto: Canadian Scholars' Press Inc.

Murray, M. (2002). Connecting narrative and social representation theory in health research. *Social Science Information, 41,* 653–73.

Naficy, H. (1993). Exile discourse and televisual fetishization. In N. Hamid & G. Teshome (Eds.), *Otherness and the media: The ethnography of the imagined and the imaged* (pp. 85–116). Reading, England: Harwood Academic Publishers.

Novac, S., Serge, L., Eberle, M. & Brown, J. (Eds.). (2002). *On her own: Young women and homelessness in Canada*. Ottawa: Canadian Housing and Renewal Association.

Novins, D.K., Beals, J. & Mitchell, C.M. (2001). Sequences of substance abuse among American Indian adolescents. *Journal of the American Academy of Child and Adolescent Psychiatry, 40*(10), 1168–74.

Panter-Brick, C. (2002). Street children, human rights, and public health: A critique and future directions. *Annual Review of Anthropology, 31,* 147–71.

Public Agenda. (2003). Crime rate in schools. www.publicagenda.org.

Razack, S.H. (1998). *Looking White people in the eye: Gender, race, and culture in the courtrooms and classrooms*. Toronto: University of Toronto Press.

Razack, S.H. (2002). When place becomes race. In S. Razack (Ed.), *Race, space, and the law: Unmapping a White settler society*. Toronto: Between the Lines. 1–20.

Reid, S., Berman, H. & Forchuk, C. (2005). Living on the streets in Canada: A feminist narrative study of girls and young women. *Issues in Comprehensive Pediatric Nursing, 28,* 237–56.

Rew, L., Taylor-Seehafer, M. & Fitzgerald, M.L. (2001). Sexual abuse, alcohol and other drug use, and suicidal behaviours in homeless adolescents. *Issues in Comprehensive Pediatric Nursing, 24,* 225–40.

Rohde, P., Noell, J., Ochs, L. & Seeley, J.R. (2001). Depression, suicidal ideation, and STD-related risk in homeless older adolescents. *Journal of Adolescence, 24*(4), 447–60.

Rosenthal, D., Ranieri, N. & Klimidis, S. (1996). Vietnamese adolescents in Australia: Relationships between perceptions of self and parental values, intergenerational conflict, and gender dissatisfaction. *International Journal of Psychology, 31*(2), 81–91.

Rotheram-Borus, M., Song, J., Gwadz, M., Lee, M., Rossem, R. & Koopman, C. (2003). Reductions in HIV risk among runaway youth. *Prevention Science, 4*(3), 173–87.

Saris, A.J. (1995). Telling stories: Life histories, illness narratives, and institutional landscapes. *Culture, Medicine, and Psychiatry, 19,* 39–72.

Scheper-Hughes, N. (1992). *Death without weeping: The violence of everyday life in Brazil*. Berkeley: University of California Press.

Shapcott, M. (2004). Where are we going? Recent federal and provincial housing policy. In J.D. Hulchanski & M. Shapcott (Eds.), *Finding room: Policy options for a Canadian rental housing strategy.* 195–214. Toronto: University of Toronto Press.

Shields, S.A., Wong, T., Mann, J., Jolly, A.M., Haase, D., Mahaffey, S., et al. (2004). Prevalence and correlates of Chlamydia infection in Canadian street youth. *Society of Adolescent Medicine, 34,* 384–90.

Sibley, D. (1995). *Geographies of exclusion: Society and difference in the west*. London: Routledge.

Statistics Canada. (2000). *Women in Canada: A gender-based statistical report*. Ottawa: Ministry of Industry.

Statistics Canada (2008). *2006 Census data*. Retrieved June 18, 2008, from www12.statcan.ca/english/census/index.cfm.

Stephens, S. (1995). Children and the politics of culture in "late capitalism." In S. Stephens (Ed.), *Children and the politics of culture*. 11–50. Princeton: Princeton University Press.

Story, M., Stevens, J., Evans, M., Cornell, C., Juhaeri, E., Gittelsohn, J., Going, S.B., Clay, T.E. & Murray, D.M. (2001). Weight loss attempts and attitude toward body size, eating, and physical activity in American Indian children: Relationship to weight status and gender. *Obesity Research, 9*(6), 356–63.

Trocme, N. & Wolfe, D. (2001). *The Canadian incidence study of reported child abuse and neglect*. Retrieved November 29, 2007, from www.phac-aspc.gc.ca/publicat/cissr-ecirc/pdf/cmic_e.pdf.

Turner, V. (1969). *The ritual process*. Chicago: Aldine.

Tyler, K.A., Hoyt, D.R. & Whitbeck, L.B. (2000). The effects of early sexual abuse on later sexual victimization among female homeless and runaway adolescents. *Journal of Interpersonal Violence, 15*(3), 323–31.

Tyndall, M.W., Currie, S., Spittal, P., Li, K., Wood, E., O'Shaughnessy, M. & Schechter, M.T. (2003). Intensive injection cocaine use as the primary risk factor in the Vancouver HIV-1 epidemic. *AIDS, 17*(6), 887–93.

UNHCR. (2008). Statistical Yearbook. New York: United Nations.

Van Maanen, J. (1988). *Tales of the field*. Chicago: University of Chicago Press.

Waldram, J.B. (1997). *The way of the pipe: Aboriginal spirituality and symbolic healing in Canadian prisons*. Peterborough: Broadview Press.

Waldram, J., Herring, A. & Young, T. (1997) *Aboriginal Health in Canada*. Toronto: University of Toronto Press.

Williams, L., Labonte, R. & O'Brien, M. (2003). Empowering social action through narratives of identity and culture. *Health Promotion International, 18*(1), 33–40.

Williams, R.J. & Gloster, S.P. (1999). Knowledge of fetal alcohol syndrome among Natives in northern Manitoba. *Journal of Studies on Alcohol, 60*(6), 833–36.

Wissow, L.S., Walkup, J., Barlow, A., Reid, R. & Kane, S. (2001). Cluster and regional influences on suicide in a Southwestern American Indian tribe. *Social Science and Medicine, 53*(9), 1115–24.

Wyatt, G.E. & Riederle, M. (1994). Sexual harassment and prior sexual trauma among African-American and White American women. *Violence and Victims, 9*(3), 233–47.

Zvolensky, M.J., McNeil, D.W., Porter, C.A. & Stewart, S.H. (2001). Assessment of anxiety sensitivity in young American Indians and Alaska Natives. *Behavior Research and Therapy, 39*(4), 477–93.

Chapter 18

IS SUBSTANCE ABUSE EVEN AN ISSUE? PERCEPTIONS OF MALE AND FEMALE COMMUNITY-BASED MENTAL HEALTH SYSTEM CONSUMER-SURVIVORS

Rick Csiernik

1. INTRODUCTION

Co-occurring mental health and substance abuse disorders have gradually and, at times, grudgingly emerged as a significant health and social issue in Canada to the point where provincial and national initiatives and task forces have been created to examine treatment concerns in greater depth (British Columbia Inter-ministry Task Group, 1999; Canadian Centre on Substance Abuse, 2002; Centre for Addiction and Mental Health, 2001; Comité permanent de lutte à la toxicomanie, 1997, 2000; Ontario Ministry of Health, 1999). This population has complex vulnerabilities, with poor housing, oppression, and poverty negatively affecting their ability to secure basic needs (Treloar & Holt, 2008). While there has been little direct examination of the issues of community-based mental health consumer-survivors who are not actively seeking counselling assistance for either substance abuse or mental health concerns, research has been conducted on other community-based populations in this area (Booth, Curran & Han, 2004; Gilder, Wall & Ehlers, 2004).

A Canadian study on co-morbidity of alcohol use and mental health disorders found that a 12-month prevalence of alcohol use problems among individuals with other mental health issues was approximately double compared to those with no such issues. The rate of illicit drug use was three times greater among those Canadians with a mental health issue compared to those without such a diagnosis. Compared to the general population, the lifetime risk for developing alcohol dependence was nearly four times greater among individuals with a mood or anxiety disorder (Rush et al., 2008). Earlier work from the United States reported that compared to the general population, the lifetime risk for developing alcohol dependence was 21 times greater among individuals with an anti-social personality; six times more likely among those suffering from mania; four times more likely in people with schizophrenia; and twice the risk among those suffering from panic disorder, obsessive-compulsive disorder, dysthymia, major depression, or somatization disorders (Helzer & Pryzbedk, 1998). Likewise, women with bipolar disorder were found to be seven times more likely than women in the general population to have a history of alcohol dependency, while men with bipolar disorder were three times more likely than the general male population to have a substance abuse issue (Frye et al., 2003). Thus, it has been well documented that substance abuse is a greater issue among those with mental health problems than the general population. Of additional concern is that those with a concurrent disorder are also more likely than those with only a mental health problem or only a substance abuse issue to have housing issues or to become homeless (Drake, Osher & Wallach, 1991; Kessler et al., 1996; Mandersheid & Rosenstein, 1992).

One area that has received less attention pertains to the differences in substance abuse by sex of community-based mental health consumer-survivors (Grella, 1996; Sinha & Rounsaville, 2002). Brunette and Drake (1998), in a study of 108 people with schizophrenia or schizoaffective disorder, found that homeless women with concurrent disorders paralleled women with only substance abuse disorders in having distinct characteristics and treatment needs when compared with men. Canadian data indicated that men are two to three times more likely than women to develop a dependency on alcohol and illicit drugs (Rush et al., 2008). Likewise, Hanna and Grant (1997), using a nationally representative sample of the United States population, found that distributions of alcohol abuse and depression were almost mirror opposites between the sexes, with men having far more alcohol-related problems and women having a greater presentation of depression. However, this could be, in part, an artefact of men who are depressed being underdiagnosed.

However, what has not been asked is how clients themselves view these issues. This Community-University Research Alliance on Mental Health and Housing allowed for an exploratory examination of this population, for despite our increasing understanding and knowledge of the complexity of concurrent disorders, there have been limited opportunities to directly examine issues at the community level and find out what, if any, differences exist between women and men in a non-institutional environment. Thus, the aim of this exploration was to learn more about how a non-clinical, non-institutional population of male and female mental health consumer-survivors perceived the significance of substance abuse in their lives.

2. METHODOLOGY

The population, from which the sample of 300 was drawn, was both non-institutional and non-clinical as study respondents were not drawn from any counselling agency's records or caseloads nor from a psychiatric facility, but were recruited through posters and word of mouth. Data collection consisted of a quantitative questionnaire administered to a sample of 150 men and 150 women experiencing chronic mental health challenges, all of whom were living in the community in London, Ontario, at the time of the interviews. Four survey instruments were used: (1) the Colorado Client Assessment Record (CCAR) (Ellis, Wackwitz & Foster, 1996); (2) the Lehman Quality of Life Scale (Lehman, Postrado & Rachuba, 1993); (3) the Childhood Trauma Questionnaire (Bernstein et al., 1994); and (4) the Utilization of Hospital and Community Services Questionnaire form (modified from Browne et al., 1990).

Qualitative information was also collected through eight focus groups consisting of 36 women and 29 men, conducted between July 5, 2002 and September 3, 2002, and ranging in size from five to 13, with a mean of 8.1 running between 60 and 90 minutes. A proximity content analysis was used in analyzing the focus group data using the following key words and derivations: alcohol, drinking, drug, substance use, and addiction. Proximity content analysis looks for the co-occurrence of explicit concepts in the text. Key words are determined and then scanned for through the transcribed interviews to find interrelated, co-occurring concepts (Krippendorff, 2004; Neuendorf, 2002).

3. RESULTS

The mean age of first contact with the mental health system of the 300 participants in the quantitative portion of the study was 21, and the mean age of initial hospitalization was 23. Women in the sample had been hospitalized in a psychiatric facility significantly more than had men—an average of nine times—while men had been hospitalized an average of six ($t = -3.518$, $df = 268$, $p<.001$). A majority of both men (n = 117, 78.0 percent) and women (n = 123, 82.0 percent) were using psychotherapeutic medications at the time of the interviews. Schizophrenia was the most frequent primary diagnosis for male participants, followed by mood disorder, while the opposite was true for women ($t = -48.662$, $df = 262$, $p <.000$) (Table 18.1). It is interesting to note the absence of post-traumatic stress disorder (PTSD) as a separate diagnosis (it is part of the other category) in light of its growing importance in the area of concurrent disorders (Brady, Sonne et al., 2005; Jacobsen, Southwick & Kosten, 2001; Najavits, 2002). This is partially a result of the length of time after many of the study participants' initial diagnosis, when PTSD was not actively considered as a causative factor. It also speaks to the power of first diagnosis and, once it is attached to an individual, how it can become a lifetime label, especially when the person becomes street-engaged.

Table 18.1: Primary Diagnosis by Sex

	Male n = 134	Female n = 129	Total n = 263
Schizophrenia	64 (47.8%)	43 (33.3%)	107 (40.7%)
Mood disorder	44 (32.8%)	51 (39.5%)	95 (36.1%)
Developmental handicap	4 (3.0%)	7 (5.4%)	11 (4.2%)
Anxiety disorder	8 (6.0%)	3 (2.3%)	11 (4.2%)
Personality disorder	0	4 (3.1%)	4 (1.5%)
Organic disorder	0	1 (0.8%)	1 (.4%)
Other	14 (10.5%)	20 (15.5%)	34 (12.9%)

Results of the CCAR indicated that only two (1.3 percent) women in the study reported that their substance abuse was a moderate problem, none reported it as any more severe, and 58 (38.7 percent) stated it was no problem at all. In contrast, 14 (9.3 percent) men stated that their drug use was a moderate to severe problem, twice as many men as women stated that it was a slight problem, and 12 percent fewer men stated that substance abuse was not an issue in their lives. While there was a significant difference between the sexes (t = 18.695, df = 299, p<.000), the majority of both men and women did not report that their use of psychoactive drugs was a major issue in their lives (Table 18.2). While underreporting the amounts and effects of drugs has been an ongoing issue in the addiction literature, this is not considered a problem in this study due to the respondents' openness in discussing their mental health and sexual abuse histories.

Table 18.2: Severity of Personal Substance Abuse

	None		Slight		Moderate		Severe		Extreme
	1	2	3	4	5	6	7	8	9
Males n=150	40 (26.7%)	56 (37.3%)	25 (16.7%)	15 (10.0%)	9 (6.0%)	4 (2.7%)	1 (.7%)	0	0
Females n=150	58 (38.7%)	70 (46.7%)	11 (7.3%)	9 (6.0%)	2 (1.3%)	0	0	0	0
Total n=300	98 (32.7%)	126 (42.0%)	36 (12.0%)	24 (8.0%)	11 (3.7%)	4 (1.3%)	1 (0.3%)	0	0

The CCAR does not distinguish between "normal" and "abnormal" results; rather, it is the dispersion of scores that highlights differences. In examining overall problem severity, it was the male participants who generally scored lower than the women (t = −44.104, df = 297, p<.000). Slightly fewer than half the female respondents (n = 68, 45.6 percent) scored 5 or greater on overall problem severity compared to 58 (38.7 percent) men, while 40 (26.8 percent) women reported that their overall problem severity was slight to none compared to 61 (40.9 percent) men (Table 18.3).

Table 18.3: Overall Problem Severity

	None		Slight		Moderate		Severe		Extreme
	1	2	3	4	5	6	7	8	9
Males n=149	1 (.7%)	18 (12.0%)	42 (28.0%)	30 (20.0%)	42 (28.0%)	14 (9.3%)	2 (1.3%)	0	0
Females n=149	0	11 (7.4%)	29 (19.5%)	41 (27.5%)	47 (31.5%)	18 (12.1%)	3 (2.0%)	0	0
Total n=298	1 (.3)	29 (9.7%)	71 (23.8%)	71 (23.8%)	89 (29.8%)	32 (10.7%)	5 (1.7%)	0	0

While more women than men reported that they would benefit from assistance in managing their medication, there was no significant difference in the overall level of functioning responses. Twenty-four (16.1 percent) men and 21 (14.1 percent) women stated that their overall level of functioning was moderate to very high, while 125 (83.9 percent) men rated their overall functioning average to moderately low compared to 127 (85.2 percent) women (Table 18.4).

Table 18.4: Overall Level of Functioning

	Very High 1	2	Moderately High 3	4	Average 5	6	Moderately Low 7	8	Very Low 9
Males n=149	1 (.7)	0	5 (3.4%)	18 (12.1%)	58 (38.9%)	57 (38.3%)	10 (6.7%)	0	0
Females n=149	0	1 (.7%)	5 (3.4%)	15 (10.1%)	65 (43.6%)	50 (33.6%)	12 (8.1%)	1 (.7%)	0

More women reported a family history of substance abuse and more problematic substance abuse by their parents, though more women than men also reported that their parents never or rarely used alcohol or other psychoactive drugs. However, overall there was no statistically significant difference regarding parental substance abuse (Table 18.5).

Table 18.5: Parental Substance Use

	Never	Rarely	Sometimes	Often	Very Often
Males n=148	56 (37.8%)	8 (5.4%)	36 (24.3%)	21 (14.2%)	27 (18.2%)
Females n=146	63 (43.2%)	11 (7.5%)	21 (14.4%)	23 (15.8%)	28 (19.2%)
Total n=294	119 (40.5%)	19 (6.5%)	57 (19.4%)	44 (15.0%)	55 (18.7%)

When asked, as part of the Childhood Trauma Questionnaire, if their parents were ever too drunk or high to care for the family, the majority of respondents, 179 (60.9%) who replied stated that this had never occurred. There had been some parenting problems because of substance use for 51 (17.3%) people, while 64 (21.8%) reported that the statement was often or very often true. However, it was again slightly though significantly more women (n = 36, 24.4%) than men (n = 28, 19.1%) who stated that there had been parenting issues due to substance abuse during their childhoods (t = −16.493, df = 293, p<.000) (Table 18.6).

Table 18.6: Parental Substance Abuse Impaired Ability to Parent

	Never	Rarely	Sometimes	Often	Very Often
Males n=147	97 (66.0%)	7 (4.8%)	15 (10.2%)	11 (7.5%)	17 (11.6%)
Females n=147	82 (55.8%)	13 (8.4%)	16 (10.9%)	12 (8.1%)	24 (16.3%)
Total n=294	179 (60.9%)	20 (6.8%)	31 (10.5%)	23 (7.8%)	41 (14.0%)

In reviewing the transcripts of the focus groups, it was very interesting to discover that during the course of the eight one-to-one and half-hour sessions, involving 65 people, that there were only four references to substance abuse—two by men and two by women. The issue of addiction was simply not a focus. Of the four responses, both those made by male participants referred to personal problematic use:

> "I built two houses right near _____ village, just before I ended up at the group home, and part of the reason I ended up there was my uncle 'cause I was looking after him 'cause he's alcoholic, and I was supposed to show up for him and this kind of stuff, and then it didn't work out, and I just got mixed up in drugs."

> "I didn't want to live on drugs and booze anymore, so I came here to get out."

The only comments made by two different female participants dealt more directly with current and past housing and living conditions:

> "We're not allowed to drink or use any kind of substance, and you have to be home by curfew.... If I'm going to go out and have a social drink with a friend, I can't. I'm not allowed. I automatically [have to] leave the house for 24 hours."

> "I had already put up with worse than that [neighbour issues], much worse than that for many years.... I had to make [a neighbour] threaten me [to get the police involved].... Well, he was just a little weasel guy, a little weasel drug dealer."

In contrast to substance abuse, themes that were discussed by every focus group were the inadequacy of their incomes and problems with finding appropriate, affordable housing, let alone having a choice in their accommodations. Other themes that were prominent were food, transportation, and the stigma of having a mental health label.

4. DISCUSSION

Not unexpectedly, there were several prominent differences observed between community-based male and female mental health system consumer-survivors, including primary diagnosis, personal and family histories of substance use and abuse, and family histories of mental health issues. Personal use of psychoactive substances was more of a primary issue for men than for women, though interestingly, women reported slightly more parental substance use and problematic use than did male respondents. In contrast, women scored greater on overall problem severity, though there was little difference found in overall level of functioning. This indicates that mental health issues were perceived as more of a problem for women than for men in this study, which is further supported by the greater number of average psychiatric hospitalizations that women reported. This first finding further supports the belief that sex-specific services for community-based mental health system consumer-survivors need to be developed and delivered with a greater focus on feminist-based interventions for women compared to the current primary male-created and -focused treatment system. Historically, residential substance abuse programs in Canada have provided more beds for men than for women (Canadian Centre on Substance Abuse, 2000), and likewise there are more concurrent disorder programs serving men than women (Centre for Addiction and Mental Health & Canadian Centre on Substance Abuse, 2001). There has been an ongoing question about whether this was warranted based on client need, and this study's findings indicate that there is justification for this disparity. However, additional female-specific programming would be beneficial, particularly in residential settings where there are issues of safety in disclosure when there are only two or three women in a facility housing a dozen or more residents.

For individuals with a mental health problem who are also abusing psychoactive substances, the risks are compounded, particularly in community-based situations, where social supports may not always be consistently present or available. Unfortunately, participants in this study reported a lack of primary and secondary social supports as the majority of them were not in a long-term intimate personal relationship, nor did the majority benefit from the stability, routine, and social support provided by having permanent employment. This finding suggests that these individuals are at risk for developing substance abuse-related problems.

Thus, it is even more striking and unexpected that there was virtually no discussion of alcohol or other psychoactive drugs or substance abuse issues in general during the eight focus group sessions. This may have to do with the stigma and oppression felt by this group. However, it also speaks clearly to the reality that there are simply much more pressing issues in this group's lives than their use of psychoactive substances. When asked direct questions regarding housing, social supports, and community service needs, only four responses related these open-ended questions to drugs or substance abuse in any way. Despite the growing attention on concurrent mental health and substance abuse disorder issues, and the consistent reporting of a greater prevalence of substance abuse issues among those with diagnosed mental health problems, substance abuse was not perceived as a significant concern by either female or male participants. While some may consider this a result of self-reporting bias or issues of sampling, over 350 individuals participated in this research and they openly talked about sexual abuse, their issues of mental health, and their homelessness. Themes that were of much greater and more direct importance to participants were finances, poverty, housing conditions, food, and transportation.

As with any study relying on secondary analysis of data, the findings are limited by how the data were collected and how the questions were posed. While several of the quantitative scales addressed substance abuse issues, the results were still all self-reported, with the inherent limitations of underreporting, including subjects wishing to provide answers that appear correct and a natural underreporting of drug use, which occurs when this content area is asked in a face-to-face interview with no anonymity. However, the data collection process itself relates to the question of perception, suggesting that what helping professionals consider issues in clients' lives do not always align with the issues that consumer-survivors consider of primary importance. This point should be carefully weighed by social workers, nurses, and other helping professionals as they engage with community-based mental health consumer-survivors.

This study provided an insight into the substance abuse concerns, or lack thereof, of a non-clinical population of community-based Canadian mental health consumer-survivors. While substantive differences by sex were observed, what was most evident was that this entire group does not prioritize their substance use as a major concern for day-to-day living. While treatment of concurrent disorders has taken on more focus in the clinical world, potential clients did not perceive any urgency to attend substance abuse counselling, whether or not it was male- or female-specific.

As Skinner (2009) recently discussed, for people with concurrent disorders, the daily practices and policies of the social and health services systems that they utilize often fail to support and actualize them. Rather, they "regularly report that they experience services as uninviting, unresponsive, disinterested, fragmented, and inaccessible, particularly if the problems are complex" (p. 4). There is a disconnect between clients' basic needs and the need to address drug use and substance abuse issues, with substance use simply not considered as significant an issue as other pragmatic problems of daily living. Thus, the increasing focus on concurrent disorder treatment will also need to consider barriers of unmet day-to-day living needs that preclude clients from accessing assistance. Monies are certainly needed in increasing treatment options and enhancing treatment opportunities. However, without taking care of basic needs, those who would benefit from the services provided by these programs may remain in a state of precontemplation regarding their drug use and may never become ready to change.

REFERENCES

Bernstein, J., Fink, L., Handelsman, L., Foote, J., Lovejoy, M., Wenzel, D., Sapartz, E. & Ruggiero, J. (1994). Initial reliability and validity of a new retrospective measure of child abuse and neglect. *American Journal of Psychiatry, 151*(8), 1132–36.

Booth, B., Curran, G. & Han, X. (2004). Predictors of short-term course of drinking in untreated rural and urban at-risk drinkers: Effects of gender, illegal drug use, and psychiatric comorbidity. *Journal of Studies in Alcohol, 65*(1), 63–73.

Brady, K.T., Sonne, S., Anton, R.F., Randall, C.L., Back, S.E. & Simpson, K. (2005). Sertraline in the treatment of co-occurring alcohol dependence and posttraumatic stress disorder. *Alcoholism: Clinical & Experimental Research, 29*(3), 395–401.

British Columbia Inter-ministry Task Group. (1999). *Meeting the challenge of serious mental illness and substance misuse.* Vancouver: Riverview Hospital.

Browne, G., Arpin, K., Corey, P., Fitch, M. & Gafni, A. (1990). Individual correlates of health services utilization and the cost of poor adjustment to chronic illness. *Medical Care, 28*(1), 43–58.

Brunette, M. & Drake, R. (1998). Gender differences in homeless persons with schizophrenia and substance abuse. *Community Mental Health Journal, 34*(6), 627–42.

Canadian Centre on Substance Abuse. (2000). *Directory of substance abuses organizations in Canada 2000.* Ottawa: CCSA.

Canadian Centre on Substance Abuse. (2002). *Best practices: Concurrent mental health and substance abuse disorders.* Ottawa: Health Canada.

Centre for Addiction and Mental Health. (2001). *Best practices: Concurrent mental health and substance use disorders.* Ottawa: Health Canada.

Centre for Addiction and Mental Health & Canadian Centre on Substance Abuse. (2001). *National program inventory: Concurrent mental health and substance use disorders.* Ottawa: Health Canada.

Comité permanent de lutte à la toxicomanie. (1997). *Avis sur la double problématique toxicomanie et problèmes de santé mentale.* Présenté au ministre de la Santé et des Services sociaux. Montréal: Comité permanent de lutte à la toxicomanie.

Comité permanent de lutte à la toxicomanie. (2000). *Drogues, alcool, et toxicomanie au Québec, des inquiétudes à l'action.* Rapport au ministre de la Santé et des Services Sociaux. Montréal: Comité permanent de lutte à la toxicomanie.

Drake, R.E., Osher, F.C. & Wallach, M.A. (1991). Homelessness and dual diagnosis. *American Psychologist, 46*(11), 1149–58.

Ellis, R., Wackwitz, J. & Foster, M. (1996). *Treatment outcomes using level of functioning and independent measures of change: An alternate approach for measurement of change.* Denver: Decision Support Services, Colorado Department of Mental Health.

Forchuk, C., Thames Valley District Health Council, Essex Kent Lambton District Health Council, Grey Bruce Huron Perth District Health Council, Waterloo Region Wellington Dufferin District Health Council, Cline, B., Coatsworth-Puspoky, R., Csiernik, R., DaCosta, B., Hall, B., Hoch, J., Jensen, E., Nelson, G., Ouseley, S., Speechley, M. & Ward-Griffen, C. (2002). Mental health and housing: Family and consumer perspectives. *Journal of Urban Health, 79*(4), Supplement 1, S89–S90.

Forchuk, C., Ward-Griffin, C., Csiernik, R. & Turner, K. (2006). Surviving the tornado: Psychiatric survivor experiences of getting, losing, and keeping housing. *Psychiatric Services, 57*(4), 558–62.

Frye, M., Altshuler, L., McElroy, S., Suppes, T., Keck, P., Denicoff, K., Nolen, W., Kupka, R., Leverich, G., Pollio, C., Gruenze, H., Walden, J. & Post, R. (2003). Gender differences in prevalence, risk, and clinical correlates of alcoholism comorbidity in bipolar disorder. *American Journal of Psychiatry, 160*(5), 883–89.

Gilder, D., Wall, T. & Ehlers, C. (2004). Comorbidity of select anxiety and affective disorders with alcohol dependence in southwest California Indians. *Alcoholism: Clinical and Experimental Research, 28*(12), 1805–13.

Greenbaum, T. (1993). *The handbook of focus group research.* Toronto: Maxwell MacMillan Canada.

Grella, C. (1996). Background and overview of mental health and substance abuse treatment systems: Meeting the needs of women who are pregnant or parenting. *Journal of Psychoactive Drugs, 28*(4), 319–43.

Hanna, E. & Grant, B. (1997). Gender differences in DSM-IV alcohol use disorders and major depression as distributed in the general population: Clinical implications. *Comprehensive Psychiatry, 38*(4), 202–12.

Helzer, J. & Pryzbeck, T. (1988). The co-occurrence of alcoholism and other psychiatric disorders on the general population and its impact on treatment. *Journal of Studies on Alcohol, 49,* 219–24.

Jacobsen, L., Southwick, S. & Kosten, T., (2001). Substance use disorder in patients with posttraumatic stress disorder: A review of the literature. *American Journal of Psychiatry, 158,* 1184–90.

Kessler, R.C., Nelson, C.B., McGonagle, K.A., Edlund, M.J., Frank, R.G. & Leaf, P.J. (1996). The epidemiology of co-occurring addictive and mental disorders: Implications for prevention and service utilization. *American Journal of Orthopsychiatry, 66,* 17–31.

Krippendorff, K. (2004). *Content analysis: An introduction to its methodology.* Thousand Oaks: Sage Publications.

Krueger, R.A. (1994). *Focus groups: A practical guide for applied research.* Thousand Oaks: Sage Publications.

Lehman, A., Postrado, L. & Rachuba, L. (1993). Convergent validation of life assessments for persons with severe mental illnesses. *Quality of Life Research, 2*(5), 327–33.

Mandersheid, R.W. & Rosenstein, M.J. (1992). Homeless persons with mental illness and alcohol or other drug abuse: Current research, policy, and prospects. *Current Opinion in Psychiatry, 5,* 273–78.

Morgan, D. (1988). *Focus groups as qualitative research.* Beverly Hills: Sage Publications.

Najavits, L.M. (2002). *Seeking safety: A treatment manual for PTSD and substance abuse.* New York: Guilford.

Neuendorf, K. (2002). *The content analysis guidebook.* Thousand Oaks: Sage Publications.

Ontario Ministry of Health. (1999). *Making it happen.* Toronto: Integrated Policy and Planning Division, and Mental Health System Management.

Rush, B., Urbanoski, K., Bassani, D., Castel, S., Wild, T.C., Strike, C., Kimberley, D. & Somers, J. (2008). Prevalence of co-occurring substance use and other mental disorders in the Canadian population. *Canadian Journal of Psychiatry, 53*(12), 800–09.

Sinha, R. & Rounsaville, B. (2002). Sex differences in depressed substance abusers. *Journal of Clinical Psychiatry, 63*(7), 616–27.

Skinner, W. (2009). Essaying complexity: Exploring the gap between holistic values and integrated practices. *Mental Health and Substance Use: Dual Diagnosis, 2*(1), 4–7.

Treloar, C. & Holt, M. (2008). Complex vulnerabilities as barrier to treatment for illicit drug using with high prevalence mental health co-morbidities. *Mental Health and Substance Use: Dual Diagnosis, 1*(1), 84–95.

Section V

INTRODUCTION:
MOVING FORWARD

This final section brings us back to the beginning—back to Margaret. The final two chapters recap her legacy to the community and the ripples her presence has created.

Chapter 19 provides the history of Margaret's Haven, its origins, the partnerships that were created in developing this unique initiative, and the issues that eventually led to its closure. However, the measure of Margaret's Haven is not just what it was, but what it has led to and continues to create in the community. This legacy is further described in Chapter 20. The final chapter of *Homelessness, Housing, and the Experiences of Mental Health Consumer-Survivors: Finding Truths—Creating Change* provides an overview of what has been accomplished through the CURA and highlights the question of "Why should communities be involved in research?" In addressing this question, Chapter 20 examines who was and who is the community, and what the various partners gained from being involved in this unique process. Margaret's Haven's achievements led to concrete changes in policies and practices, as well as the more elusive enhancement of "voice." The greatest cost of this type of process is the time that must be invested to make it successful, though the process itself is often the most significant reward for all those who participate.

Chapter 19

MARGARET'S HAVEN: THE STORY AND THE PROCESS

Elsabeth Jensen, Cheryl Forchuk,
Rick Csiernik, Katherine Turner,
and Pamela McKane

1. INTRODUCTION

As has been demonstrated by the previous chapters, homelessness is an increasingly pressing social, economic, and political issue. Also, the diversity of those who are homeless and the factors that lead to homelessness are becoming clearer. However, still, as throughout history, there are those who are blamed for their homelessness—now they are labelled "hard to house." What are the factors that contribute to someone being "hard to house," and what kind of housing and/or supports would contribute to the successful housing of the "hardest to house"? These were some of the critical questions that a group of people in London, Ontario, attempted to address in the mid-1990s. They came together to develop a solution to the problem of housing women who were deemed "hardest to house." This would lead not only to the CURA that has been described in great detail thus far, but also to one specific housing project that typifies the entire process, Margaret's Haven (MH).

The planning group for Margaret's Haven was formed after staff at LIFE*SPIN (LS), a grassroots-oriented social service agency that provided assistance to low-income families and individuals, became aware of one particular client who was chronically homeless. In the spring of 1997, "Margaret" (a pseudonym), a long-time resident of London who was homeless at the time and a consumer-survivor of the health care and social service systems, approached LS seeking help. Margaret had lived in women's shelters and found that the programs did not meet her needs. The shelters lacked adequate resources and staff to support her. She did not trust anyone and feared readmission to the London Psychiatric Hospital. LIFE*SPIN was able to support her by treating her with dignity while helping her obtain financial support and a place to live. However, she remained caught in the cycle of homelessness and the criminal justice system. Margaret had "fallen through the cracks" as she had run out of housing options because she refused to be medicated for a mental health issue and had significant rental arrears. Margaret's experience was the inspiration for the creation of a unique housing project, one whose goal would be to create a permanent home for Margaret and those like her who had been labelled "hard to house." The initiative was formally called Margaret's Haven Non-profit Housing (MH), and this chapter is the story of its evolution.

2. LIFE*SPIN

Margaret's Haven came to exist because of LIFE*SPIN, a community-based social service organization established in 1989 whose mandate is to provide information, support, advocacy, and community-based programs for low-income residents of London, including involvement in community economic development initiatives. LS has historically had an emphasis on women's issues. However, LS is far more than just another community-based, non-profit organization. It was and is a nurturing place where people could come together in a community of practice to share, learn, and challenge. Many of the staff and volunteers of LS were drawn together because, as individuals, their life experiences had forced them to face difficult questions about society and their place in it. This, in turn, led the organization as a collective to develop unique commitments to social change. Many of LIFE*SPIN's staff and volunteers were also attracted at a very intuitive level to the idea of community economic development (CED) and the holistic frame of reference for sustainable development it represents.

In February 1997, the Collective Common Market Enterprises (CCME) committee of LS began to explore the potential for creating a housing project using community economic development strategies and tools. Many of the staff of LS believed that CED was not just about project development alone, but envisioned a movement toward a broader, sustainable, long-term solution to poverty, mental illness, and homelessness. For this reason, advocacy and education for structural and policy change were seen as foundational and integral to the initiative. This belief was also at the root of the origins of the CURA, and the two projects developed simultaneously and became intertwined over time.

LIFE*SPIN staff were involved in other CED initiatives, including the research, development, and implementation of peer-lending circles for entrepreneurs and provision of small business supports. LS also assisted in implementing a community forum for the Affordable Housing Task Force of the City of London, developed the framework for a community development loan association focused on community development activities, and laid the groundwork for the bricks-and-mortar operations of Margaret's Haven. LS staff wrote policy position papers on income supports, affordable housing, community reinvestment, mental health, homelessness, and other vital concerns, all with a focus on making this information accessible to both the public at large and individuals who might be in a position to create change in the existing systems. The organization participated in community forums, committees, and local, regional, and national conferences, often facilitating workshops on housing and CED-related issues. LIFE*SPIN took every opportunity possible to participate in local, provincial, and federal government consultations on the issues in which the organization was involved. As the staff of LS discovered, the community learned because the root of the work attempted was collaborative. It was a major undertaking to develop and sustain these networks of connection, support, and learning, but it paid dividends over and over again.

3. MARGARET'S HAVEN

The Beginning

Staff from LIFE*SPIN began to consider what kind of accommodation would be required to house Margaret and others like her in order to successfully end their homelessness. A staff member, Janet Kreda, held focus groups with mental health consumer-survivors to determine the desired features of this new housing. In the winter of 1998, a team of 17 people, including the staff of LS, mental health professionals, planners, and housing specialists, formed an advisory committee to guide the development of this new housing project, which had the following stated objectives:

- to create affordable housing for women with psychiatric support needs that is safe, attractive, and supported
- to create a project with the long-term potential to be self-sustaining
- to create a model for future creation of supportive housing for consumer-survivors
- to provide an environment that is private, safe, and secure
- to provide accommodation that is affordable
- to provide permanent housing
- to provide community space, including a common room, kitchen, and garden space
- to provide access to flexible support services
- to provide the potential for intimate community living
- to be consumer-survivor–run
- to conduct a formal evaluation of the project

From these objectives a mission statement was developed:

> Margaret's Haven Community Housing Project is community-based, women-centred, permanent housing that is safe, attractive, supportive, and affordable. Margaret's Haven is a place where women with psychiatric challenges and a history of housing difficulties can live independently in a co-operative environment with dignity and respect. All residents contribute to the community of Margaret's according to their abilities.

By the spring of 1998, seven committees had been struck: (1) finance and fundraising, (2) by-law, (3) tenant selection, (4) site, (5) social policy, (6) legal, and (7) community education and promotion to focus on the specific tasks associated with the development of this unique housing project. In the fall of 1998, Janet Kreda was hired as project coordinator, and a logo contest, needs survey, and consultations with housing planners across Canada were undertaken. By the end of the year, funds had been obtained for a demonstration project grant from the Federal Homelessness Secretariat.

The Development

The tenant selection committee's application process focused on two key criteria: tenants must be homeless or at risk of homelessness, and they must also have a history of psychiatric illness. Throughout the winter and spring of 1999, fundraising activities were organized, including preparation of a formal funding proposal, while the site committee focused on determining potential sites for the housing project. Given the importance of safety, potential sites were identified and they were toured during the day and night to ascertain the relative security of the area. However, finances were also a determining factor in selecting potential sites for this new housing project, as was access to public transit because most of the tenants would rely exclusively on this form of transportation. In May 1999, the site committee selected a potential location and a conditional offer on that site was accepted. In June, a needs assessment was prepared and a neighbourhood education campaign that included public meetings and written materials was begun.

It was determined that tenancy would be on a month-to-month basis, and residents would not be required to sign a one-year lease. Units would be either one or two bedrooms with access to a common green space, including a garden. However, tenants were required to have mental health supports in place when they applied. Margaret's Haven would supplement this by providing seven-day-a-week, individual, flexible, on-site housing-related supports. These supports were also envisioned as having a role in linking MH tenants with other community-based supports they might require. An agreement was struck so that the required housing supports would be provided by London East Community Mental Health Services (LECMHS), an agency with experience in providing community-based mental health. The funding for such supports would be sought from the Ontario Ministry of Health and Long-Term Care.

The development of Margaret's Haven occurred at a time when federal and provincial involvement in affordable housing development and management had been downloaded to municipalities in Ontario. The government of the day argued that the private sector should develop affordable housing since it could do so more efficiently than the government. Consequently the finances for purchasing a property for MH was a combination of federal funding for capital expenses, private donations, and grants from philanthropic foundations, including a capital grant of $60,000 from the City of London to LS. Bridge financing for the same amount was arranged with the Canadian Alternative Investment Co-operative, and it was repaid directly through the grant once it was released. Thus, when the site was finally purchased in 2000, Margaret's Haven became one of the few new housing projects to be undertaken in Ontario that year, a truly extraordinary accomplishment regardless of the purpose of the project.

During this time, academics at the University of Western Ontario and King's University College[1] were approached about the possibility of assisting with an evaluation of this new housing project. Out of this initial discussion and discussions with other community housing and homelessness agencies, a letter of intent for a much larger initiative—a Community-University Research Alliance (CURA)—was developed and ultimately funded by the Social Sciences and Humanities Research Council (SSHRC). As part of its activities, the CURA would conduct a formal evaluation of Margaret's Haven.

The Project

LIFE*SPIN took possession of the new property on June 1, 2000, and a collaboration agreement and proposal for funding was formalized with the Ministry of Health by London East Community Mental Health Service to provide support services for residents. The Ontario Trillium Foundation was instrumental in providing initial funding to MH for the supports during the initial functioning of the project. Unfortunately, strains developed in the relationship between LS and the MH advisory committee regarding who would manage Margaret's Haven now that it was a reality. While Margaret's Haven had been developed by an advisory board, the LIFE*SPIN board had operated under the belief that MH would remain a component of that organization and not operate as a stand-alone entity.

During the developmental period, there was great personal stress on those most intimately involved in the project because of inadequate funding for administration and project development. All staff worked full-time or more and received, at best, part-time pay and, at worst, no pay at times. Nevertheless, each person had reasons for choosing to commit to this work. There was huge satisfaction in the opportunity to learn, grow, and chart a new path.

Throughout the fall of 2000, the MH office was moved to the site, lease negotiations continued, and renovations proceeded with the usual challenges and hiccups that accompany any complex endeavour. Arrangements for supports for the women were finalized through the use of Trillium's interim funding and, finally, Ministry of Health funds. During the winter and spring of 2000, MH separated from LS as an independent, incorporated, charitable, non-profit organization. A five-person board of directors, along with a 12-person advisory committee, was established and the MH board offered to purchase the property from LS over time.

The tenant selection committee conducted interviews and selected tenants for MH on an ongoing basis from the spring of 2000, with the slate of tenants approved by the new board in September. On November 1, 2000, the first tenants moved into MH, followed by additional tenants throughout 2001. The idea had become a concrete reality.

Although great care had been taken to choose the best possible site with the financial limits of the project, drug and sex trade issues within the area became a substantial problem for residents. Relationships with the local Business Improvement Area (BIA) and the police department were developed to address these concerns, which led staff and residents of MH to become very involved in local community development and homelessness initiatives in the neighbourhood. However, the issue would be one of concern throughout the lifespan of Margaret's Haven.

Margaret's Haven struggled to balance the physical needs of tenants with the psychosocial supports they also required. This was an ongoing challenge, particularly as the financial realities of running a housing project conflicted with the desire to provide optimal housing and support for the women. This created tension between MH and LECMHS, and in the end proved to be insurmountable, which ultimately contributed to a decision to terminate the project at the site. Extensive efforts continued for an extended period to identify a new site that was both affordable and safe, but in the end, no other property could be found.

The realities of working with a high-need population were part of the project from the onset and the goal of the project. While one tenant experienced the longest period of stable residency as an adult because of Margaret's Haven, and while others were able to stabilize their lives, not every resident had a successful experience. The greatest problem involved a woman who, after more than two years of living at MH, lived in squalor as a result of her illness. MH staff tried to work with her and hoped that she could remain with the assistance of outside supports to deal with the health and safety concerns. MH was seen as the last resort in terms of housing for her, and eviction was never part of the philosophy or mandate of the project. However, after a great deal of research and advocacy, it was clear that the only option available to MH as a landlord to address this problem and to protect the other residents was to evict the tenant. Supports to deal with senile squalor were simply not available through the resources MH could provide.

This fundamental issue raised questions in how the supports were structured at MH and to whom the staff on site was ultimately responsible—MH or LECMHS? In March 2003, LECMHS informed MH that it would end its partnership with MH to provide support services for the tenants, and that it would move the MH tenants to WOTCH Housing, an organization with which LECMHS had entered into a new partnership. The MH board met, discussed this issue, and decided with deep regret that the only option, given the time frame of these changes and finances, was for MH to cease property management operations at its current site and for its tenants to move to the new housing option. Margaret's Haven ceased to operate housing on May 1, 2003.

The Structural Legacy

In spite of the outcome, throughout its years of operation, MH developed significant credibility in the community, which was invaluable in securing funding and also in partnering with other community agencies in other projects. MH's credibility within the community was evident as its most significant funder agreed to work with MH in developing a proposal to bring together key stakeholders within the community to discuss the role that MH had played and the impact it had on the community, and to identify ways in which MH's work could be continued in other ways.

Other than the creation of housing for the women of Margaret's Haven, the most important legacy is the CURA and the networks that have developed among community members and between community members and academics as a result of it. The impact that this alliance's advocacy and research has had at the policy level is difficult to fully quantify, but should not be underestimated. Nor should the value of the lasting networks developed within the community as a result of the alliance be underestimated in terms of moving forward the initial agenda of Margaret's Haven.

The Personal Legacy

While Margaret's Haven no longer exists, it met its intended mandate in a way no other organization had done previously in the London community. Eleven residents of Margaret's Haven agreed to voluntarily participate in an evaluation of the housing project, and three additional women provided information through exit interviews, which were conducted after they left Margaret's Haven for more permanent housing. The average age of the residents interviewed was 41, with a range from 23 to 52. Two women were separated, two were widowed, and seven described themselves as single/never married. Nine lived alone, while two had a household of two. Three reported that they had children under the age of 18 years with whom they would have liked to live. The group had four members who had completed post-secondary education, four who had completed high school, and three who did not give information about their level of education. One woman described herself as employed part-time, while 10 described themselves as unemployed.

The women reported a variety of housing histories, ranging from living in one home in the two years before coming to Margaret's Haven to experiencing 10 moves in two years. Five of the women interviewed came from living in an apartment in the preceding year, and one left her apartment in order to escape a violent situation. Unfortunately, the data do not contain any information about the quality of the apartments where these women lived. Two women came directly from shelters, while two others had been housed by Regional Mental Health Care in London. One of these women had been in hospital for two years, while the other had entered hospital after losing housing when her relationship ended. One woman moved to Margaret's Haven from a group home, while the last woman had lived in a rooming house after residing in a shelter.

The participants' average age of first contact with the mental health system ranged from five years of age to 38, with an average of 20.5. Age of first psychiatric hospitalization ranged from age 13 to 38, with an average age of 22.4 years. The group averaged 19.7 hospitalizations to date, with the fewest hospitalizations being two and the greatest being estimated at 100. While seven women had been in hospital in the preceding two years, only one had been hospitalized in the month preceding the interview.

Of the three women who had stayed at Margaret's Haven and were then able to move on, one had been homeless for most of a year, while two had lived in poor-quality housing before being accepted at MH. In general they found their time at MH to be a positive experience, and all indicated that they felt they were in a better place as a result of their experience at Margaret's Haven.

Several themes recurred throughout the exit interviews. Safety was discussed repeatedly, particularly a fire, which led to a feeling of insecurity. Other factors that caused the women to feel unsafe were the presence of the sex and drug trades in the neighbourhood. Living with others who at times exhibited disturbing behaviours was a problem mentioned several times, although no solution was suggested. In contrast, the presence of consistent expectations and rules provided a structure that supported a feeling of security. Having people available to talk to and who could help with problem solving was also considered a significant positive feature. The garden was likewise described as an asset. Two women identified clearly during their exit interviews that they had been helped throughout their stay at MH and were better off as a result.

Physical environmental issues at MH included the need to climb stairs, which was difficult for those with mobility problems, and the lack of secured entry to the complex. Having strangers knock on the door in the early morning hours was a problem mentioned several times by different respondents. This negatively affected their sense of security. The presence of vermin was a detractor as well. The need for controlled entry for safety was a recurring theme. The women also recommended the need for a safe neighbourhood to walk around in, even in the middle of the night. The need for laundry facilities was also mentioned.

It was clear throughout all the interviews that poverty was a huge issue for the women. While Margaret's Haven could not have a direct role in solving this problem, there might have been a greater role that MH could have played through advocacy or by developing programs to help the women get at least part-time work of some kind.

4. CONCLUSION

Margaret's Haven existed because a small, talented, committed, dedicated, and passionate group of people chose to look beyond the limits they saw to create a vision of how the community could move beyond them. MH was special because these same people were willing to put themselves on the line and turn at least part of this vision into a reality. They did this in as open, transparent, and collaborative a manner as possible. In retrospect, while this initiative could not be sustained in its conceived format, it succeeded brilliantly in many ways. Margaret's Haven ultimately met its mandate by housing women with serious mental illness who were, for the most part, experiencing difficulty in being housed. The limited number of exit interviews also cautiously support Margaret's Haven as an experience that improved the lives of the women who lived there during its brief existence.

Housing and mental health legislation is, in theory, geared to protect tenants' rights in housing situations and patients' rights in care situations. However, the implementation can create situations that limit the ability to intervene and provide needed supports. For landlords, this means that often the only recourse they have is eviction. For the mental health system, this means that they sometimes cannot act when they know they are needed. To this, of course, is added the obligation of helping professionals to support the self-determination of clients.

We can understand exactly what a person wants most and what is best to support his or her development, but if society is unable or unwilling to provide it because of inadequate resources or competing priorities, it is unrealistic to insist that these things be provided regardless. A space must be created to negotiate a new way through the impasse. Similarly, policies need to be created in a more strategic and sustainable fashion. That is why long-term, cross-sectoral dialogue and development are so important. One size does not fit all in policy or housing type. The process always affects outcomes. Flawed processes create flawed and skewed results. Consequently, if individuals do not trust enough to engage in difficult and tense conversations with each other, they cannot influence each other's understanding of the situation and create a new approach to the situation, so the same old problems will continue to be repeated. Mutual trust and commitment to two-way communication around all issues are essential in maintaining partnerships and good decision making in any community development initiative. Time and effort must be dedicated to creating and maintaining this. New initiatives, even if they do not totally succeed, are critical in determining what works and what does not as we put the needs of consumer-survivors at the centre of the process.

NOTE

1. Cheryl Forchuk, Elsabeth Jensen, and eventually Rick Csiernik.

Chapter 20

WHY SHOULD COMMUNITIES BE INVOLVED IN RESEARCH?

Cheryl Forchuk

1. WHY SHOULD COMMUNITIES BE INVOLVED IN RESEARCH?

The tapestry of the various studies of this book have illustrated the richness of the final product when all parts of the community—those affected by the situation, those working to aid those affected by the situation, and those studying the situation—all come together in a collaborative research endeavour. To understand why communities should do this, we need to ask the following:

- Who is the community?
- Who benefits and how?
- What are the costs and who bears them?

It also begs the question: Why should researchers include communities?

2. WHO IS THE COMMUNITY?

There are obviously many perspectives from which one can address this critical question. In considering the "community" in relation to mental health and housing, it is not simply the geographical location that constitutes the community. We asked ourselves: Who knows about this? Who is affected by this? Whose voice needs to be brought forward? The last question also forces us to consider whose voice has been historically silenced in the dialogue and how to ensure that it is now clearly heard. It is important to consider the voices of as many stakeholders as possible, and to ensure that all will be in a position to speak.

There were several times when we thought we had identified the community, only to find we had inadvertently left out an important constituent. For example, in the beginning, the project leaders identified the critical need to include the consumer-survivor voice. However, they soon realized that representation came only from housed consumer-survivors, so we also needed to ensure that homeless individuals would be invited to be part of the process and be included in the dialogue. The organizing group identified the need to include service providers from shelters, hospitals, community mental health agencies, and housing providers, but then found that we also needed to include representatives of income support groups and community legal clinics. Among the stakeholders identified early in the process were family members, but we found that our family volunteers tended to be from the more politically involved families who have learned to confront the vicarious stigma of mental illness and who were able to openly self-identify. When we thought of policy and decision makers, we thought of government and service providers, but we did not initially identify other obvious groups such as landlords, the media, the police, and employers who make very key decisions regarding the issue at hand. To tell the story as fully as possible, we needed this full spectrum of stakeholders. No doubt, some readers will identify other groups that were missed and that could have added further to our understanding. However, by keeping our understanding of community open throughout, we were able to address many shortcomings of our original conceptualization.

Who is community? It is the people who collectively live the issue.

3. WHO BENEFITS AND HOW?

Ideally, the most vulnerable, the invisible, the disempowered in our population will benefit the most through participatory research. In our example, mental health consumer-survivors were the *raison d'être* of all our efforts. If, at the end of the day, consumer-survivors are no better off despite our efforts, what was the point? In our first round of focus groups, one participant eloquently and succinctly stated, "Be my voice." He described the disempowerment he experienced and the importance of having his story told, collectively, with those of other consumer-survivors. It is no coincidence that the name of our lead consumer-survivor group in this CURA was "Can-Voice." This name had been chosen many years earlier when, as part of a visioning process, the lack of voice for consumer-survivors was identified as one of the key reasons to come together. Norma-Jean Kelly, the Can-Voice representative at the start of the project, is a gifted artist who has drawn a series of portraits of people without mouths to depict the lack of voice among consumer-survivors. The vital importance of voice should never be underestimated, especially by those privileged to have theirs regularly heard and respected.

Many strategies were used to ensure that the voices of consumer-survivors would be heard. Consumer-survivors were not simply the subjects of the studies. They were active participants on all committees and, for the final two years of the project, were the community directors of the CURA. They represented between 20 percent and 30 percent of the participants at the annual conference. They co-wrote papers. They co-presented at conferences. They were hired as staff. Their stories were included in peer-reviewed publications, one-page summaries, web pages, and newspaper articles. They became more than the product of the project—they became the key texture of the tapestry.

Voice without action is only marginally better than having no voice at all. We cannot solve such a complex problem as homelessness for all consumer-survivors. However, we can work together to create some progress. One of the fastest policy changes resulting from research occurred after our first set of focus groups in the summer of 2001. Issues related to the Ontario Disability Support Program (ODSP) were frequently identified. In the fall, while discussing the results, the policy committee member from the Ontario Ministry of Health and Long Term Care said that although he had frequently heard about problems, he did not have specific details regarding one specific concern. He had a meeting planned with ODSP staff in Toronto and requested a summary of the CURA findings regarding this problem. The committee, which consisted of consumer-survivors, community agency representatives, and academics, quickly summarized all the related comments into a four-page document and gave it to him so he could present the concern at his forthcoming meeting. This small document could not address all the issues, but pertinent concerns were presented along with supportive materials and examples. This document concerning direct deposit for ODSP cheques and direct payment to landlords contributed to a small change in policy within one month throughout Ontario, thus benefiting all people with disabilities in securing housing. The following month, the housing advocate from the Canadian Mental Health Association, who sat on the same committee, apologized for being late for the policy meeting. She had just finished arranging a direct landlord payment for a client and, by doing so, had averted her client's imminent eviction. We were subsequently able to deal with other related issues, such as revising the form letters used with ODSP clients. Not all problems identified on the original list were addressed by the research findings. However, some were, and subsequent policy changes were implemented to benefit current and future consumer-survivors.

Clearly, consumer-survivors also benefited from strategies such as that developed to prevent discharge from psychiatric wards to homelessness (Chapter 12). Our current work in this area is suggesting over a 90 percent reduction in this problem despite the current worsening economy. We still have not solved the problem of homelessness for this population, but we have shown that it is possible to prevent it for many when they are most vulnerable, such as when they are hospitalized, by connecting the domains of health, income support, and housing, and putting the individual first above the separate system silos.

Consumer-survivors were the most important group that we hoped would benefit from the collaborative, participatory approach. However, many others also benefited. Community agencies frequently commented that they did not always learn something new from research findings, but they regularly found data that they could use to strengthen their positions, such as lobbying for specific resources or for better coordination of services. Services were able to examine specific practices. For example, the hospitals in the London community can now more quickly determine the frequency of discharge to no fixed address with their documentation systems. Ontario Works was able to look at the importance of outreach services, which have since been incorporated into several other programs. The Canadian Mental Health Association was able to obtain clear data on the effectiveness of their housing advocate, and has looked at plans to increase this resource.

There were almost 300 students who benefited from research placements, clinical placements, access to data sets and the policy library, and paid research positions. Master's, doctoral, and post-doctoral students from a host of disciplines were able to use the data for theses and publications, and to work collaboratively with students from different disciplines and the full range of stakeholders invested in this issue. The CURA's work was instrumental in receiving a large grant from Health Canada to develop an interprofessional educational program on housing and mental health at the University of Western Ontario. The project included nursing, social work, undergraduate medicine, psychiatry, psychology, physiotherapy, and occupational therapy to promote client-centred interprofessional care in this area. Over 700 students took part in these workshops and interprofessional clinical placements over several years.

The number of publications, many of which are included in this book, as well as the spin-off projects, such as the work on diversity and homelessness, the project on preventing homelessness, and the one on interprofessional education, were of direct benefit to academics and community researchers. This partially addresses the question: Why should researchers include communities? However, the larger answer to this question is that doing so increases the relevance of the work.

4. WHAT ARE THE COSTS AND WHO BEARS THEM?

The greatest cost for all this complex, integrated research is time. It takes time to work together. It takes time to trust each other before the real work can begin. As mentioned earlier, the organizing committee worked together for more than a year before officially beginning this Community-University Research Alliance. However, it was time well spent.

This type of process takes much more time for researchers to engage in than does traditional research, which is time-consuming enough. All parts of the CURA research process were discussed in extensive detail with all the partners, so each component took longer to enact. The various agencies and community representatives needed time to discuss issues within their own agencies to understand the research process, identify the concerns, and bring it back to the larger group. There were entire days of meetings that a group of professional researchers could have likely completed in a one-hour teleconference. The various committees came up with very creative solutions, such as the preventing homelessness initiative, but then had to step back and look for funding sources—often several times—as the process progressed through several phases.

There are also financial costs for this type of research. The project needed to have extensive staffing to assist in data collection, data entry, analysis, and report writing. There were many financial costs related to the meetings themselves. There had to be teleconferencing, transportation, and food available for most meetings. However, these costs pale compared to the gift of time from all the participants in the process.

5. WHAT HAVE WE ACCOMPLISHED TOGETHER?

While working together over the past few years, we have demonstrated the devastating effect on people's lives created by the disconnection between housing, income, and the mental health systems. We have also demonstrated that by bringing these threads back together, we can begin to mend the torn tapestry and create a lasting work. The various policy and practice implications all address the disconnections in different ways. The tapestry is but the beginning of a work of art that we hope will cover many walls. In the process, consumer-survivors have gained a voice and used it well. The alliances formed will endure long after the funding of this CURA. Through this book we hope others will be inspired to create similar partnerships and alliances, for the benefits far exceed.

Appendix A

GLOSSARY OF HOUSING TERMS

Cheryl Forchuk, Pamela McKane,
Jim Molineux, Ruth Schofield,
and Rick Csiernik

INTRODUCTION

Over the course of the Community-University Research Alliance on Mental Health and Housing, a variety of terms were frequently used, but initially members of the advisory committee and subcommittees did not always interpret or use the terms in the same way. As a result, a directory of housing definitions was developed. This glossary is presented for the same reason—to assist with understanding the terminology and concepts associated with housing and housing policy in Canada. The definitions are derived from both the housing and mental health systems, as well as from local, provincial, and federal levels of government, though the list is far from exhaustive. The glossary is divided into five categories:

1. Permanent Affordable Housing
2. Group Living or Boarding Home Housing

3. Transitional Housing
4. Emergency Shelters and Hostels
5. Related Definitions

1. PERMANENT AFFORDABLE HOUSING

Permanent affordable housing involves a landlord and tenant relationship, with the tenant generally choosing the length of stay. The challenge in defining the countless definitions for housing in this category is to understand the basic differences between private versus public housing models, and the many variations of public housing. Numerous government-funded programs have been developed over the years, which, in turn, have spawned their own distinct vernaculars. As social housing developed, gaps in the housing system became apparent, leading to more and more varied programs, which led to yet more new housing terms. This section includes the range of terms that have emerged.

Accessible Housing
This kind of housing is accessible to those who are intended to occupy it, including those who are disadvantaged by age, physical or mental disability, medical condition, or by being victims of a natural disaster.
Source: Davies (2001).

Adequate Housing
Housing that is habitable and structurally sound, and that provides sufficient space and protection against cold, damp, heat, rain, wind, noise, pollution, and other threats to health.
Source: Davies (2001).

Affordable Housing
Housing that is modest in terms of floor area and amenities, based on household needs and community norms, and priced at or below average market housing rents or prices for comparable housing in a community area.
Source: British Columbia Housing (2001).

Adequate shelter at a cost that does not exceed 30 percent of household income.
Source: Canadian Mortgage and Housing Corporation (2004).

Housing that is affordable at a cost that does not compromise the attainment and satisfaction of individuals over other basic needs of life, including needs for food, clothing, and access to education.
Source: Davies (2001).

Housing that is suitable for basic household needs and that has a market price or rent that is affordable for the household, i.e., the household would not be required to pay more than 30 percent of its gross income for rent.
Source: Affordable Housing Task Force (2004).

Affordable permanent housing is targeted at low-income individuals or families who are determined to be in deep core housing need.
Source: Corporation of the City of London (2004).

Co-op Housing
Co-operative housing is rental housing that is owned and managed directly by a co-operative corporation. All tenants are members and they elect a board of directors among themselves. Co-op housing members are of mixed income, with approximately 75 percent paying rent geared to income and the remaining 25 percent paying market-level rent.
Source: Ontario Non-profit Housing Association (2004).

In this form of housing, tenancy is controlled by the members of the co-op and is run by a board of directors. There is no outside landlord. All residents must become members and agree to follow certain by-laws. Residents pay a monthly charge that is set by the co-op in its annual budget to pay for common necessities. Co-ops obtain government funding to support a rent-geared-to-income program for low-income residents. In addition to affordable housing, some co-ops service the needs of specific communities, including seniors and people with disabilities.
Source: Citizenship and Immigration Canada (2009).

Core Housing Need
Core housing need, as defined by the Canada Mortgage and Housing Corporation, pertains to households that fall below standards for adequacy, suitability, and affordability, and that would have to spend more than 30 percent of household income to pay the average rent in their local housing market for adequate, suitable housing.
Source: Affordable Housing Task Force (2004).

Independent Living

Independence is defined as "living in the community, requiring the least intervention from formal service and, to the greatest extent possible making one's own decisions."
Source: Ontario Ministry of Health and Long-Term Care (2004).

Modified Unit

This is any unit that has been modified in order to be accessible to an individual with a physical disability or so as to allow an individual with a physical disability to live independently.
Source: Ontario Ministry of Housing (2000).

Non-profit Housing

Non-profit housing can be municipal, private, or co-operative, with each of these variants having its own unique definition of this concept.

Non-profit housing is owned and managed by private non-profit groups, such as churches or ethnocultural communities, or by municipal governments. Non-profit housing uses private funding and government subsidies to support a rent-geared-to-income program for low-income tenants.
Source: Citizenship and Immigration Canada (2004).

Non-profit and co-operative housing creates mixed-income communities and provides secure, affordable housing for families, seniors, and people with disabilities.
Source: British Columbia (2004).

Private non-profit housing is owned and managed by independent, community-based non-profit groups, such as church groups, service clubs, ethnic organizations, YMCA/YWCAs, or associations for community living. Approximately 80 percent of non-profit housing residents pay rent based on their income (what is known as rent-geared-to-income or RGI). The remaining 20 percent pay market rents.
Source: Ontario Non-profit Housing Association (2004).

Private non-profit housing is owned by non-governmental groups, such as churches, ethnic groups, service clubs, labour unions, or local community groups.
Source: Co-operative Housing Federation of Canada (2007).

A non-profit housing co-operative is jointly owned and run by its resident members. It provides housing at near cost in a community setting. If there is a surplus, the co-op may use it to pay for future expenses, improve the co-op, or reduce housing charges for low-income members.
Source: Co-operative Housing Federation of Canada (2007).

Public Housing
Local housing corporations are non-profits owned and operated by 47 "service managers," typically regional governments established across Ontario to be responsible for housing, social welfare, and ambulance services. This is the publicly owned, formerly provincial housing stock that was often referred to as "public housing." All residents pay rent geared to their income.
Source: Ontario Non-profit Housing Association (2004).

Public housing is residential units built under a federal public housing program and originally owned wholly by a province or by a partnership of the federal and provincial or territorial governments. In Ontario, public housing is now owned by local housing corporations.
Source: Co-operative Housing Federation of Canada (2007).

Rent-Geared-to-Income Assistance Housing/Rent Supplement Program
The reduced housing charge a person of low or modest income pays. The payment is based on household income.
Source: Co-operative Housing Federation of Canada (2007).

The rent supplement program is a government initiative that helps co-ops to house low-income members. These households pay a fixed portion of their income toward housing charge. The rent supplement makes up the difference between what the member pays and what the co-ops normally charge.
Source: Co-operative Housing Federation of Canada (2007).

Rent supplement is a subsidy tied to a particular unit covering the gap between the market rent and the rent that the household can afford to pay based on their total household income.
Source: Affordable Housing Task Force (2004).

Rent-geared-to-income subsidy is paid to social housing providers and equals the difference between the market rent of a unit and the actual rent paid by low-income tenants. The allocation and the amount of this subsidy are subject to various policies of the municipal government.
Source: Ontario Non-profit Housing Association (2004).

RGI assistance is financial assistance provided to a household under a housing program to reduce the amount a household must otherwise pay to occupy a unit in a housing project.
Source: Co-operative Housing Federation of Canada (2007).

Social Housing

Social housing is rental housing integrated for a variety of mixed-tenant groups, such as low income, single parents, and refugees. It is primarily operated on a non-profit basis by municipal corporations, private non-profit corporations, or co-operative housing groups, and contains some proportions of units with rents geared to household income.
Source: Ontario Ministry of Health and Long-Term Care (2004).

Housing that has been supplied and continues to be maintained through the payment of government subsidies according to the terms of agreements between the housing provider and the federal and/or provincial government under a variety of programs.
Source: Affordable Housing Task Force (2004).

Special Needs Housing (see also Modified Unit)

Special needs housing refers to a unit that is occupied by or made available to a household of one or more individuals who require accessibility modifications or provincially funded support services in order to live independently in the community.
Source: Ontario Ministry of Housing (2000).

Supported Housing

Affordable and adequate supported housing is integrated within the community, including an arrangement of individualized mental health support services, which are de-linked from the housing itself. This housing option includes regular non-profit or rental housing, housing owned by the person, and people living with

families/key supports. People with mental illness can be supported in either private settings or when they are living with families.
Source: Ontario Ministry of Health and Long-Term Care (2004).

Supportive Housing
This is housing for people who need support to live independently. Support-service funding is provided by ministries of health or social services. Some non-profit groups also provide housing for homeless/hard-to-house individuals who do not receive additional funding from provincial ministries.
Source: Ontario Non-profit Housing Association (2004).

Supportive housing for seniors helps seniors in their daily living by combining a physical environment that is specifically designed to be safe, secure, enabling, and home-like with support services such as meals, housekeeping, and social and recreational activities.
Source: Canadian Mortgage and Housing Corporation (2004).

Dedicated supportive housing in Ontario is funded by the Ministry of Health and Long-Term Care, and consists of non-profit subsidized housing spaces that include communal living accommodations with varying levels of supports, including group homes, as well as independent apartment units with varying levels of support. The housing is owned or "reserved" by the community mental health agency for their clients. The units can be reserved through formal or informal agreements in non-profit rental housing. The Ministry of Health and Long-Term Care funds both the support services and the accommodation components, and provides rent subsidies to housing providers. Through the provision of flexible support services, skills training, and counselling, the person works toward independence and community integration.
Source: Ontario Ministry of Health and Long-Term Care (2004).

Housing augmented by support service for individuals and families who require support services to live independently. Groups targeted for supportive housing typically include those suffering from mental illness, addiction, or developmental disabilities; victims of violence; frail elderly people; and individuals released from corrections facilities.
Source: Affordable Housing Task Force (2004).

2. GROUP LIVING OR BOARDING HOME HOUSING

Boarding homes are either aggregate or independent living arrangements with social and health supports ranging from none in rooming houses to 24-hour nursing care in long-term care (LTC) facilities (formerly called nursing homes). In Ontario these living arrangements are funded in various ways, such as for-profit, not-for-profit, cost shared between municipalities (20 percent) and province (80 percent) (Ministry of Community and Social Services) or 100 percent (Ministry of Health and Long-Term Care). Except for rooming houses, there are eligibility criteria for the various living arrangements, which depend on income, or functional ability, or legal conditions.

Boarding House
A boarding house offers tenants food and other services in addition to accommodation. Boarding houses often house elderly people, former psychiatric patients, or the disabled. In Ontario a program called Habitat Services helps ensure that certain boarding houses maintain adequate standards of cleanliness and care. This program requires that the owner/operator of the boarding house sign a contract with Habitat Services. In return for funding, the owner/operator agrees to accept periodic inspections of the house and regular visits from service providers.
Source: Rupert Coalition (2004).

Domiciliary Hostels
Domiciliary hostels provide long-term, supervised accommodation, including board and care homes, for adults with psychiatric or related disabilities who require supervision of their daily living activities. This program is funded on a cost-shared basis between the Ontario Ministry of Community and Social Services (80 percent) and local municipalities (20 percent). Many of the clients served would live as "street people" if the hostel program did not exist. Clients who are eligible for the program receive subsidies from the local municipality to access an approved hostel bed. The amount of subsidy depends on the client's income, with the province setting the formula for determining the subsidy.
Source: Corporation of the City of London (2004).

Halfway Homes

Halfway homes are community-based residential facilities for individuals in conflict with the law and that are classified based on the assessed security risk of the residents. The facilities provide accommodation, 24-hour supervision, counselling, and programming with the goal of safely reintegrating the individual who had been in conflict with the law back into the community. Halfway homes are operated by non-profit agencies or private corporations contracted by Correctional Service of Canada.

Source: Correctional Service of Canada (2005).

Long-Term Care Facilities

These facilities provide care, programs, and services designed to meet the physical and psychosocial needs of people 18 years of age or over whose needs cannot be met through in-home services. Access to these facilities is coordinated through the Community Care Access Centres (CCAC) across Ontario. People admitted to a long-term care facility must pay a co-payment for their accommodation. A reduced rate is offered to people without sufficient income to pay the maximum rate for basic accommodation. In addition to resident co-payment, long-term care facilities receive funding from the Ontario Ministry of Health and Long-Term Care for nursing and personal care, as well as for various programs and services.

Long-term care facilities are designed for people who require 24-hour nursing care and supervision within a secure setting. In general, long-term care facilities offer higher levels of personal care and support than those typically offered by either retirement homes or supportive housing. In Ontario access to long-term care homes is only through CCAC's eligibility process, which includes assessing medical and functional information.

Long-term care facilities are owned and operated by various organizations including:

- Nursing homes are usually operated by private corporations.
- Municipal homes for the aged that are owned by municipal councils. Many municipalities are required to build a home for the aged in their area, either on their own or in partnership with a neighbouring municipality.
- Charitable homes that are usually owned by non-profit corporations, such as faith, community, ethnic, or cultural groups.

Source: Ontario Ministry of Health and Long-Term Care (2004).

Residential Care Housing

This form of housing provides room and board, 24-hour supervision, and basic assistance with activities of daily living such as bathing, dressing, and dispensing of medication. These include both homes for special care and domiciliary hostels. Both are mainly for-profit, private residential homes. Homes for special care are monitored by provincial psychiatric hospitals and consist almost exclusively of former patients of provincial psychiatric facilities who have a serious mental illness. Domiciliary hostels are typically private residences administered through municipal agreements, and cost shared between the province (80 percent) and municipality (20 percent). It is estimated that approximately two-thirds of the residents of domiciliary hostels are psychiatrically disabled.
Source: Ontario Ministry of Health and Long-Term Care (2004).

Rest and Retirement Homes

These are privately operated facilities whose services and prices are market-driven. Some beds in these facilities, usually those in wards, are subsidized by the government. In these settings, individuals are provided with room and board. In some cases, people may have their own apartments. If people require supports, they must purchase these services. The housing provider may provide the supports on a fee-for-service basis or a separate provider is called upon to provide supports.
Source: Ontario Ministry of Health and Long-Term Care (2004).

Rooming House

A rooming house is any building in which renters occupy single rooms and share kitchens, bathrooms, and common areas. The building may be a converted single-family house, a converted hotel, or a structure built specifically for this purpose. Rooming houses may have as few as three rooms or more than 100.
Source: Rupert Coalition (2004).

Supportive Housing for Seniors

Supportive housing for seniors is designed for people who need only minimal to moderate care, such as homemaking or personal care and support, to live independently. Accommodations usually consist of rental units within an apartment building. In a few cases, the accommodation is a small group residence. Supportive housing buildings are owned and operated by municipal governments or non-profit groups, including faith groups, seniors' organizations, service clubs, and cultural groups. Accommodations, on-site services, costs, and the availability of government

subsidies vary with each building. The care arrangements between a tenant and a service provider are usually defined through a contract between the two parties.
Source: Ontario Ministry of Health and Long-Term Care (2004).

3. TRANSITIONAL HOUSING

Transitional housing is meant to meet the needs of people making the transition from homelessness to permanent accommodation, but, unlike emergency shelters, is not intended to meet urgent needs. As with emergency shelters, however, transitional housing has stipulations related to the length of time an individual can remain in transitional housing, which is dictated by legislated funding criteria. Transitional housing providers have some discretion over the length of stay, which can be anywhere from six months to two years. Often, though not always, support and assistance—such as developing budgeting skills, life skills programs, support with housekeeping and cooking skills aimed at assisting individuals in making the transition to permanent accommodation—are provided in transitional housing. Transitional shelter also encompasses safe homes, and second-stage housing.

Safe homes provide temporary accommodation in communities where transition houses do not exist. The safe home may be a rental apartment, private home, or hotel unit.

Second stage housing assists women who have left abusive relationships make long-term plans for independent living. British Columbia housing has developed multi-serviced housing for this population. Women and their children usually stay in a second-stage housing for nine to 12 months.
Sources: British Columbia (2004); Corporation of the City of London (2004).

4. EMERGENCY SHELTERS AND HOSTELS

Emergency shelters encompass a range of short-term, temporary shelter options for individuals who are homeless. This can range from crash beds to hostels for homeless individuals and families to shelters for refugees and victims of domestic violence. Typically people can stay a maximum of four to six weeks in emergency shelters before they must leave. The length of time is stipulated by legislated criteria attached to the funding that emergency shelters receive to cover the costs of housing and providing supports for homeless individuals on an urgent/crisis basis.

Emergency shelters and hostels provide temporary accommodations for individuals and families who must leave their homes during a crisis or who do not have a permanent place to live. Typically they provide shared bedrooms or dormitory-type sleeping arrangements, though some shelters have individual or dedicated single bedrooms. Families with children are most commonly housed in a motel or similar accommodations. Some shelters also offer a higher level of support for individuals, an approach that is viewed as a model of best practice. This is accomplished with additional sources of funding, either through other government agencies or fundraising.

Transitional emergency housing may include shelters and community crisis beds. Emergency shelters provide short-stay housing for those who are homeless or in need of transitional housing. A bed or sleeping mat on the floor is provided. Motel rooms are used as needed, mostly for families.

Sources: British Columbia (2004); Ontario Ministry of Health and Long-Term Care (2004).

5. RELATED DEFINITIONS

Absolute Homelessness
Absolute homelessness means living on the street or in places unfit for human habitation, such as abandoned buildings or vehicles.
Source: Canadian Institute for Health Information (2007).

Hidden Homelessness
Hidden homelessness relates to individuals who are temporarily staying with friends or with family. It is also referred to as couch surfing. The hidden homeless are not staying in shelters or on the streets, so they can be difficult to count.
Source: Canadian Institute for Health Information (2007).

Homeless–At-Risk Housing
Households that spend more than half of their total income on housing costs.
Source: Canadian Institute for Health Information (2007).

Programs that serve low-income people who have been homeless or are at risk of homelessness and need program assistance to maintain their independence. In some jurisdictions may be referred to as "second-stage housing." They may provide an intermediate stage of accommodation from short-term to fully independent housing. They may also provide permanent housing for people who are able to live independently as long as they have access to support programs. Eligible client

groups include women and their children who have left their abusive relationships and need counselling and assistance to re-establish themselves, and youth who have decided to end their "street involvement," but need support and assistance to make the transition. People with mental illness are also eligible if they are able to live independently with regular support.
Source: British Columbia (2004).

Homelessness
When one has no home and must live either outdoors or in emergency shelters or hostels, and when homes do not meet the United Nations basic standards of adequate protection from the elements, access to safe tenure, and personal safety and accessibility to employment, education, and health care.
Source: United Nations (1987).

At present there is no universally agreed-upon definition of homelessness. There is a lack of consensus on who to encompass in the definition (for example, those living in shelters only, or those living in public places outside of shelters), the minimum duration of homeless periods (for example, a specific number of days or weeks), and age ranges (particularly in research involving youth).

Most definitions of homelessness include those without physical shelter who sleep outdoors or in emergency shelters. Others are more inclusive and encompass those with shelter that lacks basic standards of health and safety, including protection from the elements, access to sanitary facilities, personal safety, and security of occupancy.
Source: Canadian Institute for Health Information (2007).

Homelessness and Housing Insecurity
Those affected by homelessness and housing insecurity include those who are visible on the streets or staying in local shelters; those who have been homeless in the recent past and continue to be at risk; those who live in unsafe, overcrowded, illegal, temporary, or transitional accommodation; and those at imminent risk of losing their housing.
Source: Affordable Housing Task Force (2004).

Shelter Allowance
An income supplement not tied to a particular unit but based on a household's income and housing needs.
Source: Affordable Housing Task Force (2004).

REFERENCES

Affordable Housing Task Force. (2004). Affordable Housing in London. London: City of London

British Columbia. (2004). *Homelessness—causes and effects: A profile, policy review, and analysis*, vol. 2. Retrieved October 26, 2010 from www.housing.gov.bc.ca/housing/docs/vol2.pdf.

British Columbia Housing. (2001). *Affordable housing program agreement*. Retrieved March 14, 2009, from www.bchousing.org/programs/housing.

Canada Mortgage and Housing Corporation. (2004). *Affordable housing*. Retrieved October 26, 2010, from www.cmhc-schl.gc.ca/en/corp/faq/faq_002.cfm.

Canadian Institute for Health Information. (2007). *Improving the health of Canadians: Mental health and homelessness*. Ottawa: Canadian Institute for Health Information.

Co-operative Housing Federation of Canada. (2007). *Glossary of terms*. Retrieved March 14, 2009, from www.chfcanada.coop/eng/pages2007/glossary.asp.

Corporation of the City of London. (2004). *Ideas, sites, and buildings to create affordable housing*. London: City of London.

Correctional Service of Canada. (2005). *Employment needs, interests, and programming for women offenders*. Ottawa: Correctional Service of Canada.

Davies, L., MP. (2001). *Bill C-416 A Housing Bill of Rights for Canadians*. Retrieved from www2.parl.gc.ca/HousePublications/Publications?aspx?pub=bill&doc=c416&parl=37&uses=1&language=E.

Ontario Ministry of Health and Long-Term Care. (2004). *Mental health implementation task forces—north east MHITF final report*. Retrieved February 16, 2004, from www.healthgov.on.ca/english/providers/pub/mhitf/north_east/sec_8.pdf.

Ontario Ministry of Housing. (2000). *Social Housing Reform Act, S.O.2000*. Retrieved October 26, 2010, from www.e-laws.gov.on.ca/html/statutes/elaws_statutes_00s27_e.htm.

Ontario Non-profit Housing Association. (2004). *About non-profit housing*. Retrieved February 16, 2004, from www.onpha.on.ca/about_non_profit_housing.

Rupert Coalition. (2004). *Community residential services of Toronto*. Retrieved February 16, 2004, from www.web.net/rupert/faq.htm.

United Nations. (1987). *International year of shelter for the homeless*. New York: United Nations.

Appendix B

CURA FACT SHEETS

As part of the dissemination initiative of the Community-University Research Alliance on Mental Health and Housing, three one-page fact sheets were developed that summarized the formal research findings of three major studies:

1. Surviving the Tornado of Mental Illness: Psychiatric Survivors' Experiences of Getting, Losing, and Keeping Housing (Chapter 4)
2. Canadian Families Caring for Members with Mental Illness: A Vicious Cycle (Chapter 5)
3. "It's Important to Be Proud of the Place You Live in": Housing Problems and Preferences of Psychiatric Survivors (Chapter 7)

Each fact sheet had the Community-University Research Alliance on Mental Health and Housing logo at the top of the sheet to identify and "brand" the source of the information. The fact sheets consisted of a brief abstract of the research, along with key findings and implications. The fact sheets were forwarded to the media, politicians, and key community stakeholders. They were also distributed at all candidates meetings held during the course of the CURA to inform a broader audience of the research outcomes and their implications.

SURVIVING THE TORNADO OF MENTAL ILLNESS: PSYCHIATRIC SURVIVORS' EXPERIENCES OF GETTING, LOSING, AND KEEPING HOUSING

University of Western Ontario / London Health Science Centre—Research
375 South St., Room D227NR, London, Ontario N6A 4G5 (519) 685-8500 ext. 75720

Homelessness and housing stability have become important concerns for consumer-survivors of the mental health system. Although many studies have focused on issues of homelessness, housing stability, and housing preference, the subjective experiences of consumer-survivors have remained relatively unexplored.

This qualitative study explored the housing-related experiences of consumer-survivors of the mental health system. Nine focus groups, involving 90 people, were conducted in urban and rural southwestern Ontario. The metaphor of a tornado was proposed to express the degree of upheaval and loss experienced by consumer-survivors.

Key Findings

- The focus-group participants described three levels of upheaval, loss, and destruction, similar to the devastating effects of a tornado: (1) losing ground, (2) struggling to survive, and (3) gaining stability.
- **LOSING GROUND:** The themes associated with this first and most destructive phase of the tornado were living in fear and losing control of basic human rights.

  "They made me give up my apartment.... I left everything behind—my couch, my TV, everything, my fish tank, everything. I left it all behind because they said I wasn't well enough to go back. I wasn't able to look after myself."

- **STRUGGLING TO SURVIVE:** This phase, in which consumer-survivors described picking up the pieces from the destruction caused by the tornado, included gaining access to social supports and receiving professional services.

  "[T]he food bank is here, but it is only going to feed you for two days, and when you have no money, what do you do for the other 28 days?"

- **GAINING STABILITY:** The final phase included the securing of personal space, and building relationships.

  "I am in my fifth home ... but this one I know I can stay for two years and I can finally go to a permanent home after that. So I know I'll finally be able to have a home that I can call home for quite a while."

Key Implications

- This study prompts us to ask: What is the tornado? Is it the experience of mental illness, or the experience of society's response to mental illness?
- Findings suggest that the destructive tornado experienced by consumer-survivors may have more to do with *society's response* to mental illness than with the illness itself.
- Health care providers and policy decision makers need to be aware of the losses that are not simply a result of the symptoms of mental illness, but are a result of the responses to the illness.
- Timely availability of supports and services, including adequate housing, income support, and community care, will help people rebuild their lives.

Acknowledgement: This research was supported by a grant from the Social Sciences and Humanities Research Council of Canada.

Forchuk, C., Ward-Griffin, C., Csiernik, R., Turner, K. (2006). Surviving the tornado of mental illness: Psychiatric survivors' experiences of getting, losing, and keeping housing. *Psychiatric Services, 57*(4), 1–5.

APPENDIX B

CANADIAN FAMILIES CARING FOR MEMBERS WITH MENTAL ILLNESS: A VICIOUS CYCLE

University of Western Ontario / London Health Science Centre—Research
375 South St., Room D227NR, London, Ontario N6A 4G5 (519) 685-8500 ext. 75719

Families caring for members with mental illness are too often forgotten in health promotion work. Research has shown that families are a major source of support for people living with serious mental illness, yet more research must be done to discover the perspectives of family caregivers.

This qualitative study explored the experiences of individuals who are caring for a family member with a mental illness. Eleven focus groups, involving 75 participants, were conducted during a three-year period. The study found that family caregivers were part of a "circle of care," supporting the independence of individuals with mental illness, while trying to protect them from the inadequacies of the health care and social service systems. Family caregivers expressed anger, frustration, and fear related to the inadequate supports available. However, family members also expressed hope that the system would change.

Key Findings

- The "circle of care" frequently led to a "vicious cycle" of caregiving.

- Three central themes were identified within the "vicious cycle" of caregiving: (1) witnessing inadequacies, (2) working behind the scenes, and (3) creating a better world.

- **WITNESSING INADEQUACIES:** Families caring for a member with mental illness witnessed a number of inadequacies. Poor living conditions, inappropriate or unsafe housing, neglectful landlords, and limited access to qualified staff were all problems expressed by family members.

- **WORKING BEHIND THE SCENES:** In response to poor housing conditions, family members worked behind the scenes to provide care. Family caregivers working behind the scenes assumed a number of different roles, paid for various expenses, and dealt with the lack of support and assistance.

- **CREATING A BETTER WORLD:** In their quest to break free from this "vicious cycle," families expressed a desire to create a better world. Families were hopeful that changes in the system would improve care for people with mental illness and their families. To this end, family members made a number of suggestions for change, including a need for affordable, safe, and conveniently located housing, and a call for supports to be put in place to help families who act as primary caregivers.

Key Implications

- Findings suggest that family caregivers working behind the scenes are not adequately supported by the health care and social service systems. Changes in mental health legislation are needed.

- Health care providers need to build trusting collaborative relationships with families who care for a member living with mental illness.

- If families' hopes for creating a better world are to be realized, nurses need to collaborate, advocate, and support caregiving families.

Acknowledgement: This research was supported by a grant from the Social Sciences and Humanities Research Council of Canada.

Ward-Griffin, C., Schofield, R., Coatsworth-Puspoky, R. & Vos, S. (2005). Canadian families caring for members with mental illness: A vicious cycle. *Journal of Family Nursing, 11*, 140–61.

"IT'S IMPORTANT TO BE PROUD OF THE PLACE YOU LIVE IN": HOUSING PROBLEMS AND PREFERENCES OF PSYCHIATRIC SURVIVORS

University of Western Ontario / London Health Science Centre—Research
375 South St., Room D227NR, London, Ontario N6A 4G5 (519) 685-8500 ext. 75720

People with severe mental illness are at risk of losing their housing, living in substandard housing, or being placed in inappropriate housing that does not satisfy their preferences. In order to understand these housing and mental health issues as lived experiences, it is important that we hear the perspective of consumer-survivors of the mental health system.

This qualitative study explored the housing needs and preferences of consumer-survivors of the mental health system. Consumer-survivor groups across southwestern Ontario recruited participants for 14 focus groups, involving 133 people. Participants identified a number of central problems or concerns related to their current housing situations, and also identified their housing and support preferences.

Key Findings

PROBLEMS/CONCERNS	PREFERENCES/DESIRES
Oppression, stigma, discrimination	➡ Acceptance, advocacy
Social networks, social supports, and being forced to choose between support and independence	➡ A balance between support and independence
Lack of affordable, desirable, stable, and safe housing	➡ Affordability, choice, stability, security, privacy
Poverty, low-income, disability program difficulties	➡ Financial support, access to desirable housing
Accessing crisis support, transportation, medical and mental health services	➡ Readily available support, affordable transportation, accessing the right services in the right places

Key Implications

- Participants expressed a preference for independent living arrangements, and emphasized the importance of having adequate access to support, yet participants' housing choices were significantly limited. The dilemma of choosing between where one wanted to live and where one can access services was a common experience. Moreover, issues of oppression and poverty were consistently identified as central problems.

- These issues are systemic, and require systemic responses. Nurses and nursing organizations can play an important role in advocating for the systemic solutions that are needed, such as increased funding for income supports and public awareness of stigma and discrimination.

- As a society, we need to meet the challenge placed before us by one participant who poignantly requested, "Be my voice."

Acknowledgement: This research was supported by a grant from the Social Sciences and Humanities Research Council of Canada.

Forchuk, C., Nelson, G. & Hall, G.B. (2006). "It's important to be proud of the place you live in": Housing preferences of psychiatric survivors. *Perspectives in Psychiatric Care, 42*(1), 42–52.

LIST OF CONTRIBUTING AUTHORS

EDITORS

Cheryl Forchuk is a professor at the School of Nursing, Faculty of Health Sciences, with a cross appointment to the Department of Psychiatry, Schulich School of Medicine and Dentistry, University of Western Ontario. She is a scientist and program leader for the Health Outcomes and Health Services Group at Lawson Health Research Institute, London, Ontario. She received her Bachelor of Science in nursing and Bachelor of Arts in psychology from the University of Windsor. She received her Master of Science in nursing from the University of Toronto, with a clinical specialty in mental health-psychiatric nursing and her PhD from the college of nursing at Wayne State.

Dr. Forchuk has published on many topics, including: denial, therapeutic relationships, and sexuality. She has published a book through Sage Publications on Peplau's interpersonal theory of nursing. Her current research includes exploring the nurse–client relationship, recovery from psychosis, the transition from psychiatric hospital to community, housing issues related to mental health, and diversity issues related to homelessness.

Richard Csiernik received his BA, BSc, and BSW from McMaster University in Hamilton, Ontario. He holds an MSW from the University of Toronto, a Graduate Diploma in Social Administration from Wilfrid Laurier University in Waterloo, Ontario, and his PhD in social work from the University of Toronto. He is Professor and past graduate program coordinator at the School of Social Work, King's University College, at the University of Western Ontario, London, Ontario, where he teaches research, group work, field practice, and addictions. Rick is a member of the Ontario College of Registered Social Workers and Social Service Workers.

Rick has written and edited seven books including: *Wellness and Work: Employee Assistance Programming in Canada*, *Substance Use and Abuse: Everything Matters* and *Responding to the Oppression of Addiction* (with Dr. Bill Rowe), published by Canadian Scholars' Press Inc., along with *Practicing Social Work Research* with Rachel Birnbaum and Barbara Decker Pierce. He is also the author of over 100 peer-reviewed articles and book chapters, and has been an invited and peer-reviewed presenter at over 150 national and international conferences and workshops. Rick also teaches in the Addiction Studies program at McMaster University in Hamilton, Ontario, where he was recipient of the Instructor of the Year Award in 1997. He has also been on the Dean's Honour Roll of Teaching Excellence at King's University College for 11 consecutive years.

Elsabeth Jensen received her Diploma in Nursing from Hamilton Civic Hospitals School of Nursing in 1972; earned a BA in sociology in 1981 and a BSCN in 1989 from the University of Western Ontario; and an MSN in 1998 and a PhD in nursing in 2004 from Wayne State University. Dr. Jensen is an advance practice nurse, specialized in mental health, and is currently an associate professor in the School of Nursing at York University. She is a past president of the Registered Nurses' Association of Ontario, and recently completed a second term as member at large, nursing research. She is one of 100 nurses to receive a Centennial Award from the Canadian Nurses Association in recognition of her outstanding contributions to the nursing profession.

Her areas of research include interpersonal violence, program evaluation, knowledge integration/translation, models of discharge care, homelessness/housing and health, and health policy. Dr. Jensen received funding from the Ontario Mental Health Foundation to evaluate a community-based discharge planning model in an acute care mental health program. She is an author of 15 peer-reviewed articles and five book chapters, and has presented her work at professional conferences nationally and internationally.

CONTRIBUTING AUTHORS

Gloria Alvernaz Mulcahy is from California, of Tsalagi ancestry. Gloria is a registered psychologist, having received her PhD from the Institute for Child Study, University of Maryland. She is adjunct professor, Faculty of Education, and academic research associate, Centre for Research and Education on Violence against Women and Children, at the University of Western Ontario, Canada. Gloria serves as UN/NGO representative, vice president, North America, World Council for Psychotherapy. Her community work includes being the president, board of directors, At^lohsa Native Family Healing Services, and vice president, Ganaan De We O Dis^Yethi Yenahwahse, Southwest Ontario Aboriginal Health Access Centre. She is a documentary filmmaker, poet, and research consultant for *Embodied Trauma: The Influence of Past Trauma on Women during the Transition to Mothering*.

Heather Atyeo, RN (EC), received her BScN (2002) and Primary Health Care Nurse Practitioner certificate (2008) from the University of Western Ontario. Her clinical focus has been on mental health as a crisis counsellor in a community-based crisis service and as a nurse case manager with a variety of outpatient mental health programs. She also works as research assistant with the Mental Health Nursing Research Alliance at the Lawson Health Research Institute in London, Ontario.

Helene Berman, RN, PhD, is associate professor in the School of Nursing at the University of Western Ontario, and Scotiabank research chair, Centre for Research and Education on Violence against Women and Children. Her research has focused on violence in the lives of children, and has included homeless, Aboriginal, and newcomer youth who have experienced marginalization, trauma, uprooting, and displacement. She was the principal investigator on two national studies examining how girls and young women are socialized to expect violence, its effects on their health, and implications for policy-makers and programmers. Her research has been funded by the Canadian Institutes of Health Research (CIHR), SSHRC, and Status of Women Canada. The theoretical and methodological perspectives used are informed by critical and feminist theory, intersectionality, participatory approaches, and narrative analysis. She is past chairperson of the Alliance of Canadian Research Centres on Violence.

Richard Booth is a registered nurse and works clinically in mental health/psychiatry. He has a BScN from McMaster University and a Master of Science in

Nursing from the University of Western Ontario, with a focus on distance education and eLearning. Currently, he is pursuing doctoral education at the University of Western Ontario, with a focus on nursing education, eHealth, and information systems. Richard has consulted on various nursing- and eHealth-related projects to date, including the Registered Nurses' Association of Ontario nursing and eHealth project and curriculum. He also maintains an active membership on the executive of the Ontario Nursing Informatics Group.

Stephanie Brown, BA (University of Western Ontario), MSW (Wilfrid Laurier University), RSW, is a social worker, forensic services, Regional Mental Health Care, St. Thomas, Ontario. Stephanie currently works with individuals, families, and groups on the Forensic Rehabilitation Readiness Unit, which opened in September 2007. She worked as a research assistant for the CURA while completing her undergraduate degree in physiology and psychology, and since that time has worked collaboratively on secondary analyses of the CURA data, examining issues of health, housing, and parenting among mental health consumer-survivors.

Robin Coatsworth-Puspoky, RN, MScN, is a professor at Lambton College. She teaches in first year of the Practical Nursing Program. Robin's clinical area of expertise is geriatric mental health. She has held positions with the Regional Psychogeriatric Program and Regional Mental Health Care as a clinical nurse specialist in geriatric psychiatry, and as a research assistant with the research project titled "Therapeutic Relationships: From Hospital to Community." Robin holds undergraduate degrees in sociology and nursing from the University of Western Ontario. She received her Master of Science of Nursing degree from UWO in 2001, with a specialty in nursing education. Her thesis research focused on exploring and comparing peer and nursing support relationships in mental health from the perspective of the people receiving support. Robin's research interests include nurse–client relationships, geriatric mental health, knowledge translation, and transcultural nursing.

Susan Dill has been director of residential programs and services, Women's Community House, London, Ontario, since 2004, providing strategic direction and management for all programs and services at two shelters for abused women and their children. She has also been an instructor at Fanshawe College in London, and served on the Site Committee for a Health Canada-funded project to create interprofessional collaborative teams for comprehensive mental health services in the community.

LIST OF CONTRIBUTING AUTHORS

Kathryn Edmunds, RN, BN (University of Manitoba), MSN (Wayne State University), is currently a doctoral student in the Arthur Labatt Family School of Nursing at the University of Western Ontario. She is also an adjunct assistant professor in the Faculty of Nursing at the University of Windsor, and has extensive experience as a public health nurse with the Windsor–Essex County Health Unit, practising in rural southwestern Ontario. Current theoretical and research interests include the health experiences of women temporary agricultural workers within the contexts of prolonged and recurring uprootedness, social determinants of health, and globalized gendered migration.

Carolyne A. Gorlick is an associate professor at the School of Social Work, King's College, University of Western Ontario. As principal investigator, she has completed a federally funded, four-year research project on welfare-to-work programs in Canada. A final report, *Welfare to Work in Canada: Policy Intentions and Program Realities*, has been produced, along with a *National Inventory of Welfare to Work in Canada*, volumes I and II, and, with G. Brethour, *Welfare to Work Programs: An Overview*. Dr. Gorlick is also a member of the CURA/UWO research project on homelessness, community economic development, and former psychiatric patients. This project has focused on health factors, housing, and the centrality of poverty, diversity, and multiculturalism in the context of those homeless in Canada.

Amy M. Haldenby, RN, was raised in a rural community in southwestern Ontario. Amy completed her undergraduate nursing degree at the University of Toronto, received her Master's in health promotion from the University of Western Ontario, and completed the Primary Health Care Nurse Practitioner program at Ryerson University. Working with marginalized individuals in an urban community is her primary practice interest.

G. Brent Hall, after completing his PhD in geography at McMaster University in 1980, worked at the University of Guelph before returning to New Zealand to take up a position in geography at the University of Auckland in 1982. In 1985 he and his family returned to Canada, where he worked at Sir Wilfrid Laurier University. In 1987 he was appointed to develop a program in geographic information systems (GIS) at the University of Waterloo. He became full professor and associate dean in 1995, and worked there until September 2007. During this time he held the Belle van Zuylen Visiting Chair in geography at the University of Utrecht (The Netherlands) in 1992, and an Erskine Fellowship at the University of Canterbury in 2004.

Brent has co-authored one book, edited one book, and written numerous book chapters and 59 papers in peer-reviewed journals. He is a recipient of the Horwood Critique Prize from the Urban and Regional Information Systems Association (1997), a university-wide award in teaching excellence at the University of Waterloo (2003), and a national award for excellence in teaching geography from the Canadian Association of Geographers (2006).

Jeffrey S. Hoch received his PhD in health economics from the Johns Hopkins Bloomberg School of Public Health. Dr. Hoch also holds a Master's in economics from the Johns Hopkins University and a Bachelor of Arts degree in quantitative economics and decision sciences from the University of California at San Diego. Dr. Hoch has taught health economics and economic evaluation classes in Canada and internationally. Currently, Dr. Hoch is pursuing research on the statistical methodology and application of health economics. Special interests include health services research related to mental health, and other health issues affecting poor and vulnerable populations.

LiBbey Joplin, BA, MTS, CAPPE, is citizen development researcher.

Shani Kingston-MacClure, who was born in Ireland, received her BSW degree from King's University College and her MSW from Wilfrid Laurier University in Waterloo, Ontario. Since 2000 Shani has been a social worker in the Adult Mental Health Care Program, London Health Sciences Centre, London, Ontario. She has also worked for the Canadian Mental Health Association, Paramed Health Services, and the Children's Aid Society of London and Middlesex.

Raquel Lopez was born in El Salvador, settling in London, Ontario, when her family fled their homeland in 1990. Raquel obtained her Social Service Worker diploma from Fanshawe College in London in 1994, her BA in sociology from King's University College in 1999, and her MA in sociology from Queen's University in Kingston in 2005. She is presently an addiction and mental health counsellor with Addiction Services of Thames Valley, London, Ontario.

Pamela McKane is honoured to have been involved with the CURA from 2002 to 2005. Initially involved in various research projects in her capacity as housing development assistant, Pamela was also part of the administrative team of the CURA as community director of the CURA during her term as acting executive director of Margaret's Haven. Currently, she is a doctoral candidate in political science at York University.

James Molineux is retired from the City of London. Jim, a long-term civil servant, concluded his distinguished career as the manager of Coordinated Access and Social Housing Policy.

Phyllis Montgomery, RN, MScN, PhD, is an associate professor in the School of Nursing, Laurentian University, Sudbury, Ontario, and coordinator of the MScN program. Phyllis's research interests focus on women's mental health, with many of her research projects exploring women's efforts to craft a life in the context of adversity.

Geoffrey Nelson is professor of psychology and a faculty member in the graduate program in community psychology at Wilfrid Laurier University. He has served as senior editor of the *Canadian Journal of Community Mental Health* and chair of the Community Psychology Section of the Canadian Psychological Association. Professor Nelson has held a senior research fellowship from the Ontario Mental Health Foundation, and in 1999 he was the recipient (with the Canadian Mental Health Association/Waterloo Region Branch) of the Harry McNeill Award for Innovation in Community Mental Health from the American Psychological Foundation and the Society for Community Research and Action. In 2004–05, he was university research professor at Laurier. His research and practice has focused on community mental health programs and supports for people with serious mental illness and community-based prevention programs for children and families.

Susan L. Ray, RN, PhD, is an assistant professor at the School of Nursing, Faculty of Health Sciences, with a cross appointment to the Department of Psychiatry, Schulich School of Medicine and Dentistry, University of Western Ontario. She is an associate scientist at the Lawson Health Research Institute. Her research program focuses on the impact of psychological trauma on contemporary peacekeepers and their families, male survivors of sexual abuse/incest, and the immigrant/refugee population. Dr. Ray is also interested in testing the efficacy of interventions for posttraumatic stress disorder. Her research methodology is primarily qualitative, using interpretative phenomenology and grounded theory. Currently, she is the Principal Investigator of a funded research grant exploring compassion fatigue among front-line mental health professionals and a co-investigator of a SSHRC-funded public outreach grant examining homelessness and diversity. She is also a member of the International Honor Society of Nurses, Iota Omicron chapter.

Gord Russell is a graduate of York University, where he earned a BA in geography and anthropology, and the Ontario Theological Seminary (now Tyndale Seminary), where he earned his Master's in Divinity degree. Gord has been involved with the Men's Mission and Rehabilitation Centre, an emergency and transitional shelter for men in London since 1991, and is currently the acting executive director of Mission Services of London. He is involved with the London Homeless Coalition and the Evangelical Fellowship of Canada Roundtable on Poverty and Homelessness.

Ruth Schofield received her BScN and MSc(T) from McMaster University. Ruth is an assistant professor at McMaster University School of Nursing, with a teaching focus on community health nursing. She previously taught family and community health nursing at the University of Western Ontario. Her clinical and administrative practice includes over 23 years in public health related to child and family health, and mental health. Ruth is the past president of the Community Health Nurses Initiatives Group, an interest group of the Registered Nurses' Association of Ontario, an RNAO board member, the Ontario representative on the Community Health Nurses Association of Canada (CHNAC) board. She is co-chair of CHNAC's Certification, Standards, and Competence Standing Committee. She was co-chair for the past two National Community Health Nurses Conferences, and past member of the Ontario Public Health Association's board of directors. Her research focus is on mental health and housing, family health, community health nursing, and interprofessional education.

Cheryl Smith is manager of Community Partnerships and Funding, City of London. Cheryl's work involves helping people by investing in neighbourhoods, developing leaders, supporting families, and working with communities. Through community investment and planning, the City of London provides opportunities to build social infrastructure and strengthen neighbourhoods as key strategic investments in the health and well-being of our local communities. Through this type of upstream investment in our people, neighbourhoods, and communities, we are working to deter downstream costs and impacts such as reduced crime and violence, reduced reliance on the social safety net, and a reduction in poverty. Upstream investment will also result in improved outcomes such as increased literacy rates and improved health and physical activity levels and improved quality of life.

Mark Speechley received his PhD in epidemiology and biostatistics from the University of Western Ontario, which was followed by a post-doctorate in chronic disease epidemiology at the Yale University School of Epidemiology and Public Health. His areas of primary research interest include fall prevention in older adults, for which he has received funding from Health Canada–Veterans Affairs Canada and the Ontario Neurotrauma Foundation. With collaborators he has received funding from NIH, CIHR, Heart and Stroke, SSHRC, and other agencies for studies on genetic screening, systematic reviews of published studies of rehabilitation for various conditions, and the housing circumstances of psychiatric consumers. He has been involved in over 100 peer-reviewed papers, and has been primary supervisor for 10 PhD and 16 MSc students. He teaches epidemiology in the MD and BMSc degree programs at the University of Western Ontario.

Katherine Turner, BA, LLB (University of Western Ontario), CED (Concordia University), was the inaugural community director of the CURA on Mental Health and Housing and executive director of Margaret's Haven Non-profit Housing, in London, Ontario. She is presently FedNor Initiatives officer, Industry Canada, Government of Canada, Thunder Bay, Ontario. Katherine's research interests focus on trying to understand how we take collective responsibility for, and control over, the version of reality we have created. How do we put people and society at the centre of the systems we create and how can we ensure that longer-term development and evolution will serve the interests of people and society? How do we use research to challenge our assumptions and the assumptions of others, while maintaining dialogue and relationship that can result in the creative tension necessary to productive change? How do we support individuals and communities to make good, well-grounded decisions and create strong structures and institutions that work in their best interests?

Michele Van Beers has been providing community-based support for individuals with intellectual and mental health disabilities since 1985. She commenced her career by working in and subsequently managing residential treatment facilities. In 1999, she initiated the development of the Housing Advocacy Program at Canadian Mental Health Association in London, Ontario. Michele believes that a shared commitment to quality of service ultimately streamlines and enhances the services that individuals receive. This results in sustainable outcomes for clients and improved system design due to the development of relationships between key stakeholders. This philosophy was the basis for the development of the Housing Advocacy Program, with a primary function to assist individuals with mental health issues to secure stable, safe, and affordable housing of their choice. Currently, Michele's commitment to system design and development is expressed through her role as director of operations with the Canadian Mental Health Association–London Middlesex.

Sandra Vos, RN, MScN. Considerable nursing experiences have framed Sandra's career over the last 27 years. Public health nursing was a springboard for health promotion, teaching, and clinical service work and long-term care. After completing her Master's in 1988, she undertook research and project jobs that focused on mental health, policy and procedure development, preschool vision health, and the CURA project. She taught at Ryerson University and the University of Western Ontario. When not involved in local food projects, she can be found applying best management practices to her herd of cows and the land she farms.

Catherine Ward-Griffin, RN, PhD, is a professor at the School of Nursing, University of Western Ontario, and a scientist at the Lawson Health Research Institute in London, Ontario. Working in the areas of caregiving, community and family health promotion, women's health and social policy, her program of research focuses on relationships between formal and informal systems of care, as well as the interpersonal relationships among health care providers, older adults, and their families in both home care and long-term care settings. Using a critical theoretical lens, Dr. Ward-Griffin is particularly interested in examining the experiences and health effects of double-duty caregiving—those women and men who provide care at work and at home to older relatives. She has received peer-reviewed funding from a number of national funding agencies, and findings of her research have been widely published in gerontology and nursing research journals.

Linda S.Y. Wan received her BSc from the University of Western Ontario and worked as a research assistant on the CURA. Born and raised in Ontario, Linda completed her Master of Art's degree in counselling psychology at Simon Fraser University, where her thesis examined the personal growth attained by Chinese-Canadian immigrants during the migration experience.

COPYRIGHT ACKNOWLEDGEMENTS

Chapter 3: Cheryl Forchuk, Ruth Schofield, Libbey Joplin, Rick Csiernik, Carolyne Gorlick, and Katherine Turner, "Housing, Income Support and Mental Health: Points of Disconnection," *Health Research Policy and Systems*, vol. 5, no. 14 (2007). Reprinted with permission from the authors.

Chapter 4: Cheryl Forchuk, Catherine Ward-Griffin, Rick Csiernik, and Katherine Turner, "Surviving the Tornado of Mental Illness: Mental-Health Consumer-Survivor Experiences of Getting, Losing and Keeping Housing," Psychiatric Services, vol. 57, no. 4 (2006), pp. 558–562. Reprinted with permission from *Psychiatric Services*, (Copyright 2006). American Psychiatric Association.

Chapter 5: Catherine Ward-Griffin, Ruth Schofield, Sandra Vos, and Robin Coatsworth-Puspoky, "Families Caring for Members with Mental Illness: A Vicious Cycle," *Journal of Family Nursing*, vol. 11, no. 2 (2005), pp. 558–562. Reprinted with permission from the authors.

Chapter 6: Rick Csiernik, Cheryl Forchuk, Mark Speechly, and Catherine Ward-Griffin, "De 'myth' ifying mental health – Findings from a Community University Research Alliance (CURA)," *Critical Social Work*, vol. 8, no.1 (2007), pp. 1–15. Reprinted with permission of the publisher.

Chapter 7: Cheryl Forchuk, Geoffrey Nelson, and G. Brent Hall, "'It's important to be proud of the place you live in": Housing Problems and Preferences of Mental-Health Consumer-Survivors," *Perspectives in Psychiatric Care*, vol. 42, no. 1 (2006), pp. 45–52. Reprinted with permission of John Wiley and Sons.

Chapter 8: Geoffrey Nelson, G. Brent Hall, and Cheryl Forchuk, "Current and Preferred Housing of Mental Health Consumers-Survivors," *Canadian Journal of Community Mental Health*, vol. 22, no. 1 (2003), pp. 5–19. Reprinted with permission of the publisher.

Chapter 9: Ruth Schofield, Cheryl Forchuk, Elsabeth Jensen, and Stephanie Brown, "Perceptions of Health and Health Service Utilization among Homeless and Housed Mental Health Consumer-Survivors," *Journal of Psychiatric and Mental Health Nursing*, vol. 15, no. 5 (2008), pp. 399–407. Reprinted with permission of John Wiley and Sons.

Chapter 10: Amy Haldenby, Helene Berman, and Cheryl Forchuk, "Homeless and Health in Adolescence," *Qualitative Health Research*, vol. 17, no. 9 (2007), pp. 1232–1244. Reprinted with permission of the publisher.

Chapter 11: Cheryl Forchuk, Gord Russell, Shani Kingston-MacClure, Katherine Turner, and Susan Dill, "From Psychiatric Wards to the Streets and Shelters," *Journal of Psychiatric and Mental Health Nursing*, vol. 13, no. 3 (2006), pp. 301–308. Reprinted with permission of John Wiley and Sons.

Chapter 12: Cheryl Forchuk, Shanni Kingston-MacClure, Michelle Van Beers, Cheryl Smith, Rick Csiernik, Jeffrey S. Hoch, and Elsabeth Jensen, "An Intervention to Prevent Homelessness among Individuals Discharged from Psychiatric Wards to Shelters and 'No Fixed Address,'" *Journal of Psychiatric and Mental Health Nursing*, vol. 15, no. 7 (2008), pp. 569–575. Reprinted with permission of John Wiley and Sons.

Chapter 13: Richard G. Booth, "Using Electronic Patient Records in Mental Healthcare to Capture Housing and Homelessness Information of Mental Health

Consumer-Survivors," Issues in Mental Health Nursing, vol. 27, no. 10 (2006), pp.1067–1077. Reprinted with permission of the publisher.

Chapter 15: Cheryl Forchuk, Phyllis Montgomery, Helene Berman, Catherine Ward-Griffin, Rick Csiernik, Carolyne Gorlick, Elsabeth Jensen, and Patrick Riesterer, "Gaining Ground, Losing Ground: The Paradoxes of Rural Homelessness," Canadian Journal of Nursing Research, vol. 42, no. 2 (2010), pp.138–152. Reprinted with permission of the publisher.

Chapter 16: Cheryl Forchuk, Elsabeth Jensen, Rick Csiernik, Catherine Ward-Griffin, Susan L Ray, Phyllis Montgomery, and LindaWan, "Exploring Differences Between Community-Based Women and Men with a History of Mental Illness," *Issues in Mental Health Nursing*, vol. 30, no. 8 (2009), pp. 495–502. Reprinted with permission of the publisher.

Chapter 17: Helene Berman, Gloria Alvernaz, Mulcahy, Cheryl Forchuk, Kathy Edmunds, Amy Haldendy, and Raquel Lopez, "Uprooted and Displaced: A Critical Narrative Study of Homeless, Aboriginal, and Newcomer Girls in Canada," *Issues in Canadian Mental Health Nursing*, vol. 30, no. 7 (2009), pp. 418–430. Reprinted with permission of the publisher.

Chapter 18: Rick Csiernik, "Is Substance Abuse Even an Issue? Perceptions of Male and Female Community-Based Mental Health Consumer-Survivors," *International Journal of Mental Health and Addiction*, vol. 5, no. 1 (2007), pp. 29–37. Reprinted with permission of the publisher.

INDEX

Aboriginal girls
  current knowledge/understandings of, 262–63
  as diverse group, 265
  health/safety issues of, 262–63
  violence against, 262–63, 269
Aboriginal girls, as uprooted/displaced, 258
  and ambiguous/dangerous spaces, 269
  by being "different," 268, 269
  families of, 267, 268, 269, 274, 276
  by frequent moves, 267, 268, 269, 274, 279
  and impact of, 276–77
  by poverty, 273
  and reserves, 267, 269, 273, 276, 277
  in study sample, 258, 260, 264, 265, 266
  and teen motherhood, 269, 274, 276–77
Aboriginal peoples
  health/safety issues of, 262–63, 267
  housing assistance for, 148, 214
  "nested identities" of, 278
absolute homelessness, 332
abuse
  see also specific types of abuse; adolescents, homeless
  and access to housing, 18, 136, 148, 173, 235
  of elderly, 211
  and mental illness, 250

of rural residents, 235, 237
accessible housing, 322
access to services
    and diversity of homelessness, 209, 210, 211, 220, 222, 223
    vs. housing preferences, 95–96, 99–102, 108, 118–19
    by mental health consumer-survivors, 99–101, 101–2
    by rural residents, 230, 232–36
    by shelter residents, 128, 157
    by substance abusers, 294, 295–96
adequate housing, 322
adolescent girls. *See* girls, *and entries following*
adolescents, homeless, 123–24, 143–61, 209–11
    see also girls, homeless, *and entry following*
    abuse of, 144, 145, 147, 148, 153–55, 156, 158, 209, 210, 271
    affordable housing for, 148, 159, 160–61
    background/significance of, 144
    contemporary policy context of, 147–48
    criminal behaviour by, 210
    as diverse group, 147, 211
    employment of, 145, 148, 152, 158, 159
    experiences of, 145–47, 151–58, 267–68, 270–76, 278, 279
    family abandonment/betrayal of, 153–54, 155, 273
    and health care system, 144, 146, 156–58, 159–60, 210
    health concerns of, 124, 144, 145–46, 156–58
    narratives/themes of, 151–58
    as "outcasts," 154, 273
    perceptions of, 145, 146, 159
    in rural areas, 234, 237
    sexual activity of, 145–46, 155
    sexual violence against, 146–47, 155–56, 159–60, 161, 210
    in shelters, 151, 152–53, 154, 210, 222
    specific disorders of, 145–46, 147, 152, 156
    street "families"/peer groups of, 153, 154–55, 273, 275–76
    substance abuse by, 145, 147, 210
    and suicide, 145, 147, 210
    violence against, 146–47, 152–53, 155–56, 159–60, 161
adolescents, homeless, study of, 124, 148–61
    data collection/analysis of, 150–51
    design of, 148–49
    discussion of, 158–61
    narratives/themes of, 151–58
    sample used in, 149–50
adolescents, homeless, study narratives/themes of, 151–58
    dangers of street life, 152–53
    employment/education, 152, 158, 159
    exiting street life, 151–52
    females' safety issues, 155–56, 159–60, 161
    health/health care system, 156–58, 159–60
    public policy, 158, 159
    rethinking family, 153–55
affordable housing
    see also social housing *and other housing types*
    for adolescents, 148, 159, 160–61
    assistance in finding, 183
    barriers to finding, 37, 78–79, 91–92, 96–97, 209, 217–18, 293
    CMHC definition of, 36
    decrease in, 35, 36–37, 44, 64, 110–11, 175, 176, 182
    definitions of, 322–23

for discharged patients, 168, 175–76, 180, 182–83, 191, 198
for elderly, 211
family concerns over, 64, 69, 72, 73
government involvement in, 32, 35–37, 107–8, 110–11, 147–48, 211–12, 307
for immigrants/refugees, 209
and NIMBY syndrome, 78–79
permanent, types of, 322–27
in U.S., 110
waiting lists for, 37, 96, 136, 235
Affordable Housing Task Force (London), 305
assertive community treatment (ACT), 235
Australia, issues studied in, 110, 210

boarding homes/houses, 110, 328
Booth, Richard, 125

Canada Mortgage and Housing Corporation (CMHC), 36
Canada Pension Plan (Disability), 37–38
Canadian Alternative Investment Co-operative, 307
Canadian Mental Health Association (CMHA), 7, 43, 183, 318
Canadian Multiculturalism Act, 207
Can-Voice, 5, 9, 317
Centre for Addiction and Mental Health (CAMH), 49
Childhood Trauma Questionnaire, 22, 289, 292–93, 293*t*
churches, 54, 56, 236, 324
"circle of care," families' provision of, 32, 65–66, 66*f*, 68
Colorado Client Assessment Record (CCAR), 21–22, 81, 289, 290–92

in results data, 133–34*t*, 246*t*, 247*t*, 248*t*, 291*t*, 292*t*
community economic development (CED), 304–5
community involvement in research, 301–2, 315–20
accomplishments of, 320
beneficiaries of, 316–19
and community identification, 316
costs of, 319
Community-University Research Alliance. *See* CURA on Mental Health and Housing, *and entry following*
Constitution Act, 1867, 36
Consumer Housing Preference Survey Instrument, 23, 112
co-op housing, 36, 323, 324–25, 326
core housing need, 323
couch surfing, 18, 152, 220, 221, 235, 267, 275, 332. *See also* hidden homelessness
critical social theory (CST), 148–49, 212, 213, 263
critical time intervention (CTI), 169, 181, 192, 193–94
Csiernik, Rick, 6, 7
CURA on Mental Health and Housing, 3–10
annual conference of, 7–8
committee structure of, 7*f*, 7–9
fact sheets of, 8, 335–38
member participation in, 7–10, 317
origins of, 6–7, 8, 305, 308, 310
research by, 8, 13–29
students on, 9, 15, 19, 124, 130, 318–19
CURA on Mental Health and Housing, research by, 8, 13–29
and community involvement, 301–2, 315–20
context of, 13–14

data collection in, 20–23, 289
flexibility of, 28–29
focus groups for, 8, 23–27, 92–103, 317–18
goal/overall approach of, 14–15
policy changes resulting from, 317–18
qualitative methodology of, 8, 14, 23–28
quantitative methodology of, 14, 15–23
sampling in, 15–20
custodial housing, 107, 110

data collection instruments, 20–23, 289. *See also specific instruments*; sampling, in CURA research study
DeCosta, Betty, 5
deinstitutionalization, 14, 32, 59, 79, 91, 107, 191–92, 198, 211–12
and housing/income support issues, 42–45, 49, 55
and poor discharge procedures, 70–71, 179
demographic form, 20–21
determinants of health, social, 44, 60, 72
housing as, 4, 60, 180, 192
Diagnostic and Statistical Manual (DSM) diagnoses, 16, 208
disability support. *See* Ontario Disability Support Program
disabled, housing for, 324, 326
discharge to shelters/streets, 9, 124–25, 167–76, 179–87, 192
and critical time intervention, 169, 181, 192, 193–94
CURA intervention study on, 182–87, 194–95
data on, 168–69, 170–72, 171t, 172f, 181–82, 193–95
and electronic patient records, 125, 191–99
health/safety issues of, 179

implications of, 175, 175f, 176, 186–87
and income supports, 55, 124, 175, 183, 187, 317–18
and in-patient treatment, 194
as invisible problem, 124, 125, 168–69, 176, 192
and lack of affordable housing, 168, 175–76, 180, 182–83, 191, 198
London/St. Thomas study of, 124–25, 169, 170–76, 181–82, 194–95
poor procedures for, 70–71, 179
U.K./U.S. intervention studies on, 180–81, 193–94
discharge to shelters/streets, intervention study on, 182–87, 194–95
advocacy/financial assistance in, 183
findings of, 124–25, 185–86, 186t
implications of, 186–87
limitations of, 187
methodology of, 183–85
participants in, 183–84, 184t
discharge to shelters/streets in London/St. Thomas, study of, 124–25, 169, 170–76
case studies of, 172–74
discussion of, 176
findings of, 170–72, 171t, 172f, 181–82, 194–95
implications of, 175, 175f
methodology of, 170
district health councils (DHCs), 23–24, 25–26, 92
diversity and homelessness, 201–2, 205–12
and access to services, 209, 210, 211, 220, 222, 223
current knowledge of, 207–12
and family life, 218–21
and generational differences, 222

and immigrants/refugees, 208–9, 218–19, 220, 223
and multiculturalism, 206–7
and "othering," 205–6, 207, 215, 223–24
and poverty, 206–7, 208–9, 211, 215–18
in socio-political context, 206
and transience, 221–22
diversity and homelessness, current knowledge of
elderly, 211
immigrants/refugees, 208–9
mental illness, 208
public policy, 211–12
youth, 209–11
diversity and homelessness study, 207, 212–24
discussion of, 223–24
and ethnography, 212–13
findings of, 215–22
methodology of, 213–15
participatory approach to, 201–2, 212, 213
diversity and homelessness study, themes of, 215–22
family life, 218–21
generational differences, 222
poverty, 215–18
transience, 221–22
domiciliary hostels, 328, 330
downloading, of social housing, 36–37, 206, 211–12, 238, 307

Edwards, Betty, 9
elderly
homelessness among, 211
supportive housing for, 327, 330–31
electronic patient records (EPRs), 125, 191–99
barriers to using, 197–98

compared to paper records, 195, 196–97
generic/specific data in, 196–97
and homelessness, 195–97
and homelessness/mental health context, 193–95
and longitudinal information, 195–96
off-site access to, 197
privacy/security of, 197–98
and psychiatry, 192–93, 195–96
eligibility, for income support, 37–42, 158, 160, 196, 217
emergency shelters and hostels, 144, 148, 331–32, 333
emotional abuse, 22, 145, 153–54, 155
employment
of adolescents, 145, 148, 152, 158, 159
as determinant of health, 4
diminished access to, 78, 79, 206, 208, 209, 333
and education, 78, 80–81, 81t, 85–86, 152, 158, 159
of immigrants/refugees, 218
and income support eligibility, 37–42, 217
of mental health consumer-survivors, 80, 81t, 86, 92, 96, 113t
and mental illness stigma, 93, 102
of rural residents, 202, 237
of substance abusers, 294
ethnography, 212–13

families, as mental illness caregivers, 32–33, 59–73
advocacy by, 62, 71, 73, 316
"blame" and "burden" issues of, 60–61
cost issues of, 60–61, 68–69, 72
focus groups of, 25–27
health of, 60–61, 63–65

and health care providers, 62, 63, 69, 70–71, 72–73
and inadequate/substandard housing, 66–68, 84
and lack of affordable housing, 64, 69, 72, 73
and mental health legislation, 72, 73
and mental health reform, 73
myths about, 84, 86
perspectives of, 61–63
recognition of, 62, 72, 73
in rural areas, 62–63, 65, 239
and schizophrenia, 27, 60, 61, 62, 68, 71, 73
and stigma, 62, 63, 316
support for, 63–65, 70
women's role in, 61, 65
family abandonment/betrayal
of adolescents, 153–54, 155, 273
as myth, 84, 86
family care and mental illness study, 65–73
discussion of, 72–73
methodology of, 65
themes/findings of, 32–33, 65–72
family care and mental illness study, themes/findings of, 32–33, 65–72
"circle of care" concept, 32, 65–66, 66f, 68
creating a better world, 69–72
witnessing inadequacies, 66–68, 84
working behind the scenes, 68–69
family life, and homelessness, 218–21
and government policy disconnects, 220
and health care/service providers, 219–20, 221
for immigrants/refugees, 218–19, 220
and policies geared to individuals, 220–21
and poverty, 220–21
and separations, 219–20, 220–21, 222
in shelters, 219–20, 222
fear, living in, 52, 53, 56, 81, 85
Federal Homelessness Secretariat, 306
First Nations Market Housing Fund, 148
focus groups, in CURA research study, 8
see also mental health consumer-survivors, themes identified by
of consumer-survivors, 23–27, 92–103, 317–18
in diversity/homelessness study, 213–15
of families, 25–27
feedback process for, 27–28
interviews in, 25, 26
of other non-consumer groups, 27
policy changes resulting from, 317–18
themes identified by, 93, 94t, 95–103
Forchuk, Cheryl, 5–6, 9
Freire, Paulo, 213

gay/lesbian individuals. See LGBT individuals, issues of
gender, 243–45
gender differences, of mental health consumer-survivors, 202–3, 243–45
see also men; women
age of illness onset, 246, 246t
education, 80–81, 246t, 247
employment status, 80, 81t
health of homeless/housed, 130, 131t, 136
hospitalization, 80, 85, 247, 290, 294
housing/living arrangements, 82–83, 82t, 112, 113t, 249, 250–51
illness severity, 249, 250–51
legal issues, 81
levels of functioning, 248–49, 251, 292, 292t
marital status, 80, 80t, 247, 247t, 250

personal strengths/resources, 249, 250, 251
primary diagnosis, 80, 80*t*, 247–48, 248*t*, 249–50, 252, 288, 290, 290*t*
substance abuse, 80, 202–3, 203–4, 248, 248*t*, 249–50, 287–96
gender differences, of mental health consumer-survivors, study of, 245–52
   discussion of, 249–52
   methodology of, 245
   results of, 246–49
generational differences, and homelessness, 222
girls
   see also adolescents, homeless, *and entries following*; women
   devaluation of, 144, 260–61, 278
   in homelessness studies, 124, 151, 211
   sexual abuse of, 147, 172–73, 262, 268, 271
   in uprooting/displacement study, 203, 258, 260, 264, 265, 266
   violence against, 203, 211, 260, 261, 262–63, 269
girls, homeless, 144, 146–47, 155–56, 159–60, 261–62
   see also adolescents, homeless, *and entries following*
   current knowledge/understandings of, 261–62
   as diverse group, 265
   and health care system, 146, 156, 157–58
   health issues of, 261
   safety issues of, 145–47, 155–56, 159–60, 161, 210, 211
   sexual activity of, 145–46, 155
   sexual violence against, 146–47, 155–56, 159–60, 161, 210
   substance abuse by, 147
   and suicide, 147
   unique challenges of, 146–47
girls, homeless, as uprooted/displaced
   by being "different"/"outcasts," 268, 273
   and dangerous environments, 271–72
   families of, 270–71, 273, 274–76
   by frequent moves, 267–68, 270, 271–72
   reasons for, 270–71
   and spaces of belonging, 274–76
   and spaces of hope, 276
   "street families" of, 275–76
   in study sample, 258, 260, 264, 265, 266
   tenuous connections of, 273
girls, uprooted/displaced, 203, 257–79
   see also Aboriginal girls, *and entry following*; girls, homeless, as uprooted/displaced; immigrant and refugee girls, *and entry following*
   background/significance of, 258
   conceptualizing, 259–60
   current knowledge/understandings of, 260–63
   liminal spaces of, 259, 266, 268, 274–75, 277, 278
   "nested identities" of, 278
   as "Others"/different, 260–61, 266, 268, 269, 273
   shelter/"accommodations" of, 267–68
girls, uprooted/displaced, study of, 263–79
   "core narrative" of, 265, 266–67
   research methods of, 264–66
   results/discussion of, 266–79
   sample groups of, 264, 265, 266
   theory/methodology of, 263
girls, uprooted/displaced, study narratives/themes of, 266–79
   and "core narrative," 266–67

disconnection/dangerous spaces, 266, 268–72
liminal spaces, 266, 268, 274–75, 277, 278
negotiating spaces of belonging, 267, 274–77
tenuous connections/spaces of hope, 266–67, 272–74, 279
uprooting experiences, 267–68
government policies, inadequacies/ disconnects of, 31–32, 35–45
see also specific programs
and family life, 220
health care/service providers and, 44–45, 217–18
on housing, 32, 35–37, 110–11, 147–48, 211–12, 307
on income supports, 37–42
on mental health, 14, 31–32, 42–44
group homes, 6, 110, 311
adolescents in, 157, 293
as considered substandard, 235
and CURA samples, 8, 14, 16–17, 18, 19, 20, 24–25, 26
and health study, 130, 136
as housing preference, 23, 84, 112
NIMBY reaction to, 78
residence in, 82, 82t
as supportive housing, 108, 327
group living/boarding home housing, by type, 328–31
Guaranteed Annual Income Supplement for the Disabled (GAINS-D), 41

Haldenby, Amy, 124
halfway homes, 108, 329
Harris, Mike, and Conservative government of
and mental health reform, 14, 43–44

and Ontario Disability Support Program, 40–42
and Ontario Works, 38–40
and psychiatric hospitals, 14, 43
and social housing, 36–37, 206, 307
Health, Ontario Ministry of (MOH), 107
mental health reports by, 43–44
Health and Long-Term Care, Ontario Ministry of (MHLTC)
and CURA, 7, 317
and CURA focus groups, 25–27, 92–93, 317–18
and Margaret's Haven, 6, 307, 308
mental health reform by, 14, 73
Health Care Consent Act (Ontario), 73
health care/service providers, 22, 27
and discharge to shelters/streets, 186–87, 192, 195–97
and family caregivers, 62, 63, 69, 70–71, 72–73
in focus/research groups, 8, 27, 28, 214, 316
and government policy disconnects, 44–45, 217–18
and homeless adolescents, 144, 146, 156–58, 159–60, 210
and homeless families, 219–20, 221
and housing preferences, 119
and immigrants/refugees, 218–19, 223
and mental illness "tornado," 52, 56
negative/discriminatory behaviour by, 78, 208, 210
on poverty, 217–18
on "revolving door" of service access, 222
in rural areas, 231, 232, 233–34, 236, 239
and substance abuse, 250

health of mental health consumer-survivors, 123, 127–38
　disorders of, 127, 132, 135, 136–37
　and health services use, 128–29, 134–35
　in homeless/housed individuals, 127–30, 132–38
　in men and women, 130, 131*t*, 136
　and mortality rates, 128
　perceptions of, 123, 129–30, 135, 135*t*, 137
health of mental health consumer-survivors, study of, 130–38
　and barriers to health care, 137–38
　demographics of, 130, 131*t*, 132, 136
　and level of functioning, 134*t*, 134
　methodology of, 130
　and perceptions of health, 135, 135*t*, 137
　and problem severity, 132, 133*t*, 134, 136–37
　and schizophrenia, 131*t*, 132, 136
　and use of health services, 134–35, 136–37
Health Services Restructuring Committee (Ontario), 43
hidden homelessness
　see also couch surfing
　definition of, 332
　among immigrants/refugees, 209, 223
　perception of, 157
　in rural areas, 230
　studying, 16, 28–29
HIV infection, 127, 145–46, 147, 179, 262
homeless–at-risk housing, 332–33
homeless girls. *See* girls, homeless, *and entry following*
homeless vs. housed individuals
　health of, 127–30, 131*t*, 132–38
　hospitalization of, 134–35, 137, 193
　substance abuse by, 133*t*, 134, 136–37, 138

homelessness
　of adolescents, 123–24, 143–61, 209–11
　definitions of, 143–44, 332–33
　and diversity, 201–2, 205–24
　and family life, 218–21
　fluid nature of, 221–22
　generational differences of, 222
　and health/health service utilization, 127–38
　as hidden, 16, 28–29, 157, 209, 223, 230, 332
　and hospitalization, 52, 55, 193–95, 193, 196, 318
　and housing insecurity, 333
　of immigrants/refugees, 208–9, 218–19
　and mental illness, 32, 68, 127–30, 132–38, 208
　rural, 202, 229–39
　sex as used to avoid, 125, 145, 155, 182, 186
　stereotypes of, 205–6
　stigmatization of, 31
　and substance abuse, 127, 133*t*, 134, 168, 270
　types of, 332
homelessness, prevention of, 123–25
　see also entries for topics below
　and discharge to shelters/streets, 167–76, 179–87
　and electronic patient records, 191–99
Homelessness Action Task Force (Toronto), 144
homelessness, of mental health consumer-survivors, 32, 68, 208
　causes of, 191–92
　and discharge to shelters/streets, 124–25, 167–76, 179–87, 192, 193–94
　and electronic patient records, 125, 191–99

frequency of, 193
and government inadequacies/
    disconnects, 31–32, 35–45
and health, 127–30, 132–38
and health services use, 128–29, 134–35
invisibility of, 16, 29, 124, 125, 176, 230
homes for special care, 7, 20, 82, 136, 330
and resident survey, 111, 112, 113*t*, 114, 114*t*, 116
hospitalization
    and affordable housing, 129
    data collection on, 22, 168, 289
    families' experience of, 61, 62, 64–65, 67, 69, 70–71, 73
    of homeless/housed individuals, 134–35, 137, 193
    and homelessness, 52, 55, 193–95, 193, 196, 318
    low preference for, 110
    of Margaret's Haven residents, 311
    of men and women, 80, 85, 247, 290, 294
    record keeping and, 191–99
    of substance abusers, 290, 294
hospitals, discharge from. *See* discharge to shelters/streets, *and entries following*
hospitals, provincial psychiatric (PPHs), 42–43
    and deinstitutionalization, 42–45, 49, 55
    in London and St. Thomas, 14, 170, 171*t*, 304
hostels, 82, 110
    domiciliary, 328, 330
    emergency, 144, 148, 331–32, 333
housing
    see also affordable housing; social housing; supported housing; supportive housing; *and other housing by type*
    and demographics/psychiatric history, 112, 113*t*, 114
    inadequacies of, as witnessed by families, 66–68, 84
    lack of national policy on, 32, 35, 110–11, 147–48, 211–12, 307
    as social determinant of health, 4, 60, 180, 192
    substandard, 91, 143, 191, 235, 250
Housing and Urban Development, U.S. Department of, 110
housing history
    of shelter residents, 112, 113*t*, 221, 235, 238
    of study participants, 83, 83*t*, 112, 113*t*
housing insecurity, 332
housing preferences, 33–34, 49, 50, 84
    vs. accessible services, 95–96, 99–102, 108, 118–19
    as compared to current housing, 107–12, 113–14*t*, 114–19
    as current housing, 114*t*, 116–17, 118–19
    data collection on, 23, 92–93, 111–14
    and demographics/psychiatric history, 112, 113*t*, 114
    and housing problems/issues, 91–93, 94*t*, 95–104
    and housing stability, 49–50, 54–55
    and lifestyle difficulties/help needed, 115, 115*t*
    participatory action research approach to, 111–19
    qualities of, 114
    and satisfaction/quality of life, 110, 111, 112, 116–17, 118
    supports needed to obtain, 115, 115*t*, 117–18
    by type, 114*t*
    U.S./Australian research on, 109–10, 117

housing preferences, factors affecting, 91–104, 107–19
  see also mental health consumer-survivors, themes identified by
  accessible services, 95–96, 99–102, 108, 118–19
  affordability, 96–97, 98, 102, 110–11
  children, 97, 98
  independence, 92, 96, 98, 99, 101–2, 109, 114, 117–19
  oppression/stigma, 16, 78–79, 93–95, 101, 102, 103
  poverty/finances, 92, 97, 99, 101, 102–3, 115, 115*t*, 117–18
  rural location, 100, 102
  safety issues, 97–99
  social networks/social support, 95–96, 118–19
  staff support, 92, 96, 101–2, 118
  summary of, 94*t*
  transportation, 100, 102, 115, 115*t*, 117–18
housing preferences, by type, 114*t*
  homes for special care, 114*t*, 116
  independent living, 33, 50, 84, 92, 98, 101–2, 109, 114*t*, 117
  shelters, 84, 114*t*, 116, 117, 118
  supported housing, 92, 98, 101–2
  supportive housing, 64, 98, 99, 101, 110, 114, 114*t*, 116, 117, 118

immigrant and refugee girls
  current knowledge/understandings of, 260–61
  "othering"/devaluation of, 260–61, 266, 273, 278
immigrant and refugee girls, as uprooted/displaced, 258, 267, 279
  by being "different," 260–61, 266, 268
  and ethnic neighbourhoods/spaces, 270, 272–73, 274, 277–78
  and language, 272, 274, 277
  and spaces of hope/belonging, 272–73, 274, 277, 279
  in study sample, 258, 260, 264, 265, 266
immigrants and refugees, 206, 209, 258
immigrants and refugees, homeless, 208–9
  and access to services, 209, 220, 223
  family life of, 218–19
  health of, 206–7, 208–9
  and health care/service providers, 218–19, 223
  as hidden, 209, 223
  "othering" of, 207, 215, 223–24
  poverty of, 206–7, 208–9, 215–18
  in shelters, 208, 218
  social exclusion of, 206–7
income supports, 22, 44, 52, 305, 316
  and discharge problems, 55, 124, 175, 183, 187, 317–18
  eligibility for, 37–42, 158, 160, 196, 217
  inadequacies of, 31–32, 35–45, 53, 54, 55, 99, 102–3, 217–18, 229
income supports (specific), 37–42
  see also specific programs
  Canada Pension Plan (Disability), 37–38
  Ontario Disability Support Program, 37, 40–42, 183
  Ontario Works, 37, 38–40, 99, 183, 318
independent living
  definition of, 324
  as housing preference, 33, 50, 84, 92, 98, 101–2, 109, 114*t*, 117
  and lack of crisis support, 99
  sampling of people in, 16, 17, 18
  sustainability framework for, 50
influenza, 127, 145

intersectionality theory, 263
intervention, to prevent discharge to shelters/streets, 179–87
   see also discharge to shelters/streets, *and entries following*
   critical time concept of, 169, 181, 192, 193–94
   CURA study on, 182–87, 194–95
   U.K./U.S. studies on, 180–81, 193–94
intervention study on discharge to shelters/streets, by CURA, 182–87, 194–95
   findings of, 124–25, 185–86, 186t
   implications of, 186–87
   methodology of, 183–85
   participants in, 183–84, 184t
interviews, 19–20, 21–22, 25, 26

Jensen, Elsabeth, 5–6

Kelly, Norma-Jean, 5, 317
Kreda, Janet, 5, 9, 305, 306

landlords, 27, 186, 316, 322
   and custodial care, 107
   direct ODSP payment to, 317–18
   families as, 68, 84
   families' experiences with, 67
   poor treatment by, 93, 94t, 95
   and power of eviction, 95, 174, 312
   rent demands by, 55, 216–17
Layton, Jack, 143
Learning, Earning, and Parenting (LEAP) program, 40
Lehman Quality of Life Scale, 22, 112, 116–17, 118, 289
LGBT individuals, issues of, 145, 156, 160, 223–24

LIFE*SPIN, 5, 6, 304–5
   and CED approach, 304–5
   and Margaret's Haven, 5, 304–9
liminal spaces, of uprooted/displaced girls, 259, 266, 268, 274–75, 277, 278
local health integration networks (LHINs), 92
London, City of
   see also discharge to shelters/streets in London/St. Thomas, study of
   Affordable Housing Task Force of, 305
   and CURA, 7, 14
   and Margaret's Haven, 307
   Regional Mental Health Care, 310
London East Community Mental Health Services (LECMHS), 307, 308, 309
London Psychiatric Hospital, 14, 170, 171t, 304
longitudinal studies/information, need for
   and electronic patient records, 195–96
   on families, 72
   on gender/mental health, 252
   on homelessness/mental health, 138
long-term care facilities, 235, 328, 329

Margaret (mental health consumer-survivor), 3, 5, 10, 301, 304
Margaret's Haven, 5–7, 9, 301–2, 302–13
   and CURA, 6–7, 8, 305, 308, 310
   development of, 305–8
   evaluation of, 8, 307–8, 310–12
   funding of, 306–7, 308, 310
   LECMHS and, 307, 308, 309
   LIFE*SPIN and, 304–9
   management of, 308
   mandate of, 306, 309, 310, 312
   mission statement of, 306

personal legacy of, 310–12
tenants of, 306, 307, 308–9, 310–12
safety at, 308–9, 311
shutdown of, 309
site/neighbourhood of, 307, 308–9, 311
staff of, 308
structural legacy of, 310
supports at, 307, 308, 309
transportation to/from, 307
McGuinty, Dalton, and Liberal government of, 37, 43
McKane, Pamela, 9
men
  see also gender differences, of mental health consumer-survivors; women
  and mental illness, 243–52
  mood disorders in, 80t, 136, 248t, 290, 290t
  sampling of, 15, 18
  schizophrenia in, 80t, 244, 247, 248t, 249, 252, 290, 290t
  as substance abusers, 80, 287–96
mental health, 4
  de-"myth"-ifying, 33, 77–86
  government policy disconnects on, 31–32, 42–44
Mental Health Act (Ontario), 71, 73, 169
Mental Health and Housing, Community-University Research Alliance on. *See* CURA on Mental Health and Housing
mental health consumer-survivors, xii
  see also entries for topics below
  employment of, 80, 81t, 86, 92, 96, 113t
  family care of, 32–33, 59–73
  focus groups of, 23–27, 92–103, 317–18
  gender differences of, 202–3, 243–52
  health/health study of, 127–38

and homelessness, 32, 68, 127–30, 132–38, 208
housing of, by demographics/psychiatric history, 112, 113t, 114
housing history of, 83, 83t, 112, 113t, 221, 235, 238
housing preferences of, 33–34, 91–104, 107–19
level of functioning of, 134t, 134, 248–49, 251
myths perpetuated about, 33, 77–86
perceptions of health among, 123, 129–30, 135, 135t, 137
problem severity of, 132, 133t, 134, 136–37, 249, 250–51
use of health services by, 134–35, 136–37
mental health consumer-survivors, themes identified by, 32, 93–103
  see also housing preferences, factors affecting
  accessible services, 99–101, 101–2
  in family care study, 65–72
  housing, 33–34, 49–55, 96–99, 101–2
  living in fear, 52, 53, 56, 81, 85
  loss of possessions, 52–53, 55–56
  in mental illness "tornado," 32, 51–56, 51f, 186
  need for advocacy, 95, 101, 103
  oppression/stigma, 16, 78–79, 93–95, 101, 102, 103, 208, 294
  poverty/finances, 92, 97, 99, 101, 102–3, 115, 115t, 117–18
  rural services, 100–1
  social networks/social support, 95–96
  summary of, 94t
mental illness. *See* homelessness, of mental health consumer-survivors;

mental health; mental health consumer-survivors, *entries on*; stigma of mental illness
mental illness "tornado," phases/themes of, 32, 51–56, 51*f*, 186
  building relationships, 54–55
  gaining stability, 52, 54–55, 56
  government responses to, 55
  losing ground, 52–53, 55–56
  struggling to survive, 52, 53–54, 56
Ministry of Health. *See* Health, Ontario Ministry of; Health and Long-Term Care, Ontario Ministry of
Mission Services of London, 7
mobile health services, 137, 238
modified units/special needs housing, 324, 326
mood disorders, 20
  in discharge intervention study, 184*t*, 185
  and homelessness, 128, 132, 136
  of housed individuals, 113*t*, 114
  in men and women, 80*t*, 136, 244, 247, 248*t*, 249, 252, 290, 290*t*
myths, 77–78, 84–85
  and stereotypes, 79, 84–85, 86, 205–6
myths about mental illness, 33, 77–86
  as barrier to finding housing, 78–79
  and CURA study data, 80–86
  historical, 78, 85
  and public attitudes, 79
myths about mental illness, and CURA study data, 80–86
  education/employability, 78, 80–81, 81*t*, 85–86
  family abandonment, 84, 86
  homogeneity, 80–82, 80*t*–82*t*, 85
  violence/unpredictability, 78, 81, 82, 85

narrative inquiry/analysis, 148–49, 203, 263, 264
National Housing Initiative (NHI), 148
newcomers. *See* immigrant and refugee girls, *and entries following*
"no fixed address." *See* discharge to shelters/streets, *and entry following*
non-profit housing, 103, 107, 324–25. *See also* LIFE*SPIN; Margaret's Haven
"Not in My Backyard" (NIMBY) syndrome, 78–79

Ontario Disability Support Program (ODSP), 37, 40–42, 183
  eligibility for, 40–41
  inadequacy of, 41–42, 55, 99, 102–3, 217–18, 229
  and payment to landlords, 55, 317–18
  people's experiences with, 68, 217–18, 236
Ontario Disability Support Program Act, 41
Ontario Trillium Foundation, 308
Ontario Works, 37, 38–40, 99, 183, 318
  inadequacy of, 217–18
  income support provided by, 41–42
  people's experiences with, 68, 217–18, 220, 236
Ontario Works Act, 38, 39–40
"othering"
  of homeless, 205–6, 207
  of immigrant/refugee girls, 260–61, 266, 273, 278
  of immigrants/refugees, 207, 215, 223–24
  of uprooted/displaced girls, 266, 273, 278
oppression
  intersecting/overlapping forms of, 148–49, 201, 203, 252, 258, 266

and mental illness myths, 33, 78–79, 86
and poverty, 101, 102, 252, 258, 287, 338
and stigma, 16, 78–79, 93–95, 101, 102, 103, 208, 294
and violence, 252, 258
Ouseley, Sue, 9

participatory action research (PAR), 14, 15
    benefits of, 316–19
    in diversity/homelessness study, 201–2, 212, 213
    in housing preference study, 111–19
physical abuse, 22, 80, 85
    of adolescents, 145, 153, 155, 158, 210, 268
postpartum depression, 218–19
post-traumatic stress disorder (PTSD)
    of adolescents, 210
    in men and women, 247, 248t, 250
    of substance abusers, 290
poverty, 4
    of Aboriginal girls, 273
    in diversity/homelessness study, 206–7, 208–9, 211, 215–18
    and family life, 220–21
    health care/service providers on, 217–18
    and housing preferences, 92, 97, 99, 101, 102–3, 115, 115t, 117–18
    and oppression, 101, 102, 252, 258, 287, 338
    in rural areas, 229–30
    of shelter residents, 216–18
preferred housing. *See* housing preferences *entries*
privacy
    of electronic patient records, 197–98
    in shelters, 53, 167, 219, 250
provincial psychiatric hospitals (PPHs), 42–43
    and deinstitutionalization, 42–44
    in London and St. Thomas, 14, 170, 171t, 304
public housing, 37, 136, 238, 322, 325
Putting People First (Ontario government report), 43, 44

qualitative methodology, 8, 14, 23–28
quality of life, data collection on, 22, 112, 116–17, 118, 289
quantitative methodology, 8, 14, 15–23

refugees. *See* immigrant and refugee girls, *and entries following*
rent
    and affordable housing, 36, 53, 323
    burden of, 68–69, 99, 158, 209, 216–17, 221, 273
    as demanded by landlords, 55, 216–17
    of discharged patients, 55, 124, 175, 183
    first and last month's, 99, 124, 183, 216–17
rent-geared-to-income assistance
    housing/rent supplement program, 323, 324, 325–26
research
    community involvement in, 301–2, 315–20
    by CURA, 8, 13–29
research, participatory approach to, 14, 15
    benefits of, 316–19
    in diversity/homelessness study, 201–2, 212, 213
    in housing preference study, 111–19
residential care housing, 330
rest and retirement homes, 235, 329, 330
restructuring, of health care system, 43, 59, 91
rooming houses, 328, 330
rural homelessness and mental illness, 202, 229–30

adolescents and, 234, 237
and crisis intervention, 233–34, 238
and employment, 202, 237
and family caregiving, 62–63, 65, 239
grassroots/volunteer supports for, 236, 238–39
and health care/service providers, 231, 232, 233–34, 236, 239
health issues of, 234–35
as hidden, 230
and lack of access to services, 230, 232–36
mobile services for, 238
and poverty, 229–30
safety issues of, 235, 236, 237–38
and shelters, 202, 234–35, 236, 237–39
and stigmatization/social exclusion, 231, 232
transient nature of, 232, 235, 237–39
and transportation, 100, 230, 232, 236, 238, 239
and urban culture shock, 237–38, 239
and violent/criminal behaviour, 234
women and, 236, 237
rural homelessness and mental illness, as experience of gaining/losing ground, 231–39
in access to services, 232–36
in relocation, 232, 235, 237–39
in social ties, 232
in transportation, 236, 238, 239
rural homelessness and mental illness study, 230–39
discussion of, 238–39
findings of, 231–38
methodology of, 230–31

safety
of discharged patients, 179
of homeless girls, 145–47, 155–56, 159–60, 161, 210, 211
and housing preferences, 97–99
at Margaret's Haven, 308–9, 311
and rural homelessness, 235, 236, 237–38
in shelters, 53, 67, 153, 167, 210, 237–38, 250, 294
of women, 53, 82, 146–47, 155–56, 211, 236, 237, 294
Salvation Army men's shelter (London), 6, 7
sampling, in CURA research study, 15–20
see also data collection instruments, in CURA research study
of homeless individuals, 16, 17–18
inclusion guidelines for, 15–16
of independent people, 16, 17, 18
interviews in, 19–20, 21–22
issues of, 16–18
of men and women, 15, 18
participants in, 19–20
of shelter residents, 17, 18, 130
of supported housing residents, 16–17
schizophrenia, 16, 20, 195
in discharge intervention study, 184t, 185
experiences with, 6, 68, 71
and family care, 27, 60, 61, 62, 68, 71, 73
and homelessness, 128, 169, 180
of housed individuals, 113t, 114, 131t, 132, 136
and housing preferences, 110
in men and women, 80t, 136, 244, 247, 248t, 249, 252, 290, 290t
in substance abuse study, 288, 290, 290t
and suicide, 244
service providers. *See* health care/service providers

sex, as exchanged/sold for housing, 125, 145, 155, 182, 186
sexual abuse, 22, 85
    and access to housing, 82, 94, 97, 136, 237, 250
    and fear of re-abuse, 82, 94, 97
    of girls, 147, 172–73, 262, 268, 271
    of homeless adolescents, 144, 145, 147, 148, 153–55, 156, 158, 210
    of substance abusers, 291, 295
    of women, 80, 82, 97, 136, 237, 250, 268
sexual assault/violence, 146–47, 155–56, 159–60, 161, 210
shelter allowance, 333
Shelter Enhancement Program (federal), 148
shelters
    see also discharge to shelters/streets, *and entries following*
    emergency, 144, 148, 331–32, 333
    for women, 250, 294, 304, 310
shelters, issues/problems of
    access to care, 128, 157
    availability of, 148
    health/mortality, 127, 128, 145
    privacy, 53, 167, 219, 250
    for rural residents, 202, 234–35, 236, 237–39
    safety, 53, 67, 153, 167, 210, 237–38, 250, 294
    staff-resident ratios, 167
shelters, people living in
    Aboriginal girls/women, 267, 269, 271
    adolescents/youth, 151, 152–53, 154, 210, 222
    case studies of, 172–74
    diagnoses/medications of, 113t, 114, 208
    on discharge, 124, 125, 158, 167–76, 179–87, 193, 194–95
    diversity of, 208
    families, 219–20, 222
    generational tensions of, 222
    as homeless, 127, 143
    and housing preference, 84, 114t, 116, 117, 118
    immigrants/refugees, 208, 218
    interventions to prevent, 179–87
    men and women, 18, 53, 82, 82t, 128, 154, 155, 219–20, 250
    poverty of, 216–18
    prevalence of, 191
    residential changes of, 112, 113t, 221, 235, 238
    as rural residents, 202, 234–35, 236, 237–39
    sampling of, 17, 18, 130
    shelters and streets, discharge to. *See* discharge to shelters/streets, *and entries following*
siblings, 62, 153, 267
    abuse by, 153, 158, 268
Social Assistance Reform Act (Ontario), 40
social determinants of health, 44, 60, 72
    housing as, 4, 60, 180, 192
social housing
    see also affordable housing
    definitions of, 326
    downloading of, 36–37, 206, 211–12, 238, 307
    government involvement in, 32, 35–37, 107–8, 110–11, 147–48, 211–12, 307
    for immigrants/refugees, 209
Social Sciences and Humanities Research Council (SSHRC), 4–5, 6, 13, 308
stability
    housing, 49–50, 54–55, 118, 175, 175f, 192, 196–97
    personal, 32, 45, 51, 52, 54–55, 56, 180, 239, 267, 270, 274

stereotypes, 77, 202
  of mental illness, 79, 84–85, 86, 205–6
stigma of mental illness, 14, 27, 92, 208
  and employment, 93, 102
  families' experience of, 62, 63, 316
  among immigrants/refugees, 218–19
  and oppression, 16, 78–79, 93–95, 101, 102, 103, 208, 294
  in rural areas, 232
  among substance abusers, 293, 294
St. Thomas Psychiatric Hospital, 14, 170, 171*t*
students, on CURA, 9, 15, 19, 124, 130, 318–19
substance abuse
  and discharge, 175, 185, 187
  and electronic patient records, 196
  by homeless adolescents, 145, 147, 210
  by homeless/housed individuals, 133*t*, 134, 136–37, 138
  and homelessness, 127, 133*t*, 134, 168, 270
  by parents, 204, 210, 292–93, 292*t*, 293*t*, 294
  recovery programs for, 40
  and sexual abuse, 291, 295
substance abuse by male and female mental health consumer-survivors, differences in, 202–3, 248, 248*t*, 249–50, 288–89, 295
  and access to services, 294, 295–96
  and hospitalization, 290, 294
  and housing/living conditions, 293, 295
  and level of functioning, 292, 292*t*
  and parental substance abuse, 292–93, 292*t*, 293*t*, 294
  as perceived problem, 80, 290–91, 294–96
  and primary diagnoses, 288, 290, 290*t*
  and PTSD, 290
  and severity of abuse, 291–92, 291*t*, 292*t*

  and severity of overall problem, 291, 291*t*, 294
  and sexual abuse, 291, 295
substance abuse by male and female mental health consumer-survivors as perceived problem, study of, 203–4, 289–96
  discussion of, 294–96
  methodology of, 289
  results of, 290–93
substandard housing, 91, 143, 191, 235, 250
Substitute Decisions Act (Ontario), 73
suicide/danger to self, 21, 128, 132, 133*t*
  adolescents and, 145, 147, 210, 262
  schizophrenia and, 244
  women and, 80, 128
supported housing, 108–9
  definition of, 326–27
  government involvement in, 111
  as housing preference, 92, 98, 101–2
  sampling issues of, 16–17
  vs. supportive housing, 50, 108–9, 110
supportive housing, 107–8
  apartment-type, 98, 101, 116
  benefits of, 129, 180
  definitions of, 327, 330–31
  demographics of, 18, 33, 112, 113*t*, 114
  family preferences for, 64
  government involvement in, 37, 107–8, 111
  as housing preference, 64, 98, 99, 101, 110, 114, 114*t*, 116, 117, 118
  lack of, 64, 251
  vs. long-term care facilities, 329
  problems of, 108
  for seniors, 327, 330–31
  vs. supported housing, 50, 108–9, 110

Supportive Housing Coalition of Toronto, 108
supports, income. *See* income supports, *and entry following*

"tornado" of mental illness. *See* mental illness "tornado," phases/themes of
transitional housing, 331
transportation, 103, 293, 295
    and housing preference, 94t, 100, 102, 109, 114, 115, 115t, 117–18
    to/from Margaret's Haven, 307
    and rural homelessness, 100, 230, 232, 236, 238, 239
tuberculosis, 127, 145, 179
Turner, Katherine, 5, 9

United Kingdom, issues studied in
    discharge of psychiatric patients, 180–81, 194
    public attitudes to mental illness, 79
United Nations High Commissioner for Refugees, 258
United States, issues studied in
    Aboriginal children/youth, 262–63
    discharge of patients, 169, 180, 181
    family care, 59
    homeless children/youth, 261, 262
    housing preferences, 6, 110, 117
    military veterans' health, 129
    minority homelessness, 208–9, 262–63
    substance abuse and mental illness, 288
    uprooting of immigrants/refugees, 259
Utilization of Hospital and Community Services Form, 22, 289

violence
    against girls, 203, 211, 260, 261, 262–63, 269
    against homeless adolescents, 146–47, 152–53, 155–56, 159–60, 161
    as mental illness myth, 78, 81, 82, 85
    and oppression, 252, 258
    sexual, 146–47, 155–56, 159–60, 161, 210

waiting lists
    for affordable housing, 37, 96, 136, 235
    for support services, 100–1, 232
Western Ontario Therapeutic Community Housing (WOTCH), 7, 309
women
    see also gender differences, of mental health consumer-survivors, *and entry following*; girls, *and entries following*; men
    devaluation of, 144
    as family caregivers, 61, 65
    immigrant/refugee, 208–9
    and mental illness, 243–52
    mood disorders in, 80t, 244, 247, 248t, 249, 252, 290, 290t
    and PTSD, 247, 248t, 250
    in rural areas, 236, 237
    safety concerns of, 53, 82, 146–47, 155–56, 211, 236, 237, 294
    sampling of, 15, 18
    schizophrenia in, 80t, 136, 248t
    sexual abuse of, 80, 82, 97, 136, 237, 250, 268
    sexual assault of, 146–47
    shelters for, 250, 294, 304, 310
    as substance abusers, 80, 287–96
    suicide by, 80, 128
Workplace Safety and Insurance Board (WSIB), 38

Youth Homeless Strategy (federal), 148